Genocidal Nightmares

Genocidal Nightmares

Narratives of Insecurity and
the Logic of Mass Atrocities

Edited by

Abdelwahab El-Affendi

Bloomsbury Academic
An imprint of Bloomsbury Publishing Inc

B L O O M S B U R Y
NEW YORK · LONDON · OXFORD · NEW DELHI · SYDNEY

Bloomsbury Academic
An imprint of Bloomsbury Publishing Inc

1385 Broadway	50 Bedford Square
New York	London
NY 10018	WC1B 3DP
USA	UK

www.bloomsbury.com

BLOOMSBURY and the Diana logo are trademarks of Bloomsbury Publishing Plc

First published 2015
Paperback edition first published 2016

© Abdelwahab El-Affendi and Contributors, 2015

All rights reserved. No part of this publication may be reproduced or transmitted in any form or by any means, electronic or mechanical, including photocopying, recording, or any information storage or retrieval system, without prior permission in writing from the publishers.

No responsibility for loss caused to any individual or organization acting on or refraining from action as a result of the material in this publication can be accepted by Bloomsbury or the author.

Library of Congress Cataloging-in-Publication Data
Genocidal nightmares : narratives of insecurity and
the logic of mass atrocities / edited by Abdelwahab El-Affendi.
pages cm
Includes index.
ISBN 978-1-62892-071-0 (hardback)
1. Genocide–Causes. 2. Atrocities–Causes. 3. Violence–Social aspects.
4. Genocide–Causes–Case studies. 5. Atrocities–Causes–Case studies.
6. Violence–Social aspects–Case studies.
I. El-Affendi, Abdelwahab, editor of compilation.
HV6322.7.G436 2014
364.15'1–dc23
2014023589

ISBN: HB: 978-1-6289-2071-0
PB: 978-1-5013-2023-1
ePub: 978-1-6289-2073-4
ePDF: 978-1-6289-2075-8

Typeset by Integra Software Services Pvt. Ltd

For Eiman, Maha, Ahmed, Omar and Maryam

Contents

Preface ix
Foreword *Francis M. Deng* xi

1. Introduction: Narrating the Precariousness of Human Decency
    Abdelwahab El-Affendi 1
2. Killer Narratives: Collective Nightmares and the Construction of Narrative Communities of Insecurity
    Abdelwahab El-Affendi 27
3. Imagining Nationhood, Framing Postcoloniality: Narrativizing Nigeria through the Kinesis of (Hi)Story
    James Tar Tsaaior 53
4. Sudanese Stories: Narratives of Grievance, Distrust and Fatalism in Recurrent Violence
    Alex de Waal 73
5. General Elections and Narratives of Violent Conflict: The Land Question and Civic Competence in Kenya
    Kenneth Inyani Simala 91
6. The Violence of Security, Lethal Representations and Hindu Nationalism in India
    Dibyesh Anand 103
7. Memories of Victimhood in Serbia and Croatia from the 1980s to the Disintegration of Yugoslavia
    Slobodan G. Markovich 117
8. Insecurity, Victimhood, Self and Other: The Case of Israel and Palestine
    Ilan Pappe 141
9. Resistance Narratives: Palestinian Women, Islam and Insecurity
    Maria Holt 153
10. The State and Intergroup Violence: The Case of Modern Iraq
    Ali A. Allawi 171

11 Islamophobia as a Securitization Narrative: The Exclusionary Logic of Imperial Geopolitics
      Nafeez Mosaddeq Ahmed 191
12 Killer Narratives in Western Popular Culture: Telling it as it is Not
      Anas S. Al-Shaikh-Ali 211

Concluding Remarks   *Abdelwahab El-Affendi* 231
Authors' Biographies 239
Index 242

Preface

The core idea of this book has been under development by the editor since the early 1990s when he published an article entitled: 'The Eclipse of Reason: the Media in the Muslim World', in which he reflected on the link between the successful suppression of critical narratives and the durability of authoritarian regimes in the Middle East. A few years later, he began to point to a link between the pervasive narratives of fear, mistrust and insecurity and the overall political climate in the region, which did not only permit and entrench authoritarianism, but also encouraged political violence (including mass terrorism).

In this book, this insight is developed further with the help of a number of prominent colleagues, and generalized in an attempt to fill an important gap in our understanding of how mass violence and terrorism link to other political pathologies, including dysfunctional political systems. By bringing together divergent disciplinary perspectives on the link between the construction and dissemination of narratives of insecurity on the one hand, and the production and reproduction of mass violence on the other, the book aims to offer a new explanation of the sudden resort of otherwise 'normal' and 'rational' actors to acts of apparently irrational brutality. The core hypothesis is that when otherwise outrageous actions are framed within plausible and compelling narratives, they appear rational, even imperative, from certain perspectives. The appropriate 'script' can portray the most inhuman act (up to, and including genocide) as not only acceptable, but as 'humane'. One has just to watch a 'zombie' movie to perceive how indiscriminate slaughter can be made to look absolutely a commendable endeavour, or even hilarious!

The book starts with an introductory chapter setting out the theoretical framework for the discussion, and then proceeds to examine case studies, including former Yugoslavia, Sudan, Nigeria, Iraq, India and Israel-Palestine. It also examines the rise of Islamophobia as a distinct narrative of insecurity infecting and threatening otherwise stable democracies.

In addition to raising the important question of mass violence from a novel angle focusing on the role of the narrative construction of insecurity, the book also brings together the work of renowned authors who bring to the endeavour insights from disparate regions of the world, as well as from diverse disciplines and fields of inquiry, including history, philosophy, political science, International Relations, sociology and literary criticism. The authors write from within the communities involved – with a couple of exceptions where deep and extensive expertise makes up for it – and are thoroughly familiar with the perspectives they are exploring. This includes familiarity with the language, history and the nuances of the discourses being deployed. They thus offer important and deep insights into the questions being tackled and correct some widespread misperceptions about those conflicts.

In a work such as this, one is indebted to such a large number of people and institutions that it is impossible to enumerate these benefactors in such short a space. But we start with the AHRC and ESRC, whose generous funding for this project through the Global Uncertainties Programme was indispensable. Special thanks are due to Dr Chris Wyatt at the ESRC, who has been liaising with me closely throughout the project. I also thank all the contributors, who have been admirable in their dedication and patience. In particular, I thank Dr Francis M. Deng, who has taken time off his busy schedule as Special Adviser to the UN Secretary General on the Prevention of Genocide to read and comment extensively on the draft, adding many important insights in the process.

Thanks are also due to the many colleagues at the Centre of the Study of Democracy (CSD) and the Department of Politics and International Relations at the University of Westminster for their continuous support. CSD has always provided a uniquely stimulating environment for research, enhanced by the generosity of spirit which pervades it. In particular, thanks to Suzy Robson, our dedicated administrator, Simon Joss, Roland Danreuther, Chantal Mouffe, Bhikhu Parekh, John Keane and David Chandler. Special thanks are due to Mona El-Koueidi, my research assistant, who has worked hard at all stages of the research, offering invaluable support. Thanks also to Amr Magdi for his assistance.

Thanks are also due to the anonymous reviewers at the various stages of this work, whose generous and insightful comments have made this work a much better product than it would otherwise have been. Gratitude is also due to our editors at Bloomsbury, in particular the indefatigable Matthew Kopel and Kaitlin Fontana, and all the staff who worked on bringing out this work.

Foreword

Francis M. Deng

Dr Abdelwahab El-Affendi has produced an edited volume that addresses one of the most daunting challenges for humanity – genocide and mass atrocities. He does so with an intellectual rigour and stimulating probing characteristic of his work. From a wide variety of interdisciplinary perspectives, the book poses serious dilemmas that rotate around the philosophical narratives about hate and evil, and their manifestations in genocidal violence and mass atrocities. These are more than 'nightmares', for people wake up from nightmares with a sigh of relief, while the calamitous consequences of responding to exaggerated and sometimes misconceived nightmarish fears are tragically real.

The normative and moral dilemmas which the book successfully exposes centre on the role of the individual culprit, the communal violence that propels killings to the level of mass atrocities, the contextual dynamics that trigger the frenzy of mass murder, and the luring culture that nurtures a deeper propensity towards the elimination of 'them' that presumptively threaten 'us'. These dynamics are enormously complex and do not lend themselves to easy summation in this brief preface. Whether focus is placed on 'evil' personalities, their 'evil' deeds, mass obedience to the dictates of deranged authoritarian leaders, or the devastating incitement of hostile environments, the moral dilemma in the perception of the perpetrators categorically dichotomizes between the risk of being eliminated by a perceived enemy, and waging a pre-emptive attack aimed at eliminating that supposedly threatening enemy. From the perspective of the victims, to try to explain the source of the threat to address the root causes would be tantamount to condoning the atrocity or dulling the moral outrage, even implying that 'all of us are potential perpetrators of evil' under similar circumstances. On the other hand, countering the perceived threat in kind logically means that 'responding to genocide must then be genocide', as El-Affendi graphically puts it.

A tragic example of this was reflected in the massacres in South Sudan between the Dinka and the Nuer, triggered by what the government considered a coup attempt on December 15th, 2013, and the opposition leaders attributed to clashes within the Presidential Guard. The interethnic violence that followed rapidly spread beyond the capital, Juba, to several states in the country. While investigations into what happened are still being conducted, and hostilities continue, this is a double tragedy, given that South Sudan had suffered half a century of devastating wars, including mass atrocities of historic proportions.

The book highlights another moral dilemma in the choice between the threat of punishment as deterrence and pre-emptively removing the source of fear that provokes resort to genocide. This, of course, echoes the classic and unresolvable question of whether capital punishment is a deterrence to murder. I would, however, tend to agree with El-Affendi that it is unlikely for those set on a course of committing mass murder to stop and reflect on any punishment they might incur for their criminal acts. On the other hand, if the expectation can credibly be established that individual leaders who plan, incite and direct genocide and other atrocity crimes will sooner or later be held accountable, that could conceivably deter prospective culprits from committing those crimes. Nonetheless, I would contend that the indictment of incumbent leaders in conflict situations who are still needed to play a role in resolving atrocious conflicts poses a genuine moral dilemma.

Notwithstanding the controversy surrounding the indictment of incumbent leaders accused of responsibility for genocide and other atrocity crimes, both as a punishment for their wrongful deeds and as a deterrence to others, the book makes a plausible case for prioritizing up-stream prevention. This in turn requires a proper diagnosis of the problem and developing appropriate strategies for addressing the root causes of genocide and mass atrocities. According to the authors of the volume, 'the thesis we are defending here is that the production, dissemination and successful promotion of narratives that instil a deep sense of collective insecurity are usually the tipping point which convinces ordinary people that engaging in mass murder is perfectly rational, even unavoidable'. As a premise of their thesis, El-Affendi singles out Islamophobia (as) an interesting instance of a 'narrative of insecurity' which 'is evolving and beginning to have a serious and tangible impact in front of our very eyes, thus offering a "laboratory case" for exploring how this type of narrative originates, evolves and works'. And, indeed, while some of the case studies in this volume, Kenya, former Yugoslavia, India, Palestine, Iraq, Nigeria and Sudan in that order, deal with ethnic and other religious conflicts than with Islam, Islamophobia still figured prominently in the volume. This focus is by no means surprising, even though the editor notes, 'It has not been our conscious plan, but the theme of Islam and Islamophobia appears as a thread connecting almost all of the cases marshalled here to illustrate how the narrative of insecurity frame and justify mass violence.'

While I agree with the authors that fear is a central factor in the root causes, my own focus is on the implications of identity conflicts that degenerate into genocidal violence, with fear, of course, as a major contributing factor. Conflict of identities has indeed been an area of concern for me for decades, both through my studies of Sudan's national identity crisis and in the context of my UN mandates, first as Representative of the Secretary-General on Internally Displaced Persons (IDPs) for twelve years (1992–2004) and then as Special Adviser of the Secretary-General on the Prevention of Genocide (2007–2012). Both UN mandates involve very sensitive issues of national sovereignty, especially as they concern acutely divided societies where gross inequalities, discrimination, marginalization and denial of rights associated with a national identity crisis often trigger genocidal conflicts, and determine the response of the state to the humanitarian consequences of the identity-related conflicts. Put in other words, the crisis of national identity results in a vacuum of national responsibility to protect populations under the threat of mass violence or in need of humanitarian assistance. The international community becomes the alternative source of protection and assistance to the needy populations.

However, in countries divided between the 'in-group' in control of state power, and the denigrated and often persecuted 'out-group,' the state is likely to invoke sovereignty as a barricade against international involvement. Short of military intervention, which is very costly in both material and human terms, a more pragmatic and potentially effective approach is to engage governments on the basis of 'sovereignty as responsibility,' a concept I developed in collaboration with colleagues in the African Studies Project at the Brookings Institution in Washington DC in response to the post-Cold War challenges of conflicts in Africa. During the Cold War, regional and even internal conflicts used to be seen in a distorted way as part of the proxy confrontation between the Super Powers. The end of the Cold War meant seeing internal conflicts in their proper context and reassigning the responsibility for preventing, managing and resolving them to the state, with regional and international cooperation, if needed. This is the essence of the synthesizing volume in our series which carried the title *Sovereignty as Responsibility* (Brookings, 1996). The concept has since been recast and developed as the 'Responsibility to Protect,' and although RtoP or R2P, the acronyms for which it is more popularly known, is still controversial because it tends to be associated with military intervention and a threat to sovereignty, it is gaining wide support as the most practical strategy for preventing, and responding to, the atrocity crimes of genocide, war crimes, ethnic cleansing and crimes against humanity.

Both 'sovereignty as responsibility' and the 'responsibility to protect' have three pillars: the responsibility of the state to protect its own populations; the responsibility of the international community to assist the state to enhance its capacity to discharge its national responsibility; and the responsibility of the international community to take collective action to provide the needed protection when a state is manifestly failing to protect its own populations. Measures under the third pillar range from diplomatic intercession, to the imposition of sanctions, and, under certain compelling circumstances, to military intervention.

Internal displacement is clearly one of the areas that pose a special challenge to international cooperation with the states concerned. At the time of my appointment as Representative of the Secretary-General on IDPs, there were some 24 to 30 million internally displaced persons in over 50 countries. These are people who have been forced to flee their homes or areas of normal residence by armed conflicts, internal strife, and systematic violations of human rights, but who have remained within their national borders. Had they crossed international borders, they would have been refugees for whom the international system has a legal and institutional framework for their protection and assistance. Although internally displaced persons remain within their own countries, where, unlike refugees who have escaped internal conflicts, they continue to be within domestic danger zone, they have no legal or institutional bases for receiving protection and assistance from the international community. It is worth emphasizing that internal displacement is only a symptom of conflict that may involve genocide and other mass atrocities, in turn the result of acute crises of national identity in sharply divided nations, the very reason international involvement is needed, but often resisted.

Yet, since the crisis is by definition internal, it raises particularly sensitive issues of sovereignty, which is why the establishment of the mandate of the Representative of the Secretary-General on IDPs was highly controversial. From the beginning, I had to factor this into my approach to the mandate. If my role was seen as a threat to national sovereignty, doors would be closed, and I would not have access for dialogue with the national authorities and to internally displaced populations whose cause I was supposed to advocate. Sovereignty as responsibility became the normative basis for my dialogue with governments.

As I have often explained, the first five minutes with the president or minister concerned were crucial to getting the message across. I would thus start by conveying the message that I realized the problem was internal, and fell under state sovereignty, but that I did not see sovereignty negatively as a barricade against international involvement; I saw it positively as a concept of state responsibility for protecting and providing humanitarian assistance to its needy populations, and, if necessary, request assistance from the international community. I then added discreetly, but firmly, that if the state failed to discharge that responsibility, with the consequence that the population concerned was threatened with suffering and death, the international community would not stand by and do nothing; it would find one way or another to intervene. The best way to safeguard sovereignty was therefore to discharge the responsibility of sovereignty.

In my reports and statements on the countries concerned, I always noted that not only was internal displacement a consequence of internal conflicts, but that those conflicts were themselves symptoms of deeper structural problems involving serious national identity crises. I urged the authorities to see in the crisis of internal displacement an opportunity for addressing that deeper structural crisis of national identity and endeavour to bridge the cleavages involved and fill the vacuum of responsibility associated with the national identity crisis.

On the whole, my approach to the mandate was well received. It made internal displacement a legitimate and acceptable concern for state cooperation with the international community. Building on human rights law, humanitarian law, and analogous refugee law, a team of international legal experts developed under my guidance, the Guiding Principles on Internal Displacement, which have been widely accepted, enshrined in the legislation of many countries, and provided a basis for the African Union Convention for the Protection and Assistance of Internally Displaced Persons in Africa (Kampala Convention), the first binding instrument on the subject.

Genocide, even more than internal displacement, is a highly emotive phenomenon. Although it is one of the most heinous crimes that humanity is expected to unite in preventing, stopping and punishing, for the same reason, it is an issue about which both perpetrators and those called upon to prevent or stop it are usually in denial. That is why we generally recognize genocide after the fact, in historical terms, when the perpetrators are gone, in most cases defeated. Determining that genocide has occurred becomes a judgement of the victor over the vanquished. In the contemporary context, genocide often calls to mind Rwanda, Bosnia, Cambodia and the Holocaust, and is seen as too sensitive for comfortable discussion, too difficult to touch, and, therefore, conveniently avoided.

For this reason, in undertaking the mandate on genocide prevention, I had to address myself to the challenges of carrying out a formidable, if not impossible, mandate. I decided to conceptualize the problem in a way that would make it comprehensible and manageable, and to look for practical ways of doing what needed to be done collaboratively. I thought the best way was to de-mystify genocide from being viewed as something that is untouchable, something too difficult to deal with, to a problem that is the result of extreme identity-related conflicts that target specific groups of people, identified either by the factors specified in the Genocide Convention, which include nationality, race, ethnicity and religion, or by some other criteria. This is not to say that the subject itself is inherently too sensitive to discuss, but that alleging genocide generates extreme emotional reactions on the side of both, the alleged perpetrators and those called upon to intervene, which tends to make denial a defensive response that discourages meaningful discussion of the subject.

It is not the mere fact of being different that causes genocidal conflicts; it is the implications of these differences in terms of how much people are differentiated and stratified. As is generally the case with acutely divided nations, whereas some groups enjoy the dignity and the rights of citizenship, others are discriminated against, marginalized, excluded, dehumanized and denied the rights that normally accrue from citizenship. It is the reaction of these extremely denigrated groups that generates conflict, often emanating from despair, with no constructive, peaceful ways of promoting their interest in achieving equality and a sense of belonging to the nation. Their reaction paradoxically then generates a vicious cycle of fear and a counter-reaction by the state or the dominant groups that have a vested interest in the status quo.

From this analytical perspective, it is obvious that the most effective strategy for preventing genocide and mass atrocities is constructive management of diversity, aimed at promoting inclusivity, equality, and the enjoyment of human rights and fundamental freedoms. In my own experience, while genocide discussion is fraught with emotionalism and denial, calling for constructive management of diversity nearly always receives positive response. It then becomes a question of developing appropriate norms, institutions, and operational strategies for its realization. Towards that end, we have developed a Framework of Analysis that provides a tool for assessing the risk of genocide and formulating practical ways of addressing them preventively. The Framework provides a means by which states can look at themselves 'in the mirror,' so to speak, to assess how they are performing, and identify areas where reform is needed for effective preventive purposes. Strategies for promoting this normative framework can include advocacy, training, workshops, and education, formal and informal.

The book recognizes the centrality of the identity factor and notes that in extreme conflict situations, the target group is 'dehumanized and placed outside the moral universe of the perpetrators'. We are familiar with the application of such terms as 'cockroaches' and 'rats' used against the Tutsis by the Hutus and by Gaddafi against the Libyan protesters. The popular usage of the word 'animal' to express indignation about a person's conduct is a mild indication of the moral denial of humanity to such a person. Quoting from Jacques Semelin's article, 'Toward a vocabulary of massacre and genocide', El-Affendi makes the point that 'it is for this reason that the study of tales... belonging to a culture... is important for comprehending the massacres that have been committed within them'.

The dehumanization of the hostile 'out-group' as part of the 'animal world' came across to me dramatically in my study of Dinka folktales. In those tales, the characteristics which are attributed to animals, always lions, the most dangerous animal they come in contact with, are so interchangeable with human behaviour that a lion is often mistaken for a human being until its aggression or other animal behaviour patterns and characteristics begin to manifest themselves. Likewise, human beings begin to acquire lion-like tendencies in a manner that is not always indicative of basic physical transformation. The process by which animal characteristics emerge sometimes includes biological reference to the animal's tail or fur, but often the person is simply described as 'turning wild'. A person who violates culturally prescribed fundamental precepts of the Dinka moral code is often identified in the folktales as turning into a lion. Moral derelicts who turn into lions, even when they are close relatives, are usually killed, without any remorse. But in less severe violations, culprits are subjected to severe punishment, mostly beating, and redeemed to their erstwhile human status.

Even in their everyday language, the Dinka refer to excessively greedy people or those who unscrupulously receive more than they give as 'lions'. In one 'Ox song,' a man whose brother-in-law had misappropriated his favourite bull and sold it to buy grain during a period of famine accuses him of having become a lion:

> I asked Abyei, 'Father, why are gossipers whispering in a language I do not understand?
> Father, have you brought a lion into our family?'
> Father smiled and said, 'What lion has such perfect set of teeth?'
> O lion with perfect teeth,
> Have you truly devoured my bull?
> The man to whom we gave our sister has turned into a beast.

If a Dinka who violates the moral code is seen as a lion, it is easy to understand how foreign aggressors could even more readily be identified as ferocious beasts. The Dinka have been in contact with other peoples for centuries, and particularly witnessed waves of invaders during the nineteenth century. Yet, the tales do not refer to those strangers by any ethnic, racial or national terms, although their behaviour patterns are considered vile and notably non-Dinka. Those who consort with members of the 'lion world' eventually turn into lions themselves, and unless re-tamed by severe punishment, are brutally killed.

This is, however, only part of the story about Dinka attitude towards foreigners. As human beings, Dinka moral codes dictate that they be treated with the deference due to all human beings as God's creatures. Indeed, even animals and inanimate entities deserve respect as God's creatures. Gross violation of their fundamental dignity is believed to invite divine wrath that could result in severe illness and even death. The dividing line then is the extent to which foreigners are considered so morally depraved that they forfeit their fundamental dignity as human beings.

As noted earlier, the book underscores the widely held view that it is fear which motivates the supposedly threatened group to respond with genocidal onslaught. Fear is 'the most important motive' for engagement in mass atrocities, states El-Affendi. The grounds for fear do not have to be tangible. Fear is mostly perceived or contrived, not only by the vulnerable, but also by the relatively powerful. The existential threat which the more powerful feel from the weaker antagonists creates a mutually reinforcing dynamic that the groups in conflict can no longer control or manage. It usually requires a third party to mediate between the parties in conflict.

The irony is that the subjectivity with which people define themselves, as opposed to the objective realities of their identities, often means that what divides the parties has a lot to do with myth rather than reality. The people at war are often not as different from one another as they think they are, generating what El-Affendi calls 'the fear of pollution'. This was dramatically brought home to me in many of the countries I visited in connection with my IDP mandate. Looking at the people in conflict, it was not always easy to tell who belonged to which side of the identity divide. I remember addressing crowds in Burundi, some of whom looked typical Tutsis in the way we are told Tutsis look, and some of whom looked typical Hutus, but with many in between whom I could not identify ethnically. I asked the foreign minister after one of those meetings: 'Can you always tell a Tutsi from a Hutu?' His response was, 'Yes, but with a margin of error of 35 per cent'. And that margin of error is common in most divided countries. The 'fear of pollution' or of being cast into the wrong group because of the ambiguities at the borderline of identities makes those in the grey areas assert their belonging to their constructed identity with a distorting vengeance. It is noteworthy, for instance, that in the Sudan, in the tribal wars between the Dinka and their Baggara Arab neighbours, with whom there has been much inter-racial mixing, it is the progeny of this admixture who are often on the frontline to prove their belonging and loyalty to their adoptive group. And in the recent mass atrocities in South Sudan, the groups involved, the Dinka and the Nuer, are ethnically and culturally the closest in the country, virtually one kindred group.

The policy implication of the analysis adopted by the volume is that 'it is at the level of these narratives which frame conflicts that action must start, by providing both practical assurance against perceived threats, but also a more realistic assessment of threats and a responsible debunking of xenophobic, racist or other paranoid narratives branding whole categories of human beings as "evil" or unworthy of human dignity'. The envisaged action is largely intellectual articulation of the problem and the development of alternative, more constructive narratives. This is a challenge for education, formal and informal, institutional and public. The objective of such education must include exploding the divisive myths of distorted identities, removing unwarranted differentiating factors, and exploring the common ground.

The right policy-oriented education, embracing diversity as a source of enrichment rather than conflict, must begin early in life, ideally at home, during the most formative years. I recall that during our first visit to Muglad, the administrative centre of our Missiriya Arab neighbours, as we walked along a dirt path, a boy four or five years old, smeared in mud, dressed in rags, looked at us with a deceptively innocent smile on his face, and said, '*abeed*.' Those of us who were not familiar with the local Arabic intonation thought that he was greeting us. To our surprise, our cousin, who had correctly understood the boy to say 'slaves,' went and slapped him on the face. Many years later, we had a similar experience in Europe. I was visiting relatives who were studying medicine in Italy. As we strolled on the streets of Venice, a boy of about the same age as the one in Muglad uttered a racial slur, calling us 'niggers'. Where could such small boys have learned to use those insulting terms, but from their families and communities?

It is also important to note that formal education, even to the highest level, does not necessarily guarantee the right moral outcome. The genocides, mass atrocities, racism, xenophobia, apartheid and various forms and degrees of discrimination, have been conceived, planned, instigated, and directed by highly educated individuals, including PhD holders. Education at all levels must comprise the right moral content, if it is to address the major societal ills of our time. The concept of human dignity, which can be assumed to be shared by all cultures in varying degrees, and which is the foundation of universal human rights, provides the basis for the right policy oriented education to inculcate a culture of peace, mutual respect and unity in diversity.

Here, the role of belief systems becomes vital. It has always been my view that since virtually all religions or beliefs share the same fundamental moral values, even though they are antagonistic on institutionalized practices, perhaps a modem code based on their shared essential values could be developed to be used as a basis for moral education. It is well documented by anthropologists that some of the people considered by adherents of universalizing religions are among the most religious in the world. Their belief systems could be documented, incorporated in the global spiritual and moral code, and used in promoting the universal goal of human dignity.

What is needed is early structural prevention of potentially genocidal conflicts and adequate responses to the humanitarian consequences that conflicts generate, in addition to addressing the root causes of conflict to restore peace, security, stability and equitable socio-economic development. These are essential elements of good governance, based on democratic values and respect for fundamental rights and civil liberties. It is also the primary responsibility of the state to protect its citizens and all those under its jurisdiction, if need be with the support of the international community.

Our experience so far shows that conceptualizing genocide as an extreme form of identity-related conflicts resonates well with many governments, and provides a basis for constructively engaging them. From this premise, it is easily understandable that the best way of preventing genocidal conflicts is to promote constructive management of diversity, the objective being to ensure inclusivity, equality, and respect for the human dignity of all groups, irrespective of their nationality, race, ethnicity or religion, among other identity factors. The normative framework of cooperation between the state and the international community is well reflected in the three pillars of shared responsibility for prevention, response and re-building, as embodied in the dual concepts of 'sovereignty as responsibility' and 'the responsibility to protect'.

All this should be seen as part of a process towards universal ideals that may not be achievable in the short run, but which humanity must strive to approximate incrementally. The challenge is to bridge the gap between long-term aspirations towards ideals and short-term pragmatic engagement with governments for immediate results. Respect for human rights as an element in the universal quest for human dignity must be the Overriding Guiding Principle. But it has to be pursued collectively and cooperatively to minimize obstruction by vulnerable governments that are defensively guarding their narrow notions of sovereignty. It is one thing to say to governments that, in the name of human rights and humanitarian principles, the international community will override their sovereignty by whatever means necessary, including coercive force; it is quite another thing to say to them: 'Sovereignty itself means responsibility, and the dignity you enjoy in the international community, the respect you have, your legitimacy at home and abroad, all have a lot to do with the degree to which you positively discharge the responsibilities of sovereignty'. No self-respecting leader or government, desirous of gaining legitimacy at home and abroad, can object to this constructive formulation of the challenge.

The authors of this volume have provided us with a refreshing basis for approaching the most daunting challenges of addressing the awesome threat of genocide and mass atrocities. They focus in their policy-oriented analysis on the narratives of fear between identity groups, while I have adopted in this foreword a broader approach to genocidal conflict of identities. We however share the same premise based on identity conflicts, and come to basically similar conclusions about the urgent need to address the root causes behind the narratives of fear or mismanaged diversity. Our shared goal is to facilitate the prevention of genocide and mass atrocities, which, tragically continues to be elusive. Humanity has repeatedly pledged 'Never again' to genocide, and has repeatedly failed to honour that pledge. Every failure however raises the level of guilt and enhances the determination to do better to make the words 'Never again' a reality. This incremental consciousness and the determination to do better should provide ground for optimism. In any case, optimism, provided it is not blind, is a source of motivation for action; pessimism leads to a dead-end. Principled optimism, combined with pragmatic incremental moves towards realizing 'Never again' should mean that genocide can indeed be prevented.

1

Introduction: Narrating the Precariousness of Human Decency

Abdelwahab El-Affendi

[Man] is... essentially a story-telling animal... I can only answer the question 'What am I to do?' if I can answer the prior question 'Of what story or stories do I find myself a part?'

Alasdair MacIntyre, 1981[1]

The killing starts with the use of words disqualifying [the victim's] humanity... simple words, a few short phrases, pronounced in the context of threat and fear, open the country's future to apocalypse of mass murder.

Jacques Semelin, 2007[2]

The right narrative in politics can win an election, gather a mob, destroy an enemy, start a war.

L. Timmel Duchamp, 2010[3]

Nabokov... helps us get inside cruelty, and thereby helps articulate the dimly felt connection between art and torture.

Richard Rorty, 1989[4]

In August 2012, just as Norwegian mass murderer Anders Behring Breivik was being sentenced to twenty-one years in jail for killing seventy-seven people a year earlier in a shooting spree preceded by a car bomb, a French intellectual published an essay that appeared to praise the mass killer. Richard Millet, an editor at Gallimard, provoked outrage when he described Breivik as an artist whose atrocities had attained 'formal perfection ... in their literary dimension'.[5] While insisting that he did not approve of the terror, Millet said Breivik was 'what Norway deserves'. His acts were 'what awaits our societies' that remained in denial to the impact of multiculturalism on European nations, which were 'dissolving socially' and 'losing their Christian essence'.[6]

Breivik, it is to be recalled, detonated a two-ton car bomb in the heart of Oslo on 22 July 2011, killing seven people before starting a shooting spree at a youth camp on a nearby idyllic island. By the time he surrendered to the police, sixty-nine more people were killed and nearly 200 injured. Prior to embarking on his massacre, Breivik, (described by the police as a 'right-wing fundamentalist Christian', and styling himself as a 'Marxist Hunter') emailed a 1,518-page 'compendium' to over a thousand people. In this work, he explained how and why he planned his acts, detailing his motives and reproducing literature which influenced his beliefs and actions. He even included an 'interview' he conducted with himself, as an aide for those wanting to decipher his motives and sources of inspiration. He was so keen to get his 'story' to the world, since without it this 'work of art' would not make sense.

Precisely because of this 'due diligence', the Oslo massacre provides explanatory clues about the motives and drives behind the type of mass atrocities that are the focus of our present study. In the light of all this, we can see a clear linear link between the nightmare scenarios (which Millet also reproduced in his own 'literary' compendium) of a Europe teetering over the abyss of cultural oblivion and the atrocity perpetrated. The act makes no sense outside the narrative in which it is embedded and 'is meaningful not only because a story can be told about it after the fact' but equally because 'we are called to action by beckoning scripts'.[7]

In this chapter, we outline and explore the thesis that atrocities are embedded in narratives of insecurity and make sense mainly within nightmare scenarios of the type expounded by Breivik and Millet. We begin by offering conceptual clarifications and definitions of key terms, tracing their interconnections before proceeding to explore difficulties that usually hamper the search for adequate explanations for such atrocities. Finally, we indicate how we seek to provide novel explanations to overcome these difficulties. Summaries of the chapters will then follow.

Conceptual clarifications

The key terms used in this study ('mass violence', 'terrorism', 'genocide', etc.) are heavily contested and notoriously difficult to pin down. However, on closer scrutiny, the contests surrounding concepts like terrorism appear to be more about justification than meaning. A report by the United Nations' High-level Panel on Threats, Challenges and Change (2004) underlined this point by trying to overcome two sets of objections to an agreed definition: demands to exempt either acts perpetrated by states or by peoples under foreign occupation. To resolve the issue, the Panel first sought consensus on the principle that attacks on innocent civilians could not be justified under any circumstances, including when resisting foreign occupation. Then it reaffirmed the principle that atrocities perpetrated by states are already covered in international law as war crimes and crimes against humanity, and need not be designated 'terrorism'.[8] That attacks on innocent civilians represented the core defining feature of terrorism was made explicit in the Panel's proposed definition of it as encompassing 'any action ... intended to cause death or serious bodily harm to civilians or non-combatants, when the purpose of such act, by its nature or context, is to intimidate a population, or to compel a Government or an international organization to do or to abstain from doing any act'.[9]

For Alex Schmid, a leading expert in the field, the difficulty to agree a definition is due, among other things, to the wide variety of terrorist acts, the deeply emotive character of the term, and the tendency to use it for purposes of condemnation and de-legitimation.[10] Schmid offers a list of ten elements for an act to qualify as terrorism, including attacks on non-combatants, a political motive, being directed to larger audience (for purposes of intimidation and propaganda) and the illegal/criminal nature of the act.[11] We believe the High Panel's indicative definition (together with Schmid's list of 'ingredients') will be sufficient for our purposes. Terrorism is mainly politically motivated attacks on non-combatants for the purposes of political intimidation and coercion.

Arriving at an internationally agreed legal definition of a term is no guarantee that it will stop being contested, as the case with the term 'genocide' proves. The 1948 UN Convention on the Prevention and Punishment of the Crime of Genocide (UNGC) states in Article II that an act qualifies as genocide if it targets any national, ethnic, racial or religious group, with the intent of destroying it 'in whole or in part', either through killing its members, causing them serious bodily or mental harm, deliberately inflicting on the group conditions calculated to cause physical destruction, imposing measures intended to prevent births or forcibly transferring children of the group to another. However, that did not protect the term against 'inflationary' use (and abuse, such as describing inter-racial marriage or birth control as genocide).[12] As is the case with terrorism, this ambiguity has to do with the tendency to use the term in an evaluative sense, to denote a category of the most abominable, and the least morally defensible, crimes imaginable. However, it is safe to say that, as with terrorism, the difficulty is usually not about the definition but again about numbers and 'mitigating circumstances'. For in spite of difficulties with intent, and the ambiguity surrounding acts short of murder, it is not that difficult to recognize acts that qualify as genocidal, in the sense of being 'extensive, group-selective violence whose purpose is the destruction of that group in a territory under the control of a perpetrator'.[13]

Benjamin A. Valentino chose the term 'mass killing' (defined 'simply as *the intentional killing of massive numbers of noncombatants*') as a generic term that encompasses genocide and ethnic cleansing, 'in order to avoid ... difficulties with the term "genocide"'. Additionally, 'massive' is defined as 'at least fifty thousand intentional deaths over the course of five years or fewer'.[14] In a later work, Valentino modifies the definition to denote 'any event in which the actions of state agents result in the intentional death of at least 1,000 non-combatants from a discrete group in a period of sustained violence'. The period in question is also deemed to start when the number of killings surpasses 100 and ends if the numbers dip below this figure for three consecutive years.[15]

For Christian Gerlach, mass violence is 'widespread physical violence against noncombatants', which goes beyond direct killings to incorporate 'forced removal or expulsion, enforced hunger or undersupply, forced labor, collective rape, strategic bombing, and excessive imprisonment'.[16] Jacques Semelin proposes 'massacre' (defined as '*a form of action that is most often collective and aimed at destroying non-combatants*', italics in original) as the basic unit ('lowest common denominator') of mass violence. Genocide and acts of mass violence are then defined in terms of a series of massacres.[17]

There may be a case for using such a limited and carefully delineated concept as a starting point and building up from there. But even here several problems crop up. Massacres could be committed against combatants, if they are captured (the 1943 Katyn massacre of captured Polish officers by Stalin's troops) or when they are practically unarmed because of unevenness in fire-power (Kitchener's massacre of the Mahdists in the Battle of Omdurman in 1898 or the 'Turkey shoot' of fleeing Iraqi soldiers in Kuwait in 1991). It is also not always 'collective', since a lone gunman or a couple could indulge in massacres, as in Breivik's case.

From our perspective, what matters is not just the numbers but the message being sent and the limits the perpetrators observe. In this regard, Valentino's own alternative rendering of the problem in terms of the 'systematic murder of noncombatants'[18] is a good starting point. When acts of murder are 'systematic', the perpetrators do not foresee a limit or upper ceiling for potential victims. That could be used as the defining characteristic of incidents of mass violence: it is where at least one side in a conflict either deliberately seeks to maximize casualties as a conscious objective, or does not care how many victims, including non-combatants, were targeted in order to achieve a given political objective. This definition covers genocide and mass terrorism, where the maximization of casualties is a direct aim, but also cases of 'ethnic cleansing' (defined in one UN report as 'a purposeful policy designed by one ethnic or religious group to remove by violent and terror-inspiring means the civilian population of another ethnic or religious group from certain geographical areas').[19] It also covers the phenomenon Semelin calls 'genocide of subjugation', aiming to subdue, rather than to exterminate, a group, including 'collateral damage' during carpet bombing, mass shelling or the use of weapons of mass destruction. This definition avoids objections that subsuming genocide under mass murder is 'simplistic' and does not capture core aspects of the crime.[20] For it captures Arendt's important insight about totalitarian and genocidal regimes being 'the fullest expression of a distinctly modern pathological ambition for power that rejected any sense of limits'.[21]

It is indeed this manifest preparedness to accept no limits or restraint which characterizes the phenomena grouped by Scott Straus under the rubric 'mass atrocities'. This concept covers a range of acts of violence that include crimes against humanity, genocide, ethnic cleansing and war crimes. It also implies 'a vague degree of scale consistent with genocide' but without being restricted to 'group-selective or group-destructive violence'. Straus recommends that the concept should evolve towards incorporating 'a high threshold of deliberate lethal violence against civilians'.[22] We believe our definition of mass violence fulfils this requirement by highlighting the preparedness to inflict, or tolerate, a limitless number of casualties and totally unrestrained brutality. It also bypasses the problematic question of intention, since preparedness can be inferred from actual conduct. We did not need Breivik's trial confession to discover that he was not going to stop killing voluntarily. We can also see clearly from the conduct of the Syrian regime since the March 2011 uprising that it was prepared to inflict as much brutality as it took to suppress the popular uprising. Not all mass killers have extermination as an objective, as most hope intimidation would do the trick.

The term 'mass atrocity' is also employed by Gareth Evans to refer to 'what is now embraced by the description "genocide, war crimes, ethnic cleansing, and crimes against humanity"'.[23] The term is used to refer to discreet instances of mass violence as defined above, an equivalent to Semilin's 'massacre', but with more emphasis on the specially abhorrent nature of such crimes.[24]

A number of authors have found, from different perspectives, common features linking mass atrocities. For Neil Kressel, genocide and mass terror are manifestations of 'mass hate'.[25] Helen Fein argues that acts of 'modern collective terrorism' could 'fit under the definition of the genocide of the UNGC' but prefers to describe them as 'genocidal massacres'.[26] In another work, Fein adds slavery and trafficking to genocide and terror as instances of the violation of 'life integrity rights' (which include rights to life and personal inviolability, protection from arbitrary incarceration, maintaining control of one's body and labour, freedom of movement and protection of family life).[27] Claudia Card adds torture to genocide and terror as varieties of 'atrocities' and a 'paradigm of evil'. She only provides an ostensive definition of 'atrocity', however, listing acts of genocides, terror bombings, lynchings, assassinations and war rampages as instances. These acts are also 'uncontroversially evil' (with 'evil' defined as 'reasonably foreseeable intolerable harms produced by *inexcusable* wrongs').[28]

This convergence and 'overlapping' agreement reflect important insights about what is common to 'atrocities'. Our contribution is to add another dimension of overlap: the types of narratives used to incite or justify such acts. The term 'narrative', which is central to our thesis, is also problematized by its application to an increasingly wider number of contexts, causing it to 'become rather inflationary', and lose some of its 'conceptual and analytical force'.[29] With 'the narrative turn' everywhere, as one author noted, 'few words have enjoyed so much use and suffered so much abuse as narrative and its partial synonym, story'. The term could be used to signify 'explanation', 'theory', 'hypothesis', 'evidence', 'ideology' or 'message', not to mention Jean-François Lyotard's celebrated invocation of 'Grand Narratives' (as 'global explanatory schemes').[30] However, attempts to make the concept more precise by setting up criteria for exclusion, while theoretically feasible, run into difficulties because of the sheer variety of narrative forms, genres and texts (including images and visual 'texts').

But there is a further challenge. For the alleged 'abuse' of the term, in particular by postmodernist writers, is often an intentionally 'subversive' device. As part of a deliberate attack on established notions and disciplines, it seeks to undermine the claims of social science (even science as a whole) to a status different from (and superior to) other types of discourse, such as literary criticism. But while purists like Jürgen Habermas deplore this 'levelling of genres',[31] pragmatists like Richard Rorty argue that this is the whole point of the exercise. For them, the distinction between mathematics and literary criticism lies merely in the fact that it is much easier to reach consensus among mathematicians about a theorem than among literary critics about the merits of a text.[32]

Ordinarily, I am more sympathetic to the Habermasian position, but our current enterprise is closer to the 'subversive' side of this debate. It is, in fact, doubly subversive in not just sitting astride a number of different social science disciplines but in also ignoring the even more solid boundary between the social sciences and humanities. We are also bringing into one focus a number of phenomena (terrorism, mass violence, genocide, abuse of democratic rights) which are usually treated separately. We do not thus want to define the term 'narrative' too narrowly.

For this reason, we select Freedman's slightly colourful definition of narratives as 'compelling story lines which can explain events convincingly and from which inferences can be drawn',[33] (in preference to Michael J. Toolan's more austere and schematic 'minimalist' definition: 'a perceived sequence of nonrandomly connected events',[34] which echoes a host of other conventional definitions). It must be recognized, in addition, that the narrative form is ubiquitous, having been internalized in each culture since early childhood. It is thus 'universally present in everything we say, do, think, and imagine. Even our dreams are, to a large extent, organized as narratives. In consequence, its taken-for-granted existence can easily be seen as a natural existence, as a natural and given mode of thought and action'.[35]

As the quote above from MacIntyre suggests, all action is embedded in some narrative, a view also ascribed to Hannah Arendt, who argued that nothing captures the intensity and richness of the meaning of action as 'a properly narrated story'. According to this interpretation, Arendt should best be understood as 'as a theorist of action who understood its intrinsically narrative nature'.[36] In addition to taking on board this point about all action being embedded into some narrative or another, we further narrow the focus by concentrating on 'narratives of insecurity', a term that is being widely used, but mostly without a direct definition. Martin and Petro offer what amounts to an ostensive definition by enumerating instances such as 'strategic fictions' (scenarios of possible security threats), 'tales of catastrophic future wars', politicians' attempts to justify wars or extraordinary political measures by citing possible threats, media coverage of wars and conflict, fictional narratives (films, novels, etc.) dealing directly or indirectly with security issues, philosophical reflections about epochal social transformations and interpretations of satellite images, among others. Most of these narratives, the authors argue, are being deployed to justify (and sometimes contest) 'a revitalized national security policy based on a permanent war strategy'.[37] Taking a cue from Martin's own use of the term to discuss the relevance of horror fiction to the security debate, we provisionally define 'narratives of insecurity' as 'horror stories which protagonists in political contests tell about themselves and others'.

Narratives are by necessity shared accounts – social constructs that are communicated or meant to be communicated. In this regard, we discount paranoid narratives of seriously mentally disturbed people, even when they lead to violence, since such narratives cannot by their nature be shared. However, beyond that there are many levels or possibilities of sharing. When a narrative of insecurity is shared only within a small group, we have a cult or an 'extremist' or a 'fringe' group or network (such as networks of conspiracy theorists). But such a narrative becomes a precursor to mass violence only when it goes mainstream or is espoused by a determined extremist group. The process can go full circle, as when a paranoid cult becomes a state ideology and comes to resemble in some sense psychotic paranoid delusions that are difficult to share except through a process of intimidation and forced indoctrination. Today's North Korea epitomizes this inversion.

The challenge this study is trying to tackle is to explore how fringe narratives of cults and conspiratorial theorists (which will always exist) can go mainstream and gain wider currency and with it power.

Narrating insecurity

A number of studies of genocide and mass violence recognize insecurity as a primary factor and motive. Daniel Chirot and Clark McCauley argue that the most important motive behind mass violence is fear, especially when a group is seen to threaten the very existence or vital interests of the would-be perpetrators. In particular, fear of 'pollution', especially from a moral or religious or a racial perspective, represents a special category of fear that provokes violent reactions against groups perceived as the source of threat.[38]

Fear and the obsession with countering 'pollution' are also seen by Jacques Semelin in his important study as central to genocidal violence. As he puts it, 'fear is indeed present, behind the scenes and at the front of the stage, at the root of it all'.[39] For Midlarsky, threat (fear by the perpetrator of loss of something valuable) and vulnerability (both of the intended victims and the perpetrators) are 'two necessary conditions for the occurrence of genocide'.[40] For Semelin, the greatest fear emanates from a perceived threat to a nation's or a social group's components of identity, 'which give meaning to those who share them and to what brings them together'. But if that basic point of reference, 'which allowed people to say "us"' suddenly disappears, then this 'us' becomes 'a grievance, a wound, an affliction'.[41] This loss could be the effect of a 'collective trauma' (equivalent to individual post-traumatic state) affecting the group, such as military defeats.

Social and political actors respond to this sense of insecurity by 'using metaphors and symbols which resonate deeply with their [people's] own history', so as to 'transform collective (diffuse) anxiety into intense fear directed towards a highly dangerous enemy'. But while the final aim of this social-affective process is 'to treat the afflicted "us" and reshape it in order to help it emerge from its state of crisis', some political actors might attempt to 'tap into the trauma of defeat for their own benefit by offering a narrative that could rescue the nation's honour and provide it with a new incentive'. Those actors who 'know how to tug at these strings of the *imaginaire* have in their possession a powerful weapon'.[42]

In this context, ideology (itself an 'accretion of imaginary representations') can be seen as the 'springboard towards massacre', providing the tipping point from fantasies of annihilation to actual engagement in mass murder. In actual genocide episodes, the rhetoric of these ideologies is built around three main themes: identity, purity and security. 'Since these pertain to life, death and the sacred, they can leave no-one indifferent: they "speak" to everyone, inter-mixing imagination and reality'.[43] Here, 'narratives of identity' are used to 'verbalise anxiety and at the same time to assuage it restoring meaning to what no longer seems of have any'.[44]

The insecurity in question is intimately linked to an imagined identity, which is the object of the threat. For some theorists, '*all* social insecurities are culturally produced'. In this sense, insecurity and the objects to be secured are 'mutually constituted', since 'insecurity is itself the product of processes of identity construction in which the self and the other, or multiple others, are constituted'.[45] The acute perception of a major threat to the in-group from a designated out-group is often accompanied by stereotyping, the exaggeration of differences and over-emphasis on the homogeneity of both groups. In extreme cases of conflict, the other is also dehumanized and placed 'outside the moral universe' of the perpetrator.[46] Accompanied by a manifestation of Freudian 'narcissism of minor differences' in the context of essentializing the Other, this tendency could provoke fear of 'pollution' by proximity, since the other could conceivably 'infiltrate' the group, precisely because he/she is so similar.[47] And, finally, we encounter a narrative which frames this antagonistic relationship and defines the threat.

The role of narratives is also affirmed by Sternberg and Sternberg, who devote at least two chapters to discussing the use of stories instigate and promote hate.[48] Semelin similarly emphasizes the role of propaganda and framing narratives in instigating massacres and genocide by 'cultivating fear and suspicion'. The resulting collective paranoia, or 'delusional rationality', would then structure 'the figure of the enemy to be destroyed into a sufficiently elaborate ideological discourse' that helps 'precipitate destructive action'.[49] Svendsen speaks of 'presentation' as one of the key influences pushing 'normal' people to engage in atrocities. In this context, it can be said that '*ideas* about evil have caused more evil than just about anything else'.[50] Key to this factor is the presentation of the target of atrocities as both 'evil' and a threat to the perpetrators, who are in turn portrayed as potential victims. Atrocity can therefore appear as legitimate self-defence, a process of getting rid of 'pests and vermin'.

In presenting the target group as an immediate existential threat, leaders and political entrepreneurs take advantage of 'the human predilection for historicizing our fears and angers, our hates and loves, and for nursing our past humiliations and errors in order to turn them into vengeful action'.[51] The two processes are linked, as Semelin tried to show: the inherent precariousness of imagined identities is intimately linked to an acute sense of insecurity that is deployed to mobilize the in-group in 'self-defence' against imminent danger.[52]

> [T]he discourse of the other to be destroyed feeds upon a rhetoric of the threat that he represents. Whether this threat is fictional … or real … the other to be destroyed must create fear because it is this feeling of fear that legitimates his destruction … Everything happens as if it were an urgent problem of security … The enterprise of destruction appears to be an operation of prevention and of group survival.[53]

This sense of urgency is shaped, conveyed and disseminated through the appropriate narratives which portray the other as threatening, *regardless of appearances*. This involves the deployment of multiple images and constructions of identities while appealing to deep collective feelings and memories.

> It is for this reason that the study of tales, rumours and memories belonging to a culture … is important for comprehending the massacres that have been committed within them. It is in fact this plunge into the imaginary that gives historical and emotional resonance to the ideological discourse.[54]

Securitization theory, as propounded by the Copenhagen School, also views insecurity as discursively constructed by the means of 'a speech act of securitization', where an actor bestows the security label on an issue, thus designating it an existential threat. This justifies demands for acquiescence from the relevant audience in tolerating (otherwise unacceptable) extraordinary measures to deal with the perceived threat. In this respect, 'it is the utterance itself that is the act' that shifts an issue from 'normal politics' to the realm of the exceptional. It is crucial here to determine when 'an argument with this particular rhetorical and semiotic structure achieves sufficient effect to make an audience tolerate violations of rules'.[55] For some analysts within this broad school, the efficacy of securitization speech-acts (and their form) must take account of 'the fact that contemporary political communication is increasingly embedded within televisual images'. This, in turn, 'requires broader techniques for "reading" the rhetorics of securitizing acts', focusing 'not only on the ways in which images impact on the speech-act of securitization in an age of images, but on the way in which visual representations of different policy options influence security practices'.[56]

Didier Bigo and his collaborators add an emphasis on the 'role of the professionals of the management of unease' in this 'social and political construction of (in)security'. What is at work here is a 'field of professionals' incorporating 'domestic and EU politicians, police and intelligence officials, army officers, security experts, journalists, and the part of civil society enrolled in the (in)security games'.[57] This would signify that influences on securitization outcomes are often conflicting, competitive or contradictory, and always negotiated.

In our analysis, we critically build on these insights, following an approach, similar to the one recommended by Scott Watson, of drawing simultaneously on the insights of securitization theory and the 'framing' literature, which examines the construction of threats from a broader perspective.[58] Framing designates a broad field of studies whose focus is to 'describe the power of a communicating text', mainly by exploring the impact of selecting a particular aspect of 'a perceived reality' and making it 'more salient in a communicating text'. This could in turn 'promote a particular problem definition, causal interpretation, moral evaluation, and/or treatment recommendation'.[59] Research in this area is vast, both empirical and theoretical and covers fields ranging from sociology and psychology to media studies; but its conceptual 'foundations' are found in sociology and psychology, with a focus on the use of words, images and presentation styles to construct a new story and with what impact on audiences.[60] The research also deals with how the audiences deploy their own 'frames' for selecting and responding to communicated texts, exerting in turn influence on communicators, including politicians and media professionals.[61]

Our approach

In synthesizing and building on the valuable insights of all these fields of research, the approach adopted in this book complements and helps shed more light on previous explanations of the incidence of mass atrocities. The added value also includes helping resolve some of the problems and contradictions posed by some competing and partially valid explanations. For example, the contribution of traumatic memories to genocidal mobilization could be subsumed under the 'narrative of insecurity' paradigm, as has been shown by some case studies in this volume (in particular Yugoslavia, Nigeria and Islamophobia). Additionally, this approach could resolve some of the contradictions posed by explanations of mass violence centring on regime type. While many authors argue that genocide and mass killings are usually perpetrated by despotic or totalitarian regimes,[62] others hold that emerging or unstable democracies are more likely to produce such atrocities.[63] Our approach could solve this problem by pointing out that it is in fact *insecure* regimes, whether democratic or not, that are usually dragged onto such a course. Similarly, important new light can be shed on debates such as those provoked by Daniel Goldhagen's controversial 1996 book, *Hitler's Willing Executioners* and Christopher Browning's earlier work, *Ordinary Men: Reserve Police Battalion 101 and the Final Solution in Poland* (1992).[64] While Goldhagen argued that only a deeply ingrained and widely shared 'eliminationist anti-Semitism' could explain the enthusiastic, and often sadistic, German participation in the Holocaust, Browning sees a more nuanced picture, involving the impact of the Nazi regime, the traumas and uncertainties of the time and the atmosphere of war on the Eastern Front, as contributing factors. Our approach can reconcile the two positions by pointing out that German behaviour and attitudes can be explained by the horror stories embraced about various existential threats facing Germany at the time. As Omer Bartov perceptively notes, Germany emerged from the traumatic experience of the First World War with contradictory sentiments that glorified war on the one side and entertained a deep sense of victimhood on the other. 'Elusive' enemies lurked everywhere and needed to be unmasked and eliminated before they 'stab Germany in the back' once more.[65] These traumas and uncertainties could be exploited (given the prevalence of racist attitudes in Europe at the time) to generate and promote such horror stories.

More generally, the narrative-focused approach makes it easier to reconcile agency-centred and structure-centred explanations of the incidence of mass violence. As opposed to the problematically deterministic psychological or sociological explanations, the narrative approach salvages agency in the sense that the acceptance of narratives involves choices, at least theoretically. Certain structural factors favour certain narratives at the expense of others. For example, 'modernity' has made it easier to embrace nationalist narratives as well as some narratives about 'race', including pseudo-scientific narratives about racial stratification (but not narratives about 'malicious witches'). Similarly, 'modern' ideas about the capacity of man to control his world facilitated the acceptability of utopian ideologies and narratives about bright futures that could be attained at a 'reasonable' price in suffering. At another level, wars and conflict made it easier to promote and sell stories of intense insecurity and thereby made drastic policies sound acceptable, even unavoidable.

Confronting (and explaining) evil: The precariousness of human decency

A number of authors have pointed out the near impossibility of 'understanding' or explaining atrocities, given the moral indignation they provoke.

> Can we study the event of 9/11 with [an] intellectual and ethical distance, and if not, can we be said to be 'studying' it – as opposed to invoking, or denouncing, or mourning, or memorializing it – at all?[66]

In her initial reflections on the 'evil' excesses of modern genocidal totalitarianism, Hannah Arendt argued that these excesses represented 'the unpunishable, unforgivable absolute evil which could no longer be understood and explained by the evil motives of self-interest, greed, covetousness, resentment, lust for power, and cowardice'.[67]

The affirmation of the radical and absolute nature of genocidal evil entailed the impossibility, even inappropriateness, of seeking to explain it within the framework of modern social science, which seeks to fit events into familiar patterns. For the early Arendt, to adopt a detached 'objective' stance towards the Nazi concentration camps was not only to misunderstand and misrepresent but to condone.[68] The methodology of the social sciences emphasized function at the expense of 'substance' and could not thus capture a unique and unprecedented phenomenon such as the Holocaust. Nor could it incorporate the sense of horror and indignation that must be an integral part of viewing such phenomena and could not be added as an optional extra.[69]

This assumption of a fundamental incompatibility between understanding and condemnation is symbolized by the divergent attitudes towards using terms such as 'evil' in describing atrocities. For some, the label does reflect 'an intuitive sense that there is a difference between radical evil and more common forms of immoral behaviour'.[70] Arendt has famously (and significantly) adapted the Kantian term 'radical evil' to refer to the horrors of the Holocaust and Soviet mass atrocities.[71] For Claudia Card, what distinguishes 'evil' from lesser wrongs, and what is really shocking about it, is the infliction of foreseeable and intolerable harm on others that is 'utterly without moral excuse'.[72]

However, the central problem resides in the fact that the perpetrators of atrocities usually *do* present 'excuses' they regard as moral. In its most interesting and disturbing sense, the Kantian concept of evil as 'diabolical' (i.e., being perpetrated for its own sake) appears untenable. Following Kant, who had argued that humans were not capable of pure or diabolical evil, most recent commentators agree that pure evil, if it exists at all, is rather rare and thus irrelevant for tackling the wider issues relating to recurrent atrocities. Even sadists inflict pain for their enjoyment.[73]

Card, however, still argues for the retention of the notion of diabolical evil in the case of perpetrators who adopt evil methods to attain objectives that are in themselves evil.[74] Others concur, arguing that replacing the concept of 'evil' with a less loaded alternative could have serious *moral* consequences. Reducing evil to a social, psychological or genetic dysfunction robs the perpetrator of agency and causes moral evil to vanish 'into natural evil'.[75] It could even entail 'treating evil as a kind of sickness that we can cure by putting somebody on a couch, or giving them an injection later on'.[76] Shifting the onus on 'context' for turning ordinary decent people into perpetrators of evil acts can be 'troubling'.

> If Serbian rapists, Hutu machete-wielders, and Nazi camp commandants differ from the average citizens in Western democracies principally by being at the wrong place at the wrong time, by what right could the rest of us condemn them?[77]

So we appear to have a paradox here. In avoiding loaded terms like 'evil' in describing major atrocities, we seem not only to set aside the moral dimension, but to misunderstand the phenomenon we are confronted with. On the other hand, it has also been argued that the 'all too familiar rhetoric of "evil"', fashionable at the time of crisis, can obstruct serious thinking about the challenge and threatens to 'demonize what we refuse to understand'.[78] While there may be a case for a concept to 'designate a level of immorality and depravity beyond the mere immoral', a secularized concept of evil 'has an in-built tendency towards redundancy', becoming 'obscure, difficult, and, in the end, deeply unhelpful'.[79] Additionally, the invocation of 'evil' automatically shifts the gear up in a 'hyper-securitization' direction (see next chapter) with the enemy deemed to be worthy only of annihilation.

> When confronted with an evil foe such as 'the terrorist', self's appropriate response ceases to be simply to defend itself, resist, or even defeat; but instead to stamp out, annihilate, and eradicate, in order to make normal 'friend–enemy' politics possible.[80]

Paradoxically, therefore, invoking the label 'evil' to forcefully condemn mass atrocities ends up leaving extermination as the only viable (even morally sanctioned) option. The 'appropriate' response to genocide must then be genocide, or something pretty close. It is to be ominously recalled here that part of the narrative justification of the Holocaust was to promote a 'belief that the Jews represented a cosmic evil enemy bent on the destruction of the German people and civilization'.[81]

Herein lies the dilemma: the perpetrator does not accept the charge of committing 'evil', so the explanation must show how, from his perspective, this was not an atrocity. However, this explanation cannot be a valid explanation if it does not preserve the full meaning of 'atrocity' without overlooking or diminishing the moral dimension of the problem. To sum up, the challenge is to comprehend the 'incomprehensible' without diminishing or diluting its intrinsic quality as fundamentally 'incomprehensible'. How can we account for the 'ordinariness' of perpetrators of 'evil' without accepting the 'ordinariness' of evil? For, 'explanation' entails, in some sense at least, looking at the matter from the perspective of the perpetrator, which is problematic, to put it mildly.

Hannah Arendt has framed the parameters of this debate by putting forth two apparently contradictory propositions on the 'evil' of modern genocide. Her above cited stance on the evil of genocide as unique, absolute and defying explanation was apparently later modified by her observations on the 'banality of evil' at Adolf Eichmann's trial.[82] The shocking discovery here was that the character of perpetrators of extraordinary evil did not conform to the general notion of the 'demonic' but were rather 'terribly and terrifyingly normal', tending to treat their crimes as mundane tasks which they performed unthinkingly. Their characteristic 'manifold shallowness' meant that, in spite of 'the uncontestable evil of their deeds', the perpetrators appeared 'quite ordinary, commonplace and neither demonic nor monstrous'.[83]

Each characterization has consequences: treating atrocities as instances of absolute evil entails that they defy explanation while the 'banality' thesis 'allowed evil to be situated in totally secular terms, as a function of everyday tasks done by individuals who refuse to make, or prove themselves to be incapable of making, moral decisions'.[84] It also highlights the disturbing revelation that 'evil' is ubiquitous and that, 'under certain conditions individuals might well act no differently than had Eichmann'. As Arendt herself put it, 'Therein lies the horror and, at the same time, the banality of evil.'[85]

In some interpretations, the theses on the radicalness and banality of evil are not incompatible. Responsibility for atrocities is shared by the 'thoughtless' majority that plays various roles in the schemes of the 'monstrous' minority, without fully grasping the full picture. And while the thesis on the unique, emergent and 'incomprehensible' nature of murderous totalitarian systems discouraged generalizations about them, the notion of the ordinariness of evil encourages probing into those 'certain conditions' which could easily turn anybody into an Eichmann. One should add here that, even while asserting the thesis of uniqueness, Arendt hinted at inherent tendencies in the processes of modernity that could easily turn 'normal' societies into murderous enterprises. Due to 'a silent conspiracy with totalitarian instruments devised for making men superfluous', totalitarian solutions 'may well survive the fall of totalitarian regimes in the form of strong temptations which will come up whenever it seems impossible to alleviate political, social, or economic misery in a manner worthy of man'.[86] So the precariousness of moral decency transcends individual 'thoughtlessness'. Whole societies may also lack the moral fibre to face the serious challenges thrown up by modernity.

Arendt's thesis on 'banality' has encountered intense critiques, both at the moral-philosophical and at the political-empirical levels. Many have questioned her picture of Eichmann, whose role could not be plausibly characterized as peripheral or banal, given what is needed to climb the ladder within the brutal Nazi hierarchy.[87] The banality of his motives was only apparent, since he had consciously made the moral choice that led him into perpetrating evil.[88] However, what was remarkable about these critiques of Arendt was 'how far [the] research goes to reinforce her fundamental arguments'.[89] Even critics agree that Arendt has 'got much right by bringing evil down to a concrete level as it might appear in the figure of the cliché-ridden, unthinking bureaucrat'. The banality concept, in fact, 'did some heavy lifting for Arendt, and others that followed in her wake'.[90]

On the basis of Arendt's insight, some observers were forced 'to confront the ordinariness of most perpetrators of mass killing and genocide' who could scarcely be 'distinguished by background, personality or previous political affiliation or behavior as having been men or women unusually likely or fit to be genocidal executioners'.[91] This point is summed up by Stanley Milgram's provocative suggestion that 'If a system of death camps were set up here in the United States of the sort we had seen in Nazi Germany, one would be able to find sufficient personnel for those camps in any medium-sized American town.'[92]

In order to capture the essence of Arendt's deep and provocative insight, it might be helpful to go beyond the Eichmann controversy, which has many other dimensions, and even abandon the very concept of the 'banality of evil' itself. The core of Arendt's insight lies in the point we raised earlier about the precariousness of moral human decency, at both the individual and collective levels. There is a thin line separating decent human beings and morally constituted societies from the abyss of utter barbarism. The question this volume aims to address relates to what is it that propels too many people to cross this line.

The central challenge is thus to account for the ordinariness of the perpetrators of extraordinary atrocities, for the 'humanness' of their appalling inhumanity. If we were to do away with simplistic assumptions about the 'evil' character of the perpetrators (at least as an explanatory variable) and eschew psychological and social determinism, then we are left with a puzzling enigma about the 'magical' triggers which effect the transition from normality to frenzied mass murder. Our suggestion is that the key to resolving this issue lies in examining the narratives put forth by the perpetrators themselves. It is our argument here that acute insecurity induced via narratively constructed panics provides the bridge for crossing the thin line from normality to barbarism.

The advantage of this approach stems from doing away with any assumptions about the perpetrators being 'demonic', evil or psychologically disturbed but without sacrificing agency or moral responsibility. Within the context of narratives constructed (or assimilated) by the perpetrators about themselves, they do not see themselves as 'evil'. In their own story, they were choosing the proverbial 'lesser evil' if not engaged in heroic exploits.

The fierce debate provoked by Millet's take on Breivik's 'atrocious but necessary' acts illustrates this when the issue is framed within a context of a threat to Europe's very existence. Here, we have two ways of constructing the same narrative: one crude and marginal and the other sophisticated and highly intellectual. A number of analysts have already blamed the xenophobic anti-immigrant rhetoric of mainstream European politicians (themselves panicked by the threat of resurgent populist parties) for paving the way for the atrocity.⁹³ Thus, 'Breivik may be a loner, but he's not alone.'

> Transcribing the anti-Muslim blogosphere into his text is his way of showing he is part of a movement... [his text] gets its compositional energy from the phenomenon of crowd-sourcing. This is not a brainless cut-and-paste job. It's a wiki for right-wing terrorism.⁹⁴

Breivik wanted his atrocity to provide a seminal story of 'heroism' and 'direct action' that would broaden this movement. In his self-conducted 'interview', he outlined a plan of action for his presumed followers and issued a chilling warning to the liberal elites of Europe ('cultural Marxists') to 'surrender by 2020' or face extermination. If they stopped all Muslim immigration and began deporting Muslims, they will be forgiven. Otherwise, we 'will eventually wipe out every single one of them'.⁹⁵

However, the hostile reaction to Millet's take on the issue indicates that his hopes remain elusive. Widespread prejudice may be necessary, but not sufficient, to instigate genocidal violence. While you cannot have a Salem witch-hunt where belief in witches is absent, still, not every American town in the late seventeenth century was Salem. So we may need to be cautious about the argument that we are getting dangerously close to genocidal outbursts in Europe as anti-Muslim 'dehumanizing metaphor' becomes more and more prevalent in mainstream political discourse in the context of the 'war on terror'. This may provide 'a cultural platform for acts of war and a potent cognitive framework for interpreting such acts'.⁹⁶ But this begs the question about the transition from political rhetoric that justifies wars and assaults on civil liberties to fantasies of extermination and actual atrocities. In other words, what causes the shift from securitization to hyper-securitization?

Our argument

This book is an attempt to answer these questions, starting with a reminder that 'ordinary' people do not cease to be ordinary when they engage in mass atrocities, but they are transported by the narratives they embrace into a new (constructed) universe where neighbours become demons and poor refugees the vanguard of a conquering army. How this process takes place, and how it works, is the subject of the chapters of this book, where it is argued that the observed 'precariousness of human decency' cannot simply be explained by individual traits or 'collective madness' but by people being in the grip of fear and insecurity. But our specific focus is on *narratives* of insecurity as the main tools of the construction of insecurity and the core variable signalling the shift towards hyper-securitization. We see this in the context of a 'dynamic' narrative which does not just see others as alien, disgusting, inferior or threatening but also as actors in a 'drama' in which the would-be perpetrator is potential victim or probable hero.

In this collection of essays, these tenets are explored, argued further, substantiated and tested in a variety of contexts. While this approach takes into account that the 'dynamics by which mass murder develops are extremely varied',[97] the central hypothesis is that a script which portrays communities as on the verge of losing everything they hold dear is a clarion call to mass atrocities.

The narratives in question must be minimally plausible and also need to be sufficiently gripping to energize the target audiences. Ironically, memories and experiences of past massacres, as was the case in Rwanda, the Balkans, Iraq, Palestine, etc., tend to make wider sections of society more receptive to such narratives, especially at times of turmoil and uncertainty. 'Never again!' then becomes: 'Right Now!' One also needs some skilful story tellers: orators, writers, public intellectuals, artists, media personnel or gifted politicians who could vividly invoke old and new nightmares. When in the grip of these nightmares, actors see no alternative to taking (or at least tolerating) drastic action to avert the perceived catastrophe. Far from regarding what they were about to do as 'evil', they see it as heroic, exhilarating, cleansing and necessary to save the nation, even the world.

The contributions to this volume come from a variety of disciplinary backgrounds and cover diverse regions. They have thus naturally adopted a variety of methodologies, ranging from literary criticism to historical analysis and ethnographic field research and much in between. This gives added value to the contributions, since any corroborations they offer to the main thesis were not 'built-in', so to speak, but were the outcome of independent investigations.

The contributors, in addition, have the advantage of in-depth knowledge of the countries and regions they write about. The intimate knowledge they have of the cultural and historical background and, no less important, of the languages, is important – as some explicitly point out – since some of the crucial cultural and linguistic nuances that shape the key contests are often lost in mainstream debates. The reliance on this intimate knowledge and the marshalling of an impressive number of case studies covering Africa, Europe, the Middle East and Asia enable us to illustrate and shed important light on the processes which cause societies to slide into mass violence.

In Chapter 2, Abdelwahab El-Affendi explores the insecurity-inducing impact of several forms of narrative constructs (TV documentaries, popular fiction, political rhetoric, etc.) to assess the contribution of certain forms of narrative to tolerance for atrocities. Basing his analyses on a critical examination of genocide studies, popular culture, securitization theory and theories of identity construction, El-Affendi introduces the concept of 'hyper-securitization' to account for shifts from minimal securitization polities (usually liberal democracies), to high securitization (authoritarian) regimes, to maximum securitization (totalitarian) regimes and finally hyper-securitization (genocidal) polities. On this basis, he rejects the claim about the 'state of exception' instituted in the context of the 'war on terror' being a manifestation of inherent tendencies in liberal democracies. Rather, what is at issue is the intriguing resilience – and precariousness – of democracies in the face of constant threat from demagogues promoting destabilizing narrative of insecurity. This resilience stems from a capability for producing counter narratives that neutralize the horror narratives of the extremists. As 'minimal securitization' polities that tend to favour desecuritization and minimal state intervention, democracies thrive by rejecting destabilizing narratives through constant contestation but also through memories of previous disasters. This contestation is vital, since atrocities are often scripted in advance into narratives that stir the deepest emotions, unite and divide, generate intense fear and high hopes, demonize rivals and adversaries and ascribe divine affinity to one's group. Some of these narratives (such as the cowboy–Indian contrast in Western films) are so powerful and universally gripping that even Native American children would rather play cowboys than Indians in children's games! The power of compelling narratives can thus hardly be over-estimated.

The competing narratives of Nigerian nationhood offer another compelling example of the impact of rival stories on the escalation of ethnic conflict. Anchored in a colonial past, simultaneously blamed for having dreamt up Nigeria as an anomaly of a nation, and for having sown the seeds of pathological fear and mutual mistrust among its ethnic components, these narratives continue to shape Nigerian politics in the present, with disastrous consequences. In Chapter 3, James Tar Tsaaior explores these narratives, which are defined by tragedy and a major contributor to it. Narratives of extreme insecurity and mistrust have begun to circulate even before independence, as the three men credited with being the 'fathers of the nation', fought duels through autobiographies. In the first salvo, one leader accused his main rival of being a potential Hitler, eager to install his ethnic group as a 'master race' to lord it over the country. Such narratives prompted sections of the nation to engage in pre-emptive or retributive violence, as happened during the events surrounding the disastrous series of coups and counter-coups of 1966 and the subsequent Biafra war. These events in turn became the subject of myth and gist for endless horror narratives of victimhood, conspiracies and tragic heroism, further enhancing animosities and setting the stage for yet more violence. And even though the country appeared since 1999 to be making steady progress towards a stable democracy, it continues to be plagued by new, more localized, if extremely virulent types of violence legitimated by narratives of ethnic or religious victimisation and insecurity. As a result, Nigeria, Africa's giant, is, in Mazrui's phrase, in danger of becoming 'the Lilliput of the world'.

Sudan is another 'African giant' (at least geographically) that has continued to suffer diminution in stature, physically and in every other sense. In July 2011, it lost its status as African's largest country when the South seceded, and before that it has come to symbolize all that could and have gone wrong with a modern state. In Chapter 4, Alex de Waal, a seasoned observer of the country, contemplates one of the paradoxes which have puzzled many over the years: Sudan's notoriety as a country plagued with endemic violence and brutality, as well as the country's reputation of being the site of legendary civility among the elite and the population at large. This 'paradox of civility and barbarity' is underpinned by the coexistence of a multiplicity of competing and conflicting narratives of mutual mistrust and victimhood, together with narratives and traditions of accommodation and civility. Together with persistent claims and counter-claims of betrayal and bad faith, these narratives had led to a relentless degradation of political life, generating a fatalist expectation of violence. This in turn discouraged compromise and helped perpetuate violence, in spite of traditions of inter-elite civility which ensured the rarity of flare-ups of violence in urban areas (or maybe because of them). Direct inter-communal violence in general remained very rare, at least until the Darfur conflict from 2003. The fact that the rival elites rarely experienced personal insecurity may have encouraged intransigent rhetoric and hasty resort to violence. It also contributed to a 'market-place' mentality, where violence was used as a bargaining chip in inter-elite haggling over power and resources. But the consequences for the grass-roots were often tragically costly. De Waal's chapter raises thought-provoking challenges, and we will revisit some of his arguments in our concluding remarks.

In Chapter 5, Kenneth Inyani Simala looks at the flare up of violence in Kenya in the wake of the disputed 2007 presidential elections as an illustration of the ways in which elite rivalry tended to be expressed through 'killer narratives' that foreground ethnicity as a focus of mobilisation. The overt and covert manipulation of ethnic loyalties in the context of short-term political rivalry is anchored in deeply internalized narratives of deprivation and victimisation connected to land ownership (or lack of it). Some of these narratives cover periods going back to pre-colonial times, but they are still the object of fervent contemporary contests. The narratives deployed, mainly through the media, but also in electoral rhetoric, do not just frame identity, but also define the parameters of the conflict and make it intelligible to the protagonists. Each flare-up is exacerbated by memories of past conflicts, recalled grievances, publicized fraudulent land grabs and ever-shifting political/ethnic alliances. In view of the multiplicity of stories and competing interpretations of Kenyan history, the responsibility for the absence of civility that characterized the 2007 elections falls on the shoulders of the political elite who peddle the self-serving stories framing Kenyan nationhood. Reading between the lines in Simala's chapter, one can already discern latent narratives that could frame forthcoming contests and conflicts.

While many of the above cases illustrate how national nightmares of insecurity and memories of victimisation and genocide can generate extreme violence, the case of extremist Hindu nationalism in India illustrates another dimension of the issue: how violence can be enlisted in the construction and vindication of narratives of insecurity. In Chapter 6, Dibyesh Anand explains how the ultra-nationalist Hindutva movement evolved an exclusivist identity narrative in which the 'Muslim' figures as a source of multiple threats to 'the security of Hindu body politic'. In particular, 'myths and stereotypes about the marauding and libidinous Muslim, the innocent and motherlike Hindu woman, the tolerant Hindu man' are constantly enlisted to mobilize hostility to the minority. As a result, 'dehumanized representations of the Other as a danger' become tools for 'the normalization of abnormal violence'. More important, Hindutva activists advocate violence as a means for 'awakening the nation', thus deliberately generating insecurity to make their narratives more plausible for the majority of Hindus, who have not yet espoused these narratives. According to Anand, the Hindu ultra-nationalists 'borrow heavily from the orientalist and imperialist writings' to support their narrative demonizing Muslims. One result is that the 'most common image of the Muslim amongst Hindutva today is of [the] "terrorist"'.

The disintegration of Yugoslavia in the 1990s has become emblematic of the way haunting narratives of insecurity and victimhood could translate themselves into actual horror stories of mass murder. In Chapter 7, Slobodan G. Markovich provides an intriguing insight into the evolution and function of these competing narratives of victimhood, and in the process dissipates many common misperceptions about the context in which these narratives emerged. Markovich highlights the role of a few intellectuals, mostly disillusioned Communists, in developing competing Serb and Croat historical accounts of victimhood and genocide, which in turn enthused and energized rival and conflicting national identities in the decaying phase of the Yugoslav Communist state. These narratives partly reflected disenchantment with the universalist and pan-Yugoslav Communist narrative, and contributed to the discrediting and disintegration of that narrative (centred around the Tito cult and a rosy image of a progressive Yugoslav haven of brotherhood). The resulting ethical vacuum was filled by rival ultra-nationalist narratives. In the process, Croat narratives of inter-war victimhood and post-WWII massacres emerged to counter rival Serbian narratives of 'perennial' victimhood: from WWI sacrifices to WWII genocide (in which the Croats were the 'villain'). The imaginatively crafted narratives, first rehearsed among émigrés, gained immense popularity in the 1980s, and drew the battle lines of that era. Markovich argues that these authors did not intend to promote conflict, just to commemorate the suffering of their respective nations and recover lost identity. However, it was inevitable that narratives of martyrdom and genocide where the villain is in fact a political competitor could scarcely have led to any other outcome.

In Chapter 8, Ilan Pappe looks at the probably unique case of Israel-Palestine, where holding to competing narratives of victimhood represents an existential struggle for national survival. Both Palestinians and Israelis jealously guard and nurture their narratives of suffering, which they do not want any recognition of the suffering of the other side to dilute. This duel by narrative perpetuates the conflict and obstructs reconciliation, becoming a major source of insecurity on its own right. Pappe sees no prospect for peace unless Israel admits responsibility for the *Nakbah* and Palestinian dispossession. However, he sees this as a distant possibility, given the genuine and deep fear among Israelis of confronting this burden. Admitting to atrocities would have 'existential repercussions for Israeli Jewish psyche'; it would mean not only losing the status of the 'ultimate victim in modern history', but also shockingly suggests that Israeli Jews were becoming 'a mirror image of their worst nightmare'. To overcome this problem, Pappe suggests an approach of reconciliation along the lines of the Truth and Reconciliation process, where the object is not to punish or apportion blame but to end suffering.

In Chapter 9, the Israeli-Palestinian contest over who 'controls the story', is approached by Maria Holt from another angle, as she explores the role of Palestinian women in producing and preserving narratives of victimisation and dispossession in the contest of legitimizing resistance. Drawing from her field research in Lebanon and the West Bank, Holt examines the complex role of women as keepers of memory and 'guardians of the Palestinian resistance narrative, as well as representing voices of morality'. She finds that women favour peaceful resistance, where they could have a more equal role. However, in view of their inordinate share of suffering, they nevertheless do not shy away from supporting violence, or even becoming suicide bombers themselves (admittedly in very rare cases). Here, violence is deployed to reinforce Palestinians narratives, to ensure they get attention and not be displaced by the rival Israeli narratives. However, a paradoxical circularity emerges from this process, since the violence produced on account of narratives of self-vindication is in turn used to undermine the precarious narratives of Palestinian nationhood and rights through accusations of terrorism. The violence can also undermine the women's own quest for a role beyond the sub-roles assigned to them by tradition.

Iraq is another country that has become synonymous with genocidal violence repeatedly spiralling out of control. In Chapter 10, Ali Allawi takes the wider view, trying to contextualize the recent ethnic and sectarian violence in Iraq within the broader history of the modern Iraqi state. In the process, he throws up new and startling insights into the nature of this violence. Basing his analysis on Michael Mann's typology of mass violence and ethnic cleansing, Allawi compares six major flare-ups of mass violence in modern Iraq in terms of actors, scale, justifying narratives and outcomes. His findings indicate that, the post-Saddam sectarian mass violence was the exception, rather the norm. Although stoked by rival narratives of insecurity and victimisation (including very plausible historical allegations of genocide and ethnic cleansing), the recent signalled a radical departure from earlier forms of violence instigated by an increasingly insecure national state. The notable exception was the anti-Jewish riots of 1941, which were perpetrated by non-state actors. Responding to actual or perceived threats to its authority, the nascent and fragile Iraqi state tended to unleash progressively spiralling violence against sections of the population. Action escalated from the suppression of the Assyrian uprising of 1933 (with an estimated 600 fatalities), to the ethnic cleansing of the Fayli Kurds in the 1970s and 1980s, before reaching virtually genocidal proportions in the campaigns against the Kurds in 1988 and Shi'a insurgents in 1991. The most recent post-2003 violence, like the short-lived anti-Jewish riots of 1941, reflects the weakness of the state rather than its might. It employed similar narratives, accusing the target groups of disloyalty, treacherous activity, fealty to foreign powers and alien ideologies. These narratives, in turn, were shaped and dominated by obsessions of the Iraqi state elite, in particular in its Arab nationalist phase, with building a 'strong' centralizing state, and its 'glorification of the military [and] refusal to recognize or formally acknowledge the notion of plural identities'. In few other places had narratives of mutual insecurity claimed more victims.

It has not been our conscious plan, but the perception of Islamic identities as threatening appear as a thread connecting almost all of the cases marshalled here to illustrate how narratives of insecurity frame and justify mass violence. This may seem an indirect confirmation of Huntington's famous remark that 'Islam has bloody borders'. As extreme right-wing narratives suggest, the fact that 'Muslims' are involved in conflicts in all sorts of places (even if they were victims), is a sure confirmation that there is something wrong with Islam. In Chapter 11, Nafeez Mosaddeq Ahmed accepts that the term 'Islamophobia' may be an 'under-developed' and imprecise one, but the phenomenon it denotes is real (and alarming) enough. For Ahmed, the rise of Islamophobia is not simply the product of the progressive demonization of Muslims in the media in the post-9/11 era, but is linked to residual imperialism and increasing global uncertainties. Tending more towards the stance of the Paris School on International Security (and taking a more favourable position than El-Affendi's towards the 'jargon of the state of exception'), Ahmed argues that Islamophobia is best understood as a narrative of securitisation which enlists prejudice to deal with the increasingly unmanageable crises and uncertainties of an era of retreating Western hegemony. In fact, some securitizing discourses deliberately seek to link the 'Islamic threat' to perceived multiple crises and 'threats' which include economic uncertainties, dwindling resources, imbalanced demographics, and even climate change. The resulting progressive securitisation of the Muslim presence in the West (and in Muslim regions as well), threatens to generate a self-reinforcing process where demonization of Muslims at home and attacks on Muslim targets abroad produces a spiral of alienation and counter-violence. The institutionalization of anti-Muslim paranoia in the form of wide-ranging new domestic legal and political measures has exacerbated the problem, giving the media and extremists more anti-Muslim narratives to feed upon. While Ahmed's concern that this process could turn genocidal may sound like an exaggeration, one might be tempted to think again in the light of recent alarming ascendancy of extreme right-wing groups and the artificially induced anti-Muslim hysteria in the United States.

In Chapter 12, Anas Al-Shaikh-Ali explores Islamophobia from a more literary perspective, tracing the bewildering proliferation of Islamophobic narratives in Western popular culture in the past couple of decades, with increasingly violent consequences. What Al-Shaikh-Ali finds more intriguing is the uncanny continuity between tendentious story-telling about Muslims over more than three centuries. Thus one can find recurring themes in the narratives of nineteenth-century 'travellers' (who pontificated about the barbarism of 'Turks' without ever having set foot in a Muslim country), in films that consistently painted the 'Arab' in the dimmest of lights, or in new-old fabricated 'real life stories'. There seems to be a ready template on which all stories about Muslims are modelled, and it is worryingly reproducing the narratives that presaged earlier genocides. It is no surprise then that indiscriminate anti-Muslim violence is also on the rise. Perpetrators of atrocities have been exposed to these narratives in myriad forms: news, film, TV shows, computers games, novels or embellished 'factual' fantastic narratives about very improbable religious conversions. There is a clear line from the ubiquitous demonizing narratives to the atrocities. In fact, there were times when the narrative and violence merged into each other, as happened from the late eighteenth century when Muslim prisoners of war were forced to attend plays with 'appropriate Near Eastern' themes in American port cities, both as a form of abuse and as a spectacle. Interestingly, however, Al-Shaikh-Ali finds that alternative narratives had existed as far back as the eighteenth century, where genuine eyewitness narratives challenged the fabulous stories of the make-believe travellers, just as today alternative news reports, films and books continue to challenge dominant narratives, even if usually from the periphery. The truth tellers of the nineteenth century also found it difficult to get people to believe them, but it is a start in the right direction.

The chapters in this book add a number of important and novel perspectives to the ongoing discussions on mass violence. By their focus on justifying narratives, and by treating mass violence in a variety of regions and contexts, the contributions have generated new and important insights. As mentioned above, they complement and enhance a number of structural explanations which would otherwise remain incomplete or unconvincing. Thus while the chapters confirm theses about links between mass violence and modernity, wars, the modern nation state, divided societies and even democracy, they go beyond this to give these presumed links a specific meaning. The common thread running through these factors is the incongruence between new powerful institutions and the narratives of self, identity and empowerment simultaneously generated and encouraged by modernity. Thus the reformulation of pre-existing ethno-religious identities into proto-nationalist narratives (Iraq, Yugoslavia, Nigeria, Sudan, Kenya), in conjunction with the removal of an authoritarian order (colonialism, Communist or nationalist dictatorship) and the establishment of a new state that attempts to extend its powers to previously unregulated areas, create conditions for intense conflict. The processes are self-reinforcing: the narratives of empowerment and self-determination encourage groups to reject conditions that they would have tolerated in the past, while any exclusivist construction of the state automatically designates 'outside' groups as a threat. The aspirations of excluded groups and memories of earlier traumas are marshalled to mobilize new identities, while threatened states and groups then take drastic action, generating new grievances. Wars either consolidate new states or bring about their disintegration, providing cover for atrocities in the process, which in turn generate new grievances and contests over narratives. The case studies also show that the construction of new narratives builds on existing repertoires, by seeking to confirm, modify or contest them. The versions which gained most traction in mobilizing groups behind mass violence were those most successful in consecrating victimhood on one side and villainy on the other. This was achieved, for example, in Nigeria by re-telling the stories surrounding the 1966 coups, and in Yugoslavia by recounting (in both senses of the world) the events of the Second World War. In sum, when narratives depict an existing situation as intolerable or threatening, drastic action that recognizes no limits is called for or legitimized.

Thus in spite of starting from diverse points of view and disciplinary backgrounds, and with no prior obligation to support the core hypothesis, the chapters have provided compelling evidence in support of the thesis that narratives of victimhood and insecurity play a central role in precipitating and legitimating mass atrocities. This, we hope, is sufficient to encourage others to explore this theme further. In the following chapter, we explore in more detail the intricacies of the interconnection between narrative construction and mass atrocities, and in the concluding chapter, we revisit again some of the core points raised by the present contributions, some of which indicate the need for further research in this area.

Notes

1 Alasdair MacIntyre, *After Virtue*, New York: Bloomsbury Academic, 2013, p. 250.
2 Jacques Semelin, *Purify and Destroy: The Political Uses of Massacre and Genocide*, New York: Columbia University Press, 2007, p. 38.

3   L. Timmel Duchamp, ed., *Narrative Power: Encounters, Celebrations, Struggles*, Seattle, WA: Aqueduct Press, 2010, p. 2.
4   Richard Rorty, *Contingency, Irony and Solidarity*, Cambridge: Cambridge University Press, 1989, p. 146.
5   Richard Millet, *Langue fantôme, suivi de Éloge littéraire d'Anders Breivik*, Paris: P.-G. de Roux, 2012.
6   Jessica Elgot, 'French Writer Richard Millet Says Anders Breivik Gave Norway "What It Deserved"', *The Huffington Post*, 30 August 2012, http://www.huffingtonpost.co.uk/2012/08/30/french-richard-millet-norway-anders-breivik-deserved_n_1842337.html.
7   Leslie Paul Thiele, 'The Ontology of Action: Arendt and the Role of Narrative', *Theory & Event*, Vol. 12, No. 4 (2009), http://muse.jhu.edu/login?auth=0&type=summary&url=/journals/theory_and_event/v012/12.4.thiele.html.
8   *A More Secure World: Our Shared Responsibility*, Report of the High-level Panel on Threats, Challenges and Change, New York, United Nations, 2004, pp. 51–52, 160–161.
9   *A More Secure World*, p. 52, § 164d.
10 Alex Schmid, 'Terrorism – The Definitional Problem', *Case Western Reserve Journal of International Law*, Vol. 36, Nos. 2 and 3 (2004), pp. 372–420.
11 Schmid, 'Terrorism', pp. 403–404.
12 Samuel Totten and Paul R. Bartrop, *The Genocide Studies Reader*, London: Routledge, 2009, p. x.
13 Scott Straus, 'Identifying Genocide and Related forms of Mass Atrocity', Working Paper, United States Holocaust Memorial Museum, 7 October 2011, pp. 19–20, http://www.ushmm.org/m/pdfs/20111219-identifying-genocide-and-mass-atrocity-strauss.pdf [accessed 7 December 2013], p. 4.
14 Benjamin A. Valentino, *Final Solutions: Mass Killing and Genocide in the Twentieth Century*, Ithaca, NY: Cornell University Press, 2004, pp. 10–12.
15 Jay Ulfelder and Benjamin Valentino, 'Assessing the Risks of State-Sponsored Mass Killing', *Political Instability Task Force*, Washington, DC, 1 February 2008. Available at SSRN: http://ssrn.com/abstract=1703426 or http://dx.doi.org/10.2139/ssrn.1703426, pp. 2–4.
16 Christian Gerlach, *Extremely Violent Societies: Mass Violence in the Twentieth-Century World*, Cambridge: Cambridge University Press, 2010, p. vii.
17 Semelin, *Purify and Destroy*, p. 4.
18 Valentino, *Final Solutions*, p. 10.
19 Benjamin Lieberman, '"Ethnic Cleansing" Versus Genocide', in Donald Bloxham and A. Dirk Moses, eds., *The Oxford Book of Genocide Studies*, Oxford: Oxford University Press, 2010, p. 44.
20 Martin Shaw, 'Darfur: Counter-insurgency, Forced Displacement and Genocide', *The British Journal of Sociology*, Vol. 62, No. 1 (2011), pp. 56–61.
21 Douglas Klusmeyer, 'Beyond Tragedy: Hannah Arendt and Hans Morgenthau on Responsibility, Evil and Political Ethics', *International Studies Review*, Vol. 11, No. 2 (2009), p. 335.
22 Straus, 'Identifying Genocide', pp. 4–5, 21.
23 Gareth Evans, *The Responsibilty to Protect: Ending Mass Atrocity Crimes Once and For All*, Washington, DC: The Brookings Institution, 2009, pp. 11–12.
24 Claudia Card, *Confronting Evils: Terrorism, Torture, Genocide*, Cambridge: Cambridge University Press, 2010, pp. 5–8.

25 Neil Kressel, *Mass Hate: The Global Rise of Genocide and Terror*, New York: Westview, 2002, pp. 1–11.
26 Helen Fein, 'Defining Genocide as a Sociological Concept', in Samuel Totten and Paul R. Bartrop, eds., *The Genocide Studies Reader*, London: Routledge, 2009, p. 51.
27 Helen Fein, *Human Rights and Wrongs: Slavery, Terror, Genocide*, Boulder, CO: Paradigm Publishers, 2007
28 Card, *Confronting Evils*, pp. 6, 16.
29 Jens Brockmeier and Rom Harré, 'Narrative: Problems and Promises of an Alternative Paradigm', in Jens Brockmeier and Donal A. Carbaugh, eds., *Narrative and Identity: Studies in Autobiography, Self and Culture*, Amsterdam: John Benjamins Publishing Company, 2001, p. 40.
30 Marie-Laure Ryan. 'Toward a Definition of Narrative', in David Herman ed. *The Cambridge Companion to Narrative*, Cambridge: Cambridge University Press, 2007, p. 22.
31 Jürgen Habermas, *The Philosophical Discourse of Modernity: Twelve Lectures*, Cambridge, MA: MIT Press, 1990, pp. 185–210.
32 Richard Rorty, *Philosophy and Social Hope*, London: Penguin Books, 1999, pp. 179–180.
33 Lawrence Freedman, 'Networks, Culture and Narratives', *Adelphi Papers*, Vol. 45, No. 379 (2006), p. 22.
34 Quoted in Roberto Franzosi, 'Narrative Analysis-or Why (and How) Sociologists Should be Interested in Narrative', *Annual Review of Sociology*, Vol. 24 (1998), p. 519.
35 Brockmeier and Harré, 'Narrative', p. 47.
36 Thiele, 'The Ontology of Action'.
37 Andrew Martin and Patrice Petro, eds., *Rethinking Global Security: Media, Popular Culture, and the 'War on Terror'*, New Brunswick, NJ: Rutgers University Press, 2006, p. 2.
38 Daniel Chirot and Clark McCauley, *Why Not Kill Them All? The Logic and Prevention of Mass Political Murder*, Princeton: Princeton University Press, 2010, pp. 20–45.
39 Semelin, *Purify and Destroy*, p. 42.
40 Manus I. Midlarsky, *The Killing Trap: Genocide in the Twentieth Century*, Cambridge: Cambridge University Press, 2005, p. 4.
41 Semelin, *Purify and Destroy*, p. 15.
42 Semelin, *Purify and Destroy*, pp. 16–17, 23.
43 Semelin, *Purify and Destroy*, p. 22.
44 Semelin, *Purify and Destroy*, pp. 22–27.
45 Jutta Weldes et al., eds., *Cultures of Insecurity: States, Communities, and the Production of Danger*, Minneapolis: University of Minnesota Press, 1999, pp. 1, 10.
46 James Waller, *Becoming Evil: How Ordinary People Commit Genocide and Mass Killing*, New York: Oxford University Press, 2002, pp. 239–247.
47 Chirot and McCauley, *Why Not Kill Them All?*, pp. 81–89.
48 Robert J. Sternberg and Karin Sternberg, *The Nature of Hate*, Cambridge: Cambridge University Press, 2008.
49 Semelin, *Purify and Destroy*, pp. 46, 72–74.
50 Svendsen, *A Philosophy of Evil*, pp. 123, 185.
51 Chirot and McCauley, *Why Not Kill Them All?*, p. 91.
52 Semelin, *Purify and Destroy*, pp. 42–47.

53 Jacques Semelin, 'Toward a Vocabulary of Massacre and Genocide', *Journal of Genocide Research*, Vol. 5, No. 2 (2003), p. 197.
54 Semelin, 'Toward a Vocabulary of Massacre and Genocide', p. 196.
55 Barry Buzan, Ole Wæver and Jaap de Wilde, *Security: A New Framework for Analysis*. Boulder, CO: Lynne Rienner, 1998, pp. 25-26; See also, Ole Wæver, 'Securitization and Desecuritization', in Ronnie D. Lipschutz ed. *On Security*, New York: Columbia University Press, 1995, pp. 46-86.
56 Michael C. Williams, 'Words, Images, Enemies: Securitization and International Politics', *International Studies Quarterly*, Vol. 47 (2003), pp. 512, 527.
57 Didier Bigo and Anastassia Tsoukala, eds, *Terror, Insecurity and Liberty: Illiberal Practices of Liberal Regimes After 9/11*, London: Routledge, 2008, pp. 3-4.
58 Scott D. Watson, '"Framing" the Copenhagen School: Integrating the Literature on Threat Construction', *Millennium: Journal of International Studies*, Vol. 40, No. 2 (2012), pp. 279-301.
59 Robert M. Entman, 'Framing: Toward Clarification of a Fractured Paradigm', *Journal of Communication*, Vol. 43, No. 4 (1993), pp. 51-52.
60 Porismita Borah, 'Conceptual Issues in Framing Theory: A Systematic Examination of a Decade's Literature', *Journal of Communication*, Vol. 61 (2011), p. 247.
61 Dennis Chong and James N. Druckman, 'A Theory of Framing and Opinion Formation in Competitive Elite Environments', *Journal of Communication*, Vol. 57 (2007), pp. 99-118.
62 For example, Irving Horowitz, *Genocide: State, Power and Mass Murder*, New Brunswick: Transaction Books, 1976.
63 Michael Mann, *The Dark Side of Democracy: Explaining Ethnic Cleansing*, Cambridge: Cambridge University Press, 2005.
64 See Cole, *The Myth of Evil*, pp. 174-191, for a summary of this debate.
65 Omer Bartov, 'Defining Enemies, Making Victims: Germans, Jews, and the Holocaust', *The American Historical Review*, Vol. 103, No. 3 (June, 1998), pp. 771-816; see also, Omer Bartov, 'Genocide, Barbaric Others, and the Violence of Categories: A Response to Omer Bartov: Reply', *The American Historical Review*, Vol. 103, No. 4 (October, 1998), pp. 1191-1194.
66 Alan Nadel, 'Terror, Representation, and Postmodern Lessons in Hitler Studies', *Postmodern Culture*, Vol. 20, No. 1 (September 2009), http://muse.jhu.edu/login?uri=/journals/postmodern_culture/v020/20.1.nadel.html.
67 Hannah Arendt, *The Origins of Totalitarianism*, New York: Meridian Books, 1958, p. 459.
68 Peter Baehr, 'Identifying the Unprecedented: Hannah Arendt, Totalitarianism, and the Critique of Sociology', *American Sociological Review*, Vol. 67, No. 6 (2002), pp. 805-807.
69 Baehr, 'Identifying the Unprecedented', pp. 808-809.
70 Richard J. Bernstein, *Radical Evil: A Philosophical Interrogation*, Cambridge, MA: Polity, 2002, p. ix.
71 Richard J. Bernstein, *The Abuse of Evil: The Corruption of Politics and Religion since 9/11*, Cambridge, MA: Polity Press, 2005, pp. 6-9.
72 Card, *Confronting Evils*, p. 9.
73 Lars Svendsen, *A Philosophy of Evil*, (trans. Kerri A. Pierce), London: Dalkey Archive Press, 2010, pp. 111-122; Cf. Phillip Cole, *The Myth of Evil: Demonizing the Enemy*, New York: Greenwood Publishing Group, 2006, p. 3.

74 Card, *Confronting Evils*, p. 57.
75 Svendsen, *A Philosophy of Evil*, pp. 21–24.
76 Philip Hallie, 'Response to Jeffrey Burton Russell', in Paul Woodruff and Harry A. Wilmer, eds., *Facing Evil: Confronting the Dreadful Power Behind Genocide, Terrorism, and Cruelty*, Chicago, IL: Open Court, 1988, p. 63.
77 Kressel, *Mass Hate*, p. 1457.
78 Bernstein, *Radical Evil*, p. x.
79 Phillip Cole, *The Myth of Evil: Demonizing the Enemy*, New York: Greenwood Publishing Group, 2006, p. 7.
80 Farid Abdel-Nour, 'An International Ethics of Evil?', *International Relations*, Vol. 18, No. 4 (December 2004), pp 432–433.
81 Cole, *The Myth of Evil*, p. 236.
82 Hannah Arendt, *Eichmann in Jerusalem: A Report on the Banality of Evil*, London, Faber & Faber, 1963.
83 Hannah Arendt, *The Life of the Mind* Vol. I, London: Secker and Warburg, 1978, pp. 3–4 (Quoted in: Barry Clarke, 'Beyond "The Banality of Evil"', *British Journal of Political Science*, Vol. 10, No. 4 (October, 1980), p. 420.
84 George Cotkin, 'Illuminating Evil: Hannah Arendt and Moral History', *Modern Intellectual History*, Vol. 4, No. 3 (2007), pp. 463–490.
85 Cotkin, 'Illuminating Evil', pp. 480–481.
86 Arendt, *The Origins*, p. 459.
87 David Cesarani, *Becoming Eichmann: Rethinking the Life, Crimes, and Trial of a 'Desk Murderer'*, New York: DaCapo Press, 2006; Yaacov Lozowick, *Hitler's Bureaucracies: The Nazi Security Police and the Banality of Evil*, trans. Haim Watzman, New York: Continuum, 2000.
88 Clarke, 'Beyond "The Banality of Evil"', p. 439.
89 Barry Gewen, 'The Everyman of Genocide', *The New York Times*, 14 May 2006, http://www.nytimes.com/2006/05/14/books/review/14gewen.html.
90 Cotkin, 'Illuminating Evil', pp. 485–486.
91 Waller, *Becoming Evil*, p. 8.
92 Kressel, *Mass Hate*, p. 145.
93 Nicholas Kulish, 'Norway Attacks Put Spotlight on Rise of Right-Wing Sentiment in Europe', *The New York Times*, 23 July 2011, http://www.nytimes.com/2011/07/24/world/europe/24europe.html.
94 Moustafa Bayoumi, 'Breivik's Monstrous Dream—and Why It Failed', *The Nation*, 21 May 2012, http://www.thenation.com/article/167682/breiviks-monstrous-dream-and-why-it-failed.
95 Beau Friedlander, 'An Interview with a Madman: Breivik Asks and Answers His Own Questions', *Time*, 24 July 2011, http://www.time.com/time/world/article/0,8599,2084895,00.html#ixzz1rSNtZKUI.
96 Erin Steuter and Deborah Wills, *At War with Metaphor: Media, Propaganda, and Racism in the War on Terror*, Lanham, MD: Lexington Books, 2009, (loc. 83, Kindle edition).
97 Semelin, *Purify and Destroy*, p. 168; Cf. Chirot and McCauley, 'Why Not Kill Them All?', pp. 90–94.

2

Killer Narratives:
Collective Nightmares and the Construction of Narrative Communities of Insecurity

Abdelwahab El-Affendi

In this chapter, we explore at length this book's core hypothesis: that constructed nightmares provide the best clue to accounting for the precariousness of human decency by accounting for the 'ordinariness' of perpetrators of 'evil' without accepting the 'ordinariness' of evil. We start by showing how one type of narrative (the TV documentary) could be used to deconstruct and puncture the rival nightmare scenarios that underpin the 'war on terror'. Then, we offer a brief overview of the various explanations seeking to account for mass violence and genocide, with a special focus on explanations which foreground the construction of identity and victims. We then explore the construction of 'communities of insecurity' in the process of constructing and expressing identity, followed by a critical look at Securitization Theory's take on the construction of insecurity. We then explore how popular culture and political rhetoric combine to construct, accentuate, and exploit insecurity, before proceeding to question how particular narratives gain wider currency at the expense of rivals.

Several conclusions are drawn from this wide-ranging discussion. First, securitization and the construction of identity do not automatically initiate the escalation towards violent exclusion and mass violence. Up to a certain level, they are functional for the health of the community. Only when extreme narratives of insecurity manage to displace more measured accounts do we see a slide towards mass atrocities. In this context, the slide towards excessive securitization in liberal democracies under the influence of the 'war on terror', while disturbing, does not (yet) warrant the exaggerated claims about looming totalitarianism. Even less the claim that the 'state of exception' has only revealed the true nature of liberal democracies as 'disguised' totalitarian systems. Rather, recent developments have highlighted the paradoxical precariousness and resilience of democratic systems, and the threat posed to them by paranoid narratives of extreme insecurity. We end by showing how destabilizing narratives could be, and have been, challenged in democracies by equally powerful rival narratives of inclusion.

Constructing nightmares to inhabit

In its attempt to chart the convoluted prehistory the 'war on terror', Adam Curtis's TV documentary series *The Power of Nightmares* focuses on what the two protagonists in this saga (Islamic militants and American neoconservatives) had in common. Their gurus were contemporaries with similar (anti-liberal) frames of mind, and the two tendencies even became allies at one point (in the anti-Soviet war in Afghanistan). Each had directly and indirectly helped further the other's agenda by confirming its nightmarish visions of the world.

> Both were idealists who were born out of the failure of the liberal dream to build a better world. And both had a very similar explanation for what caused that failure. These two groups have changed the world, but not in the way that either intended. Together, they created today's nightmare vision of a secret, organized evil that threatens the world. A fantasy that politicians then found restored their power and authority in a disillusioned age. And those with the darkest fears became the most powerful.[1]

According to one critic, the series 'is best watched as an epic political cartoon': it bends, simplifies and distorts the facts; 'yet, as only a cartoon can, it captures an aspect of its subject that has so far escaped even the most skeptical observers of the war on terror'.[2] No less intriguing is the fact that the narratives produced by these two protagonists appeared to vacillate between supremacist narratives of world domination, and horror stories of decline and vulnerability. America (or Islam) was in a position to shape the world, but is at the same time, worryingly vulnerable, besieged by external threats. No less dangerous, in the eyes of the neoconservatives, were local rivals ('paleoconservatives (anti-Semites to a man), and fainthearted, détente-addicted Democrats and their lackeys in the press and in Europe'). Indeed, from this perspective, the terror threat fades when compared to 'the combined forces of Michael Moore, Bill Clinton, Brent Scowcroft, Pat Buchanan, Robert Novak, and *The New York Times*'.[3] This is mirrored by the rhetoric of radical jihadists, who also fear and detest their local rivals ('traitors', 'hypocrites', 'sell-outs', etc.), while projecting themselves as a 'force of history' in exhilarating and dangerous times, at once invincible and extremely vulnerable.

This lethal combination of supremacist rhetoric and narratives of extreme vulnerability tends to characterize potentially genocidal discourses, as indicated by Nazi narratives. These feature the 're-creation of the Germans as an Aryan master race in a new thousand-year Reich', simultaneously with the terror of an enemy that was at the same time inferior and all-powerful, 'a real, albeit elusive, enemy lurking behind all other evils that plagued Germany'.[4] The same narrative of 'hagiography of the Self' contrasted with 'the representations of Other as threatening' characterizes the discourse of the ultra-nationalist Hindutva movement in India.[5] Elsewhere, former Israeli Prime Minister Ehud Barak described the Middle East in an August 1999 speech as a brutal jungle, with 'no pity or respect for the weak... whoever is incapable of defending himself does not get a second chance'.[6] Similar narratives circulated in

Darfur, where the term 'holocaust' first appeared in 1987, nearly two decades before 'genocide' became the widely used term to depict the atrocities there.[7]

What Curtis demonstrates is the power of a good story: in this case, the re-telling of a familiar story by juxtaposing the histories of two distinct groups as *one* integrated narrative, where the trajectories of the main protagonists converge as in a Greek tragedy. This can help puncture the narratives of the protagonists, but maybe at the expense of constructing an alternative narrative of insecurity, a type of 'conspiracy theory'. Powerful techniques for framing and selectiveness are also common in fiction, where authors use them to generate reader empathy for their characters, including telling the story from their vantage point, or selectively highlighting incidents of injustice, misery, heroism, etc.[8] The same happens in politics. A study of two decades of American presidential rhetoric found that presidents seeking to build a case for foreign military intervention 'turn to narrative descriptions of specific atrocities'. Conversely, presidents wishing to avoid involvement in war use 'abstract terms and statistical information' on human rights crises, 'but refrain from detailing personalized stories of abuse'.[9]

Curtis's 'story' about imperative of 'government by fear' for elites fearing the loss of control in an era of 'communicative abundance' is echoed by others. The argument is that mistrust of elites who lost their top-down monopoly information has forced the intensification of professionalization of political communication.[10] Under conditions of uncertainty and loss of trust in the ability of the elite to build a more secure future, nightmares had become a tool for governing and disciplining societies. 'For a society that believes in nothing, fear becomes the only agenda'.[11] The 'securitization' of immigration policies within the EU is one such bid for control over 'security knowledge', now constitutive of ruling elites as 'security experts' or security practitioners. Visions of insecurity frame 'a functionally defined policy domain of security' (differentiated from health care, for example), and also determine 'visions of the nature of politics, i.e. of the political organization of social relations'.[12]

The deployment of security rhetoric to identify and frame threats tends to constitute 'political communities of insecurity', where political identity and the normative framework of the political community rest on 'the distribution of fear and intensification of alienation'.[13] It is easier to promote 'Western' unity by 'systematically articulating an Islamic threat' than by seeking agreement on what defines 'Western civilization'. This way, one can 'facilitate nurturing an idea of unity without having to make its content explicit'.[14]

At the extreme, reducing perceived vulnerability may even demand that the 'other' be made to disappear through assimilation; but also through physical elimination.

> Securitization has the capacity to frame systematic killing as a strategy of survival. The ultimate aim of destroying outsiders is to preserve and guarantee the optimal survival of the community of people who are endangered. Killing is thus justified as life-saving and/or life optimizing.[15]

It is intriguing to observe here how the deconstruction of the official security rhetoric can itself become an instance of 'narratives of insecurity', a 'nightmare' about nightmare construction.

The genesis of mass atrocities

The idea that there is a continuum between identity construction, securitization strategies and genocidal nightmares and fantasies needs to be critically examined. According to Maureen Hiebert's classification of theories of genocide, the argument from securitization theory (of which more below) could be deemed to fall within identity-construction approaches (in contrast to 'structural' or 'agency-oriented' approaches).[16] Like all classifications, Hiebert's is helpful up to a point, since authors do not always oblige by sticking to one line of argument. As Hiebert is first to admit, explanations tend to posit mutual influence among the various factors. So while we may adopt a parallel schema to hers for the sake of simplicity, we will take account of disciplinary classifications and the inter-connection of various factors.

Social scientists naturally propose structural analyses, with many political scientists emphasizing the role of the state, arguing that 'no form of mass violence, and least of all genocide, erupts spontaneously'.[17] This is almost a truism, given that in the current state-centric world order, it is almost impossible for non-state actors to engage in mass violence without state collusion, except in areas where the state has collapsed partially or completely. (Ironically, in this case, the international system traps such troubled states into a cycle of violence with little outside help.) In some 'hybrid' cases, as in Iraq under US occupation or Sudan during the past three decades, both state and non-state actors (opposed to the state or allied with it) shared responsibility for atrocities.

In any case, the majority of states do not engage in atrocities, forcing questions about what context and what regime types are more prone to mass violence. The intuitive notion is that despotic or expansionist regimes are the more likely to perpetrate mass atrocities.[18] Democratization becomes, therefore, the best remedy.[19] For some sceptics, however, democracies, especially fledgling or transitional ones, are as likely to engage in mass murder as autocracies.[20] For yet others, shaky democracies are in fact more likely to engage in mass atrocities than relatively stable democracies.[21]

In this view the problem is not nationalism; rather, 'murderous ethnic cleansing is the product of the modern era of democracy, and specifically the aspiration towards "rule by the people"'.[22] More precisely, 'democratization' is singled out as the decisive element, as it paradoxically tends to increase the insecurity of certain sections of society. It was indeed no less than that pioneer student of democracy, Alexis de Tocqueville, who noted that the prejudices of the Whites against the Blacks appeared to increase in proportion as slavery is abolished, tending eventually to produce prejudice-driven genocides.[23] Minorities begin to be perceived as a threat when they become potential bearers of equal rights. Southern confederates were not too concerned with the presence of black slaves in their estates; it was 'black citizens' they could not stomach. It is significant to note the relative absence of securitization of immigration in Arab Gulf countries, where expatriates often make up to 80 per cent of the population but lack social and political rights. Things may change if the question of rights comes into the picture. The securitization of ethnicity was also absent in the dynastic Habsburg and Ottoman Empires, but ethnicity became a serious challenge in successor states.

Emerging elites in the new states saw in the enfranchisement of minorities a threat to the identity of the new states.

Transition and change, in particular drastic revolutionary change, thus appear as the decisive factors in precipitating mass violence. This is especially the case in deeply divided societies, where momentous political upheavals accentuate social and political polarization.[24] Revolutions and political upheavals are often precipitated by wars, or lead to them. Wars could in turn precipitate revolutions, and are central factors in genocide, according to many authors. Wars offer both opportunity and motive for genocide, since the attendant social mobilization makes it easier to round up 'enemy' civilians. Wars can also provide a pretext for mass killings as 'collateral damage'. In case of insurgencies, there are additional motives to target the civilian supporters of the rebels so as to 'drain the sea' in which the guerrillas swim.[25] In casting genocide as a war strategy, Markusen and Kopf go so far as to see a comparable rationale for the Holocaust and the 'strategic bombing' of German cities by the Allies during the Second World War.[26]

In Hiebert's schema, cultural influences are also subsumed under structural factors. They include widely held racist views or other exclusivist notions of community, as well as certain perceptions of conflict as a zero-sum game. This links, in turn, to local influences and manipulations of deeply ingrained beliefs and prejudices by disaffected elites.[27] Such analyses can merge into agency-focused arguments that see acts of genocide as the result of rational decisions by state elites who coldly calculate costs and benefits. Here, genocide is adopted as a strategy or 'final solution',[28] often only as a last resort. Usually states drift into genocidal action by default, rather than based on prior planning. Invariably, these acts turn out to be extremely costly blunders, and are thus in fact irrational.[29]

The construction of self and victims

The discussion of culture also merges into that of processes of 'enemy construction', since it touches on issues of language, beliefs and threat perceptions. Students of mass violence have noted the important role of language in making extreme violence palatable, even urgent. A war time Nazi poster in Warsaw depicted a bearded Jew with the caption: 'Jew-louse-typhoid',[30] suggesting that getting rid of Jews was *also* an urgent 'public health' issue. This was an insidious, if powerful and direct, appeal to feelings of personal insecurity among even the most ordinary people. The adoption of metaphors that equate potential victims with 'vermin', 'virus', etc., plays multiple roles in 'dehumanizing', or 'devaluing the humanity' of victims, and creating a sense of aversion and 'disgust' towards them,[31] as well as portraying them as a threat. The construction or appropriation of myths of identity could also help categorize enemies and rivals (or merely marginal groups) as less than fully human (usually in contrast to the 'divinely favoured' self), and thus make it acceptable to maltreat them without moral scruples. Such categorization places potential victims outside the 'universe of obligation' (defined by Fein as 'the limits of the common conscience; those whom we are obligated to protect, to take into account, and to whom we must account').[32]

Against the background of a 'permissive political culture', characterized by exclusionary perceptions and a tolerance of authoritarian approaches to conflict management, genocidal violence could be triggered by major crises that generate massive re-alignments in perceptions of identity. This is what happened with the crises which triggered the First World War, but were not resolved by it. In fact, the problems were exacerbated by war's massive cost. War traumas in turn generated 'fantasies of glory', followed by 'traumatic disillusionment',[33] triggering a search for an 'elusive enemy' to be blamed for the defeat and carnage. In Germany, a target was selected that was both a low-cost (Jews, rather than the working class, as the former could be targeted without endangering the unity of the *Volk*), and 'high return' (serving as 'a metaphor for all other domestic and foreign opponents of the nation').[34]

In both accounts, the role of culture remains elusive. 'Political culture' is as a difficult concept to pin down as the 'elusive enemies' being chased: it is 'layered', multifaceted and open to many possibilities.[35] And if the search for the enemy, as Bartov argues, precedes the location and identification of one, this poses the question raised by Arendt and others about the inter-changeability of victims. For the bureaucratic machines of modern genocidal totalitarian states, the identity of the victim is often irrelevant.[36] This issue continues to be the focus of intense debates. But, as Hiebert rightly notes, it is the conception of a target group as a threat, rather merely as sub-human or an outsider that precipitates genocidal violence. For it is possible to ignore, even co-exist with, groups regarded as sub-human or alien; it is another matter when confronted with 'powerful forces' that are 'mortally imperilling the survival of the entire political community'.[37] Thus for specifically genocidal policies to be adopted (as opposed to other forms of persecution up to and including ethnic cleansing), one must entertain the belief that the very existence of the group in question is a mortal threat to the community. This reconceptualization of victim groups passes, according to Hiebert, through three stages or 'switches'. First, the target group is excluded from the political community and treated as 'alien'. Then it is portrayed as a powerful and threatening 'enemy within', 'the bearer of death and therefore the embodiment of evil'. Finally, the target group is dehumanized and depicted as non-human or sub-human (monster, vermin, agent of pollution, etc.).[38]

We can see here how the construction of insecurity and the construction of victims are intimately related to identity construction and delineation of a 'universe of obligation'. The very maintenance of identity presupposes, even requires, the construction of difference and the conceptualization of threats to this identity. Insecurity, thus, 'rather than being external to the object to which it presents a threat, is both implicated in and an effect of the very process of establishing and re-establishing the object's identity'.[39]

Speaking from personal childhood experience during India's tragic partition, Amartya Sen describes the impact of a sudden shift of identity perceptions:

> I recollect the speed with which the broad human beings of January were suddenly transformed into the ruthless Hindus and fierce Muslims of July. Hundreds of thousands perished at the hands of people who, led by commanders of carnage, killed others on behalf of their 'own people'.[40]

This dramatic shift was mediated by institutional change, the rise of the national state, confirming Bartov's point about the pivotal role played by the consolidation of the nation state and its insecurities. The accompanying radical transformations of identities and solidarities 'tended to create a mechanism of self-definition and legitimization based on two mutually dependent conceptual and material requirements, namely, the need to define enemies and the urge to make victims'.[41] Andreas Wimmer similarly argues xenophobic and racist views are an inevitable outcome of the modern international system which bases 'collective identities, participatory rights and state institutions on the idea of a national community':

> In other words, xenophobia and racism are an integral part of the institutional order of the nation-state; or, as Etienne Balibar elegantly expresses it, they are 'an inner complement of nationalism that always exceeds it'.[42]

'Imagined communities' of equals that replaced earlier hierarchical, but inclusive, societies required these communities to consolidate themselves on the basis an actual solidarity of shared interests, further reinforced by the exclusion 'outsiders'.[43] Xenophobia, racism and ethnic conflict are thus inherent to modernity itself, 'because modern institutions of inclusion (citizenship, democracy, welfare) are systematically tied to ethnic and national forms of exclusion'.[44]

But this leaves unresolved the question about when and why identity cleavages become threatening. For Sen, the source is 'the imposition of singular and belligerent identities on gullible people, championed by proficient artisans of terror'.[45] No less problematic is the 'well-intentioned but rather disastrous support' offered by 'the practitioners of a variety of respected – and indeed highly respectable – schools of intellectual thought'. These include advocates of multicultural 'recognition' of diversity, 'communitarians', or proponents of 'clash of civilizations' theses.[46] However, Sen is the first to recognize that the imposition of exclusivist and inescapable identities may not always be a matter of choice. More often than not, identities are imposed on the victims *in spite of themselves*.[47] 'Blacks' in America or South Africa, or Jews in Nazi Germany, or lower cast groups in India, only wanted to be recognized as fellow human beings (or just fellow Americans, South Africans or Germans, etc.). But they were instead trapped into a stigmatized and excluded identity that became truly inescapable.

Narrative communities

However, it is important to note that the 'other' is not 'de-humanized' by simply being given a description, but within the context of a structured narrative, complete with myths of origin, accusations of past misdeeds and the ascription of malicious plans and conspiracies. Similarly, securitization is not merely achieved by 'saying the word security' but by framing the situation within the context of a plausible story.

At a more basic level, the depiction of nations as 'imagined communities' could suggest that the nation is, in fact, a 'mythical' narrative-like creation, 'a system of cultural signification'.[48] One could add that nations are 'communities of shared narratives'. The point was inherent in Anderson's 'view of the space and time of the modern nation as embodied in the narrative culture of the realist novel',[49] whose emergence has been facilitated by the impact of print capitalism (literacy in vernacular languages, the mediation of such artefacts as the newspaper). This enabled the imagining of new, secular, territorially based communities, displacing traditional religious or dynastic-centred political loyalties as the focus of identity.[50] Nations are also, as Cole argues following Rousseau, 'communities of fear', constructed around shared narratives about imagined evil enemies (vampires, witches, Jews, immigrants, etc.), which in turn become the basis of authority for those purporting to protect against them. Since this communal identity is constructed in the same process of the construction of those threatening 'monsters', its content tends to be shaped 'by those who wish to mobilise fear'.[51]

In this regard, a modern nation's 'biography' is constructed from a special type of identity narrative, incorporating myths of origin and selectively remembered/forgotten formative events. Past atrocities are not 'forgotten', as Ernest Renan had recommended, but are in fact remembered as part of a shared history, a family feud, so to speak, or 'reassuring ancient fratricides'.[52]

Emphasizing the 'near-pathological character of nationalism, its roots in fear and hatred of the Other, and its affinities with racism', is not the whole story, however. For as Anderson points out, it may be 'useful to remind ourselves that nations [also] inspire love'.[53] Marc Sageman, commenting on the remarkable cohesiveness and intimate bonding among mujahedin groups remarked that 'It may be more accurate to blame Salafi terrorist activity on in-group love than out-group hate.'[54]

This volatile mix of love and hate is epitomized the Yugoslav narratives, where the nation is presented as a heroic protagonist, 'unique in suffering', while depicting 'the national narratives of rival nations as illegitimate'.[55] In Slobodan Markovic's chapter in this volume, we glimpse the unifying, as well as divisive, features of narratives of 'reassuring fratricide' as well as exclusivist narratives, where history is constantly invoked and enlisted. As Ed Vulliamy pithily put it, 'The answer to a question to a Serb about a Serbian artillery attack [on Sarajevo] yesterday will begin in the year 925 and is invariably illustrated with maps.'[56]

From securitization to 'Hyper-Securitization'

Both the construction of identity and the securitization process reveal the *potential* for genocidal violence, but they do not offer clear answers as to how and when this potential is actualized. The tenets of 'securitisation theory', as outlined by the Copenhagen School, have been summed up succinctly thus:

> In securitization theory, 'security' is treated not as an objective condition but as the outcome of a specific social process: the social construction of security issues (who or what is being secured, and from what) is analyzed by examining the 'securitizing speech-acts' through which threats become represented and recognized. Issues become 'securitized', treated as security issues, through these speech-acts which

do not simply describe an existing security situation, but bring it into being *as* a security situation by successfully representing it as such.⁵⁷

Of central relevance to the current discussion is the decisive role assigned to the 'particular speech act of securitization' deployed by a 'securitizing actor' (usually, but not exclusively, a state actor) 'claiming an existential threat to a valued referent object in order to make the audience tolerate extraordinary measures that otherwise would not have been acceptable'.⁵⁸ The speech act in question is 'performative' in that, like a promise or a marriage vow, it creates a new situation by the mere fact of being uttered. The act itself transforms a given issue (such as immigration) into 'an existential threat, requiring emergency measures'.⁵⁹ A successful securitization act, however, depends on the persuasiveness of the securitizing actors, imposes on them choices of techniques: 'which heuristic artifacts' (including analogies, metaphors, metonymies, emotions, stereotypes) to deploy in order 'to create (or effectively resonate with) the circumstances that will facilitate the mobilization of the audience?'⁶⁰

Huysmans' provocative suggestion of securitization as a probable first step on a genocidal slippery slope echoes claims that the 'state of exception' invoked by securitization reveals the true nature of modern liberal politics. Rather than being an aberration, the 'state of exception' had merely 'uncovered the mask of liberal democracy and shown the true face of modernity (revealed in the holocaust and the reduction of the human bare life)'.⁶¹ This perception is linked to Schmittian interpretations of securitization theory, where the 'politics of insecurity' invokes the 'exception' as a defining dimension of the political. Here, 'fear is mobilized to break through the formalism and neutrality of the technocratic and pluralistic political sphere of liberal democracy for the purpose of reasserting authoritarian sovereignty'.⁶² One cannot challenge this political construction of insecurity in the name of freedom, since it frames the whole debate, where 'freedom is rendered in relation to and by means of questions of security'.⁶³

Departing from a similar Schmittian interpretation of securitization theory, Claudia Aradau chastises the Copenhagen School for failing to confront the normative dimensions of its theory. For if securitization is 'enacted through the non-democratic constitution of authority in various institutional locales', then it inevitably introduces 'an exceptionalism that is unsettling for democratic politics'. This makes it imperative to espouse desecuritization (the deliberate removal of issues from the security agenda) as 'a normative project which reclaims a notion of democratic politics'. However, the founders of the Copenhagen School conspicuously fail to 'normatively endorse democratic politics'.⁶⁴

One of the founders contends that securitization theory incorporates 'a Schmittian concept of security and an Arendtian concept of politics', adding in a note that 'the concept of security is Schmittian, because it defines security in terms of exception, emergency and a decision (although not by a singular will, but among people in a political situation)'.⁶⁵ However, the claim of a built-in Arendtian concept of politics, (where 'politics is productive, irreducible and happens *among* people as an unpredictable chain of actions') only serves to highlight the link of the theory to liberal democratic politics. This is an issue the School wrestled with from the beginning, noting in its seminal work that drawing its illustrations of the theory solely from liberal democratic polities did not preclude it having a broader relevance. In some polities, 'secrecy or violation of rights is the norm, and ... security arguments are not needed to legitimize such acts'. But even such polities still had rules of 'normal politics', which needed securitization arguments to override.[66]

However, attempts to apply the theory to non-democratic contexts remain problematic, given that 'normal politics' is such contexts looks more like the 'exceptional politics' of securitization theory.[67] Vuori's treatment of China confirms this point, in spite of limiting the securitization audience to the ruling elite. For one thing, the two instances of securitization cited (the student revolt and the Falun Gong group) pertain either to a limited period when the system relatively opened up or to a consistent policy of restrictions on religious freedoms. Even here, a 'speech act' acquires a whole new meaning when it is seen as a tool to 'intimidate' and 'control',[68] rather than to persuade, as Securitization Theory originally envisaged. The process takes a whole new meaning when the 'audience' is not part of the discussion on securitization but the object of a security crackdown. It becomes additionally problematic when one speaks of intimidation and propaganda as just different functions of securitization. The concept becomes almost redundant 'where most opposition has been suppressed', holders of power remained 'highly secretive', and a debate on security remained merely a ploy in inter-elite rivalry.[69]

Buzan et al. have already pointed out that, in weak or insufficiently institutionalized states or in states mobilized for total war, 'much of normal politics is pushed into the security realm'.[70] Here 'securitization' appears largely redundant and functions merely as a propaganda move or an intimidation device, as totalitarian regimes use propaganda mainly as an adjunct of terror or to address the outside world.[71] As a form of 'autocommunication', the purpose of propaganda is also 'to maintain the political order by repeating political "mantras" or "codes"', or as a 'ritual of conformity'.[72] But this is a qualitatively different practice from that of deliberation over security in a relatively open society.

We may thus need to move beyond criticism of the theory for being too Eurocentric and tending to impose a 'Westphalian straitjacket' on its analytical subject.[73] It is also insufficient to issue exhortations for the school to overcome its mistrust of popular mobilization (said to be born out of theory's emergence 'in the shadow of the Holocaust, on a continent that has come to see "the people" mainly as part of the problem').[74] Recognizing a built-in liberal democratic bias in the theory, partly evident in the theory's avowed tilt in favour of desecuritization, is also not enough; rather, the point is to recognize an in-built theoretical presupposition of liberal democracy as the template for normal politics.

In order to salvage the universal applicability of the theory, this fact has to be acknowledged and made explicit. This could be done by classifying and grading regimes according to their level of securitization, with liberal regimes classified as minimal securitization systems, while dictatorial or authoritarian regimes as high-level securitization systems. Totalitarian regimes would fit a category of maximum or saturated securitization systems, while a category of 'hyper-securitization' is needed to account for genocidal regimes, where the very existence of certain groups is securitized. 'Hyper-securitization' goes beyond maximum securitization, where almost everything is securitized, including most aspects of private life. If securitization denotes, according to the Copenhagen School, an intensification of politicization, then hyper-securitization denotes an intensification of securitization through the ratcheting up the rhetoric of existential threat, and promoting narratives which 'securitize' the very existence of certain targeted groups and where narratives of insecurity border on the hysterical.

Beyond the liberalism of fear

On this basis, we need to challenge the claims of liberal democracy being 'on a continuum with totalitarian and authoritarian regimes',[75] and the related argument by Giorgio Agamben and others that the state of exception has become the norm in modern liberal polities with the return of 'concentration camps' (such as Guantanamo).[76] Huysmans (in a later work) distances himself from this 'jargon of exception', rejecting the claim that modern politics is defined by 'the concentration camps, that is, loci where the exception has become the rule'. But one cannot define the political in terms of phenomena that represent 'the absolute limit of democratic governance'. Seeing the 'concentration camp' (where naked power confronts bare life) as the paradigm of modern politics means disregarding the complex picture that even Foucault recognizes, where 'power operates through dispersed, fragmented practices that nevertheless weave a diagram of constituting and governing societal relations'.[77] It also means disregarding 'the societal as a realm of multi-faceted, historically structured political mediations and mobilizations'.[78]

The desecuritizing tendencies of liberal democracies and their mistrust of the state, thus problematize Foucault's claim that 'There is no liberalism without a culture of danger.'[79] Liberal thinkers since Montesquieu have mistrusted the politics of fear as a short-cut to despotism and agree with Judith Shklar that 'Systematic fear is the condition that makes freedom impossible.'[80] Richard Rorty follows Shklar in defining liberals as 'the people who think that cruelty is the worst thing we do'.[81] The 'fear of fear', inherent in liberalism 'can in a specific sense be seen as a desecuritizing move' which can restore and safeguard 'normal' politics against excessive intensification and securitization.[82] This argument could be carried further, recognizing that, as 'minimal securitization regimes', liberal systems are qualitatively different from 'hyper-securitization' regimes. A double corrective move is thus needed: to recognize the threat 'hyper-securitization' poses to democratic systems but without falling into the trap of self-defeating hyperbole. Rather, a clear dividing line must be drawn between regimes that believed in restraints on power and those accepting no limits at all on their destructive power.

The 'state of exception' currently overshadowing liberal polities cannot thus be deemed their 'essence' (otherwise it would be meaningless to discuss 'exception') but as a mark of liberal democracy's vulnerability to narratives of insecurity. We may not know when the 'State of Exception' will ever end, but 'we all know when it began'.

> We can no longer quite 'remember' that moment, for the images have long since been refitted into a present-day fable of innocence and apocalypse: the perfect blue of that late summer sky stained by acrid black smoke... Since that day ten years ago we have lived in a subtly different country.[83]

The significance of this imperceptible migration to a 'different country' stems from the remarkable transparency of the process of wholesale securitization (Macrosecuritization, as Buzan and Waever put it)[84] that brought it about. Nevertheless, the camps at Guantánamo Bay and Baghram are not (yet) Auschwitz, and their significance is seriously eroded by such comparisons. The argument has often been made, sometimes by towering intellectual figures, that genocidal excess reflects the 'dark side of Enlightenment' (Adorno and Horkheimer), or the 'dark side of modernity' (Hinton, Zygmunt Bauman) or the 'dark side of democracy' (Michael Mann).[85] The reflections in question present important and deep insights into the unintended or unforeseen consequences and by-products of intellectual and social trends: the arrogance of self-validating reason preached by the Enlightenment, utopian grand schemes to control nature and humanity's future; the foregrounding of instrumental reason; the evolution of modern armies and bureaucracies as formidable (and self-perpetuating) instruments of control; the fragmentation and dilution of individual ethical responsibility; the rise of new ideologies and exclusivist national mythologies; imperialist hubris; etc.

However, the term 'dark side' (as in 'dark side of the moon'), implies being an integral and indivisible part of something, even of its essence. Such narratives become problematic, not because of the absurdity of suggesting that 'civilized modernity' is just another form of barbarism but that the 'irrationalism of totalitarian capitalism' is no better than medieval despotism or Communist totalitarianism. They are so also because such 'critiques' of liberalism were precisely what had engendered the genocidal utopias of the modern era. Like the rhetoric on 'evil', the argument that we are constantly the victims of mass deception (as portrayed *in extremis* in films like *The Matrix* (1999)), are the stuff upon which scenarios of mass violence feed.

It is incontestable that the combined insecurities relating to xenophobia and the 'war on terror' (including the insecurities of political elites pressurized by extremist rivals) threaten to 'transform the liberal polity into one that undermines its own self-defining practices' and norms.[86] In fact, the valid point that 'the so-called war against terrorism recognizes no boundaries as limits to its practices'[87] is a stark reminder of our definition of mass violence as action that recognizes no limits. However, this does not warrant the inference that anti-terror measures 'are simply a continuation of practices that define and indeed sustain liberal governmentality'.[88] Nor does it support the self-contradictory claim that not only has the exception become the norm for liberal polities, but that *it has always been the norm*. It is revealing to note, incidentally, how often law enforcement agents in recent American crime dramas regularly threaten to invoke anti-terror legislation to intimidate suspects: cooperate or we will cast you to the 'dark side'!

The threatened reversal of decades of post-War gains in international protection for human rights cannot thus be expressed in terms of a 'revelation' that the Hobbesian realm of perpetual war is just the reverse side of civil society.[89] Rather, it is an announcement that the Hobbesian outside is threatening to collapse into the 'civil' inside, as narratives of insecurity begin to undermine democratic politics, marginalizing narratives of pride in identity and mutual love. Liberalism has based itself on a narrative of human rationality and belief that human freedom is desirable, irresistible and universally beneficial. Rival ideologies held that substantial sections of the human race are evil, superfluous, not fully rational, or victims of 'false consciousness'/delusion. The 'vanguard' thus have a duty to steer history in the 'right direction', even at the expense of many who did not know what is good for them.

Narratives depicting liberal democracy as 'totalitarianism in disguise' belong in this category, since it is in effect argued that the vast majority of 'citizens' in these democracies are no better than the 'zombies' of films like *World War Z*, or the sedated residents of *The Matrix*. It is a recipe, at least, for 'education camps' that could help wake up the 'living dead'.

The power of popular culture

There is a sense in which the whole world is retrospectively complicit in the genocide against Native Americans. When children in the four corners of the globe play 'Cowboys and Indians', it is usually the 'savage' Indians who get a raw deal. So much so that even children of Native Americans would prefer to play cowboys, leading one shocked commentator to exclaim: 'It's as if Jewish children wanted to play Nazis'.[90] That is probably what would have happened if it were the Nazis who were making films about the Holocaust in Hollywood today!'[91]

This graphic illustration of the power of selective narratives in general, and popular culture artefacts in particular, is key to understanding the otherwise inexplicable shifts like the ones Bosnia (or Rwanda) witnessed, where friendly neighbours suddenly turn into vicious killers. The script of a Western movie forces us to take sides against the 'savage' Indians, while a tense action movie disposes us to accept, even demand, the brutal demise of the sadistic villain. Few people today raise questions about the suffering of the Native Americans and often treat their predicament as a matter of amusement or fun. By the same token, the 'right' type of narrative would dispose otherwise peaceful citizens to find it perfectly acceptable, even imperative, to take part in mass violence against their neighbours. Intellectuals and makers of popular culture play a crucial role in shaping collective feelings of (in)security, and thus justifying or inciting exceptional policy measures, including the perpetration of atrocities.

Recent times witnessed the proliferation of fictional narratives, such as *The Truman Show* (1998) or *The Matrix* (1999), and non-fictional ones which problematize the boundaries between fiction and reality in contemporary media-saturated societies.[92]

Both films depict manipulation in terms of extreme cases, where 'reality TV' becomes the only reality for one person, or where brain control takes a physical form. Security analysts and policymakers often deploy fictional narratives (so called 'strategic fictions') as they 'routinely invoke narrative fictions from the past and project them into an imaginary future to buttress current security strategies and policies'.[93] In recent years, imagined scenarios of mass terror attacks have displaced the various scenarios of global nuclear war, and are reproduced in elaborate detail to urge (or justify) certain 'pre-emptive' measures. Here again, fiction and security briefings appear to merge into one other. Senior Bush administration figures publicly lauded the film *The Sum of All Fears* (2002), which depicts a nuclear terror threat to an American city. As one commentator put it, such fictional scenario-building ends up pitting the United States into 'a grand fight against its own worst enemy – its future'.[94]

A prominent security analyst even recommended the popular TV teen horror series, *Buffy the Vampire Slayer*, as an inspiring 'paradigm' for dealing with major security threats.[95] A more enthusiastic endorsement concurred that the series dealt 'with uncertainty and the grim side of life better in some ways than many experts in national security'.[96] Resort to tropes from popular culture in this context reminds us of the embeddedness of its narratives 'to the point where they form a seamless web of naturalised and invisible referents'.

[Popular culture narratives] are vehicles for working through anxieties and insecurities; they are mechanisms that offer fictive solutions to real social and political contradictions and threats…They also work to transform real social and political desires and insecurities into manageable narratives in which these can be temporarily articulated, displaced or resolved.[97]

One needs to add, however, that such narratives as *Buffy* or *Independence Day* (1996), present us with a 'two-tier' fiction, so to speak. They deal not just with fictional human characters, but also with encounters with the supernatural. Here the 'other', the demons and extra-terrestrial invaders, are irreducibly evil, and can never be pacified or reasoned with. Their actions or mode of intrusion into our world are also entirely unpredictable. This is precisely the manner in which the Bush administration tended to depict the terror threat: as emanating from ubiquitous and inherently evil actors, and therefore unmanageable and totally unrelated to US policy options. One can derive similar lessons from films like Marc Forster's *World War Z* (2013), in which the hero battles to save the world from a virus that was turning the bulk of humans into marauding zombies. In any real-life scenario of this type, if a whole city catches the virus, then you have no option but to eradicate its inhabitants. Even if a member of your family catches it, then you will have no option but to get rid of them. Given the limited resources, also abandoning the majority of healthy people to their fate appears perfectly justified. The terror scenes in the movie make these measures incontestable.

In this light, the parallel narratives offered by politicians on terrorism are far from reassuring, and in fact generate deep and uncontrollable anxiety. All one can do is wait, like Buffy, for the next demon to turn up and proceed to slay it. This in turn could cause policymakers, and even whole communities, to behave irrationally, thus generating more insecurity and instability. In horror fiction, thrillers and similar genres, reassurance is provided by harnessing the idea of manageable threats, usually through the mechanism of the 'superhero', a person endowed with supernatural or superhuman powers, or just an extremely talented and/or lucky individual. Thus a threat which, if real, would have become deeply disturbing and disorienting, is turned instead into an adventure or 'thrill'. The fascination with the lure of risk and danger is said to be inherent in bourgeois society, due to boredom with sedate bourgeois life, as well as to its constantly expanding and self-transforming nature.[98] In fact, 'irrational' and frenzied American reactions to the 9/11 attacks were seen as a reflection of this paradoxical simultaneous search for security and thrill, where danger is as much a value as security.

> The state of crisis manifests something that both attracts us and repels us. It figures as an internal part of our appointment with destiny … We have to have imagined ourselves changed, and continuing to change, until we disappear from our own clear sight. This is the character of modernity.[99]

It is here that we catch a glimpse of the actual dynamics which combine to affect the shifts in attitude that could turn ordinary people into fervent agents of destruction. It is this deep sense of insecurity and mortal threat, combined with a sense of elation and thrill, even intoxication with this threatened identity and pride in the opportunity to defend it, which characterizes these situations of implacable conflict. In rising up to the threat, one is espousing a 'manifest destiny', and attaining self-realization. Like mountain climbing, hang gliding or parachuting, one is gripped by a simultaneous sense of imminent danger and limitless power. This precisely the situation Bartov described in relation to the First World War and its disastrous consequences.

There is an analogy here with action thrillers, often the favourite genre (as opposed to horror) for fictionally framing and commenting on the 'war on terror'. As Slavoj Žižek perceptively notes, successful thrillers, such as Fox TV's popular series *24* (2001–2010, starring Kiefer Sutherland as agent Jack Bauer, anti-terror superhero), provide convincing narratives of 'ticking bomb' scenarios that justify the excesses of the 'war on terror'. But they also shed light on how front-line terror warriors could easily drift into the 'heart of darkness', like Kurtz in Francis Ford Coppola's *Apocalypse Now* (1979). One can compare here the double reversal in the narratives of the perpetrators of the Holocaust, who blame the victims for 'forcing us to perpetrate or watch such terrible things'! For such perpetrators, the 'ethical' imperative becomes one of 'resisting the temptation not to murder', rather than the other way round. Also the question of 'Why do normal decent people commit atrocities?' turns into: How could the executioners who perform these terrible acts 'remain human and retain their dignity'?[100]

Thrillers and adventure tales belong to the romantic genre of narratives (in contrast to tragedy, comedy and satire), which also occasionally mirror the narratives of the protagonists of the 'war on terror'. For example, the Bush administration's portrayal of the Iraq war as a 'heroic' enterprise to rid the world of evil and tyranny echoes familiar American narratives. The 'story it tells about America, Iraq and the world is in many ways only the latest instalment of the serialized romance which is the history of the US'.[101] However, this picture is problematized when the same alliance also peddles a 'tragic' narrative of perpetual and ubiquitous terror threats, thus emulating the horror genre. Usually, the discrepancy is dealt with by alternating between narrative types: at one level, terrorists are depicted as the tip of the iceberg in a worldwide anti-liberal resurgence of 'Islamo-fascism' threatening the West and the whole world; at another, the superiority of Western values and civilization, and the unstoppable march of freedom, are projected as sure to vanquish the backward, morally bankrupt and isolated terrorists.

In a related context, Patrick Colm Hogan argues that nationalist feelings are bound up 'in precise and consequential ways' with 'universal prototypical narrative structures: heroic, romantic, and sacrificial tragicomedy'. The rise of Nazism in Germany is closely linked to a specific sacrificial emplotment of nationalism, of which F. W. Murnau's 1922 film, *Nosferatu, a Symphony of Horror*, offers a very illuminating example.[102] The film tells a story of a small town devastated by a plague caused by a 'vampire' introduced into the community because a naïve young man decided to sell his house to Jewish-looking East European. Only a great sacrifice, where 'a woman with a pure heart' should willingly offer her blood to the vampire and keep him by her side until the cock crows, will end the suffering. The seller's young wife undertakes this sacrifice and the plague comes to an end.

In the complex narrative, the 'Eastern European' alien vampire is deliberately projected in ways that conform to the stereotype of a Jew: 'blood-sucker', vermin-like invasive alien presence associated with devastation and the plague. His local collaborators are motivated by greed and are too dumb to spot the danger signals. Most of the themes (including the need for sacrifice to purge the nation) also recur in Hitler's *Mein Kampf* and other contemporary German discourses.[103] Along with novels, plays, political speeches and ordinary discourse, the film influenced the purgative sacrificial emplotment of German nationalism in the interwar years. Audiences necessarily linked the events and characters of the film to pre-existing stereotypes and tacitly drew these connections in the context of persistent anxieties regarding the devastation of their society.

We can see here how works of art and other artefacts of culture can simultaneously reflect and sublimate shared fears and prejudices, and also feed these fears and play a decisive role in enhancing the appeal of genocide-inducing narratives.

Selling narratives

This interaction of narratives of popular culture with political narratives offers important insights on how the skilful deployment of narratives can both stabilize and destabilize societies. This takes us to our starting point, and Curtis's own 'tragic' narrative about the encounter between militant Islamism and neoconservatism. Here, we see framing in action: this compelling retelling of a familiar story has the form of an extremely sophisticated 'conspiracy theory', portraying the neoconservatives as just another 'sleeper cell', as intent as Al-Qaeda on subverting American democracy. Conspiracy theories ('defined as accounts of events as the deliberate yet concealed product of a powerful few'), are a peculiar species of narratives of insecurity that are rife among extremist groups, often forming the core of their ideologies.[104] However, while conspiracy theories habitually appeal only to fringe paranoid minorities, Curtis's account is more ambitious in intent, but nevertheless very revealing about the mechanisms and impact of skilful retelling of stories.

The question of receptiveness to particular narratives remains crucial. Grave crises may increase receptiveness to formulas for the reconstruction of identity, re-describing the trauma and (re)assigning blame, while prescribing action to recover dignity and peace with oneself.[105] In this context, a narrative that calls for a collective mobilization to deal with crises and proliferating threats is more likely to be embraced by a traumatized community.[106] Bartov, like Semelin, sees trauma as a key to understanding the processes which led from disillusionment with narratives of glorification of war to the adoption of narratives of competitive victimhood and the construction of 'elusive enemies' (who in turn become victims). Linked to this is the urge to create and celebrate new identities, or to enact utopian visions linked in complex ways to the glorification and disillusionment with the industrial proportions of modern war and its transformative potential. However, this still leaves open the question of why certain narratives predominate in such circumstances, unless we accept Hogan's idea that certain narrative structures fit better than others in a given context. For Hogan, the heroic narrative is the default one when a community feels under threat. However, in conditions of utter devastation, sacrificial narratives predominate. In the former, God is with us and we will prevail; in the latter, God is against us and we are being punished. So atonement is in order, either by collective sacrifice or by sacrificing the sinful among us, or purging the evil alien presence from our midst.[107]

The successful formula must be a perfect fit for a gaping hole left by the trauma, as happened with the 2004 report of the '9/11 Commission', which, in depicting the 'war on terror' as essentially a 'war of ideas', provided for many Americans a 'Eureka moment': the missing piece of the puzzle.[108] To achieve this status, the successful narrative must displace divergent and competing ones. This, in turn, depends on many factors, including resonance with dominant beliefs and widely shared moods and attitudes, providing reassurance and restoring lost self-confidence. While many faulted the Bush administration for framing the post-9/11 challenge as a 'cosmic war on terror', it is doubtful whether a more moderate and measured tone would have fitted the mood at the time. Few other options were open, at least in the short-term, as shown by the public reaction against intellectuals (e.g., Susan Sontag) who dissented from the dominant narrative.[109]

This reaction underlines another aspect of insecurity: job insecurity for politicians and top officials. Presenting the wrong type of narrative at the wrong time, especially to a traumatized audience, could be disastrous for one's political or diplomatic career. In this regard, the peddlers of narratives of insecurity need not be completely possessed by their own nightmares. They may have to tailor their narratives to audience demands, or even respond to those demands. Depending on the timing, context and delivery, some stories resonate more with the public in a given cultural context than others.

The skilful re-telling of stories (and its perfect timing), since Marc Antony's eulogy of Caesar, could have dramatic and explosive consequences. Commenting on the notorious 1968 'Rivers of Blood' speech by the late conservative politician Enoch Powell (1912–1998), the conservative politician Lord Heseltine said that the maverick Powell had 'set fire to a tinderbox', and wrong-footed the whole political establishment.[110] Powell's dire warnings that Britain was about to be taken over by black immigrants was on the brink of giving the world a pre-taste of Yugoslavia, if not worse, by instigating a popular revolution against the ruling elite over immigration. However, decisive collective action by the establishment successfully ostracized and marginalized Powell.

Richard Rorty holds George Orwell as an example of the decisive impact of 'the right books at the right time', in this case for the future of liberal politics. Orwell managed to break 'the power of... "Bolshevik propaganda" over the minds of liberal intellectuals in England and America', thus giving them a twenty year lead over their French counterparts. The latter 'had to wait for *The Gulag Archipelago* before they stopped thinking that... solidarity against capitalists required ignoring what the Communist oligarchs were doing'.[111]

Timing and framing are thus crucial, and securitization can be seen as 'one unique master frame' that works to 'integrate the specific agendas of diverse groups into central interpretive frameworks'. This angle helps a better understanding of context in which target audiences of securitization discourses 'interact and negotiate with securitised representations'.[112] As an interactive and 'complicated cultural process', framing 'prioritizes the data which make an event into one kind of story or another'. In this context, securitization can be seen as 'a form of framing that highlights the existential threat' dimension of a given issue. This involves negotiations (mainly through media) among multiple audiences.[113]

Media framing plays a crucial role here by 'empowering certain actors' and marginalizing others.

> [It] bestows prestige and authority and allocates linguistic competence, through various mechanisms such as media ownership and capitalist interests, representation of opposing voices, and the relationship between journalists and political elites.[114]

However, just as it is possible to over-state the significance of the 'state of exception' for liberal politics, it is easy to over-state the point about the influence of the media and the hegemonic control of the power-elite according to the 'propaganda model' of Herman and Chomsky.[115] Such critiques may be useful to counter the advocacy (or assumption) of Habermasian 'ideal speech situations' in 'a properly functioning marketplace of ideas' where contested narratives are evaluated on merit.[116] But complicating factors need to be taken into account. We are indeed confronted with 'a communicative environment ever more structured by televisual media and by the importance of images'. This makes the emphasis on analyzing the 'rhetorical and discursive structure' of securitization moves problematic, since such moves become increasingly one-sided. For it is difficult to voice dissent in the face of 'self-validating images of danger'.[117] However, even before the 'Arab Spring' of 2011 demonstrated the possibilities of the interactive, image-driven, features of the new public sphere, it was becoming clear that this was not entirely a one-sided affair. Episodes such as the tragic death of Princess Diana in 1997, or the debate on banning the building of minarets in Switzerland in 2009, have shown that the masses could dictate mood and wrong-foot the elite. The same was demonstrated by the way graphic images depicting the torture of Iraqi prisoners in Abu Ghraib prison in 2004 trumped the communication strategies of the US establishment. However, in other situations, the convergence of 'tragedy, public danger and threats to national security' tends to generate 'hyper-patriotic' narratives that can override the habitual restraint and 'objectivity', making dissent taboo.[118]

Thus while narratives represent a much more effective communication and mobilization tool than abstract discourse, images can still be more powerful. That is also why the combination of image and narrative (in film or TV) remains one of the most potent tools of communication.[119] The most powerful narratives are in fact those which evocatively conjure up an image, like Enoch Powell's nightmare of a black man whipping a white native of Britain or, conversely, Martin Luther King Jr's 'dream' of white and black children holding hands. Commenting on the motives of the perpetrators of the 9/11 atrocities, Don DeLillo argued that the terrorist encircles himself by narratives that help him 'live a certain kind of apartness, hard and tight'.

> Plots reduce the world. [The terrorist] builds a plot around his anger and our indifference... Does the sight of a woman pushing a stroller soften the man to her humanity and vulnerability, and her child's as well, and all the people he is here to kill? This is his edge, that he does not see her... there is no defenceless human at the end of his gaze.[120]

The same thing could be said about the drone operator obliterating a family in distant Afghanistan by pushing a button at his desk in a mid-Western US city while sipping his latte. We make (up) our stories, and our stories make us. We live our lives within plots we have inherited, adopted, invented, encountered, dreamt (up). Then catastrophes like the First World War or 9/11 come up, and that whole universe comes crashing down and has to be rebuilt again. That is why the role of skilful artists in story-telling and re-telling has been seen, since Cicero, as vital for 'republican' orders (one could add, all orders). In this context, events like 9/11 offer 'a monumental occasion for would-be rhetorical heroes to display their talents as they sought to disclose the truth, make sense of the horror and chaos at hand, and thereby help in the treatment and guidance of an anxious and terrified American public'.[121] Like many American intellectuals, DeLillo was trying to make his own 'heroic' contribution to this endeavour, offering a more nuanced and credible account than the official version.[122] In this context, this narrative fulfils primarily the function of therapy, providing necessary reassurance, and is thus more likely to find enthusiastic reception than does the unsettling narrative of Sontag and other brave souls.

Conclusion

In contemplating the context in which mass atrocities are perpetrated, one can think of scripts like that of *World War Z*, where you do not know who will be the next 'zombie' to attack you. Or one can contemplate the script of a horror film where an attack on 'innocent children' is shown to be in fact a heroic targeting of dangerous demons who have disguised themselves as children. When 'normal' people perpetrate atrocities, they are usually enacting a script in which their acts cannot be seen as crime, but either as 'necessary evil', or heroic acts to save humanity.

There is a significant element of contingency (and unpredictability) in the emergence and acceptability of narratives, since a lot depends on the creativity and talent of the narrator as well as audience receptiveness. The Islamophobia narratives currently sweeping Europe are a case in point. They vary in quality (from crude racist slurs to sophisticated constructs about 'culture') and provenance but resonate with deeply ingrained cultural tropes about identity. They are also influenced by genuine fears provoked by recent terror acts and by anxieties about immigration or economic insecurity. However, reception to such narratives continues to vary with country, region and social group.

Narratives of securitization are integral to, and up to a certain level, essential for, the health of all communities. In democratic societies, such narratives are contested and competitively assessed. That is why Islamophobic narratives have not yet provoked destabilizing hyper-securitization. They remain, in spite of worrying and disturbing exceptions, reasonably contained. Even disturbing narratives about their hyper-securitization potential, exemplified by films like Edward Zwick's *The Siege* (1998), end up providing a reassuring message about the capability of democratic procedures to tame such tendencies. The plot depicts New York under martial law following an escalation of mass terror atrocities, with parts of the city turned into concentration camps for all those of Arab descent. Torture was routinely used on suspects as the frantic search for the terror cell gets under way. In the meantime, the skilful work of intelligence operatives (including an Arab FBI agent whose son was in the detention camps) brings the crisis to an end by locating and eliminating the terror cell. The general whose soldiers occupied Brooklyn is arrested (after a brief stand-off that threatened to ignite another American 'civil war') and normal life is restored.

The film offers an intriguing insight into how narratives of hyper-securitization could evolve and lead to carnage but also how they could be contained and neutralized. The precariousness of human decency is graphically illustrated, as is its capacity to endure and bounce back. In real life, we have also seen how Martin Luther King Jr's counter-narratives of 'brotherhood' eventually displaced the narratives of insecurity peddled by racist groups, as did Nelson Mandela's narratives of coexistence and reconciliation in opposition to narratives of victimhood, revenge and mistrust. Rorty's claims about the impact of novels by Orwell, Nabokov and Solzhenitsyn are also relevant here. One thus need not subscribe to Rorty's pragmatism and historical nominalism to agree with his point that 'genres such as the journalist's report, the comic book, the docudrama, and, especially the novel' are becoming the primary arena of moral discourse in our time, displacing the sermon and the treatise as vehicles for promoting human solidarity and sensitizing people to cruelty.[123] Political scientists did not need to be skilled in literary criticism to gauge the decisive political impact of works like *Animal Farm, 1984, Dr Zhivago, The Gulag Archipelago, Orientalism* or Martin Luther King Jr's 'I Have A Dream' speech. But we need to reflect more deeply on the 'how' and 'why' questions.

Notes

1 *The Power of Nightmares*, a three-part television series by Adam Curtis. BBC Two, 20 and 27 October and 3 November 2004. The text is from the BBC website, 'The Power of Nightmares: Baby It's Cold Outside', 14 January 2005, http://news.bbc.co.uk/1/hi/3755686.stm.
2 Jonathan Raban, 'The Truth about Terrorism', *New York Review of Books*, 13 January 2005, http://www.nybooks.com/authors/231 [accessed 31 May 2009, 23:52].
3 Raban, 'The Truth about Terrorism'.
4 Omer Bartov, *Mirrors of Destruction: War, Genocide, and Modern Identity*, New York: Oxford University Press, 2000, p. 108.
5 Dibyesh Anand, 'Fear and Political Mobilization', *CSD Bulletin*, Vol. 15, No. 1 (Winter 2007–2008), pp. 1–2.
6 Prime Minister and Defense Minister Ehud Barak's speech to the National Defense College on Thursday, 12 August 1999, published on the Israel Foreign Ministry website: http://www.israel-mfa.gov.il/mfa/go.asp?MFAH0fh80 [accessed 15 August 2003].
7 Sharif Harir, ' "Arab Belt" versus "African Belt": Ethno-political Conflict in Dar Fur and Regional Culture Factors' in Sharif Harir and Terje Tvedt, eds., *Short-cut to Decay*, Uppsala: The Scandinavian Institute of African Studies, 1994, pp. 144–185.
8 Suzanne Keen, 'A Theory of Narrative Empathy', *Narrative*, Vol. 14, No. 3 (2006), pp. 207–236.
9 Eran N. Ben-Porath, 'Rhetoric of Atrocities: The Place of Horrific Human Rights Abuses in Presidential Persuasion Efforts', *Presidential Studies Quarterly*, Vol. 37, No. 2 (2007), p. 181.
10 Jay G. Blumler and Dennis Kavanagh, 'The Third Age of Political Communication: Influences and Features', *Political Communication*, Vol. 16, No. 3 (1999), pp. 209–230.
11 Mark Jensen, 'DOCUMENTARY: "The Power of Nightmares" by Adam Curtis – summary of argument', at United for Peace, 11 September 2005, http://www.ufppc.org/content/view/3394/ [accessed 1 June 2009, 01:33].
12 Jef Huysmans, *The Politics of Insecurity: Fear, Migration and Asylum in the EU*, London: Routledge, 2006, p. 11.
13 Huysmans, *The Politics of Insecurity*, p. 47.
14 Huysmans, *The Politics of Insecurity*, p. 51.
15 Huysmans, *The Politics of Insecurity*, p. 57.
16 Maureen Hiebert, 'Theorizing Destruction: Reflections on the State of Comparative Genocide Theory', *Genocide Studies and Prevention*, Vol. 3, No. 3 (2008), pp. 309–339.
17 Anton Weiss-Wendt, 'The State and Genocide', in Donald Bloxham and A. Dirk Moses, eds., *The Oxford Handbook of Genocide Studies*, Oxford: Oxford University Press, 2010, p. 81.

18 Irving Louis Horowitz, *Genocide: State Power and Mass Murder*, New Brunswick, NJ: Transaction Publishers, 1976; Arendt, *The Origins of Totalitarianism*.
19 R. Rummel, *Death by Government*, New Brunswick, NJ: Transaction Publishers, 1994.
20 Helen Fein, 'The Three P's of Genocide Prevention: With Application to a Genocide Foretold – Rwands', in Niel Riemer, ed., *Protection Against Genocide: Mission Impossible?*, Westport, CT: Greenwood Publishing Group, 2000, pp. 42–66.
21 Mann, *The Dark Side of Democracy*; Daniele Conversi, 'Demo-skepticism and Genocide', *Political Studies Review*, Vol. 4, No. 3 (2006), pp. 247–262.
22 Michael Mann, 'Reply: Is Democracy, and was Fascism, Sacred?', *Political Studies Review*, Vol. 4, No. 3 (2006), p. 290.
23 Roger M. Smith, 'Beyond Tocqueville, Myrdal, and Hartz: The Multiple Traditions in America', *The American Political Science Review*, Vol. 87, No. 3 (1993), p. 552.
24 Robert Melson, *Revolution and Genocide: On the Origins of the Armenian Genocide and the Holocaust*, Chicago: Chicago University Press, 1992; Barbara Harf, 'The Etiology of Genocides', in I. Wallimann and M. N. Dobkowski, eds., *Genocide and the Modern Age, Etiology and Case Studies of Mass Death*, New York: Greenwood Press, 1987, pp. 41–59; Leo Kuper, *Genocide: Its Political Use in the Twentieth Century*, New Haven, CT: Yale University Press, 1983.
25 Martin Shaw, *War and Genocide: Organized Killing in Modern Society*, Cambridge, MA: Polity, 2003; Benjamin Valentino, Paul Huth and Dylan Balch-Lindsay '"Draining the Sea": Mass Killing and Guerilla Warfare', *International Organization*, Vol. 58 (2004), pp. 375–407.
26 Eric Markusen and David Kopf, *The Holocaust and Strategic Bombing: Genocide and Total War in the Twentieth Century*, Boulder, CO: Westview, 1995.
27 Hiebert, 'Theorizing Destruction', pp. 316–318.
28 Scott Strauss, 'Political Science and Genocide', in Bloxham and Moses, ed., *The Oxford Handbook of Genocide Studies*, pp. 174–175.
29 Strauss, 'Political Science and Genocide', p. 174; Valentino, *Final Solutions*, pp. 67–69; Manus I. Midlarsky, *The Killing Trap: Genocide in the Twentieth Century*, Cambridge: Cambridge University Press, 2005.
30 Herbert Hirsch and Roger W. Smith, 'The Language of Extermination in Genocide', in Israel W. Charny, ed., *Genocide: A Critical Bibliography*, vol. II, London: Mansell, 1991, p. 389.
31 Chirot and McCauley, *Why not Kill them All?*, pp. 80–81. Cf. Sander L. Gilman, *Difference and Pathology: Stereotypes of Sexuality, Race, and Madness*, New York: Cornell University Press, 1985; also Steuter and Wills, *At War with Metaphor*.
32 Hirsch and Smith, 'The Language of Extermination', pp. 388–389; Helen Fein, 'Genocide and Other State Murders in the Twentieth Century', lecture delivered on 24 October 1995, US Holocaust Memorial Museum, Committee on Conscience.
33 Hiebert, 'Theorizing Destruction', pp. 316–318; Maureen S. Hiebert, 'Constructing Victims: Reconceptualizing Identity and the Genocidal Process', http://www.cpsa-acsp.ca/papers-2004/Hiebert.pdf; Omer Bartov, *Mirrors of Destruction*, pp. 45–51.
34 Bartov, *Mirrors of Destruction*, pp. 91–111.
35 Hiebert, 'Constructing Victims'; Abdelwahab El-Affendi, 'Political Culture and the Crisis of Democracy in the Arab World', in Ibrahim Elbadawi and Samir Makdisi, eds., *Democracy in the Arab World: Explaining the Deficit*, London: Routledge, 2010, pp. 11–40.

36 Bartov, *Mirrors of Destruction*, p. 130.
37 Hiebert, 'Theorizing Destruction', pp. 332–333.
38 Maureen S. Hierbert, 'The Three "Switches" of Identity Construction in Genocide: The Nazi Final Solution and the Cambodian Killing Fields', *Genocide Studies and Prevention*, Vol. 3, No. 1 (2008), pp. 6, 12–13.
39 Jutta Weldes, Mark Laffey, Hugh Gusterson and Raymond Duvall, 'Introduction: Constructing Insecurity', in Jutta Weldes et al., eds., *Cultures of Insecurity*, p. 11.
40 Amartya Sen, *Identity & Violence: The Illusion of Destiny*, London: Penguin Books, 2006, p. 2.
41 Omer Bartov, 'Defining Enemies, Making Victims: Germans, Jews, and the Holocaust', *The American Historical Review*, Vol. 103, No. 3 (1998), p. 772.
42 Andreas Wimmer, *Nationalist Exclusion and Ethnic Conflict: Shadows of Modernity*, Cambridge: Cambridge University Press, 2002, pp. 208–210, 217.
43 Wimmer, *Nationalist Exclusion and Ethnic Conflict*, pp. 212–213.
44 Wimmer, *Nationalist Exclusion and Ethnic Conflict*, pp. 4–5.
45 Sen, *Identity & Violence*, p. 2.
46 Sen, *Identity & Violence*, p. 4.
47 Sen, *Identity & Violence*, pp. 6–8.
48 Benedict Anderson, *Imagined Communities*, London: Verso, 2006; Homi K. Bhabha (ed.), *Nations and Narration*, London: Routledge, 1990.
49 Bhabha, *Nations and Narration*, p. 2.
50 Anderson, *Imagined Communities*, pp. 12–46.
51 Cole, The Myth of Evil, pp. 89–92.
52 Anderson, *Imagined Communities*, p. 201.
53 Anderson, *Imagined Communities*, p. 143.
54 Marc Sageman, *Understanding Terror Networks*, Philadelphia: University of Pennsylvania Press, 2004, p. 135.
55 Ben Lieberman, 'Nationalist Narratives, Violence between Neighbours and Ethnic Cleansing in Bosnia-Hercegovina: A Case of Cognitive Dissonance?', *Journal of Genocide Research*, Vol. 8, No. 3 (2006), pp. 298–299.
56 Ed Vulliamy, *Seasons in Hell: Understanding Bosnia's War*, New York: St Martin's Press, 1994, p. 5.
57 Michael C. Williams, 'Words, Images, Enemies: Securitization and International Politics', *International Studies Quarterly*, Vol. 47, No. 4 (2003), p. 513.
58 Ole Wæver, 'Politics, Security, Theory', *Security Dialogue*, Vol. 42, No. 4 (2011), p. 469.
59 Barry Buzan, Ole Wæver and Jaap de Wilde, *Security: A New Framework for Analysis*, Boulder CO.: Lynne Rienner, 1998, p. 24.
60 Thierry Balzacq, 'The Three Faces of Securitization: Political Agency, Audience and Context', *European Journal of International Relations*, Vol. 11, No. 2 (2005), p. 179.
61 Bigot and Tsoukala, *Terror, Insecurity and Liberty*, p. 3.
62 Huysmans, *The Politics of Insecurity*, pp. 141–142.
63 Huysmans, *The Politics of Insecurity*, p. 103.
64 Claudia Aradau, 'Security and the Democratic Scene: Desecuritization and Emancipation', *Journal of International Relations and Development*, Vol. 7, No. 4 (2004), p. 392.
65 Ole Wæver, 'Politics, Security, Theory', *Security Dialogue*, Vol. 42, No. 4–5 (2011), pp. 470, 478.

66 Buzan et al., *Security*, pp. 24–25.
67 See for example Juha A. Vuori, 'Illocutionary Logic and Strands of Securitization: Applying the Theory of Securitization to the Study of Non-Democratic Political Orders', *European Journal of International Relations*, Vol. 14, No. 1 (2008): pp. 65–99, for China, and Claire Wilkinson, 'The Copenhagen School on Tour in Kyrgyzstan: Is Securitization Theory Useable Outside Europe?', *Security Dialogue*, Vol. 38, No. 1 (2007), pp. 5–25, for Kyrgyzstan.
68 Vuori, 'Illocutionary Logic and Strands of Securitization', pp. 80–87.
69 Vuori, 'Illocutionary Logic and Strands of Securitization', pp. 69–72, 81–82.
70 Buzan et al., *Security*, p. 28.
71 Arendt, *The Origins of Totalitarianism*, p. 341.
72 Vuori, 'Illocutionary Logic and Strands of Securitization', p. 71.
73 Wilkinson, 'The Copenhagen School on Tour in Kyrgyzstan', p. 8.
74 Vibeke Schou Tjalve, 'Designing (de)security: European Exceptionalism, Atlantic republicanism and the "public sphere"', *Security Dialogue*, Vol. 42, No. 4–5 (2011), p. 442.
75 Dana Villa, 'Review Article: Arendt and Totalitarianism: Contexts of Interpretation', *European Journal of Political Theory*, Vol. 10, No. 2 (2011), p. 293.
76 Giorgio Agamben (trans. Kevin Attell), *State of Exception*, Chicago: University of Chicago Press, 2005.
77 Jef Huysmans, 'The Jargon of Exception – On Schmitt, Agamben and the Absence of Political Society', *International Political Sociology*, Vol. 2, No. 2 (2008), pp. 178–179.
78 Huysmans, 'The Jargon of Exception', pp. 180–181.
79 Michel Foucault (ed. Michel Sennelart), *The Birth of Biopolitics: Lectures at the Collège de France, 1978–1979*, London: Palgrave Macmillan, 2008, p. 67.
80 Judith N. Shklar and Stanley Hoffmann, *Political Thought and Political Thinkers*, Chicago, IL: University of Chicago Press, 1998, p. 11.
81 Richard Rorty, *Contingency, Irony and Solidarity*, Cambridge: Cambridge University Press, 1989, p. xvi.
82 Michael C. Williams, 'Securitization and the Liberalism of Fear', *Security Dialogue*, Vol. 42, No. 4–5 (2011), p. 459.
83 Mark Danner, 'After September 11: Our State of Exception', *The New York Times Review of Books*, 13 October 2011, http://www.nybooks.com/articles/archives/2011/oct/13/after-september-11-our-state-exception/?pagination=false.
84 Barry Buzan and Ole Waever, 'Macrosecuritization and Security Constellations: Reconsidering Scale in Securitization Theory', *Review of International Studies*, Vol. 35, No. 2 (2009), pp. 253–276.
85 Max Horkheimer and Theodor W. Adorno (ed. Gunzelin Schmid Noerr, trans. Edmund Jephcott), *Dialectic of Enlightenment: Philosophical Fragments*, Stanford: Stanford University Press, 2002; Alexander Laban Hinton, *Annihilating Difference: The Anthropology of Genocide*, Berkeley, CA: University of California Press, 2002; Michael Mann, *The Dark Side of Democracy: Explaining Ethnic Cleansing*, Cambridge: Cambridge University Press, 2005; Bartov, *Mirrors of Destruction*; see also A. Dirk Moses, 'Genocide and Modernity', in Dan Stone, ed., *The Historiography of Genocide*, Houndmills: Palgrave MacMillan, 2008, pp. 156–193.
86 Vivienne Jabri, 'War, Security and the Liberal State', *Security Dialogue*, Vol. 37, No. 1 (2006), pp. 57–58.

87 Jabri, 'War, Security and the Liberal State', pp. 53–54
88 Jabri, 'War, Security and the Liberal State', p. 56.
89 Jabri, 'War, Security and the Liberal State', p. 55.
90 Michael Yellow Bird, 'Cowboys and Indians: Toys of Genocide, Icons of American Colonialism', Wicazo Sa Review, Vol. 19, No. 2 Colonization/Decolonization (2004), p. 33.
91 They did have a go at it. See for example Yael Hersonski's *A Film Unfinished* (2010).
92 William Irwin, ed., *The Matrix and Philosophy: Welcome to the Desert of the Real*, Peru, Illinois: Open Court Publishing, 2002.
93 Petro and Andrew *Rethinking Global Security*, p. 1.
94 Doug Davis, 'Future-War Storytelling: National Security and Popular Film', in Petro and Martin, eds., *Rethinking Global Security*, pp. 13–44.
95 Anthony H. Cordesman, *Biological Warfare and the Buffy Paradigm*, Washington, DC: Center for Strategic and International Studies, 29 September 2001, p. 15.
96 Rita Kempley in the Washington Post, 20 May 2003; quoted in Andrew Martin, 'Popular Culture and Narratives of Insecurity', in Petro and Martin, *Rethinking Global Security*, p. 104.
97 Martin, 'Popular Culture and Narratives of Insecurity', p. 110.
98 Marcus Bullock, 'The Origins of the Danger Market', in Petro and Martin, eds., *Rethinking Global Security*, pp. 78–79.
99 Bullock, 'The Origins of the Danger Market', p. 83.
100 Slavoj Žižek, 'Jack Bauer and the Ethics of Urgency', *In These Times*, 27 January 2006, http://www.inthesetimes.org/article/2481/jack_bauer_and_the_ethics_of_urgency/.
101 Erik Ringmar, 'Inter-Texual Relations: The Quarrel Over the Iraq War as a Conflict between Narrative Types', *Cooperation and Conflict*, Vol. 41, No. 4 (2006), p. 411.
102 Patrick Colm Hogan, 'Narrative Universals, Nationalism, and Sacrificial Terror: From *Nosferatu* to Nazism', *Film Studies*, Vol. 8 (Summer 2006), pp. 93–105.
103 Hogan, 'Narrative Universals', pp. 99–103.
104 Jamie Bartlett and Carl Miller, *The Power of Unreason: Conspiracy Theories, Extremism and Counter-Terrorism*, London: Demos, 2010.
105 Semelin, *Purify and Destroy*, pp. 24–27; Chirot and McCauley, *Why Not Kill Them All?*, p. 93.
106 Semelin, 'Toward a Vocabulary of Massacre and Genocide', p. 196.
107 Hogan, 'Narrative Universals', pp. 93–95.
108 Abdelwahab El-Affendi, 'The War of Ideas as Therapy: Reflections on a Eureka Moment in the "war on terror"', in Eric D. Patterson, and John Gallagher, eds., *Debating the War of Ideas*, Basingstoke: Palgrave Macmillan, 2009, pp. 175–193.
109 Michael J. Hyde, 'The Rhetor as Hero and the Pursuit of Truth: The Case of 9/11', *Rhetoric & Public Affairs*, Vol. 8, No. 1 (2005), pp. 1–30.
110 'Rivers of Blood', BBC Two, 8 March 2008, http://www.bbc.co.uk/white/rivers_blood.shtml.
111 Rorty, *Contingency, Irony and Solidarity*, p. 170.
112 Watson, '"Framing" the Copenhagen School', pp. 4, 17–18.
113 Fred Vultee, 'Securitization as a Media Frame', In Thierry Balzacq, ed., *Securitization Theory: How Security Problems Emerge and Dissolve*, London: Routledge, 2011, pp. 78–80.

114 Watson, '"Framing" the Copenhagen School', pp. 21–22.
115 Edward S. Herman, 'The Propaganda Model: A Retrospective', *Against All Reason*, Vol. 1, No. 1–14, 9 December 2003, http://human-nature.com/reason/01/herman.html.
116 Watson, '"Framing" the Copenhagen School', p. 18.
117 Williams, 'Words, Images, Enemies', p. 528; Tjalve, 'Designing (de)security', p. 442.
118 Vultee, 'Securitization as a Media Frame', p. 81.
119 Martin Gurri, Craig Denny and Aaron Harms, 'Our Visual Persuasion Gap', *Parameters*, Vol. 40, No. 1 (2010), pp. 101–109.
120 Don DeLillo, 'In the Ruins of the Future', *The Guardian*, 22 December 2001, http://www.guardian.co.uk/books/2001/dec/22/fiction.dondelillo.
121 Hyde, 'The Rhetor as Hero', pp. 1–4.
122 Hyde, 'The Rhetor as Hero', pp. 14–15; Marco Abel, 'Don DeLillo's 'In the Ruins of the Future': Literature, Images, and the Rhetoric of Seeing 9/11', *PMLA* Vol. 118, No. 5 (October 2003), pp. 1236–1250.
123 Rorty, *Contingency, Irony and Solidarity*, pp. xv–xvi.

3

Imagining Nationhood, Framing Postcoloniality: Narrativizing Nigeria through the Kinesis of (Hi)Story

James Tar Tsaaior

Nations, then, are imaginary constructs that depend for their existence on an apparatus of cultural fictions in which imaginative literature plays a decisive role. And the rise of European nationalism coincides especially with one form of literature – the novel... It was the novel that historically accompanied the rise of nations by objectifying the 'one', yet many of national life, and by mimicking the structure of the nation, a clearly bordered jumble of languages and styles. Socially, the novel joined the newspaper as the major vehicle of the national print media, helping to standardise language, encourage literacy, and remove mutual incomprehensibility. But it did much more than that. Its manner of presentation allowed people to imagine the special community that was the nation.[1]

Since political independence in 1960, what has consistently framed and defined Nigeria's postcolonial existence is her capacity to distil narratives that negotiate her largely uncertain and unassured destiny as a nation-state in a state of becoming. This condition of national narrativity, with its constitutive representational sites, participates in an agonistic history whose trajectory is woven around the pathology of the Nigerian state. Even though this narrative possesses the capacity to rankle festering wounds, it is not always imagined and interrogated as a galvanizing force for national re-imagining and re-invention. This makes Nigeria a veritable narrative engagement with the trappings of a tragic plot as she routinely participates in what looks like a violent history and a history of violence. This tragic rite began with the colonial encounter and its empire-building machinations, reaching an anticlimax in the brutal civil imbroglio of 1967–1970. The war itself was a culmination of socio-political and cultural narratives consistent with imagined, heterogeneous communities and groups within a fractious entity. Rooted deeply in such conflictual contextual configurations, the contours of national engineering have been conditioned by centrifugal tendencies which have constantly threatened the substratum and very soul of the fragile nation-state. This chapter negotiates the contexts and contests that have structured Nigeria's efforts at (re)inventing coherent nationhood beginning with the maiden 1966 putsch, the 1967–1970 debacle between Biafra and the Federal forces through the years of military interregnum which terminated in 1999. The governing argument of the chapter is that the contentious issues at the heart of Nigeria's construction of national identity have always been over-determined by narratives of political desire, longing and belonging, weaving national and sub-national allegories that idealize Selfness and negate Otherness. The continued currency of the narratives allegorizing nationhood and the inherent contradictions that are synonymous with Nigeria have registered their presence through legitimizing strategies of violent 'killer' narrativizations. The chapter concludes that politics and power constitute the driving forces behind these narratives. Elitist manipulation has continued to violate the sanctity of the Nigerian nation-state and to create visible crevices within a supposed monolith. In the end, Nigeria remains a work in progress, a *process* which remains contingent on the motions of history and how this history is distilled for the purpose of national re-invention.

Imperial naming

Nigeria is a veritable product of the British empire-building project in Africa and other peripheral spaces of the world. This imperial process started with the penetration of what has been variously called the 'Heart of Darkness', the 'white man's grave' and the 'white man's burden'.[2] These prejudiced characterizations of Africa were executed by European explorers and writers building up to the 'pacification' of the variegated indigenous populations. The programme was achieved through fraudulent treaties for 'protection' and other obnoxious colonial policies and practices. The amalgamation of the Northern and Southern protectorates was ratified in 1914. This effectively created Nigeria, a nation of nations and institutionalized the Indirect Rule policy.

Nigeria's very name bears eloquent and compelling witness to this imperial history. It is a name which etymologically signifies 'Niger Area'. It is a derivative from the River Niger, one of the biggest rivers that traverse its vast landscape. The name was given by Flora Shaw, the mistress, and later, wife of Lord Lugard, the first Governor-General.[3] This very naming rite effectively lends credibility to the European cultural politics of assigning names to specific spaces as a culmination of the imperial arrogance of imposing epistemological authority and control over marginal spaces and inscribing Empire onto their physical landscape and cultural fabrics.

This naming rite proceeded simultaneously with the trope of 'discovery' which possesses a long history and an enduring motif. In the European imaginary, it entailed the occupation of physical space and the inscription of the self on the cultures of native others. As a powerful expression of Western cultural agency and subjectivity, the discovery trope also represented the deleterious dimensions of European cultural assertion and its entrenched, overarching interests in the cultures of others. Quite often, demonization and vulgarization was the definition fixed on these cultures. Lugard's 'dual mandate' would soon graduate into what Niall Ferguson[4] refers to as the 'new imperialism', a reality that gave concrete substance to the colonial project. As Jyotsna Singh observes,

> [...] this discovery motif has frequently emerged in the language of colonisation enabling European travellers-writers to represent the newly 'discovered' lands as an empty space, a *tabula rasa* on which they could inscribe their linguistic, cultural and later, territorial claims... Rhetorically, however, the trope of discovery took on shifting, multiple meanings... being constantly refurbished and mobilised in the service of other colonising, rescuing, and idealising or demonising their... subjects as 'others'.[5]

Nigeria is, therefore, a narrative fashioned by the imperial imagination and colonial design. The fabrication of the nation can as such be located within these historical particularities and contextual specificities of British colonial engineering. It is, therefore, received epistemology that the very fabrication of Nigeria was in the imperial interest. Britain, like other European nations with expansionist aspirations, was prospecting for raw materials, markets and profitable investments. In the main, oil, first palm oil and, later crude, featured prominently as articles of trade. These were mostly concentrated in the South in what later became known as 'the Oil Rivers'.[6]

Further inland, the articles of trade were groundnuts, beni-seed, cotton, among others in the North. This trade was lopsided as it tilted heavily in favour of the Europeans who had considerable comparative advantage. To facilitate it, the Europeans needed transportation means and hence the construction of a rail line up north in 1923. This helped in the expropriation and evacuation of these products to the ports in the coastal South for onward transportation to the metropolitan centre. The making of Nigeria, therefore, involved the throwing into relief of an elaborate colonial programme with far-reaching consequences whose life-span endures till today.

Towards a theory of the nation

Benedict Anderson's theorization of the nation as 'an imagined political community... both inherently limited and sovereign',[7] and his thesis that its fabrication is historically consistent with modernity, are particularly relevant to the present discourse. Nations are, indeed, veritable products of modernity, as their emergence in enlightenment Europe was conditioned by the historical realities which inaugurated the modern moment. They participate in modernity through the social, political and juridical institutions they create and the Gramscian notion of hegemonic state apparatuses they fashion to embody and mediate their superstructures. However, this Marxist interpretation of the nation is limited and circumvents a holistic understanding of the term. This is precisely because the nation cannot be sufficiently explained merely in terms of its political and juridical structures.

Against this significant backdrop, it is important to cast into history to implicate other coefficients of nationhood, including culture, ethnicity, racism and a diaspora community. This historicist and modernist perspective of the nation is fascinating because it constitutes the nation as a contingent socio-political, ethnic and cultural construction in a modern world, as Anderson argues. However, Anderson's concept of national sovereignty in the modern world appears to have been intensely interrogated by totalitarian military regimes, by quasi-democratic contraptions and by civilian autocrats in Africa and other parts of the peripheral world.

It is, however, necessary to distinguish between a nation and a state, since they are not synonymous with each other. A nation is a socio-culturally constructed and determined entity, a union of people with shared experiences that comprise a common ancestry, history, language and culture. Such a union as exists in a nation does not necessarily subsist on formal political arrangements. A state, on the other hand, is different from a nation. It is a legal and political entity. Such an arrangement may comprise a heterogeneous population without a commonality of shared experiences or identity. It is merely an agglomeration of populations with a defined territory, government organs/political structure, a system of enforceable laws and the capacity to cultivate relationships with others based on sovereign terms. This tension between the terms nation and state and the need to reconcile them to meet the needs of modernity necessitate their conflation to form the oxymoron called the 'nation-state'.

The idea of the nation as a social construct is also attested to by Eric Hobsbawm. As imagined communities, nations according to Hobsbawm develop national traditions and a legacy of ethical mores and values which are invented by the elite.[8] These traditions and values – anthems, symbols, emblems, names, flags, constitutions, etc. – are codified, institutionalized and so become part of the communal property which binds together the citizens in a supposed horizontal relationship. The sense of communion and comradeship, which defines *nation-ness*, is nevertheless mediated by hierarchical structures and other oppositional binaries. However, these are tempered by nationalism as an overriding concern. It is the nationalist spirit and consciousness that is central to national survival and efflorescence and serves as a veritable justification for the existence of the nation.

Timothy Brennan initiates a discourse concerning the distinction between the nation as a product of modernity and ancientness. He states:

> As for the 'nation', it is both historically determined and general. As a term, it refers both to the modern nation-state and to something more ancient and nebulous – the 'natio' – a local community, domicile, family, condition of belonging. The distinction is often obscured by nationalists who seek to place their own country in an 'immemorial past' where its arbitrariness cannot be questioned.[9]

Ideationally, Brennan's concept of the 'natio', though too restrictive in a modern sense, affords us a historical vision of the originariness of the nation and its authentic character; hence the nebulousness of its very nature in a modern sense. This historical vision and the nebulousness of the modern nation-state and its gestures to the archives of historical memory and re-memory are responsible for the dutiful constructions of mythologies and allegories which seek to spatio-temporally locate the nation in modernity.

Brennan proceeds to locate the rise of the modern nation-state in Europe in the temporal frame of the eighteenth and nineteenth centuries and attributes it to literary narrative scripts or 'imaginative literature'. He elaborates:

> The rise of the modern nation-state in Europe in the late eighteenth and early nineteenth centuries is inseparable from the forms and subjects of imaginative literature. ... On the other hand, and just as fundamentally, literature participated in the formation of nations through the creation of 'national print media' – the newspaper and the novel ... it was specially the novel as a composite but clearly bordered work of art that was crucial in defining the nation.[10]

It is this same idea of the 'natio' that Raymond Williams mobilizes in his reification of the nation.[11] Williams too situates his hermeneutic idea of the nation in historical perspective, latching on the imaginary of nativity, place and placement within a specific *topos*. To him, this symbolic attachment to a legacy of common, shared origins through birth – not necessarily in a physical sense but also metaphorically – is what socializes people into national bonds. He elaborates that the '"Nation" as a term is radically connected with "native". We are *born* into relationships which are typically settled in a place.'

Though Raymond's perspective on the original ontology of the nation gravitates precariously to what can be said to be its *folk* character, it teleologically establishes and accentuates the tension between the negotiation of the nation in its historical sense and the artificial fabrication of modern nations contemporaneous with eighteenth and nineteenth century Europe. This process also impacted positively or negatively on other marginal spaces during the defining moment of the colonialist and imperialist encounter. The artificiality and brittleness of national territorial boundaries concomitant with the project of colonial empire-building, according to Paul Ricouer, requires that indigenous colonized peoples massed in the 'natio' 'forge a national spirit, and unfurl this spiritual and cultural revindication before the colonialist's personality'.[12] In the formerly colonized world, this appears to be the grand paradox of nationhood and national becoming, particularly in Africa.

The theory of the nation and nation-ness also produces a spiritual dimension, as Ernest Renan refracts the nation as a 'spiritual principle' and 'soul'. The spiritual dimension revisions the purely historical extrapolations that over-determined the rise of the nation in Europe and elsewhere. Renan's position, however, strikes a delicate balance between the historicist-materialist and spiritualist networks that are crucial to modern nationhood. His perspective, while appearing essentialist, is actually a unitarist conflation of the two grids governed by the idea of time past and time present, which is enriched by a legacy of communal memories and the communication of consent and willingness to consolidate the traditions retrieved from history. To Renan, therefore,

> [A] nation is a soul, a spiritual principle. Two things, which in truth are one, constitute this spiritual soul. One lies in the past, one in the present. One is the possession in common of a rich legacy of memories; the other is present day consent, the desire to live together.[13]

In re/constructing this dichotomy between the historical and spiritual axes, Regis Debray also envisions the nation in terms of sacredness and spirituality. According to him,

> the nation is an invariable which cuts across modes of production … one through which life itself is rendered untouchable or sacred. This sacred character constitutes the real national question.[14]

A framing concern in the preceding arguments negotiating the nation is that it is a historical contingency that is consistent with modernity. Another defining epistemology is that the nation is a social construction which imagines itself in terms of a community with shared historical experiences and common origins. This commonality is what provides the impetus for social and cultural solidarity among the peoples that constitute a nation. But in a much more fundamental dimension, the ruminations on nationhood also imagine it as constructed by narratives which are themselves an index of modernity, the product of a literate culture and an emergent educated elite.

It must, however, be obvious that some of the narratives are primarily oral, which does not vitiate their capacity for narrating nationhood. Indeed, in narrating nationhood, both oral and written traditions intersect and overlap. It is in this regard that Homi Bhabha observes concerning the nation and its narration thus:

> It is the mark of the ambivalence of the nation as a narrative strategy-and an apparatus of power-that it produces a continual slippage into analogous, even metonymic categories, like the people, minorities or 'cultural difference' that continually overlap in the act of writing the nation. What is displayed in this displacement and repetition of terms is the nation as the measure of the liminality of cultural modernity.[15]

Thus, a dialectical bond exists between the nation and na(rra)tion: while nations will and weave into life their canon of narratives, narratives also incarnate nations and breathe life into them.

The postcolonial imaginary and the narrativization of Nigerian nationhood

If there is a brutally frank and appropriate metaphor that represents the contradictions which underwrite the Nigerian condition as a postcolonial nation-state grappling with the contingencies of modernity, it is that Nigeria is a narrative. This is, however, a narrative in transition. The transitional character of the narrative equally compels the negotiation of Nigerianness to be necessarily contingent and in strict fidelity to the historical process. Nevertheless, the narrative possesses the incredible capacity to intrigue, stir, confound and compel sustained attention. There is, indeed, a plethora of reasons why Nigeria is fascinating as a narrative. Nigeria is demographically the most populous black country in Africa and, indeed, the whole world. One in every five black people is believed to be a Nigerian.

The country is prodigiously endowed with rich human and material resources, including crude oil. Nigeria ranks as the sixth or seventh largest producer of crude in the world. But this crude oil which 'primarily sustains the economy and holds the component parts in (dis)harmonious communion as a corporate entity has the paradoxical potential of brutally wounding and healing, of sickness and therapy'.[16] The landmass is vast with rich arable soil for the production of food and cash crops. Except for the northernmost reaches of the country close to the Sahara Desert, the fertility of the soil is truly undeniable, beginning with the forest region in the south through the guinea savannah in the middle belt and the Sahel in the north. In terms of physical relief, Nigeria is drained by two major rivers, the Niger and the Benue, among several other rivers, tributaries, creeks, estuaries, etc. The nation's shores are washed by the Atlantic Ocean, itself a major source of offshore crude.

Much of Nigeria is a cultural mosaic with a heterogeneous collectivity of ethnic nationalities, home to a rich fund of cultures and traditions. Nigerians are industrious, resourceful, resilient, creative and innovative people. However, the paradox of the Nigerian nation as a postcolonial state inheres in the fact that, even with these enormous endowments, Africa's self-adulatory giant remains a dwarf, a fragmentary narrative whose strands refuse to cohere. Ali Mazrui captures this paradoxical condition by deploying the Swiftian metaphor of Gulliver and his travels among the Lilliputians. According to him, Nigeria, the 'giant of Africa' has been 'in danger of becoming the midget of the world. Africa's Gulliver faced the threat of becoming the Lilliput of the world'.[17] Though Mazrui's appropriation of the Gulliver metaphor appears conceited, it will seem that Jonathan Swift was prophetically allegorizing Africa's crippled giant well before it heaved into existence.

Tragedy is the defining character of Nigeria as a narrative. The tragic dimensions of the Nigerian narrative congeal in the fact that the nation has wilfully refused to creatively harness her diversities in the facets of ethnicity, culture, demographic preponderance, abundant human and natural resource base and the goodwill of Nature and History. Rather, it has embraced the culture of corruption, political instability, economic stagnation, ethnocentrism, social morass and cultural stasis. Nigeria, for instance, does not have what can be validly characterized as a national ethos, a Nigerian way of meaningfully engaging nationhood, and the world. As Femi Osofisan quaintly observes, Nigeria does not have a national ethos but if it exists, its profile is abysmal, conflictual and contradictory. In his words, 'formed by colonial fiat from disparate ethnic groups and rival kingdoms – can one call it a nation when ... the old suspicions and animosities have refused to die?'[18] For Osofisan,

> the nation is still in the process of becoming ... [and] our national ethos is still undefined, chaotic, self-contradictory ... our present state of incoherence that is, paradoxically and tragically, our nation's lack of a national ethos.[19]

This perspective may appear too harsh and uncharitable to Nigeria. However, it is this atrocious lack of a national ethos that drives Nigeria to the brink of a yawning precipice in its national strivings and narrativization. The old suspicions and animosities alluded to above command attention. This is because they register the gratuitous ethnic acrimonies and sharp differences which have bedevilled the Nigerian imaginary, and intensely interrogated its incoherent postcoloniality. The politics of ethnic pluralism, which should constitute an asset for national re/invention, has become a monumental liability. The yoking together by violence of the heterogeneous peoples of Nigeria by British imperial ideology, and the stoking of the embers of division by the colonial authorities, still underwrite the essential Nigerian character. It is either you are Hausa-Fulani, Igbo or Yoruba, the so-called majorities, or you are massed among the minorities such as Efik, Ibibio, Izon, Tiv and Urhobo in an ossifying ethnic oppositional binary. Ironically, the minorities constitute the majority when put together. The irony again is that there is a Nigeria but hardly any Nigerians as individual loyalty is almost always primarily to ethnicity before the nation.

In many ways, Nigeria as a narrative is a synecdochic or microcosmic representation of the African continent. According to Jideofor Adibe, who sums up the African postcolonial predicament with solid implications for Nigeria,

> No continent is pulled in as many directions and often conflictual directions as Africa. It is the continent where different countries, and even nationalities within countries, are sharply divided, and sometimes defined by emotive external allegiances. Hence, we have Anglophone Africa, Francophone Africa, Lusophone Africa, Arab Africa, Bantu Africa, Christian Africa, Islamic Africa, Diaspora Africa etc.[20]

No doubt, the idea of Africa as a continent under the curse of history has attracted a complex of interpretive possibilities. These polarizations are emblematic of that imperial curse imposed by metropolitan politics and cultural ideologies. Adekeye Adebajo has referred to this violent history with its corpus of predicaments as 'the curse of Berlin', as 'historical and structural events continue to affect and shape Africa's contemporary international relations'.[21] It was Otto von Bismarck's 1884–1885 Berlin conference that partitioned Africa and pronounced a curse on the continent which continues to haunt it in varied ways. This curse is present especially in the guise of the modern nation-state. In an insightful, counter-historical inversion of the Eurocentric notion of Africa as the white man's burden, Basil Davidson retraces this 'curse' in a compelling title casts the White man as the Black man's burden through the curse of the modern nation-state.[22] Here, Davidson alludes to the history of artificial fabrication of nations and arbitrary boundaries in Africa.

Nigeria as a nation of nations also shares in this curse of history. The invention of Nigeria by British colonial fiat constituted it as an imagined cartography for the imperial gaze, a sphere of influence for colonial domination and exploitation. The nation which was cobbled from disparate ethnic configurations existed for the pleasure of Empire. Its existence was also for its overweening lust for territories as it was consistent with the European scramble for and partition of Africa. The corollary of this zealous imperial programme was that many of the nations which emerged from the colonial laboratory were already infected with congenitally terminal pathologies that started manifesting soon after their parturition. Nigeria ended up in this category soon after political autonomy in 1960.

As it may be apparent from the discursive drift so far, the seeds of Nigeria's fractious nationhood were sown right from the moment of the colonial encounter. The totalizing divide-and-rule policies of the colonial overlords initiated a process of mutual suspicion and pathological hate and fear among the disparate ethnicities that configured the inchoate nation. The politics of nationalist struggle with the founding fathers like Herbert Macaulay, Nnamdi Azikiwe, Tafawa Balewa, Ahmadu Bello, Obafemi Awolowo, Margaret Ekpo, etc., only barely managed to wrest political autonomy from the British when it was no longer politically expedient, economically viable or morally defensible to administer the nation.

Though nationalist resistance yielded independence, the ethnic wrangling and disquiet continued unabated, culminating in the crises of the First Republic. But this was perhaps the only historical moment when Nigeria's narrativity cohered as the nationalists were united by the common goal of transcending colonial suzerainty. Anthony Giddens postulates that, in the construction of modern nationhood, the progressive forces that constitute the nationalist collective are pulled in divergent directions, based on ethnic affiliations, regional cleavages or religious sympathies. This generates complex dilemmas, the first being the dilemma of unification versus fragmentation:

> Modernity fragments; it also unites. On the level of the individual right up to that of planetary systems as a whole, the tendencies towards dispersal vie with those promoting integration... the problem of unification concerns protecting and reconstructing the narrative of self-identity in the face of the massive intentional and extensional changes which modernity sets into being.[23]

Narratives fall apart

In Nigeria, the facade of nationalist solidarity soon crumbled. In its place, ethnic solidarity became enthroned with fierce competition for the soul of the nation and its patrimony. Indications in this direction were apparent at the very beginning. Genuine feelings of apprehension of hegemonic domination were expressed when the North preferred political autonomy later than the South. The southern political elite, who were in the vanguard of resistance against colonialism, called for independence around 1956 (one year earlier than Ghana's historic success in 1957). Nationalist leaders in the North cited the excuse that the region was unprepared for independence because it was behind the South in terms of development. Personal and communal narratives, official and popular, particular and general, were mobilized in the articulation of these alternative ethnic, regional and religious perspectives. These narratives exerted profound impact on the national imagination as they were invested or imbued with ethnic/sectarian undertones, undermining the substratum for national cohesion. Besides, they instigated fear and suspicion with gross repercussions on national unity and be/longing.

Obafemi Awolowo, one of the nationalists, was to famously announce that Nigeria is not a nation but a mere geographical expression and that he was first a Yoruba before being a Nigerian. This avowal clearly meant that the basis for Nigerian unity was vacuous, as individuals owed their loyalty to their ethnicities before the nation. In his autobiographical narrative eponymously titled *Awo*, he was to ventilate his inveterate animosity for the Igbo and his political adversary, Azikiwe, in what can be said to have set the tone for the discordant orchestral notes in Nigerian politics with spiralling repercussions. He said:

> [...] in spite of his protestations to the contrary, Dr. Azikiwe was himself an unabashed Ibo jingoist. And he gave the game completely away when he said inter alia in his presidential address to the Ibo Federal Union in 1949, as follows: 'It would appear that the God of Africa has specially created the Ibo nation to lead the children of Africa from the bondage of the ages... The martial prowess of the Ibo nation at all stages of human history has enabled them not only to conquer others but also to adapt themselves to the role of preserver'.

Awolowo was not done with his regurgitation of the offensive pronouncements of his political foe. He proceeded to state:

> It was clear from these statements and from the general political and journalistic maneuvers of Dr. Azikiwe over the years that his great objective was to set himself up as a dictator over Nigeria and to make the Ibo nation the master race. It would appear according to his reckoning that the only obstacle in the path of his ambition was the Yoruba intelligentsia, and these must be removed at all costs... I am implacably opposed to dictatorship as well as the doctrine of *Herrenvolk* whether it was Hitler's or Dr. Azikiwe's.[24]

Two realities immediately emerge from Awolowo's statement: one is that the construction of divisive ethnic structures was consistent with nationalist politics and not a post-independence phenomenon. Two, it would appear that there was a crisis of motivation for the political careers of some of the nationalists as they joined the nationalist struggle, not for patriotic reasons but for self-aggrandizement, ethnic solidarity and preservation. Awo's autobiographical narrative, like many others in the same mould, possesses canonical capital and prefigures how Nigeria was imagined during the anti-colonial resistance and in postcolonial politics. Its decidedly centrifugal tendencies clearly foregrounded the path the general narrative trajectory was headed.

Till today, there is running antagonism and a contagion of hate and suspicion between the Igbo and the Yoruba. This reality was to be compounded by the civil war of 1967–1970, which figure in some Igbo narratives as 'an act of betrayal by the Yoruba' who fought with the federal forces. It is interesting that the other major nationalists, Nnamdi Azikiwe and Ahmadu Bello, have also ventilated their concerns about Nigeria in their autobiographical narratives, *My Odyssey* and *My Life*, respectively. These narratives constitute an inter-textual dialogue with Awolowo's *Awo* and sought to undermine its claims while privileging their perspectives on national issues. Significantly, the narratives have not been innocent expressions of individual subjectivity by the three founding fathers of Nigeria. Indeed, they represent entrenched sentiments of ethnicity, region and religion nourished by them and their followers. This in itself underscores the epistemological power and potency of such narratives in structuring social and cultural relations between ethnicities in a plural nation-state like Nigeria.

Complexities of ethnic nationalism and the ethic of ethnic superiority and inferiority were at the centre of these narratives espoused by Awolowo and his rivals. The North was pathologically afraid of southern domination by virtue of its disadvantage in terms of education, while the south was also embroiled in acrimony as counter-accusations defined the rhetoric of the leaders. For instance, in a response to Awolowo that the Igbo were strategizing to dominate others, Azikiwe accused Awolowo of scheming to frustrate Nigerian unity unless he became the leader. His argument was that it was *Awo* who prevented him from winning elections in Lagos, the then political capital of Yorubaland. Such an act, to Azikiwe, postponed the day all Nigerians would be free or to have a sense of belonging. It also made it impossible to win elections in any part of the nation other than one's ethnic stronghold, thereby weakening the sense of national cohesion.

In the Middle Belt, which was under the Northern Region, fears and insecurity were also expressed by the minorities of domination and oppression by the northern political oligarchy. The sentiments here were dictated by religious or sectarian causes. Most of the northern minorities were of Christian or animist backgrounds, and they feared been coerced into an Islamic culture by the northern political/religious establishment. Narratives of the Dan Fodio jihadists who conquered much of the North about 1806, with the avowed determination to 'dip the Quran in the Atlantic', continued to reverberate and haunt the minorities who were bent on resisting the 'Islamisation policy' of the northern politicians. These narratives were critical to the formation of the United Middle Belt Congress, led by J.S. Tarkaa, a Tiv minority politician. He later aligned with Awolowo's Action Group against the Northern People's Congress, which controlled the central government in the First Republic.

One of the major narratives that have commanded national attention is of communal/regional nature. The narrative is that the British colonial authorities were more favourably disposed to the North than the South. They found the northern population more amenable and governable because of their established political and religious institutions under the emirate system. In radical contradistinction, much of the South especially Igboland, was largely segmentary with some of the groups acephalous and without unified central political structures. This made the implementation of the Indirect Rule policy a real challenge in the South. Besides, southern politicians were more independent-minded, uncooperative and unyielding than their northern countrymen. As Crawford Young put it,

> Iboland was the most difficult part of Nigeria to subdue. The centralised Hausa-Fulani emirates could be conquered from the top; in Yorubaland utter fatigue from the debilitating nineteenth-century civil wars ... led to ready acceptance of British rule. But acephalous Iboland had to be subjugated segment by segment.[25]

In the estimation of the British, the narratives affirm, it served British colonial interests better to cede power at independence to the North than the South. This narrative reality resonated with diverse political possibilities on the future destiny of the Nigerian nation. One of these which compel attention today is the near monopolization of political power by the North since independence, especially through the military establishment and coup culture.

Other narratives are of ethnic nationalist colouration. The first coup of 15 January 1966 was led dominantly by Igbo army officers and hence the appellation it has received: 'Igbo coup'. It is, however, true that not all the military majors were of Igbo extraction. Indeed, some have argued that many northern soldiers were actively involved in the first coup. And in spite of mounting evidence that the coup was staged for patriotic reasons, the original narrative still inspires credibility for many. Awolowo was allegedly designated as the person to be installed as leader of the nation if the coup had succeeded. This narrative is speculative and mainly circulates among the coup sympathizers. To many, the genuine reasons for the coup could not have been patriotic, as the Igbo officers that dominated the group constituted a self-legitimizing vanguard for Igbo domination. This is also because many of the victims of the coup were the northern political and military elite, while the Igbo intelligentsia were spared.

The reprisal killings which followed the coup assumed the colouration of 'genocide' against the Igbo. This resulted in the civil imbroglio during which millions were decimated in what has been described as a senseless and avoidable war. Narratives with a killer edge were clearly at the centre of that war: that the maiden coup was an Igbo action, especially with the assassination of many prominent officers and politicians of Northern extraction. This narrative became more compelling following the eventual emergence of General Johnson Aguiyi Ironsi, an Igbo man and the then most senior officer in the Nigerian Army. Pathological fears of Igbo hegemonic domination in the Armed Forces and in the wider public reached fever pitch. This was aggravated by Ironsi's unwillingness to swiftly and decisively punish the coup's leaders and signal the construction of unitary and viable nationhood during that delicate and fleeting moment of history. This centrist policy accentuated the fears of elements within and without the military and political elite of possible Igbo hegemony.

Uncharitable narratives viscerally implicate General Ironsi in the paroxysms of violence and state of anarchy that pervaded his military administration. However, more sympathetic accounts volunteer more balanced explanations which assign General Ironsi an apparently messianic role which he did not deliberately prepare for, as he was merely reacting to circumstances imposed by an aberrant history and its exigencies. In this schema, the introduction of a unitary political system was also part of an official narrative that constituted itself as a grand plan to advance the Igbo hegemonic agenda. Ironsi was assassinated the same year in a military action that was believed to be a strategy for containing this overarching Igbo desire to exclusively appropriate the national patrimony.

Yet another narrative with an ethnic temperament suggests that the counter-coup of July 1966 was intended for the North to secede from Nigeria and form a separate nation. It claims that it was the British who persuaded the northerners to remain in a federal Nigeria because of the huge oil deposits in the South which they would lose in the event of secession. Events have demonstrated sufficiently that truth resides in this narrative as it is oil that sustains Nigeria's largely mono-cultural economy. The North is believed to be the greatest beneficiary from this rich resource, and recent youth unrest in the oil-rich Niger Delta region are a violent reaction to the continued exploitation of the area by a federal structure which sees the area as a conquered territory.

A civil war of narratives

As a monumental historical moment negotiating Nigerian nationhood, the Civil War was constructed as a grand narrative by the official testimonies of the Federal Government. Appropriately, therefore, the Biafran insurgency was an elemental rebellious rite, a wilful centrifugal tendency, which was meant to undermine national integrity and compromise the sovereignty of Nigeria. Such official narrative appropriations were themselves lent stridency and popular appeal by the state media which subscribed to the rhythms of allegorical telling and re-telling, a tissue of versions that sought to articulate the remote and immediate precipitating causes for the war.

In the same mould, such official narrativizations, not ideologically innocent in themselves, were intended to compel popular credibility/credulity and confer valuation on the accounts. However, they became intensely contested and problematized by marginal discourses. Such alternative discourses assigned radically opposed and mutually irreconcilable motivations for the violent civil disquiet. On the Biafran side, the war was a veritable act of ethnic cleansing, a slow genocide organized by the Federal Government against the Igbo. The latter became an endangered species in their own country under the flimsy, diversionary claim that Biafra was a secessionist agenda, borne out of personal aggrandizement and lust for power by Col. Emeka Odumegwu Ojukwu.

In the labyrinth between official and unofficial narrativizations of Nigeria lurk forms of telling and re-telling. The narrativizations critically re-imagine and interrogate these conventional modes of discourse on Nigerian postcoloniality. The testimonies which represent in-betweenness are embodied by the silent or, more appropriately, the silenced, as their silence also articulates large statements that define the Nigerian paradox and predicament. This inevitably remaps the discursive boundaries in radical dimensions, thereby orchestrating a re-thinking of the scripted narratives. Implicated here is Gayatri Spivak's now famous question about the ability of the subaltern to communicate through the appropriation of speaking rites. The reality of the Nigerian postcolonial condition demonstrates sufficiently that there are layers of subalternity: there are subalterns within subalterns, each straining, not just to speak but also to be heard. But even where they express individual subjectivity and agency by refusing to speak, or when silence is imposed on them by totalizing forms of hegemonic state apparatuses, their deafening silence alone constitutes an alternative discursive strain which (re)narrates the Nigerian nation.

Consistent with the contested and contestable sites of narrative representation was the construction of popular myths which sought to explain and articulate the salvific roles of particular personages in the narratives that became quintessential of the war. Ojukwu was delineated as an epic hero, both in the secessionist media and the popular Biafran imagination. He was not motivated by a cult of personality but by a survivalist instinct intended for ethnic preservation, honour and justice. General Yakubu Gowon, then head of state, was a patriotic leader, who unlike Nero, would not fiddle while Nigeria burned under the Biafran insurrection. Gowon soon became the acronym for 'Go on with one Nigeria.'

The systematic massacres of the Igbo in the North as part of the reprisal measures against the felling of prominent Northern politicians and military officers in the 1966 putsch governed the popular imagination and dictated the actions of the military and politicians. In other words, official and unofficial narratives in the aftermath of the coup determined the direction of events in the nation: Northerners were on a revenge mission against the Igbo for killing their own and for pursuing an agenda to dominate Nigeria and impose their will on the rest of the nation. The retailing of these narratives in diverse publics had nothing to do with their veracity or authenticity and hence their openness to elastic and protean interpretive possibilities, most of which had violent and killer propensities.

According to Crawford Young, 'when cultural communities collectively perceive threats to communal status in the political environment, group solidarity tends to increase'.[26] This means that a potent threat to ethnic identity or communal consciousness necessitates the strengthening of bonds and the cultural nationalism of the threatened group. This is precisely what happened in the Igbo situation when Nigerians of Igbo extraction discovered that their sense of longing for, and belonging to, a united Nigeria was severely compromised by the systematic killings of their kin in the North. The corollary to this was the rebellion against the central government and the declaration of a sovereign state of Biafra. The emergence of Biafra as an alternative national project was precipitated by what Easterners saw as the politics of 'exclusion through inclusion' and so asserted their will to self-determination so as to avoid liquidation. This discontent continues to define their attitude to political participation in Nigeria and this is obvious with the emergence of pro-Biafra bodies like the Movement for the Actualisation of the Sovereign State of Biafra, MASSOB, whose activities have been outlawed by the state.

The years of military (mis)adventure: 1984–1999

The military rule era in Nigeria's postcolonial existence has been aptly described as the 'locust years'.[27] This metaphor symbolizes the pestilential and calamitous fate the military establishment foisted on the nation in its belaboured, martial tactics of re/inventing and re/imagining nationhood. Famines had ravaged much of the Horn of Africa, not as a result of locust infestation, though this is also located within the dynamic of political instability, mis-governance and corruption, other manifestations of a history of 'locust' legacies.

This was not without its narrative possibilities in Nigeria. Since the collapse of the First Republic from 1960 to 1966, the military infiltrated the Nigerian political landscape as a 'corrective' alternative to the malfeasance and the debris of corruption that the nascent political elite plunged the nation into. From then on, successive military adventurists including General Aguiyi Ironsi (1966), General Yakubu Gowon (1966–1975), Murtala Muhammed (1975–1976) and Olusegun Obasanjo (1976–1979), introduced martial law and decrees thereby subverting and undermining the democratic process.

A brief reprieve came the way of a harried nation between 1979 and 1983, when Shehu Shagari led a civilian administration. This was, however, overthrown in another military coup led by General Muhammadu Buhari (1983–1985). The corrective aspirations and revolutionary fervour of the regime was ended in a palace coup led by General Ibrahim Babangida (1985–1993), who is reputed to have institutionalized official corruption in Nigeria. It was Babangida who ran the most serpentine political transition in Nigeria's history which ended anti-climactically in the 12 June 1993 general elections which he unilaterally annulled. Ernest Shonekan led an interim government for less than a year when military strongman, General Sani Abacha sacked him in clearly anticipated circumstances. Abacha's dictatorship ended dramatically in his sudden death, paving the way for General Abdulsalami Abubakar (1998–1999) who, after the shortest transition programme in Nigeria's political history, handed over the reins of state power to Olusegun Obasanjo, a former military head of state, as an elected president. Since then, a democratic experiment which witnessed in 2007 the first ever civilian to civilian transfer of power occurred when the late President Umaru Musa Yar'Adua was elected. He had since been replaced on his death in 2010 by President Goodluck Jonathan, the current democratically elected president of Nigeria.

A historical reconnaissance of governance in postcolonial Nigeria demonstrates the dominance of the military in political engineering processes. While the military had ruled for twenty-eight years, democratic governance held sway for only twenty-three years, suggesting an imbalance in favour of military aggression over representative democracy. Some of the misfortunes which are consistent with the Nigerian narrative have been attributed to the incursion of the military into politics, a role they were ill-equipped for. Ironsi is reputed to have promulgated the now odious Unification Decree, which changed the structure of the nation from a federal republic to a unitary state. Narratives negotiating this epoch of national life seek to maul the policy as the inaugural programme by the Igbo ethnic nationality to impose its hegemony on the rest of the nation. Gowon has the less than salutary fame of telling the world that Nigeria then had too much money from the oil boom and that money was not the problem but how to spend it.

Gowon also drove the nation into the 1967–1970 Civil War. He, however, created states, a policy which many believe, has consolidated the unity of the fragile nation. Alternative perspectives, however, interpret this state creation effort as undermining the autonomy of the constituent units of the federation. Murtala was a fierce soldier who was consumed in the revolutionary fires he stoked. His patriotic zeal was cut short by the rampaging bullets of adversarial army officers who assassinated him in 1976. He, however, moved the nation's capital from the commercial city of Lagos to the more central location of Abuja. Obasanjo enjoyed the goodwill of having to continue with Murtala's radical policies and for voluntarily relinquishing power to a civilian government. He also remains the only person who has enjoyed the fortune of twice presiding over the affairs of the nation.

It is significant that besides personal ambition and self-aggrandizement, all of the military juntas that ruled Nigeria have deployed ethnic, regional or religious sentiments in taking over state power and consolidating themselves in office. Quite often, they also thrived on the employment of narratives which undermined the cohesion of the opposition and subverted the popular will by appealing to sectional interests. Usually, these narratives drive the populace apart rather than unite them for the onerous responsibility of nation-building. Such a divide-and-rule policy has always weakened potential oppositional strongholds into divisive thresholds and compromised the potency of alternative visions to Nigerian national narrativization.

Since 1999, 'killer narratives' and their accompanying genocidal nightmares have engaged ethnic nationalist animosities in unprecedented ways. The locust years of the military created a sense of pervasive insecurity in the land based on perceived and real fears of ethnic hegemony by the dominant groups, especially the Hausa-Fulani oligarchy. Resonances of these mutual fears and insecurities have been strongly felt in the present, and the northern elite have become the victim of isolation from political power. Following the death of President Yar'Adua in 2010, power has shifted from the North to the South with the election of President Jonathan Goodluck. A number of key northern politicians have vowed to make Nigeria ungovernable unless power rotates to the North. The terror being unleashed by *Boko Haram*, the fundamentalist religious group, is located within this political dynamic of insecurities expressed by the North after losing out in the power calculus. *Boko Haram* is sometimes perceived as a religious foil for political *r*enegotiation of power since it becomes inevitable to deploy force and violence when peaceful change becomes impossible.

What is difficult to understand is why the religious unrests have been localized mostly in the northern cities like Bauchi, Maiduguri, Jos, Kano, Kaduna, Minna and the capital Abuja. What is clear is that the targets have been Christians and their places of worship. In recent times, mosques have also been targeted in what looks like a non-discriminatory campaign against religion. Yet Nigeria is constitutionally a secular nation-state (some say it is multi-religious) where religious wars have been waged with genocidal implications. But government establishments have also been attacked. The Police Headquarters in Abuja was destroyed when a powerful bomb exploded, nearly killing the police chief. The United Nations Building was also the target of a blast, with many casualties from other nations. *Boko Haram* has claimed responsibility for these acts of violence. Its justificatory narrative is that it is fighting against Westernization which is anti-Islamic. To many, religion is being used to mask a political project at the heart of the northern agenda.

It seems the Nigerian killer narrative has assumed a dramatic, climactic turn where bombings in the North and kidnappings, especially in the Niger Delta, have become the martial strategies of the belligerents. Politics is at the centre of these narratives. The North where *Boko Haram* is spreading terror wants a reconfiguration of the power equation in its favour. The Niger Delta and much of the South is agitating for the implementation of a more balanced federation where the component units will control the resources in their areas, including crude oil, the chief source of Nigeria's monocultural economy. Calls for the convocation of a (sovereign) national conference have again become vociferous by elements in the South as a way of restructuring the nation and determining better and efficacious ways of national engineering. The Nigerian narrative remains fractured and fragmented along such acrimonious grids.

Conclusion

From all indications, Nigeria, Africa's most populous democracy, is not in a hurry to abandon the negotiation of its nationhood through killer or violent narratives. If anything, as the discussion has demonstrated, the stakes based on ethnicity, region and religion are intensifying over who controls the 'national cake'. This has instituted mutual recriminations, suspicions and spiralling cut-throat competitions between the majorities and minorities in an increasingly polarized landscape. Calls for the dismemberment of the nation have become more vociferous. Another option has been the convocation of a sovereign national conference to renegotiate the basis for unity built around a true federal arrangement, fiscal policy, state police, equitable distribution of resources and a free/fair judicial system which will respect and defend the rights and freedoms of all citizens. This position is not acceptable to official state policy, though, because federalists see in it an epitaph for an indivisible, sovereign Nigeria. But for how long this resistance by the government to the convocation of a national conference will last remains to imagined.

In the immediate post-1999 political dispensation, which had seen the exit of the military and the uninterrupted practice of democracy for over a decade, ethnic animosities, regional divisions and religious violence have also risen astronomically. Ethnic groupings with centrifugal tendencies like Oodua Peoples' Congress (among the Yoruba), Egbesu Boys, Niger Delta Volunteer Force, Movement for the Emancipation of the Niger Delta, Movement for the Survival of Ogoni People, etc. (among Niger Delta communities), Arewa Peoples' Congress (among the Hausa-Fulani) and MASSB (among the Igbo) became more active and vocal in their aspirations for self-determination.

At the regional level, Nigeria has also demonstrated the uncommon capacity in how not to engineer and narrate nationhood. Organizations like Afenifere (Yoruba), Arewa Consultative Forum (Hausa-Fulani), Ohanaeze Ndigbo (Igbo), and Middle Belt Forum (ethnicities in central Nigeria) have also been complicit in ossifying relations and freezing regional interactions in the name of seeking regional solidarity, development, justice and equity. More recently, the national contradictions have been exacerbated by the emergence of fundamentalist religious groups especially *Boko Haram*, which has been involved in Al-Qaeda-style operations and the indiscriminate killing of innocent citizens. This dimension has accentuated the sharp religious differences between the North and South, Christians and Moslems, with devastating consequences on national cohesion.

The common denominator in all these sorry realities is the killer narratives which have been distilled over time and have continued to gain currency through renewed narrative assaults. In narrating the Nigerian nation, many of the strands have become coloured with bloodstains because of the killer instincts and the genocidal nightmares which have become internalized and concretized within the narrative schema. Beginning with the 1967–1970 destructive Civil War, Nigeria's narrative possibilities have been defined and conditioned by a history of violence and a legacy of unrelieved nightmares the nation is still struggling to wake up from. Whether Nigeria overcomes this culture of killer narrativization or not remains a matter of slippery conjecture as the nation slouches like a wounded beast of plural births, hoping to be reborn and to survive its protean contradictions as a postcolonial state whose jeremiad narrative refuses to cohere.

Notes

1   Timothy Brennan, 'The National Longing for Form', in Homi K. Bhabha, ed., *Nation and Narration*, London and New York: Routledge, 1990, pp. 44–70.
2   Many European explorers and writers constructed their ideas of Africa and other marginal spaces based on their warped and prejudiced imagination to meet with the exotic tastes of their metropolitan publics, ideas which were not representative of the continent. For more, see Joseph Conrad's Heart of Darkness, a fictional representation of Africa which falls into this formulaic representational pattern.
3   The imperial naming of 'Others' by the European Self was executed as a process of ideologically imposing colonial authority and the constitution of such spaces as spheres of influence. For more on the naming of Nigeria as an imperial outpost, see Wikipedia, The Free Encyclopedia under the title 'Nigeria'.
4   Niall Ferguson, *Empire: How Britain Made the Modern World*, London: Penguin, 2004.
5   Jyotsna Singh, *Colonial Narratives, Cultural Dialogues*, London and New York: Routledge, 1996.
6   Roland Oliver and Anthony Atmore, *Africa since 1800*, Cambridge: Cambridge University Press, 2004.
7   Benedict Anderson, *Imagined Communities: Reflections on the Origin and Spread of Nationalism*, London: Verso, 1991.
8   Eric Hobsbawm, *Nations and Nationalism since 1780: Programme, Myth, Reality*, Cambridge: Cambridge University Press, 1991.

9   Brennan, 'The National Longing', p. 45.
10 Brennan, 'The National Longing', p. 48.
11 Raymond Williams, *The Year 2000*, New York: Pantheon, 1983.
12 Paul Ricouer, 'Civilization and National Culture', in *History and Truth*, trans. Charles A Kelbley Illinois: Northwestern University Press, 1965, pp. 276–277.
13 Ernest Renan, 'What Is a Nation?', in Homi K. Bhabha, ed., *Nation and Narration*, London and New York: Routledge, 1990, pp. 8–22.
14 Regis Debray, 'Marxism and the National Question', *New Left Review*, Vol. 105 (September–October 1977), p. 26.
15 Homi Bhabhaed, 'Dissemination: Time, Narrative and the Margins of the Modern Nation', in *Nation and Narration*, London and New York: Routledge, 1990, pp. 291–322.
16 James Tsaaior, 'Poetics, Politics and the Paradoxes of Oil in Nigeria's Delta Region', *African Renaissance*, Vol. 2, No. 6 (November–December 2006), pp. 72–80.
17 Ali Mazrui, *A Tale of Two Africas: Nigeria and South Africa as Contrasting Visions*, London: Adonis Abbey, 2006.
18 Femi Osofisan, *Literature and the Pressures of Freedom*, Ibadan: Opon Ifa Readers, 2001, p. 26.
19 Osofisan, *Literature and the Pressures*, pp. 35–37.
20 Jideofor Adibe, 'Africa: Cursed by History?', *African Renaissance*, Vol. 2, No. 6 (November–December 2006), p. 6.
21 Adebajo Adekeye, *The Curse of Berlin: Africa after the Cold War*, London: Hurst and Company, 2010, p. 3.
22 Basil Davidson, *The Black Man's Burden: Africa and the Curse of the Nation-State*, New York: Times Books, 1992.
23 Anthony Giddens, *Modernity and Self-Identity: Self and Society in the Late Modern Age*, Cambridge: Polity, 1991, p. 416.
24 Obafemi Awolowo, *Awo*, Cambridge: Cambridge University Press, 1960, p. 172.
25 Crawford Young, *The Politics of Cultural Pluralism*, Madison: University of Wisconsin Press, 1992, p. 461.
26 Young, *The Politics of Cultural Pluralism*, p. 461.
27 The metaphor of the 'locusts' as a referent to military adventurists in Nigeria has attracted literary discourses especially in the poetic sensibility of Nigerian writers. See poet Joe Ushie's volume, *A Reign of Locusts*, for instance, whose thematic thrust negotiates military dictatorship in Nigeria and the African continent.

4

Sudanese Stories: Narratives of Grievance, Distrust and Fatalism in Recurrent Violence

Alex de Waal

Some Sudanese writers choose fiction to express their deepest insight. Francis Deng's novel *Cry of the Owl* illuminates the enmity and intimacy between southern Sudanese and Sudanese Arabs, and also the way in which racial distinction is a matter of political artifice.[1] The hero of the novel, Elias Bol, is a Dinka young man, educated in northern Sudan under the patronage of an 'Arab' Sudanese army officer. He later becomes spokesman for his oppressed community. Among the bitter experiences of his childhood was the forcible abduction of his mother by Baggara Arab raiders (she was rescued by her kinsmen) and of his brother (who was never seen again). At the denouement of the book, redolent of the last act of a Shakespeare tragedy, Elias discovers that his biological father was in fact an Arab (he was conceived during his mother's brief captivity). At the same time he finds his long-lost brother, culturally assimilated to Arabism and Islam, and also discovers that his principal political adversary, a proponent of Arab chauvinism, is in fact his half-brother.

In the middle of the novel, Elias is posted to an army unit in Darfur, where he comes to realize that the racial antagonism in Sudan is not restricted to the north south axis. Darfurians who identify themselves as non-Arab also resent what they see as the dominance of a riverain elite, self-identified as Arab. Darfurian political leaders seek a common identity with Elias under the label 'African', but their efforts to build a political alliance come to grief when riverain army officers ably sow distrust and division among them. Yet, Elias's career owes much to the generosity of his Arab army officer benefactor, a man who struggles with his background as he seeks to be a genuine Sudanese nationalist.

This story encapsulates the tragedies of Sudan and South Sudan – tragedies in the true literary sense in which the downfall of the protagonists is caused by the flaws inherent in their virtues – rather than a linear catalogue of misery inflicted by evil men for its own sake.[2] From the paradoxes and ambiguities of Sudanese identities and politics, emerge killer narratives that justify and encourage large-scale violence. Although many Sudanese believe that the identities and oppositions around which they hate, fear and kill are primordial, even a superficial analysis indicates that they are constructed, contextual, and their particular manifestation can be transient. Yet, with passion and certitude, Sudanese have been ready to kill one another on the basis of these stories.

'A state of emergency'

The Sudanese state was born in 1956 without any national consensus on the meaning of this event.³ For the Umma Party leaders, one of the two major parties at the time, it was a second independence, recalling the Mahdist revolution of the 1880s. For its main rival, the Democratic Unionist party, independence was a prelude to unity with Egypt. For southerners, it was a compromise with northern elites preparatory for an agreement on a federal system – an agreement that was never made. Only for a minority – albeit an influential elite – was it the prelude to building a unified modern nation. All, of course, were disappointed, and part of their disappointment was rooted in the unresolved divergence over the meaning of independence.

For most of the succeeding fifty years, the late A. H. Abdel Salam remarked, Sudan's normal state was a state of emergency, governed by 'the jurisprudence of the exception'.⁴ The ruler arrogated to himself exceptional powers, and the national political community – whether based on historically rooted constituencies or on the promise of national socio-political transformation – was based on excluding a large part of the population. Each of Sudan's democratic periods (1956–1958, 1965–1969 and 1985–1989) was marked by war in the south, and southerners as a whole constituted the group most persistently excluded from Sudanese national projects. The elections of 2010, intended as a transformative exercise in national democratization – and the first time in which elections were held across southern Sudan – were overshadowed by the imminent vote on self-determination. Subsequently, the independence of the Republic of South Sudan on 9 July 2011 was itself celebrated in the shadow of a reignited civil war within northern Sudan and imminent political crisis within South Sudan, that just two years later was itself approaching renewed internecine violence. Rather than a lasting peaceful resolution of Sudan's identity crisis, secession threatened only to reconfigure Sudan's and South Sudan's contested identities into new patterns of violence.

Just as the concept of 'Sudan' is a contested creation, the concept of being 'Sudanese' is historically fickle in similar ways. The people to whom the term 'Sudanese' (Arabic for blacks) refers has shifted over time. The term was first used to refer to all black people south of the Sahara and upstream from Egypt along the Nile.⁵ From the early twentieth century, it referred mostly to 'detribalized' southerners, notably those incorporated into the army during the early phase of British rule.⁶ Finally, it became the preferred label that the riverain elites used for themselves, referring to a set of social, cultural and religious practices to which others could assimilate.⁷ Possibly because of their very fragility, for both the rulers of Sudan and their peripheral subjects, the concepts of identity and nation were the focus of violence to capture the state (the largest number of attempted and successful coups d'état of any African country: four successful coups, eleven failed coups and seventeen coup plots),⁸ to define its identity or to secede. As so cogently described by Charles Tilly for sectarian conflict in Ulster,⁹ Sudanese violence has shifted its shape over the decades, yet continues to define itself along a largely unchanged set of meta-narratives around the identity of the state and the nation.

Meanwhile, among the northern political elite, Sudanese politics is characterized by a remarkable civility. Civility within this riverain elite, most of which shares a common social and ethnic background, may perhaps be unsurprising, and there are different codes of conduct for the *awlad al balad* (sons of the land) interacting with one another, than for them dealing with the people of the peripheries. However, provincial elites, including from southern Sudan and Darfur, who rise to senior positions in the army or high office in the political system, do assimilate and become part of this circle of civility. Perhaps more than they care to admit, they also observe similar norms of political conduct. Reasons for this may include the fact that these are simply the rules of the dominant political game. Those with a weaker position and fewer resources have no choice but to play or quit. As a result, socialization into the norms through common experience in the army Staff College or the University of Khartoum played a central role in sustaining the game and inculcating its rules.

The rules of civil elite politics have been violated rarely but on those occasions, bloodily. Conspicuous examples include President Jaafar Nimeiri's war against the Ansar in 1970, his crushing of the Communist Party in 1971 and the execution of the Republican Brothers' leader, Ustaz Mahmoud Mohammed Taha in 1985. Examples under the current government of President Omar al Bashir include the summary execution of Ba'athist army officers who tried to stage a coup in 1990 and the crackdown following the Justice and Equality Movement (JEM) attack on the capital in 2008. All of these were occasions when the ruler's fear of political demise veered into panic, in response to violence initiated or threatened by the other side, and the rules of the game were violated for simple self-preservation.

Far more common is violent and abusive exercise of power in the Sudanese peripheries. In peacetime, provincial administration has long been conducted with scant regard for the dignity and livelihood of rural people. Administrators and merchants have few scruples in dispossessing farmers of their land or paying starvation wages to labourers. In times of insecurity or conflict, this treatment is aggravated by routine cruelty and disregard for life. It is striking that at the close of the 1983–2005 war, the Sudan Armed Forces (SAF) had almost no prisoners of war in its custody. And when a rural insurrection causes genuine fear among the ruling elites, for example the incursions by the Sudan People's Liberation Movement/Army (SPLM/A) across the internal boundary from southern into northern Sudan in 1985 or the attack on al Fashir air base by the Darfurian rebels in 2003, the response is disproportionately savage.

In this chapter, I explore the paradox of civility and barbarity in Sudanese politics and the narratives of its politics. Sudanese newspapers and websites provide plentiful examples of rancour and racism. The comments posted on the *Sudan Tribune* discussion boards routinely veer into vitriol, while the Khartoum paper *al Intibaha* regularly publishes inflammatory and defamatory pieces. Rather than elucidating such narratives of intolerance or violence, I look instead for the enduring features of Sudanese politics that both nourish and moderate these discourses. I contend that the constant themes, which are strengthened over time by cycles of repetition of events and accounts of events, are a combination of grievance and distrust, resulting in fatalism concerning the inevitability of violence. In turn, this creates the conditions in which political leaders are ready to pursue military action in pursuit of political ends, defining their adversaries in both political and ethnic/racial terms. Over the longer term, this also leads to the erosion of national institutions, with the outcome that even the organization of violence escapes the control of those who instigate it.

This chapter examines each of the themes of grievance, distrust and fatalism, making reference to the different ways in which these are articulated by different political groups in contemporary Sudan, leading up to an examination of how these contribute to violence. The focus is mostly upon elite narratives, but how these are refracted into local narratives is also important. The essay argues that while Sudanese public political narratives have been dominated by divisive language, which is both a product of long histories of violent contestation and in turn helps reproduce such violence, there has also been a less visible counter-narrative that facilitates political accommodation, albeit in a limited and contingent manner. However, with the separation of South Sudan in 2011, divisive narratives have become decisively legitimized, especially within northern Sudan, increasing the risks of self-justifying discourses promoting violent confrontation.

My analysis reflects and further develops dominant approaches to ethnic conflict. I argue that these narratives of violence are a variant of constructivist theory of ethnic conflict.[10] Specifically, I suggest that such narratives arise from contests among and within national elite groupings and also the strategic use of oppositional ethnic identities by certain local leaders. Thus, while the narratives themselves appeal to an 'everyday primordialism' among the populace, they are instrumentalized in a tactical political manner by members of elite, who are prepared to set aside the oppositional logic as required by the dictates of realpolitik.

Grievance

The Sudanese state is a historic chameleon, taking on a series of different shapes and colours over the last two centuries and especially so in the six decades since self-rule in 1953. Nonetheless, all manifestations of the state have been constituted around projects of exclusion that naturally entail grievances among those deprived of equal access to power and resources. Meanwhile, the state itself is constituted by a sense of grievance at those external powers – Egypt, Britain and latterly the United States – in whose arbitrary hands, the rulers see their fate as lying. These two intersecting narratives of grievance help explain the peculiar intractability of Sudanese conflicts.

The history of southern Sudanese grievance against their northern brethren is well-known and is encapsulated in the continuing use of the term *abid*, 'slave' by northerners to refer to southerners.[11] Throughout recorded history, Mediterranean and Sudanic states enslaved their black southern neighbours – a process of subjugation that reached its zenith during the Turko-Egyptian conquest of the Nile Valley (1821–1885).[12] Khartoum, as a centre of trading, raiding, subjugation and imperial administration was the key locus of domination of Sudan's southern and western peripheries. It is a matter of historical controversy whether the religious-nationalist government of

Mohamed al Mahdi and his successor, Khalifa Abdullahi (1885–1898) practiced or repressed the slave trade, but it is not in dispute that the Mahdist state defined itself in religious terms in a manner that excluded spiritual believers from the south and other margins. British imperial occupation (1898–1955) protected southern Sudan from northern depredation but left it as neglected 'closed districts', bereft of education and development, so that its leaders were easily manipulated into supporting the northern Sudanese case for independence. This then left southern Sudan disadvantaged and locked into another cycle of violence. The Anyanya war (1955–1972) witnessed repression and atrocity against the southern populace. It was followed by the modest but real gains of the Addis Ababa peace agreement period (1972–1983), but this agreement was unravelled by its northern architect, President Jaafar Nimeiri, leading to another period of civil war (1983–2005). In this instance, the SPLM/A led by Dr John Garang, fought initially for a united 'new Sudan' but latterly included the option of the south voting for secession. In turn, the unresolved war mortally wounded Sudanese efforts at building a democracy, leading to a military coup in 1989 that brought to power a coalition of military officers (led by Pres. Bashir) and Islamists (led by Hassan al Turabi). The protracted war undermined the credibility of democratic and pluralistic forms of governance and radicalized the Sudanese Islamists. In parallel, the war drove the southerners towards a secessionist agenda, defined as opposition to the religious and racial agenda of the northern government and, by implication, the religious and racial identity of the north itself.

This well-rehearsed history underpins the southern Sudanese claim to the right of self-determination, recognized in the Comprehensive Peace Agreement (CPA) of January 2005, exercised in the referendum of January 2011 and finally accomplished in the establishment of an internationally recognized sovereign Republic of South Sudan on 11 July 2011. However, it is also worth noting the fundamental ambiguity in the self-designation of the new state and its citizens: they remain Sudanese in a broad sense but are *South* Sudanese, while the state from which they seceded remains simply the Republic of Sudan, referred to only intermittently, informally and hesitantly as *northern* Sudan. Having excluded Arabic as a potential national language for South Sudan, and thereby disenfranchised South Sudanese whose only language is Arabic, President Salva Kiir finds that Arabic is the preferred language for public speaking, as it is the most widely understood language in the country. Like its mother state, South Sudan also had an ambiguous birth, midwifed by the broken promises of the international guarantors of the CPA.

Southern grievance has two main components. There are the well-substantiated claims of repression, neglect, exploitation and violence, taking different forms over the decades. A common thread to these claims is racial and religious discrimination, namely that southern Sudanese have been treated as second class citizens in their own country because they are neither Arabs nor predominantly Muslim. The second component is that a succession of good faith attempts to agree on an arrangement has been consistently betrayed. The title of the book by the former head of the autonomous Southern Region during the Addis Ababa period, Abel Alier, *Too Many Agreements Dishonoured* (1992) speaks for itself.[13]

The 2005 CPA is an elaborate document – six protocols and two annexures comprising a total of 260 pages. During the negotiations, the SPLM insisted on the maximum detail and the maximum international guarantees, including an independent Assessment and Evaluation Commission, and a UN peacekeeping operation as safeguards against betrayal by the ruling National Congress Party (NCP).

Darfurian grievances against the centre have different historical roots and character. Riverain and Darfurian states were historically rivals and the absorption of Darfur into a united Sudan occurred over the period 1874–1917 in a series of steps: conquest of Darfur by a mercenary army associated with Khartoum and Cairo; resistance by Darfurians that led to a war against the colonial occupier jointly led by riverain Sudanese and Darfurians; the establishment of a Mahdist state (1885–1898) in Omdurman that was jointly led by riverain Sudanese and Darfurians; the re-establishment of an independent Darfur state (1898–1916) and then conquest and incorporation by the British. Interestingly, while Darfur became a subordinate and neglected part of Sudan, important elements of its populace and leadership were integrated into the Sudanese establishment from the earliest days.

Darfur did not join the SPLA rebellion, despite the best efforts of Garang, but it had its own resentments against the centre, notably its extremely low level of economic development. It also had internal disputes that took an inter-ethnic character. From the late 1980s onwards, Darfur was largely beyond the reach of government administration, ruled by a combination of the security services and tribal leaders, which between them mercenarized and militarized tribalism. The proliferation of local grievances and the intrusion of the Arab/African dichotomy into Darfurian identities made the links between national and local narratives more complicated. When the Darfur rebels, under the banners of the Sudan Liberation Movement (SLM) and JEM, launched their insurgency in early 2003, the army and security services counter-mobilized ethnic Arab militias, causing the war to rapidly descend into an internal Darfurian conflict. Darfur-wide agendas thus became subordinate to immediate issues of fear and anger engendered by the conflict itself and the atrocities and mass displacement. The politics of Darfur's position with Sudan became secondary to the rhetoric of human rights violations and calls for international rescue.

Having failed in its 1990–1991 attempt to extend its rebellion to Darfur, the SPLA supported the Darfur rebellion militarily from 2002 to weaken Khartoum, even while the north-south peace negotiations were ongoing.[14] That calculation was correct, but it may have also been disastrous for the prospects of a united Sudan, as the conflict in Darfur became the biggest factor undermining the CPA. In addition, the re-framing of the Darfur conflict as an international cause célèbre, focused not upon Sudanese politics but around a narrative of genocide and calls for international military and judicial intervention, obscured the need to bring the Darfurian case back within the ambit of Sudanese national political discourse.

The eruption of war in Darfur confirmed the fears of southerners. The international narratives about the Darfur war as an 'Arab genocide' against ethnic Africans demanding international intervention, in turn, appeared to vindicate the polarized viewpoint of southern separatists.

The northern political elite also have a well-rehearsed narrative of grievance, albeit one less familiar to an English-speaking audience. Its geographical reference is wider: they see an international conspiracy against 'Sudan' that is part of a wider American-led assault on the independence of Arab countries and the values of Arab-Islamic civilization. Although this account has historical references, for example late nineteenth century European imperial occupation of Sudan and the Western modernization project in the Islamic world, the narrative of international conspiracy is largely a creation of the last twenty years and centres on the accusation against the SPLM of having willingly accepted to serve as the vanguard of this plot. Even more so, NCP/SAF bitterness towards the northern opposition, and especially the armed groups in Darfur and the northern component of the SPLM in Blue Nile and Southern Kordofan, is driven by the view that they have treacherously joined this conspiracy.[15]

For the Khartoum regime, the CPA contained painful compromises. When its provisions were outlined to President al-Bashir, he reportedly said that no army would willingly withdraw, undefeated, from a major part of its sovereign territory and hand that territory over to its adversary. But he was prepared to accept the accord because he was assured by his principal negotiator, Vice President Ali Osman Taha, that it would bring peace, national unity and the normalization of Sudan's relations with the Western world.

However, within weeks of the CPA signature ceremony in Nairobi, it was clear that the third component, namely political and financial normalization, would not be delivered. The United States made it clear that it would not lift sanctions and enable Sudan to obtain debt relief or concessionary finance from international financial institutions while the Darfur crisis remained unresolved. Khartoum interpreted this shift of emphasis to Darfur as a revival of America's 'regime change agenda' in Darfur, after having stalled in the south. This fear was confirmed when, within three months, the UN Security Council referred Darfur to the International Criminal Court (ICC).

Khartoum also preferred to see the Darfur war itself as the product of SPLM/A perfidy because of its military assistance to the rebels. Nevertheless, in 2006, Bashir again accepted to sign a peace agreement that conceded far more than he considered reasonable, namely the Darfur Peace Agreement (DPA), this time on the assurance that the United States would put its normalization process back on track. Not only did this not transpire but things took a turn for the worse when the ICC Prosecutor demanded an arrest warrant for the President himself in July 2008. Shortly after this, the major Western powers backed a peace process in Doha that seemed designed to postpone any settlement of the Darfur conflict into the indefinite future and created new preconditions for engaging constructively with the Sudanese authorities on Darfur. The NCP/SAF leadership interpreted this as a Western pretext for keeping alive a bridgehead for a regime change agenda. Every reassurance that Western diplomats tried to give with regards to their appreciation of the Sudanese acceptance of the CPA was negated by the paranoia fuelled by the goalpost-shifting pattern on Darfur. This pattern continued throughout the CPA Interim Period. In the last months of 2010, as the deadline for the referendum on self-determination in southern Sudan approached, the United States signalled that it would be ready to expedite the lifting of sanctions and the relief of Sudan's debt, on the precondition that Khartoum accept the result of the vote.

On 4 January 2011, just days before the southern referendum, Bashir spoke to an audience in Juba and announced his acceptance of the southern preference for independence and promised that Sudan would be the first state to recognize the Republic of South Sudan. The southerners were taken aback and delighted by this concession. But Bashir received no international accolades let alone any material reward. In the aftermath of the referendum, Sudan received only further delayed timelines for the normalization of relations with the United States and debt relief.

Worse, from the point of view of Khartoum, the prospect of sacrificing unity for peace seemed an increasingly vain hope. A dispute between north and south over the border area of Abyei escalated to the point of armed confrontation in May 2010 and in June, disputes over the election and security arrangements in Southern Kordofan State did indeed ignite an armed conflict between SAF and the Ninth Division of the SPLA based in that northern state.

Within their respective frames of reference, both NCP and SPLM, and the constituencies they represent, are animated by bitterness. The reciprocal sense of grievance was manifest in the conduct of the post-referendum negotiations. These negotiations began, under the auspices of the African Union High-Level Implementation Panel (AUHIP) chaired by President Thabo Mbeki, in June 2010. Following bilateral meetings between the parties in four separate committees, plenary negotiations began on a framework document in November. These talks were conducted in an atmosphere of mutual estrangement in which the counter-narrative of accommodation and mutual benefit belonged principally to the African Union facilitators. The NCP and SPLM leaders committed themselves, in their draft framework document, to 'establishing and sustaining a constructive and peaceful relationship ... which will promote the viability of both the south and the north'. However, the negotiations were actually conducted with each trying to maximize the disadvantage to the other.

The negotiators were able to come to rapid agreement on a sharp separation with minimal future engagement between the two. For example, on the question of the Sudanese of southern origin resident in the north, the NCP proposed that all those eligible to vote in the southern referendum (southerners who had been resident in northern Sudan from before 1956) would automatically be stripped of Sudanese citizenship on 9 July 2011 and given six months to either register as foreign residents or leave. The SPLM leaders did not disagree with the major substantive points of the NCP proposal but asked for the six months period to be increased to twelve. In consequence, during late 2010 and throughout 2011, there was a large-scale, poorly planned migration of people of southern Sudanese origin from northern towns to the south. Many had lived most or all of their lives in northern Sudan, spoke Arabic, had livelihoods in the north and children in school there. Some had little affinity with the south other than kinship. This movement remained remarkably free of violence, which perhaps indicates that the narratives of coexistence retain considerable traction among the general populace. Nonetheless, the process of stripping these people of Sudanese nationality and relocating them southwards, entailed enormous human hardship.

The dispute over Abyei provides a microcosm of the asymmetric reciprocal grievances of the two parties and their respective constituencies and illustrates how these narratives feed off histories of violence and in turn feed into justifications for violence.[16] Abyei is a small but fiercely disputed area on the border between north and south. Its residents are mainly Ngok Dinka and also a population of Misiriya Arabs, mostly migratory cattle herders. Its status was so controversial that it was the last major issue to be resolved in the CPA negotiations and then only when the US Special Envoy stepped in with a proposal for a separate protocol. This promised the residents of Abyei a referendum on whether to have special status within northern Sudan or join southern Sudan. Unfortunately, the Protocol provided neither a definition of the geographical extent of Abyei nor identified who should count as its residents.

The southern narrative is that Abyei area is historically Dinka territory that was transferred to Kordofan in northern Sudan in 1905; that a 1972 agreement to give the residents the option of transfer back to southern Sudan was never implemented; and that a definitive settlement was agreed in the CPA. The Abyei Protocol provided for an Abyei Boundary Commission (ABC) to determine the northern boundary of the area but that contrary to this clear provision, the NCP rejected the findings of the ABC. In a spirit of compromise, the SPLM agreed to request the Permanent Court of Arbitration (PCA) in The Hague to decide on whether the ABC had acted correctly and furthermore agreed to the PCA ruling that the boundary was considerably to the south of the ABC line, reducing the territory of Abyei Area by more than half. However, despite having agreed to take the case to the PCA, the NCP again refused to accept this ruling from the international court. Contrary to demographic evidence and best practice, the SPLM argues, the NCP insisted that Misiriya Arab nomads be counted as residents of Abyei, which would make the Misiriya into a numerical majority in the referendum and thus able to determine the outcome. Finally, in May 2011, SAF invaded and occupied Abyei, burning and looting the town and displacing the entire Dinka population. A month later, under AU facilitation, the SPLM and NCP agreed temporary security and administrative arrangements for Abyei.

The southern narrative is that this has all taken place against a pattern of repeated mass violence by SAF and Misiriya militia, dating back to the 1960s (and indeed earlier), against the Ngok Dinka, marked by massacres, abductions, mass looting of cattle and seizure of land. This escalated in the 1980s, again in 2008, and was repeated once again after the SAF invasion of May 2011, with the sole difference that on this last occasion the inhabitants fled before they could be killed. The northern narrative is that the greater part of Abyei area was historically under the jurisdiction of the Misiriya Arabs, with the River Kiir/Bahr al Arab marking the boundary between the Misiriya land and the Dinka land, excepting a small enclave around Abyei town itself. The NCP and Misiriya leaders argue that the ABC was a miscarriage of justice based on a flawed method, which assumed that the Misiriya were all 'nomads' and the Dinka all 'settled', so that historical evidence for the presence of Misiriya in the area could be discounted, while evidence for any past Dinka presence was interpreted to demonstrate ownership. They argue that the PCA decision reduced the extent of the injustice but did not eliminate it. Furthermore, they say that the 2008 Abyei Area Administration, headed by SPLM nominees, provoked the Misiriya Arabs by preventing their annual southwards migration during the 2010–2011 dry season, an act tantamount to depriving the cattle herders of their livelihoods. The SAF also contends that the SPLA provoked it by two ambushes that killed SAF soldiers, the first on 1 May 2011. After SPLA refusal to acknowledge wrongdoing and UN failure to condemn the SPLA, a second ambush on 19 May was the last straw. Furthermore, SAF says it will complete its withdrawal only when the SPLA withdraws its forces from the southern part of Abyei Area, and agree to an administration that can safeguard the rights of the Misiriya.

SAF generals see this episode against the backdrop of their withdrawal, undefeated, from southern Sudan and Abyei in 2005, on the broken promise of unity, and again from Abyei in 2008 after an SPLA provocation had prompted them to act militarily. They vow that they will not withdraw their troops and hand over to a perfidious international process and be humiliated again.

Each party constructs a narrative in which it is the victim, responding to the aggression and trickery of the other, creating a situation in which it has no alternative but to use force. It is notable that, while the narratives of violence by different parties, and the violence itself, identifies the adversary in both political and ethnic/racial terms, the primary target of the violence is the armed forces of the other, not the civilian population. Civilians are routinely caught up in this violence and especially so when the intelligence services of one side have poor information and therefore act indiscriminately. However, the fact that the armed conflicts are politically defined and conducted means that there is also a counter-narrative available that can de-escalate violence against civilian communities.

Distrust

Political theorists have identified rule-governed institutions as the key to a transition from government based on patronage and elite bargaining to a stable open access order or consolidated state.[17] Sudan has not only failed to achieve such a transition, but the relatively promising political institutions of the mid-twentieth century have eroded over recent decades. Societal trust, formerly vested in structures such as religious sects, administrative tribal leaders, and modern institutions such as trade unions, has declined, and has not been replaced by new institutional politics. Indeed, the major achievement of successive governments and rebel movements has been to destroy confidence in any such institutions. Consequently, Sudanese political life operates with extremely low levels of trust. Moreover, Sudanese concur that trust in government, and - more importantly - among members of the political class, has declined over recent decades. Rather than illustrating this pervasive distrust or further rehearsing the allegations that political leaders make against one another, this section seeks a structural explanation.

Sudan has a combination of extreme disparity in power and wealth between centre and periphery and instability at the centre. This gives rise to complicated shifting alliances, with political players requiring considerable skill at second-guessing the options of a wide range of other actors. In the 1956–1989 period, instability at the centre was manifest among contending political parties, which never succeeded in establishing a dominant coalition.[18] After the 1989 National Salvation Revolution, which was intended to bring about hitherto-elusive consolidation of power, a similar instability rapidly became manifest among factions within the ruling coalition of Islamists and soldiers.[19] The constant factor, President Bashir, maintained his position because he exercised only limited day-to-day executive power and because he scrupulously maintained a reputation of never sacrificing any of his lieutenants, no matter how much they erred, provided that they did not challenge him personally.

Sudanese politics can be seen as a 'political marketplace' in which government is practiced by a series of bargains among the members of the ruling elite and between them and provincial elite leaders who control tribes, militia or local power bases within the government system itself. These bargains are all temporary and can be renegotiated when conditions in the political marketplace change. Because today's rival or adversary can be tomorrow's ally, patron or client, it is perfectly rational that any political enmities should not translate into personal animosity. By the same token, today's ally could be tomorrow's adversary, so that personal civility does not indicate enduring affinity. No one trusts anyone else.

The ever-shifting nature of Sudanese politics has contributed to recurrent failure to respect agreements. Each agreement is good only for as long as existing conditions prevail. When those conditions change, new bargains must be struck. Thus the 2006 DPA was, on paper, a comprehensive programme for transforming the governance, development and security of Darfur within the Sudanese state. But in reality it was a bargain between the NCP and just one armed group (the SLA faction headed by Minni Arkoy Minawi) that excluded others. The DPA was workable only if the others joined or were defeated, and consequently the aftermath of the agreement saw intensified military efforts by the SLA-Minawi and SAF to destroy the groups that had refused to sign and commensurate efforts by the non-signatory groups to make their military presence felt. This logic was understood by all in Darfur, and the shortcomings of the DPA were so evident that the government was never seriously asked to implement it.

Distrust is also prevalent within each group because of the constant indeterminacy of politics. In fact it is necessary for Sudanese politicians to manage parallel competing eventualities at all times, and therefore to keep open different options. Sudan's political leaders have a notable tendency to present multiple competing visions and programmes, either in sequence or in parallel. President Nimeiri was famous for his political shape-shifting. Prime Minister Sadiq al Mahdi is notorious for vacillation and indecisiveness, shifting between cooperating with the authority of the moment and campaigning against it and also between competing roles as Imam of the Ansar Movement and secular leader of the modernizing Umma Party. His contemporary and rival, Hassan al Turabi, disguises his opportunism with clever interpretations of Islamist doctrine that allow him to present diverse stratagems as consistent with the pursuit of an Islamic state. The leader of the Democratic Unionist Party, Mohammed Osman al Mirghani, addresses this dilemma through political somnolence.

The late Chairman of the SPLM, John Garang, spoke of three tracks of political activity: negotiations between SPLM and NCP for a peace agreement between north and south, continuing and expanding the armed struggle, and working with the National Democratic Alliance (that included the northern opposition) for a popular uprising to overthrow the regime. He also managed to promote both unity and separatism at the same time. Like his nemesis Turabi, Garang was both charismatic and enigmatic, to the extent that in 2001, the two even made a pact proposing to join forces against the NCP government. In the field, the most persistent characteristic of the SPLA forces was a relentless dismantling of any institutions that they encountered, replacing them with a militaristic nihilism.[20]

President Bashir has stayed in power by serving as umpire among the contending factions within the regime. Nonetheless, he is at best inconsistent. In January 2011, Bashir welcomed in Juba the imminent southern vote for secession (while insisting that he himself was a unionist) but within days he also addressed northern constituents with a hardline Islamist message.[21]

Provincial leaders operate perpetually with one foot inside the Khartoum political arena and one outside, keeping their options open. This included SPLM leadership serving in the Government of National Unity during the CPA's interim period and also of erstwhile Darfur rebels who have joined the government. The ambiguity of their position makes them vulnerable to accusations of opportunism or hypocrisy, but their stance is logical, even necessary, given the structure of Sudanese politics. Depending on who they are addressing, they will invoke divisive ethnic discourses, nationalistic rhetoric, or the language of pragmatism.

Fatalism

The combination of a well-remembered and repeatedly rehearsed history of violence and betrayal, structurally determined distrust and a host of other risk factors for conflict makes Sudanese political conflict over-determined. In turn, this contributes to narratives of violent conflict that become self-reinforcing. Such narratives are perpetuated both by Sudanese and by foreigners, with a distinct script of human rights reporting that attributes all ills in the country to the actions of evil men.[22] Even while the major pillars of the CPA were holding and Sudan as a whole was at peace, many Sudanese firmly believed that the country would return to war. Members of the political elite, in government and opposition, quite logically kept their options open and usually calculated that the worst would transpire.

A strong sense of fatalism about the inevitability of armed conflict was evident in the run up to the outbreak of war in Southern Kordofan State during May 2011, following disputed elections. This author made three visits to Kadugli, the capital of the state, during that month, and met repeatedly with the political principals, especially Governor Ahmed Haroun (NCP) and his erstwhile deputy, Abdel Aziz al Hilu (SPLM).

The two leaders, assuming the worst of one another and mobilizing their respective forces for the worst case, mentally prepared themselves for the war. Each constructed a narrative that blamed the other, making the conflict appear inevitable and thereby portraying their own decisions as dictated by circumstances imposed by the other. Most strikingly, al Hilu refused to take the legal route of challenging Haroun's electoral victory in court, arguing that losing the case was a foregone conclusion, and war was unavoidable.

Similarly, should the confrontation in Abyei become the spark for a war between the armies of Sudan and South Sudan, each has already prepared a narrative that blames the other for making the conflict unavoidable. The leaders are not taking specific decisions that start war, but are carefully preparing to respond to any incident, large or small, in such a way so as to portray themselves as the aggrieved party on whom the war has been forced.

Within South Sudan, different communities possessed well-rehearsed narratives of grievance that were invoked as soon as the first gunshots were fired in December 2013. Groups that had been living quite peaceably as neighbours for years, and in urban areas had become thoroughly integrated, suddenly fell back on stories of inter-communal violence from the early 1990s or many decades earlier. At precisely the same moment, other narratives of inter-ethnic violence, such as the conflict between the Murle and their neighbours, became politically inconvenient and were rapidly downgraded to the status of contingent disputes readily resolved by their respective leaders.

These narratives of fatalism are more pronounced at local levels than among the elites. Indeed, while the major campaigns of armed violence have been directed by the nation's political elites, most episodes of large-scale violence have a local component. In particular, tribally organized militias have been a feature of Sudan's wars since the early 1980s, and they have been responsible for the most notorious atrocities in war zones that became 'ethics free zones'. The mobilization and motivation for militiamen has been little studied. Almost all the literature on the Baggara militia of the 1980s (known as *murahaliin*), the Popular Defence Forces and the Darfurian Arab militia (*janjawiid*) consists of documentation of the atrocities they committed, allegations about their links to the government authorities and attributions of racial supremacist or extremist political agendas. The few pieces of research conducted among them reveal a more complicated mix of motivations, including fear, grievance and livelihoods.[23] The pattern of behaviour of their leaders is opportunistic, seeking the best immediate reward for the services of the group, with loyalty rented out for cash payment.

Given the ubiquity of the militarization of rural communities, it is perhaps surprising that the war has seen few examples of inter-communal violence igniting in urban areas. This is particularly remarkable given the fact that at least a million southerners migrated into northern Sudan, where they were extremely vulnerable to exploitation and abuse. Officialdom has discriminated against them in housing and employment, including programmes of forcible relocation to the edge of Khartoum. However, inter-communal violence outside areas of active combat remained extremely rare.

An exception that seems to prove the rule is the ed Da'ien massacre of 1987, when a mob of local Rizeigat, encouraged by local militia leaders and not prevented by the authorities, attacked displaced Dinka civilians, killing more than a thousand of them. The attack was in retaliation following armed encounters between the Rizeigat militia and the SPLA, which the latter had won.[24] This in turn was portrayed as a 'massacre' perpetrated by the SPLA, inflaming feelings among the locals and leading to attacks on the displaced southerners. Notwithstanding official efforts at a cover-up, the ed Da'ien massacre caused an outcry, and there have been no repetitions on that scale.

Local people are discerning about the perils of official narratives, and appreciate the importance of maintaining social relationships across political fault lines. The best-documented example in Sudan is the case of the Uduk people of southern Blue Nile State, who have been on the frontline of the war since the mid-1980s.[25] Historic experience of living on two slaving frontiers (the Sudanese and Ethiopian imperial states) had prepared the Uduk for extreme and persistent threats, and they were able to draw upon a cultural archive of survival and displacement to help them make sense of their predicament. When the war encroached upon their territory, the Uduk naturally sympathized with the SPLM's 'new Sudan' agenda and its Blue Nile leadership but were also sufficiently schooled in the realities of war, to keep a foot in each camp. Notably, in recounting their experience of the war, they put great score in the personal traits of individual administrators and commanders, some of whom had a reputation for cruelty, while others were described as fair and humane and are less concerned with which side that individual was on.

As one would expect, different groups have different and sometimes opposing narratives of violence and peace. For example, during the public consultations held by the African Union Panel on Darfur (AUPD) during 2009, Arab communities preferred to use the terms 'war' (*harb*) and 'troubles' (*mashakil*), while Fur and Masalit regularly used the terminology of 'genocide' (*ibada*). All groups used the term 'anarchy' (*fawda*), which has the implication of a complete failure of government. According to a study by Abdul-Jabbar Fadul and Victor Tanner, this usage became common in the immediate aftermath of the war, when all groups blamed the government for the disaster.[26] However, the Arabs emphasized failure to govern and the non-Arabs demanded that the government be called to account for its crimes. The authors note the re-emergence of the 'Darfur Consensus', namely that the region should be governed jointly by its diverse communities, headed by a Fur-Arab partnership. During the AUPD public hearings, a common theme was repeated by all, namely that, left to themselves, the Darfurian communities would be able to resolve their differences and achieve reconciliation and normality.

In southern Sudan, the internecine warfare of the early 1990s prompted the churches and prominent individuals to support inter-communal peace and reconciliation efforts. These fostered narratives of peace, framed around a definition of local conflict as inter-tribal and requiring a common commitment to forgiveness and good neighbourliness. Such narratives have become internalized by many southern Sudanese as well as the foreign sponsors of the initiatives. The SPLM, initially sceptical and fearful that the inter-tribal process might promote the churches as a rival political authority, came around to a supportive position, which also recognized the value in uniting southerners against the common threat from the north. In the post-CPA period, the inter-tribal reconciliation model has become the standard procedure and narrative. But it has also been questioned, on the grounds that it privileges certain categories of persons (tribal and religious leaders) and casts southern politics as principally an inter-tribal affair. It also ignores the substantive issues of the tribalization of local government, the overlap between SPLM, SPLA and local administration and the issues such as the boundaries of administrative units and the provision of services.[27]

The pattern of narratives and counter-narratives across the diverse parts of Sudan and South Sudan, and how these are changing in response to events, is a research question. Brief impressions from north, south and the transitional areas during 2011 indicate that local narratives are shifting and hardening, as different groups interpret the independence of South Sudan in different ways. Most notably, some local elites in the border zones – for example in Abyei – see conflict as inevitable and thus seek to initiate it at the time and in the manner of their own choosing.

Conclusion

Sudanese politics has become structured around common expectations of violent action in pursuit of political goals. In a poorly-regulated marketplace of loyalties, violent acts are a tool in political bargaining. As the state has lost its ability to command the allegiance of its citizens, limited but recurrent violence, by statutory and irregular armed groups, has become an ingrained feature of politics. Such violence, part political, part criminal and part societal, is now a structural part of the governance of the Sudanese peripheries.[28] Chronic low level insecurity is interspersed with occasional eruptions of much larger violence, when one party responds to an extreme threat with a panicked over-reaction, which includes escalating rhetoric. During such occasional eruptions, mass group-targeted violence is most likely to happen.

The new state in South Sudan never succeeded in commanding the loyalty of its citizens, save in opposition to the north. Born as a poorly-regulated autocracy, with its political life dominated by corruption and militarized tribalism, South Sudan quickly reproduced the most violent characteristics of Sudanese peripheral governance.

There is an unfortunate negative synergy between political grievances, identity politics, the functioning of this political marketplace and narratives that prepare people for conflict. In a context of enduring insecurity, identities are strengthened by fear-induced mobilization for the purposes of violence, whether for self-defence or for political bargaining. Contemporary Sudanese political history provides plentiful opportunities for developing and utilizing narratives that give meaning and justification for such violence. They can also feed into or reinforce local conflicts, generating the conditions for inter-communal violence that is wholly consistent with the elite-generated narratives, although perhaps not specifically authorized by the military or political command.

Even in these difficult times, members of the Sudanese elite face low personal risk of violence. Among the northern leadership, it is only rarely that rapid and ruthless killings have occurred. Among the southern elites, sporadic killings of leaders on the margins of combat occurred during the war, and there was one case of a returning militia leader murdered in 2011. These incidents remain exceptional, while lines of communication and options of reconciliation remain open, even during the depths of violence that followed the eruption of war in December 2013.

For decades, Sudan's narratives of polarization and hostility have been tempered by their opposite. The language of compromise and conciliation has tended either to be private, or at least discreet, or to figure in official nationalistic rhetoric that carries little conviction, especially in the face of the stridency of polarizing or inflammatory speeches and the invective frequently found on websites and in political newspapers. Its relevance and importance cannot be discounted, however, and it is only through understanding these counter-narratives that it is possible to understand why Sudan did not dissolve into all-out internecine warfare. Because the principal purpose of violence is political positioning, rather than eliminating the other, the options for de-escalating violence are always present. Amid the persistent structures of violence, Sudanese social and political life continued.

However, in the absence of a consensus around the identity of the national political communities or around strong and legitimate governing institutions, Sudanese political life has been subject to a gradual but relentless degradation over the decades. The main centripetal forces have become the coercive power of the army and the patronage monies dispensed by the ruling party and its affiliated security institutions, which in turn has fed counter-narratives based on local belonging: ethnicity and land.[29] The secession of South Sudan represents an enormous and potentially fatal blow both to the legitimacy of the NCP government and to the finance on which it depends, while simultaneously underwriting a political narrative that justifies the further fragmentation of the country. In a political marketplace that has run for decades on credit, the separation of the south represents a cash payment, a definitive break in the political culture. Existing crisis management methods, however well-honed by the NCP/SAF leadership, will only postpone the reckoning.

The shifting patterns of violence in Darfur during the decade after the outbreak of full-scale war in 2003 illustrate how this reckoning may come about.[30] During the peak of the violence in 2003–2004, the conflict was organized between two readily identifiable opposing coalitions of forces, engaged in a life-and-death contest for control of the state. This may be characterized as a 'Schmittian' conflict, in the senses that it was between 'friends' and 'enemies' and that it was over state power. However, as neither side was able to win a decisive victory, the conflict instead caused the fracturing of the political-military coalitions on either side. By 2008–2009, the war was a lower-scale intractable conflict of many different armed actors, each fighting for multiple motives, including most significantly position in competing patronage hierarchies. This can be characterized as 'Hobbesian' violence in a condition of anarchy.

Immediately following independence in 2011, the confidence of leadership of South Sudan in its more secure position was transmitted to those in the northern opposition advocating forcible regime change or, increasingly, the fragmentation of northern Sudan. Within South Sudan, that confidence translated into a more naked scramble for the spoils of office, which, backed with threats of force, quickly escalated into civil war. The rhetoric of inclusion and reconciliation quickly wore thin, submerged by reciprocal ethnic invective and by the logic of a scramble for the personal material privileges of office.

In the aftermath of secession, northern politics lacks a narrative of accommodation and inclusion. Speaking to an audience drawn from the University of Khartoum on the eve of the referendum, President Thabo Mbeki stressed the African character of northern Sudan and the enduring challenge of governing a diverse nation with a rich heritage.[31] However, the northern Sudanese ruling elite has not internalized this message and remain demoralized and bewildered, fearful of what they see as enemies at home and abroad and uncertain about the future. Sudanese politics is riven by paranoia and bitterness, and not without reason, as there has been conspiracy and betrayal in spades. This is a situation in which polarizing political narratives may resonate, which in turn may justify new violent conflict.

Notes

1. Francis Deng, *Cry of the Owl*, New York: Lilian Barber Press, 1989.
2. Cf. Jane Blayton, 'Human Rights Reporting on Darfur: A Genre That Redefines Tragedy', Making Sense of Darfur, 21–24 August 2009 (in three parts), http://africanarguments.org/2009/08/24/human-rights-reporting-on-darfur-a-genre-that-redefines-tragedy-3/ [accessed 16 September 2013].
3. Abdelwahab El-Affendi, '"Discovering the South": Sudanese Dilemmas for Islam in Africa', *African Affairs*, Vol. 89, No. 356 (1990), pp. 371–389; Abdelwahab El-Affendi, *Turabi's Revolution: Islam and Power in Sudan*, London: Grey Seal, 1991.
4. A. H. Abdel Salam, 'Constitutional Challenges of the Transition', in A. H. Abdel Salam and Alex de Waal, eds., *The Phoenix State: Civil Society and the Future of Sudan*, Trenton, NJ: Red Sea Press, 2001, p. 4.
5. Eva Troutt-Powell, *A Different Shade of Colonialism: Egypt, Great Britain and the Mastery of the Sudan*, Berkeley: University of California Press, 2003.
6. Martin Daly, *Empire on the Nile: The Anglo-Egyptian Sudan, 1898–1934*, Cambridge: Cambridge University Press, 1986, pp. 291–292.
7. Paul Doornbos, 'On Becoming Sudanese', in Tony Barnett and Abbas Abdelkarim, eds., *Sudan: State, Capital and Transformation*, London: Croom Helm, 1988.
8. Patrick McGowan, 'African Military Coups d'Etat, 1956–2001: Frequency, Trends and Distribution', *Journal of Modern African Studies*, Vol. 41, No. 3 (2003), pp. 339–370.
9. Charles Tilly, *The Politics of Collective Violence*, Cambridge: Cambridge University Press, 2003, pp. 111–129.
10. Cf. James Fearon and David Laitin, 'Violence and the Social Construction of Ethnic Identity', *International Organization*, Vol. 54, No. 4 (2000), pp. 845–877.
11. Jok Madut, *Sudan: Race, Religion and Violence*, New York: Oneworld, 2007.
12. Carolyn Fluehr-Lobban and Kharyssa Rhodes, eds., *Race and Identity in the Nile Valley: Ancient and Modern Perspectives*, Trenton, NJ: Red Sea Press, 2004.
13. Alier, Abel, *Southern Sudan: Too Many Agreements Dishonoured*, London: Paul and Co, 1992.
14. Julie Flint and Alex de Waal, *Darfur: A New History of a Long War*, London: Zed, 2008.

15 This part of the discussion relies heavily on the author's interaction with the NCP and SAF leadership during 2009–2011 when he was advisor to the African Union High-Level Implementation Panel for Sudan. The discussions themselves are off-the-record.
16 Francis Deng, *War of Visions: Conflict of Identities in Sudan*, Washington, DC: Brookings Institution, 1995.
17 Douglass North, John Joseph Wallis, and Barry R. Weingast, *Violence and Social Orders: A Conceptual Framework for Interpreting Recorded Human History*, Cambridge: Cambridge University Press, 2009.
18 Peter Woodward, *Sudan 1898–1989: The Unstable State*, London: Croom Helm, 1990.
19 Alex de Waal ed, 'Sudan: The Turbulent State', in *War in Darfur and the Search for Peace*, Cambridge, MA: Harvard University Press, 2007.
20 African Rights, *Food and Power in Sudan: A Critique of Humanitarianism*, London: African Rights, 1997, ch. 4.
21 English text to be found at: http://fletcher.tufts.edu/World-Peace-Foundation/Program/Research/Sudan-Peace-Archive/Timeline, at interactive timeline on 4 January 2011.
22 Blayton, 'Human Rights Reporting on Darfur'.
23 Flint and de Waal, *Darfur*, ch. 3.
24 Ushari Mahmoud and Suliman Baldo, 'El Diein Massacre and Slavery in the Sudan', Khartoum, mimeo, 1987.
25 Wendy James, *War and Survival in Sudan's Borderlands: Voices from the Blue Nile*, Oxford: Clarendon Press, 2007.
26 Abdul-Jabbar Fadul and Victor Tanner, 'Darfur after Abuja: A View from the Ground', in Alex de Waal, ed., *War in Darfur and the Search for Peace*, Cambridge, MA: Harvard University Press, 2007.
27 Mareike Schomerus and Tim Allen, 'Southern Sudan at Odds with Itself: Dynamics of Conflict and Predicaments of Peace', London School of Economics, 2010.
28 World Bank, 'Conflict, Security and Development', World Development Report 2011, Washington, DC, 2011.
29 Komey, Guma Kunda, *Land, Governance and Conflict and the Nuba of Sudan*, Oxford: James Currey, 2010.
30 Alex de Waal, 'Evidence and Narratives: Recounting Ingoing Violence in Darfur, Sudan', in Sharon Abramowitz and Catherine Panter-Brick, eds., *Medical Humanitarianism: Ethnographies of Practice*, Philadelphia: University of Pennsylvania Press, 2014.
31 Mbeki, Thabo, Speech, Friendship Hall, Khartoum, available at: http://fletcher.tufts.edu/World-Peace-Foundation/Program/Research/Sudan-Peace-Archive/Timeline, at interactive timeline on 5 January 2011.

5

General Elections and Narratives of Violent Conflict: The Land Question and Civic Competence in Kenya

Kenneth Inyani Simala

This chapter analyses political discourse and how it has influenced civic competence as a factor in violent conflict in Kenya's 2007 General Elections. It argues that although there has been a causal relationship between land disputes and violent conflict around elections since 1992, that nexus has not been easily demonstrated. Whereas narratives of violent conflicts in the country have their roots in colonial land reforms, particularly transfer and resettlement politics, a complex of interwoven land issues has conspired to place land at the centre of political communication and general elections. Anchored in an epistemological base that explores how patterns of civic identities are formed through language, the chapter focuses on how the land question legitimizes power by attempting to change, or reinforce popular views and ideological orientations. We argue that active citizenship is constantly subverted as evidenced by the cycle of violence during elections in Kenya. Since the first multiparty contest in 1992, and except for 2013, the country has been engulfed in ethnic violence at every election time, with the violence reaching a peak following the flawed 2007 General Elections.

Framed within a model that conceptualizes narrative as a system of dynamic interaction between different actors, each involved in producing, receiving and interpreting political messages that are transmitted through language, the chapter stresses that general elections are not just an event or activity that takes place over campaign periods, but rather is a continuum. The chapter examines violent conflicts around general elections as a dominant and characteristic genre that tells a story about Kenya and provides understanding of its often-taken-for-granted meanings. Read as texts, the violent conflicts are more than just isolated incidents; rather, they are part of a long national narrative.

A narrative approach to violent conflict in Kenya

Narratives are frameworks for action through which members of particular identity groups understand the socio-political worlds in which they live and explain the conflicts in which they are involved. They are the central focus and means by which people tell stories about their lives and give them meaning across time.[1] As an account of events and experiences,[2] narratives communicate ideologies and become an analytical tool to examine questions of nationalism, identity, and minority history as they reflect and reproduce social relations and shared memory.[3]

As a chain of events in cause-effect temporal relationship, a narrative may be individual or collective and begins with one situation followed by a series of changes according to a pattern of causes and effects; and finally, a new situation arises which brings about the end.[4] A narrative must have an initial situation, and a sequence leading to a change or reversal of that situation.[5] Key elements of a narrative include a story; plot; scenes; characters; cause-and-effect chain of events; actions that unfold chronologically and varyingly; a narrator voice with a discernible personality relationship to audience; and destination.[6] Narratives may move from birth to death, while others cover only sections of the life span, dealing primarily with past and present events.[7] Narratives are of two kinds: those focusing upon personal experience[8]; and those focusing upon larger contexts and appear mainly in the form of opinion-expressing discourse.[9]

Narratives bind individuals together within an active and adaptive community and change in response to events and emergent challenges. The narratives which come to dominate public discourse are often those which serve most effectively to give definition to in-group identity and values through reference to an out-group. Such narratives provide authoritative, common sense understandings about the nature of perceived threats to the *group* and its values, and connect the fears, insecurities and problems of the moment both with past tribulations and with a forward-looking political programme.[10]

Narrative analysis can provide insight into conflict situations.[11] Narratives play a causal role in conflict dynamics by ruling 'in' or 'out' certain political options, either for communal groups or for those speaking for them. Narratives that promote exclusive in-group loyalties, fears and negative images of adversaries, and escalatory conflict moves can easily exacerbate tensions; while narratives that highlight shared values and common interests can make resolution of conflict more likely. However, analysing narratives needs to ask how events are defined, which events are included and which are excluded, as well as the principles governing the selection process.[12] This is because not all events are of equal relevance to the main point of narration, and may be excluded waiting the reader's imputation in the underlying story written by law, literature, politics, and history.[13] Narratives provide an ontological condition of social life,[14] and can be used to explain history, politics, race, religion, identity and time: stories that both explain and construct the ways in which the world is understood.[15]

Thus, multiple narratives, at times competing, circulate within various levels of social realms and include stories and abstractions presented and re-presented in various mediums like newspapers.[16] Narratives which come to dominate public discourse serve most effectively to give definition to in-group identity and values through reference to an out-group and provide authoritative, common sense understandings about the nature of perceived threats to the group and its values, and connect the fears, insecurities, and problems of the moment both with past tribulations and with a forward-looking political programme.[17]

Conceptualizing civic competence and violent ethnic conflict in Kenya

Linking violent conflict to civic competence in Kenya is an appropriate approach as it is at the heart of the political activity that has become characterized by a cycle of conflicts with deep ethnic roots. While the country's experience with violent conflict may be considered lower-level, the emerging cycle is a phenomenon that deserves special attention because the conflict has a complex history and a fascinating sociopolitical narrative. A discourse analysis of narratives of violent conflict helps expose a deeper story that may not be articulated explicitly, or may not be easily accessible. A series of violent ethnic conflicts in Kenya just around election time is part of a long and intricate national history.

In Kenya, the production and recovery of historical consciousness has become an important political task for groups that create images of 'otherness' where ethnic boundaries are politicized, and where conflicts of inclusion and exclusion amplified. Prevailing narratives of violent conflict exhibit tendencies toward polarization of identity issues and adversarial framing of historical ethnic relations. Indeed, to understand narratives of violent ethnic conflict in Kenya, one must be attentive not only to history and contemporary politics, but also to subtleties of intercultural relations. Scenes of violent conflict cannot be appreciated outside a national history that has a multiplicity of stories shaped and held together by discourses that plot it into a single logical narrative.

In intergroup relations, self-perception plays a role in conditioning the way that the 'other' is perceived, and the meaning that groups give to their real and imagined differences defines the quality of relations between them.[18] 'Others' provide the collective 'self' with a means of defining own qualities and boundaries. Analysts of ethnic conflict recognize that members of communal groups tend to define their identity through contrasting 'positive' qualities manifest among members with the putatively 'inferior' traits of out-group members. This creates a sense of bounded identity, reinforces in-group solidarity, affirming shared values, strengthening individual and collective self-esteem, and facilitating cooperation to achieve common purposes.

Whereas democratization and internal conflict have been predominant themes on African politics in the recent past,[19] it has become clear that democracy requires a certain level of civic competence. Although political mobilization is a virtue of democracy, ethnic manipulation, mobilization and coalitions in Kenya's elections negate that aspiration and stifle national consciousness. Manifest in political language and public communication, these machinations can be ascribed to lack of active and responsible civic competence. Guided by communal logic, Kenyans vote along ethnic lines with expectations of rewards and favours. Consequently, violence becomes one practical approach to ensuring the protection of one's community from actual and perceived enemies.

According to Ochieng,[20] seeds of civil war have been planted since Britain forced many disparate but hitherto independent groups into a single political entity called Kenya. This was the seed that, in January 2008, broke out of the ground with such volcanic destructiveness. That is why removal of such seeds before they explode must be a nation-building task. Institutions charged with nation-building have the civic mission of preparing informed, rational, humane and participating citizens committed to the values and principles of constitutional democracy. Kenyan citizens ought to be informed, autonomous, respectful of others, participate in peaceful political processes, keep the common good in mind in their decision-making, and above all, be citizens who act responsibly. Unfortunately, what one finds in the country every election time instead is a depressing and sorry state of civic knowledge, skills and attitudes and want of civic preparedness.

While ethnic conflicts in Africa have their roots in political machinations,[21] in Kenya, ethnicity, as one among several relevant determinants of partisanship, is an important factor in explaining electoral choices.[22] However, ethnicity per se cannot account for the violence that has now accompanied every general election since the re-introduction of multi-party politics in the country in 1991.

Political discourse, ethnicity and violent conflict in Kenya

Investigations of discourses surrounding violent conflict in Kenya cannot avoid attending to the roles of narratives in political communication. Central for this kind of analysis is the idea of 'framing' as espoused by Entman,[23] who discusses frames as being ways of organizing key ideas so as to resonate with core values and assumptions held by the public. The media, both as powerful actors in their own right and as an arena used by other power groups in society, have an enormous influence on people's thoughts, actions and understanding of the world through political communication. On the other hand, language is the life blood of politics, and the two are indispensable in the transfer, creation, transformation and appropriation of innovative political messages. While language is the most important means of communication in politics, and political language and media communication having a long relationship in Kenya, this position of public language is not very often interrogated. This is despite one of the major challenges facing political communication and democratization process in the country being ethnic mobilization through linguistic manipulation in the media. The story of violent conflict in Kenya can very well be understood against the background of the totalizing and marginalizing nature of ethnic politics as a meta-narrative.

Contextualizing ethnic conflicts in Kenya in a wider historical setting firmly indicates electoral politics as a trigger to violence in a long and intricate narrative that goes beyond public political discourse A critical examination of the cycle of violence in the country reveals that it is part of the meta-narrative that defines its history. The narrative of ethnic violence provides a rich source of insight into unmasking the surface of the conflicts so as to reach the depth of the concrete historical ideology that informs them.

Before the arrival of British colonialists in the nineteenth century, the peoples of modern Kenya lived as separate entities. After 1895, a mosaic of forty-two diverse entities were cobbled together and bounded into what became known as the British protectorate, and later the Kenya colony in 1920. The artificially created boundaries can be said to be the source of the violent ethnic violence that has come to define the country. Stereotypes and hegemony started then have metamorphosed into current ethnicity, which politicians so easily exploit to their advantage every election time. But as Schutz argues,[24] it is impossible to understand human conduct while ignoring its intentions, and it is impossible to understand human intentions while ignoring the settings in which they make sense. Such settings may be institutions, sets of practices or some other contexts created by humans – contexts which have a history, within which both particular deeds and whole histories of individual actors can be and have to be situated in order to be intelligible.[25]

General elections and violent conflict in Kenya

Since independence in 1963, Kenya has held ten General elections. The 27 December 2007 poll was the ninth and most violent. While previous elections were held in 2002, 1997, 1992, 1988, 1983, 1979, 1974 and 1969, it was the 1963 independence elections and the 1966 'Little General Election' that mark the genesis of what has become a cycle of violent ethnic conflicts. The then two main parties, Kanu and KADU, were led by Jomo Kenyatta and Oginga Odinga, and an alliance of Coastal, Luyia, and Kalenjin community leaders such as Ronald Ngala, Masinde Muliro and Daniel arap Moi respectively. The latter party opposed the hegemony and domination of the former that brought together the then two largest communities, the Kikuyu and the Luo. While the former leaders favoured a unitary system of government, the latter preferred 'majimbo' (regionalism) that would guarantee minority rights. At the Lancaster House talks in London, Kanu acceded to Kadu demands for regionalism and formed the first independence government with Jomo Kenyatta as Prime Minister and Ronald Ngala as the leader of opposition.

Kenya became a Republic in 1964 and Kenyatta changed from being a Prime Minister to a President who combined the dual roles of Head of State and Head of Government. This new arrangement effectively neutered the 'federal' Lancaster Constitution and concentrated power at the centre. Kenya became a de-facto one party state with no opposition. In 1966, the Kanu Vice President, Oginga Odinga, quit his positions in the party and government and formed his own Kenya Peoples Union (KPU) that led to what became known as the Little General Election of 1966 in which KPU lost twenty-eight out of the thirty-eight seats it contested. Thus, Kenya's first ever independence elections were held in 1969, under a single party dispensation and one National Assembly. President Kenyatta appointed Joseph Murumbi, a Maasai, and later on Daniel arap Moi, a Kalenjin, as his Vice Presidents. Their appointments, from minority ethnicities, were calculated to not only dismantle Kadu but to effectively co-opt the minority communities in Kenyatta's schemes of things, with an eye on the expansive fertile Rift Valley province, which would later play an active role in the cycle of violent conflicts that has rocked Kenya since.

With a firm grip on power, places, politics and people, Kenyatta had by the 1974 General Elections transformed his into an imperial presidency that didn't allow opposition. Upon Kenyatta's death in 1978, Daniel arap Moi succeeded him and declared to follow his approach. Moi retained Kenyatta's basic ethnic principles, with Mwai Kibaki, a Kikuyu, being appointed Vice-President so as to guarantee the majority Kikuyu needed to perpetuate the dual Kalenjin-Kikuyu ethnic hegemony. Thus, the 1979 General election was used by Moi to entrench himself in power and suppress any dissent. Nonetheless, the opposition continued to operate, rather mutedly, till a constitutional amendment in 1982 that made Kenya a de jure one-party state. A 1982 failed coup contributed to the increasing paranoid behaviour exhibited by Moi, including detention of political opponents and fortification of the Rift Valley power base. The 1983 General Elections was largely a loyalty test and precursor to the 1988 General Elections that was the most blatantly rigged one in Kenya's electoral history. By the time multi-party elections were called in 1992, the country was ethnically divided, and the opposition lost in the elections.

By the 1997 elections, the opposition splintered further along ethnic crevices. However, the opposition demonstrated a purposeful unity drive to stop a continuation of the Moi legacy and picked Mwai Kibaki as their flag bearer and won the 2002 elections. After 2002, Kenya emerged with stronger democratic institutions, a more open democratic space, a cohesive society and a vibrant economy. That was until the 2007 General Elections that resulted into violent ethnic conflicts. But this was part of the horrendous cycle of violence that has become a feature of almost every elections, with politicians manipulating historical issues and ethnic tensions to set communities against each other. In almost all spectres of violent conflict in the country, land issues have become part of the discourse. Although the 2013 General Elections were devoid of violent conflict, still issues of ethnicity and the land question came into play. The Kikuyu and Kalenjin communities ganged up against the rest of the country in what became known as the 'tyranny of numbers' and won power. Before the 2013 General Elections, these two communities had been the most notorious active participants in land clashes.

The land question and violent ethnic conflicts in Kenya

Violent ethnic conflicts in Kenya are as a result of a variety of reasons. While some are about ethnic hatred, and whereas others are a reaction to disputed elections results, a tremendous amount of it has been about land. In most cases, general elections provided the spark of the violence, with the historical land question being the real reason. History shows inability to diagnose conflict over land as the cause to the cycle of violence. Kenya has never seriously addressed landlessness that exacerbates societal inequality. It is perhaps due to this realization that 'The Kenya National Dialogue and Reconciliation Talks' mediated by Kofi Anan in 2008 called for land reform:

> We recognize that the issue of land has been a source of economic, social, political and environmental problems in Kenya for many years. We agree that land reform

is a fundamental need and the issue must be addressed comprehensively and with the seriousness it deserves...so as to establish the factors responsible for conflicts over land and to formulate actionable short, medium and long-term recommendations on the issue.[26]

It can be argued that violent conflict is coterminous with Kenya's history that is itself intricately linked to the land question. Kenya was forged on land brutality and primitive land grabbing, first by Arabs who were followed by the Imperial British East African Company (IBEA), a private firm that later handed over the territory to British East Africa, which became a Protectorate and Colony by 1914. The British Empire consolidated its hold on the territory by bringing in more settlers in the White Highlands. Thus, land grabbing, landlessness and land conflicts are as old as the Kenyan state. The incessant cycle of violent conflicts occur around election time in mostly settlement schemes where there exist deep-running suspicions over land, its sharing and ownership. With magnification of ethnicity, increase in population and decrease in acreage, the emotive land issue is a powder keg.

The earliest violent conflicts over land date back to 1498 with the arrival and conquest of the Portuguese over Arabs who were rulers at the Coast of East Africa. The ensuing conflict and the resultant Ten Mile Coastal Strip was under the Sultan of Zanzibar till an 1895 agreement that placed it under British rule. Ever since the defeat of the Portuguese, the history of this piece of land has remained contentious. In 1895, the Sultan gave the British power to administer the ten-mile coastal strip subject to respecting the existing Kadhi's courts, among other conditions. The British did so by declaring a protectorate over the Coast, while the rest of the country became a colony. However, the first government-instigated evictions occurred between 1914 and 1916 when powerful Arab ruling families from Oman and other Persian Gulf regions acted in consonance with the British to displace the local people. The displaced were herded into the Nyika reserves, where they remained as squatters as their lands were taken over by other people or turned into Crown land. During British colonial rule, many Arabs acquired title deeds to vast parcels of land within the strip. But at Kenya's independence in 1963, they left the country and appointed agents to collect rent for them, with many landless indigenous coastal people becoming rent-paying squatters to absentee landlords.

Indigenous Swahili at the Coast of Kenya feel disinherited of their ancestral land by both Arab and British colonialists. Successive governments since independence have not been helpful in finding lasting solutions. During Kenyatta's rule, communal land meant for indigenous coastal communities was allocated to influential non-coastal people. This simmering problem and discontent is believed to have led to the infamous 1997 Likoni clashes, where dozens of upcountry people were killed and thousands displaced by armed gangs claiming to be defending the land rights of the coastal Digo people. The rag-tag army, The Mombasa Republican Council (MRC) that has been waging a war of independence against the Kenya Government since 2005, is also associated with the history of landlessness at the Coast. Impoverished and frustrated, the MRC is a popular resistance group because of the single issue of land. The group has received tacit support from politicians from the region. The MRC is a reminder of how the coastal land question, with a long pre-independence history, has been pathetically handled with poor coastal communities being betrayed by the political class for decades.

Modern land problems in Kenya have political and legal origins in the invasion, conquest, occupation and consolidation of British rule from the late nineteenth century. According to colonial logic, the territory was uninhabited, and indigenous people could not exercise proper territorial sovereignty. After guaranteeing jurisdictional power, the Crown enacted the East African (Lands) Orders to alienate land in the new colony. The orders were re-enacted in the Crown Lands Ordinance of 1902 and 1915, which governed the allocation of land, and the entire territory of Kenya was declared Crown Land and appropriated to colonial invaders. The British government established the Kenya Land Commission of 1933 which received petitions from groups opposed to confiscation of land by settlers, confinement of local communities into Native Reserves and alienation and designation of the most arable lands as White Highlands for allocation to foreign settlers. In a Memorandum in the Kenya Land Commission of 1933, the Kenya Missionary Council complained that:

> The root cause of trouble is the strange failure by Government to make any inquiry into Native Land Tenure systems before giving out land to other non-native races ... it is most unfortunate that when it became apparent that injuries had been committed, no attempt was made to make reparations ... In most cases, natives were evicted without knowing they had legal claim.

The colonial land policy created an explosive situation that culminated into the nationalist Mau Mau resistance war, which started in the 1940s and gathered steam in the 1950s. Less than a thousand white farmers held more than eight million acres of the nation's best land, and fighters wanted appropriated land returned to rightful owners. The Mau Mau had a Land Reform Army whose goal was to get back ancestral land. Resistance to land dispossession and the emergence of the Mau Mau insurgency forced the colonial administration to consider granting titles to indigenous people. The Synerton Land Plan of 1954, for the first time, granted individual titles to Africans and in the process attempted to establish a bulwark of landed gentry who would contain the Mau Mau insurgents. Those who got land supported the British against the Mau Mau.

Soon after independence President Kenyatta, with money borrowed from the British and the World Bank, formed the 'million acres programme' to settle the landless, but the programme failed in 1971. This was due to the fact that legal powers for allocating land, previously vested in the British Monarch, were transferred to the President, and Kenyans became tenants to an imperial president. Yet, as early as 1964, there was growing agitation over the land question just a year after independence. By 1969, alarm bells were ringing over the way communities were being settled in the Rift Valley. Back then, Kenyatta's government had received huge financial resources to back the Kenya Land Resettlement Fund so as to buy land from departing white farmers for the benefit of black Kenyans. Whereas the resettlement scheme had commenced in 1962, by 1965, the Government adopted a different approach with a Special Commissioner registering and settling squatters on ten-acre plots carved out of abandoned or mismanaged white farms which had been taken over by Kenyan Africans. Kenyatta was accused for being unwilling to direct the Settler Transfer Fund (STF) for the re-distribution of the ten million acres of arable land occupied by white settlers to benefit landless Africans. Instead, the STF scheme was hijacked by few individuals form the ruling elite, who 'lent' themselves money meant for the landless to acquire huge tracts of land at the expense of the majority poor.

Most of those who had fought against white colonialists found themselves landless, poor and pushed to the periphery by 'native colonialists'. Those who were lucky were resettled in other parts of the country, without regard for future repercussions. Kenyatta implanted his Kikuyu community in traditionally non-Kikuyu areas and made no genuine efforts to build lasting inter-community bonds. His people retained all their cultural traditions and remained 'alien' in the host communities where they were settled. The incoming Kikuyus transferred their villages with them, and never wanted to integrate with their hosts. Farms, schools, churches, markets and any institutions established bore names and character of their ancestral Central Province. Those who never took part in the independence war were the ones owning huge chunks of fertile land in the former white highlands, in Western, Central and Coast provinces. Impoverished owners of those lands became squatters on plantations that once belonged to their ancestors.

The emergence of tribal animosity was a serious problem at independence, and land redistribution was an urgent item on the national agenda. Both problems have never received genuine attention, and continue to fester, but more seriously during election time. A flawed model of property rights introduced by the British colonial authorities has served successive regimes as a weapon to dispossess, grab and use land to buy patronage. This is the genesis of land problems in most of Kenya, and by extension, it is the root cause of violent conflicts that so often characterize general elections in the country. For many years, the land question had been suppressed and buried by successive governments till 1991, a period of political agitation for the reintroduction of multi-party politics. At this time, Rift Valley Province politicians resuscitated the land ghosts by warning proponents of political pluralism, who were wrongly perceived to be against Moi, and by extension the Kalenjin, that they had to move out of the province and relocate to their ancestral lands. By the time Kenya experienced its first multiparty election in 1992, many non-Kalenjins in the Rift Valley had lost their land, lives and livelihoods through politically instigated violent ethnic conflicts.

According to the Truth, Justice and Reconciliation Commission (TJRC) Report,[27] for the majority of Kenyans, land is a basic, and in most cases, the only economic resource from which they eke out a livelihood. The ability to access, own, use and control land has a profound impact on their ability to feed and provide for their families and to establish their socio-economic and political standing in society. The Commission established that land has been, and remains, one of the major causes of intra- and inter-ethnic conflicts in the country. Politicians often exploit the real or perceived land injustices, especially around elections time, for personal gain. The dangerous mix of land-related claims with the political aspirations of specific individuals and groups remains a tinderbox that could ignite any time.

The unresolved land injustices have led to discriminatory and exclusionary practices that work against nationhood. Land injustices and land-related grievances have led to the emergence of militia groups in some parts of the country. The stated aims of these militia groups often relate to the reclamation of lands and the removal by violent means of 'settlers' viewed as 'intruders' in ancestral lands. The prevalence of these narratives focused on contested land ownership between rival ethnic communities was key to the emergence and visibility of modern day ethnic militias, like the Mungiki, Sabaot Land Defence Force, Kaya Bombo, Rift Valley Warriors and Mombasa Republican Council. The failure by the government to effectively control the criminal activities of these gangs, especially around elections time, demonstrates how dangerous these gangs can become to national survival. A deeper analysis of the conflicts between different ethnic communities that flared into national crises confirms that there is a correlation between narratives around disputed communal land ownership, general elections and violence. The political insinuations in the spiral of violence indicate that politicians are involved in the violent conflicts.

Conclusion

This chapter set out to discuss narratives of violent conflict and challenges of civic competence in Kenya. While the land question has been identified as being the epicentre of the violence, it has been argued that underlying causes are more complex as no single narrative can explain the cycle of violent conflicts that has become so characteristic of the country, especially around elections time. The violence has layered narratives and sub-texts that deserve critical analysis. While land problems are older than Kenyatta, Moi and Kibaki's reigns, violent conflicts will not end unless some very deliberate policy decisions are taken to settle the matter. Because land is the ultimate natural resource, it requires good stewardship for present and future generations.

With thousands of citizens dead, and with many more displaced and billions of shillings lost in destroyed property in what appears to be politically instigated violent conflicts, the government cannot ignore the competing narratives of identity and land ownership. No less important, politicians must resist the temptation to exploit and stoke these narratives for electoral gain, as has been the habit. Rather, the government needs to ensure that citizen rights, including land, are protected if Kenyans are to coexist peacefully. Effective civic education is necessary, and citizens must be prepared to understand and be committed to the values inherent in the Kenyan Constitution: justice, freedom, equality, diversity, authority, privacy, due process, property, participation, truth, patriotism, human rights, rule of law, tolerance, mutual assistance, personal and civic responsibility, self-restraint and self-respect.

Notes

1. Barbara Johnstone, *Discourse Analysis*, Oxford: Blackwell Publishers, 2007.
2. Sukalpa Bhattacharjee, 'Narrative as an Other History or His Story Otherwise', in Subha Chakrabuty Dasgupta, et al., eds., *Literature and Oratures as Knowledge Systems: Texts from Northeast India*, New Delhi: Akansha Publishing House, 2011.
3. Steven Hoelscher, 'Making Place, Making Race: Performances of Whiteness in the Jim Crow South', *Annals of the Association of American Geographers*, Vol. 93 (2003), pp. 657–686.
4. Kristin Thompson, *The Voice of the Past: Oral History*, Oxford: Oxford University Press, 1988.
5. J. Hillis Miller, 'Narrative', in Frank Lentricchia and Thomas McLaughlin, eds., *Critical Terms for Literary Study*, Chicago: University of Chicago Press, 1990, pp. 66–79.
6. David Bordwell and Kristin Thompson, *Film Art: An Introduction*, Reading, MA: Addison-Wesley, 1979.
7. Charlotte Linde, 'Private Stories in Public Discourse: Narrative Analysis in the Social Sciences', *Poetics*, Vol. 15 (1986), pp. 183–202.
8. William Labov, *Language in the Inner City: Studies in the Black English Vernacular*, Philadelphia: University of Pennsylvania Press, 1972.
9. Alexandra Georgakopoulou and Dionysis Goutsos, 'Revisiting Discourse Boundaries: The Narrative and Non-Narrative Mode', *Text & Talk*, Vol. 20 (2000), pp. 63–82.
10. Manfred Jahn, *Narratology: A Guide to the Theory of Narrative*, 2005, http://www.uni-koeln.de/~ame02/pppn.htm [accessed 5 October 2013]; Marc Howard Ross, 'The Political Psychology of Competing Narratives: September 11 and Beyond', in Craig Calhoun, Paul Price, and Ashley Timmer, eds., *Understanding September 11*, New York: New Press, 2002, pp. 303–320.
11. Ross, 'The Political Psychology of Competing Narratives'.
12. Michael Frisch, 'Oral History and Hard Times', *Oral History Review* Vol. 7 (1979), pp. 70–79.
13. M. J. Zaborowska, *How We Found America: Reading Gender Through East European Immigrant Narratives*, Chapel Hill, NC: The University of North Carolina Press, 1995.
14. Margaret R. Somers and Gloria D. Gibson, 'Reclaiming the Epistemological Other: Narrative and the Social Construction of Identity', in Craig Calhoun, ed., *Social Theory and the Politics of Identity*, Oxford: Blackwell, 1998, pp. 37–99.
15. Paul Wake, 'Narrative and Narratology', in Simon Malpas and Paul Wake, eds., *The Routledge Companion to Critical Theory*, London: Routledge, 2006.
16. Somers and Gibson, 'Reclaiming the Epistemological Other'.
17. Nathan C. Funk and Abdul Aziz Said, 'Islam and the West: Narratives of Conflict and Conflict Transformation', *International Journal of Peace Studies*, Vol. 9, No. 1 (2004), pp. 1–28.
18. Funk and Said, 'Islam and the West', pp. 1–28.
19. Look for example; Eghosa E. Osaghae, 'Rescuing the Post-Colonial State in Africa: A Reconceptualization of the Role of Civil Society', *International Journal of African Studies*, Vol. 2, No. 1 (2000), pp. 55–69.
20. Philip Ochieng, *Sunday Nation*, 24 June 2007, p. 11.
21. Okwudiba Nnoli, ed., *Ethnic Conflict in Africa*, Dakar: African Books Collective, 1998); Walter O. Oyugi, 'Ethnicity in the Electoral Process: The 1992 General

Elections in Kenya', *African Journal of Political Science*, Vol. 2, No. 1 (1997), pp. 141–169.
22 Michael Bratton and Mwangi S. Kimenyi, 'Voting in Kenya: Putting Ethnicity in Perspective', *Economics Working Papers*. Paper 200809, 2008.
23 Robert M. Entman, 'Framing: Towards Clarification of a Fractured Paradigm', *Journal of Communication*, Vol. 43, No. 4 (1993), pp. 51–58.
24 Alfred Schutz, 'Common Sense and Scientific Interpretation of Human Action', in M. A. Natanson, ed., *Collected Papers, Volume I: The Problem of Social Reality*, The Hague: Martinus Nijhoff, 1973, pp. 34–35.
25 Barbara Czaniawska, *Narratives in Social Science Research*, London: Sage Publications, 2004.
26 *Sunday Nation*, 24 August 2008.
27 The Truth, Justice and Reconciliation Commission of Kenya Report 2013.

6

The Violence of Security, Lethal Representations and Hindu Nationalism in India

Dibyesh Anand[1]

The chapter conceptualizes security as a discourse of violence that masks violence in the name of counter-violence, killing in the name of protection. As the case of Hindutva in India illustrates, violence against minorities is normalized in the name of personal, communal, national and international security. The will to secure the Self has as its corollary the will to insecure the Other, the desire to control and use violence. Using the example of anti-Muslim violence in Gujarat in 2002, the chapter examines some of the ways in which a stereotypical image of Muslim men (the putative figure of 'The Muslim') is seen as constituting the danger against which the Hindu body politic needs to be secured. The violence against minority Muslims is facilitated and justified in the name of achieving security for the Hindu Self at individual, community and national as well as international levels.

The chapter is a journey into a spectacle of collective communal violence in India in 2002, its (extra)ordinariness and the gestures that seek to translate corporeality of violence into abstraction. These enabling gestures can be understood as a part of a discourse of security. It is the logic of this discourse of security that enables extreme violence to be normalized, systematized and institutionalized. The politics of hate, of which the Hindu Right (Hindu nationalist, also called Hindutva) in India[2] is a good example, feeds upon, as well as shapes, local societies' conceptions of security and insecurity.[3] The global environment, with its own dynamic politics of representation of dangers, has a direct impact on the local societies' conceptions. An example of the so-called 'Hindu-Muslim' communal riot in India is from Gujarat (a state in the federal set-up of India) in 2002, where more than a thousand people (mostly Muslims) were killed in the space of a couple of months.[4]

The chapter is divided into four sections. It starts with outlining the political context of communal violence in India and then moves on to conceptualize security as a productive discourse – one that produces 'dangers' to security as well as the object to be secured. The third section discusses the centrality of particular representations of threatening Muslim masculinity (the figure of 'The Muslim') in Hindutva discourse. 'The Muslim' is seen as constituting the danger against which the Hindu body politic needs to be secured. This legitimizes the use of violence against Muslims in the name of securing the Hindu Self. The last section visits Gujarat 2002 (a shorthand I use for violence, overwhelmingly against Muslims, that took place during 2002 in Gujarat) as the most (in)famous site that can be best made sense of within the (meta)discourse of security. The chapter concludes by re-emphasizing the point that the violence of the kind witnessed in Gujarat 2002 is made possible, probable and even inevitable by the logic of violence and abstraction that is part of the discourse of security. The main argument of this chapter is that the violence against minority Muslims is facilitated and justified in the name of achieving security for the Hindu Self, individual and communal.

The Hindu Right in India

Communal violence in India should be understood within the larger context of the struggle and debate over the secularism of the postcolonial Indian state.[5] This has become especially significant since the 1990s, the decade that saw the end of the Indian National Congress's dominance and the rise of the Bharatiya Janata Party (BJP), a Hindu nationalist party. The victory of the Congress-led alliance in the national elections in 2004 and in 2009 does not signal the demise of Hindu nationalism as a political movement. It merely reminds us that the electoral politics in India, at this point in time, can absorb ideologically distinct political formations.

The history of Hindu nationalism in India is as long as that of the mainstream nationalism represented mainly by the Congress.[6] The attitude of many Congress leaders and activists toward majoritarian communalism (of which Hindu nationalism is an articulation) and even communal violence has been ambiguous. Yet, BJP and its Hindutva ideology are different and distinct from the dominant secular ideals of the Indian state. Its rhetoric of democracy, rights and nation is based on a simplistic majoritarian principle, and runs along the following lines: since Hindus are the majority, it is 'natural' and 'democratic' that their 'rights' should be promoted by the Indian state which hitherto has been 'pseudo-secular' because of its appeasement of the minorities! The Hindutva movement therefore is a 'conservative revolution', combining paternalist and xenophobic discourses with democratic and universalist ones on rights and entitlements.[7] The Hindutva is targeted at transforming the Indian state and controlling the Muslim and Christian minorities. At the same time, the primary goal is to transform the Hindus, to 'awaken the Hindu nation'.[8] There is a schizophrenic shuttling between the idea of a pre-existing monolithic Hindu nation and a lamentation that most members of this supposed nation do not fit in Hindutva's template of an ideal citizen of the Hindu nation. A Hindutva website's call illustrates this well: 'No Hindu politics is possible unless there is Hindu-Awakening. And that Hindu-Awakening is not yet in sight.'[9] Hindutva is self-recognized as being as much about representing the Hindu nation as it is about fabricating one. This has been the case throughout the twentieth century.[10]

What was different at the start of the twenty-first century was the respectability and influence gained by the exponents of Hindutva through participation in the government at the federal level, as well as in various states allowing them to gain access to the resources of the state. For instance, leaders who were seen as firebrand ideologues during the 1990s became members of the government; non-Hindutva politicians competed over who was a more authentic Hindu; school children were taught a history where militant Hinduism is normalized and minority religions such as Islam and Christianity (and as a corollary, Indian Muslims and Indian Christians) are alienated; government employees could join Hindutva organizations; Prime Minister (at the time) Atal Behari Vajpayee remarked in a cavalier manner, after the riots in Gujarat, that Muslims were a source of 'problems' everywhere in the world.[11] Thus, there was a visible shift to the Right in Indian politics in the 1990s and early 2000s, and the ascendancy of Hindutva forces was its peak.[12] Even during the election campaign in 2009, which the BJP lost, one witnessed the frequent presentation of Narendra Modi, Gujarat's Chief Minister, who was most closely associated with anti-Muslim violence in 2002, as an efficient pro-business political leader, as if his record as having presided over anti-minority violence was excusable. Hindutva's ascendancy is clearly not a foregone conclusion nor did it even manifest itself throughout the country. But, at the very least, it is there as an important force in the Indian political landscape, seeking to create a more Hinduized India (Hinduized on terms set by Hindutva forces and not in its traditional, fuzzy and fluid forms) and discipline the religious minorities.

Communal violence in India remains a contested subject among actors including politicians, activists, and scholars.[13] The Hindutva shares the neo-Orientalist belief in the primordial naturalness of Hindu-Muslim violence in India ('historic clash' as most Western media tend to report). However, 'riots' (spectacular incidents of inter-communal collective violence) are not a direct product of communalism (where communities are seen as bounded, historical, and given). Instead, 'communal' riots are exercises in the construction of communities through the mobilization (of the 'Self'), purification (erasure of commonalities) and definition (through violence of what is the Self and what is the Other). Communalism is not merely a reflection of a pre-existing community but the will to create a bounded community.[14] Communalism as an ideology operates at the level of the individual as well as the collective – the identity and interests of individuals are seen as coinciding with that of the collective, the community. In this sense, it is deterministic. For instance, in the case of Hindu-Muslim communalism, every individual is reduced as only a Hindu, or only a Muslim – no other identities matter. As several testimonies after riots have shown, identification with community becomes stronger when one suffers on account of being a member of that community.

In his film *Father, Son and Holy War* (1994),[15] Patwardhan finds that the Muslim women, who were identifying their common interests with Hindu women before the 1993 riots in Mumbai, felt during violence that it was their 'Muslimness' that marked them, while their being a 'woman' became irrelevant. The reduction of individuals to only one form of identity is generally more common in representations of the minorities by the majoritarian discourses. The idea being that while 'we' the majority can experiment with identities, 'they', the minorities are overdetermined by what marks them as minority. While the Hindus have multiple layers of identity, every aspect of a Muslim is supposed to be determined by her/his Muslimness. The determinism of communal discourses dehumanizes the Other and poses it as a danger to the security of the Self.

The productive discourse of security

Security is a central concept in the theory and praxis of International Relations, but also local, inter-local, as well as translocal relations. In positivist literature on security, it is assumed to possess an ontological and epistemological certainty, where the sources of insecurity as well as the referent of security are givens. In line with the literature of critical international relations,[16] I conceptualize security as a productive discourse that produces insecurities to be operated upon, as well as defining the identity of the object to be secured. This challenges the dominant conceptual grammar of security that treats insecurities as unavoidable facts, while focusing attention onto the acquisition of security by given entities. It foregrounds the processes through which something or someone (the Other) is discursively produced as a source of insecurity against which the Self needs to be secured. Thus, discourses of insecurity are about 'representations of danger'.[17] Insecurities, in this view, are social constructions rather than givens – threats do not just exist out there, but have to be created. All insecurities are culturally produced in the sense that they are produced in and out of 'the context within which people give meanings to their actions and experiences and make sense of their lives'.[18] Insecurities and the objects that suffer from insecurities are mutually constituted. That is, in contrast to the received view, which treats objects of security and insecurity themselves as separate things, pre-given and natural, we treat them as mutually constituted cultural and social constructions. They are thus products of processes of identity construction of Self-Other. The argument that security is about representations of danger and social construction of the Self and the Other does not imply that there are no 'real' effects. What it means is that there is nothing inherent in any act or being or object that makes it a source of insecurity and danger.

Security is linked closely with identity politics. How we define ourselves depends on how we represent others. This representation is thus integrally linked with how we 'secure' ourselves against the Other. Representations of the Other as a source of danger to the security of the Self in conventional understandings of security are accompanied by an abstraction, dehumanization, depersonalization and stereotyping of the Other. The Other gets reduced to being a danger and hence an object that is fit for surveillance, control, policing and possibly extermination.[19] This logic of the discourse of security dictates that the security of the Self facilitate, and even demand, the use of policing and violence against the Other. This can be illustrated through the case of Hindutva's politics of representation that legitimizes anti-Muslim violence in the name of securing the Hindu body politic at various levels.

'The Muslim', a stereotype of Muslim males, is posed as a danger to the body of Hindu women and through them to the purity of the Hindu nation. At the same time, it is seen as a threat to national, state and international security. These representations of 'The Muslim' as a danger to the security of Hindu body politic facilitate the politics of hate against the Muslims in India.

Representing 'The Muslim' as a danger

'The Muslim' as an object of insecurity in the Hindutva discourse inhabits the levels of the personal, local and national as well as international. 'The Muslim' is discursively constructed as a site of fear, fantasy, distrust, anger, envy and hatred, thus generating desires of emulation, abjection and/or extermination. These desires are not confined to the subscribers of Hindutva but are prevalent in the wider society among those describing themselves as Hindu. The Hindutva movement is not an inevitable result of these prejudicial desires but scavenges upon them and in turn fuels and fossilizes them. The desires of emulation, abjection and extermination are inextricably linked to certain threatening representations of 'The Muslim'. The politics of Hindutva is one where the construction of a desired masculinity (ideal Hindu male: virile, yet with controlled sexuality) requires the destruction of competing masculinities and men. In the words of V. D. Savarkar, one of the 'founding fathers' of Hindutva, the aim of the Hindu nationalism is to recuperate manliness and 'Hinduize all politics and militarize hindudom'.[20]

Hindutva's politics of representation is one replete with myths and stereotypes. Let me provide you with some snapshots.[21] Hindutva discourses construct a myth of the Hindu self as virtuous, civilized, peaceful, accommodating, enlightened, clean and tolerant, as opposed to 'The Muslim' Other, which is morally corrupt, barbaric, violent, rigid, backward, dirty and fanatic. The myth borrows from various stereotypes and motifs that are prevalent in India and elsewhere, including the West. The Prophet's sex life, licentious Arabs buying young girls and boys, men with four wives, Muslim prostitutes, lack of democracy in the Muslim world – all these motifs are mobilized to 'confirm' the immorality and corruption of Muslims. Halal meat, circumcision, the history of 'the spread of Islam through sword' and rape, forms of punishment in the Arab world, Islamic terrorism – these images are deployed to provide an alibi to the supposed barbaric and violent character of Islam and Muslims. This is encapsulated by Savarkar's statement – 'where religion is goaded on by rapine and rapine serves as a hand-maid to religion, the propelling force that is generated by these together is only equalled by the profundity of human misery and devastation they leave behind them in their march'.[22] Refusal to modernize, the veil, sharia law, low status of women – these stereotypes characterize the Muslims as rigid and backward. Muslims supposedly have a penchant to live in small houses in ghettos and walled cities, which goes with 'The Muslim' predilection for filth and dirt. As Kakar in his analysis of stereotypes about Muslims points out, 'the image of Muslim animality is composed of the perceived ferocity, rampant sexuality, and demand for instant gratification of the male, and a dirtiness which is less a matter of bodily cleanliness and more of an inner pollution as a consequence of the consumption of forbidden, tabooed foods'.[23] Fanaticism of Muslims is a motif that needs no elaboration, since it is deployed by many states and groups around the world in contemporary times. This 'fanaticism' (of which Al Qaida is the most recent incarnation) is supposed to flow out of Islam (the Prophet's personal character, Quran's rigid instructions and spread of Islam through violence). At the same time, it is claimed to be a result of the physical and moral character of Muslims. Empirical studies, anecdotal evidence and personal experience show that these myths are not confined to Hindutva forces only but are increasingly becoming a part of a 'common sense' among other Hindus (especially upper caste) too.[24] These images borrow heavily from the orientalist and imperialist writings by the West.[25] In recent times, Hindutva proponents, especially in cyberspace, scavenge voraciously from racist writings about Islam and 'Muslim mind' coming out of the West.[26] The so-called international 'war on terror' has only reinforced this association of Islam with terrorism. The most common image of the Muslim among Hindutva today is of 'terrorist'. As the writings of proponents of Hindutva show, Muslims and terrorism are seen as inseparable. For instance, Chitkara laments that 'Common Hindu is surprised why riots take place when Muslims have already been given a separate home-land Pakistan? Terrorism shows that their appetite has not been quenched.'[27] This conflation serves to criminalize large sections of Muslim males. The supposed 'terrorism' of Muslims is seen as a justification to discriminate against them and marginalize them from 'sensitive' government posts.[28]

While the 'The Muslim terrorist' is constructed as a grave threat to the national security of India today, in the long term, what is seen as even more dangerous to the existence of the Hindu nation is the spectre of 'overpopulating Muslims'. Every census in India since the late nineteenth century has been followed by a hue and cry about the relative strength of Hindus vis-à vis Muslims. The idea of demographic decline has been entrenched in Hindutva since the early twentieth century. This was encapsulated by U. N. Mukherji's analysis of Hindus as a dying race in 1909 – 'they count their gains, we calculate our losses'.[29] After an alarmist (and erroneous) report on the 2001 Census, the debate resumed about how Muslims are breeding like rabbits and are going to overtake Hindus.[30,31] There are various spectres – obliteration of the Hindu nation (in a few hundred years); defeat of the Hindus in the numbers game (in a few decades); another Pakistan as in few years' time Muslims will constitute 30% of population (the way it was during 1947) bolstering their claim for partition. Acharya Dharmendra, a Hindu religious leader proclaimed in a public meeting in 2003: 'Muslims breed like rabbits and their population would soon overtake that of the Hindus.'[32] The scientific arguments against unduly alarmist readings of demographic figures that expose lies about the alarmism or that rationalize differential population growth among religious groups[33] do not do away with the common 'knowledge'/myth of overpopulating Muslims. This becomes clear when one participates in conversations with many Hindus in middle-class drawing rooms, university cafes, tea stalls and other public and private gatherings.

The 'overpopulating Muslim' is linked not only to religion but also to the virility of Muslim men (and the over-fertility of Muslim women). This imagined virility is used to construct an image of Muslim masculinity that is marked by an uncontrolled and uncontrollable lust and is hence a danger to Hindu women. The handsome Muslim who is a master in the art of seduction, the lecherous Muslim and the Muslim rapist – all these images play upon each other as a danger to 'innocent' Hindu females.[34] This then encourages the mobilization of Hindu women for Hindutva in the name of self-defence and protection of the body of Hindu women and the Hindu nation.[35] But more crucially, it exhorts Hindu men to 'protect' their innocent Hindu mothers, sisters and daughters. This implies defending Hindu women from 'the Muslim' who is lecherous and a potential rapist. It also entails protecting Hindu women from the seduction of Muslim men by policing interactions between Hindu women and Muslim men, casting any relationship based on this interaction as an indicator of sly Muslim men polluting, converting and oppressing Hindu women. Any agency of the Hindu woman in such relationships is denied. The close connection between demonizing the Muslim and policing (Hindu) woman's sexuality is well illustrated in debates during the early twentieth century, when Hindu widow remarriage was promoted as necessary to 'control' the passion of Hindu widows who would otherwise become prey to the designs of Muslim men.[36]

Thus a militant aggressive masculinity is called for in the name of defence and security of the Self (women, family, community, religion, nation, state). The construction of 'the Hindu' draws its legitimacy from the representation of 'The Muslim' as a danger to the Hindu body and in turn legitimizes the use of 'any means' to protect and take revenge. The Hindu male is expected to protect Hindu women, and in the process, if required, is justified in castrating Muslim men and raping Muslim women. This violence is masked by the Hindutva forces as self-defence. As Bacchetta points out, 'the counterpart to the chaste Hindu male is the Muslim male polygamist or rapist, and to the chaste motherly Hindu woman is the Muslim woman as prostitute or potential wife'.[37]

Thus, 'The Muslim' as a gendered figure is constructed to mobilize the Hindu male and female and awaken the Hindu nation. The fact that Hindutva forces are not dominant politically in India does not reduce the danger of such vicious representations of the Muslim in fermenting collective anti-Muslim violence. As pointed out earlier, what is more disturbing is that these representations scavenge upon, and in turn shape and fossilize, prejudicial desires that are common in the popular imaginary among many Hindus in India and abroad. Not enough attention has been paid to the 'highly selective and manipulative process by which myths and stereotypes about the marauding and libidinous Muslim, the innocent and mother-like Hindu woman, the tolerant Hindu man, have entered and entrenched themselves in public memory and consciousness'.[38] Hindu fanaticism is seen as a contradiction in terms by some Hindus who, while politically shunning the Hindu Right, buy into the myth of Hinduism as marked overwhelmingly by tolerance. Though Hindu chauvinism is widespread, it is not hegemonic as there are many Hindus who do not subscribe to it. Rejecting the charge of Hindu communalism, the apologists of Hindutva will present communal conflicts as 'an unintended by-product of Hindu national self-assertion that results from adverse reactions from minority communities and from the Indian state'.[39] In most communal riots in contemporary India, Muslims are overwhelmingly victimized in terms of loss of life, dignity, and livelihood. Yet, this screaming fact is silenced by blaming the victims – the loss is sad, but 'they' (Muslims) asked for it! Why did they start the riots? Why do they support Pakistan? Why are they terrorists and criminals? Why do they create problems and strife everywhere in the world? Why cannot they be like us? – these questions rid many Hindus of their guilt consciousness and leave intact the self-image of the enlightened tolerant Hindu. Anti-Muslim riots in Gujarat in 2002 illustrate well this 'blame the victim' ideology and the role the imagining of 'The Muslim' as a danger to the security of Hindu body plays in making sense of this kind of violence.

Visiting a site of communal violence: Gujarat 2002

The anti-Muslim violence in Gujarat in 2002 was masked as 'inevitable' and 'understandable' acts to secure the Hindu Self. The (meta)discourse of security offered the forces of Hindutva a tool to legitimize violence as non-violence, killers as defenders, rape as understandable lust and death as non-death. I do not go into details of the violence and explanations of it here[40] but propose one of the ways in which we can make sense of the complicity of a significant number of Hindus in this violence, borrowing the analysis from various reports mentioned above.

During February 2002, the Vishwa Hindu Parishad (VHP), one of the constituents of the Sangh Parivar,[41] was carrying on with its agitation over the building of a temple in Ayodhya.[42] After some altercation, one coach of the Sabarmati Express, a train returning from Ayodhya and carrying many Hindu *kar sevaks* (activists), was burnt at the Godhra station in Gujarat on 26 February, killing fifty-eight people. What followed for the next couple of months was massive communal violence in which most of the victims were Muslims. Though Hindutva forces painted this anti-Muslim violence, in which around a thousand people were killed, as a reaction to Godhra, documented evidence points to four crucial features of this violence which challenge the 'riots-as-post-Godhra-reaction' thesis. First, there was active state complicity – through police inaction[43]; frequent police participation in anti-Muslim violence; hate speeches by members of the state government and the BJP; active participation of local and state leaders in fomenting violence; the availability of lists of Muslim establishments (data privy to the government) to the Hindu mobs. Second, there was a conscious and well-orchestrated preplanning for communal violence through activities of various Hindutva organizations. Third, organizations such as VHP used the train incident as an excuse to 'teach Muslims a lesson' through recourse to vicious brutality. Fourth, the ruling party BJP used this to buttress its political position – a strategy that succeeded with the BJP coming to power with a greater majority in a snap election. In a few months' time, the violence subsided but the hatred and its legacy remain as the struggle for rebuilding lives and securing justice continues.

What makes the spectacle of anti-Muslim violence in Gujarat 2002 extraordinary is its banality and its 'participative' nature. Class, gender, age and caste were no barrier, either for the willing participants or for the unwilling victims. It is not sufficient to explain this phenomenon in instrumental terms alone. While interests did play an important role (for instance, looting, grabbing of land, occupying houses, settling scores), it was not the sole determining factor. For the majority who did not benefit in instrumental terms but still accepted Hindutva versions of the violence and voted to re-elect the BJP in Assembly polls, it was the imagined subjectivity of the victims (dangerous, fanatic, violent and hence to be blamed for provoking Hindus) that was the important factor. It is these dehumanized representations of the Other as a danger that offer us a good handle to understand the normalization of abnormal violence and the construction of a secure Hindu identity through the humiliation and extermination of other identities.

The approving statements of a Hindu man (a non-participant middle-class professional man), quoted by Cohn, reflect a sentiment that is widespread (both in the real and the virtual world)[44]:

> Muslim boys, even married ones, try to have friendships with Hindu girls. I tell you, most Muslim guys are very good looking, and Hindu girls are very innocent – once they give you their heart, it's easily broken ... I personally feel they're spoiling the lives of these Hindu girls. Our blood gets hot ... It's time that the Hindus fight violence with violence.[45]

The need to secure the Hindu female body against the danger of 'The Muslim' was therefore seen as one of the rationales for violence against Muslims.[46] Gujarat 2002 was a lesson in masculinization showing, through the defeat and humiliation of Muslim men, who the 'real men' are. The slogan 'Jis Hinduon ka khoon na khola, woh Hindu nahin, woh hijra hain' (Those Hindus whose blood does not boil, are not Hindus, they are eunuchs), chanted by the student wing of BJP at a premier university in Delhi during a post-Godhra procession,[47] illustrates this obsession with manhood. Various forms of display of violent sexuality were seen emphasizing Hindu manhood as the violent protector of Hindus revealing the impotency of 'The Muslim'. The reaction of Praveen Togadia, a leader of the VHP, in the aftermath of Godhra is significant: 'Hindu Society will avenge the Godhra killings. Muslims should accept the fact that Hindus are not wearing bangles. We will respond vigorously to all such incidents.'[48] Pamphlets exhorting Hindu men not to feel guilty about raping Muslim women; regional Gujarati newspapers sensationalizing false stories about Hindu girls being raped; Hindutva ideologues hammering on about the historic rape of Hindu women and nation at the hands of Muslims; distribution of bangles (an ornamental marker of femininity) to Hindu men who did not participate; punishing (through killing, boycott and hate campaigns) of Hindu men and women who were seen as helping Muslims – all these show that the macabre display of 'tolerance', 'passion', and 'reaction' (these were the self-serving terms used by various proponents of Hindutva to characterize the anti-Muslim violence) was anything but spontaneous.[49] It shows the construction of a particular form of masculinity through acts of violence – a masculinity that declares itself the protector of the security of Hindu bodies as well as the Hindu body politic.

A majority of the people in the affected areas of Gujarat did not participate directly in violence. However, neither was there any strong protest against the violence. Many nongovernmental organizations and citizens groups did not speak out in strong terms condemning the violence. 'All sides should calm down' is seen as implying that no one is responsible. The silent majority's inaction in Gujarat 2002 was an action loaded in favour of those perpetrating anti-Muslim violence. The BJP state leadership, which was clearly identified as complicit with the Gujarat 2002 killing machinery, was confident of gaining electorally after the riots, and the fact that this confidence paid off is an indictment of the silent majority. This electoral victory in the State Assembly elections of December 2002, the best performance ever by BJP on its own in any state in India, challenged most factors that are seen as important in the electoral democracy in India (e.g., anti-incumbency factor, lack of development, and strength of the opposition) and showed that violence against Muslims paid off. This cannot be explained by the instrumental interests of the Hindu majority alone but by the lack of compassion for the Muslim victims. There was a curious reversal of responsibility as many Hindus blamed Muslims for the violence and saw themselves as the victims whose security was threatened by 'The Muslim'.

Conclusion: Do security narratives kill?

The chapter answers in the affirmative. Security is not a response to a pre-existing danger but is constitutive of it. Security is in a sense story-telling with a familiar plot – there is an enemy, there are threats from the enemy, there is a defender, there are victims that need to be defended and there is a constant struggle between the good (the defender) and the bad (the enemy); surveillance and violence are integral to this struggle. This constitution of danger and insecurity in the narratives of security is thus productive of violence. Security often masks violence in the name of counter-violence, killing in the name of protection. As the case of Hindutva in India illustrates, violence against minorities is normalized in the name of personal, communal, national and even international security. The will to secure the Self has as its corollary the will to insecure the Other, the desire to control and use violence. An engaged scholarship that recognizes the violence of security is a step in the direction of interrogating the theory and praxis of security that underpins the violent world we live in today.

Notes

1   Originally published as 'Violence of Security: Hindutva in India', in *The Roundtable: Journal of Commonwealth Affairs*, Vol. 94, No. 379 (2005), pp. 201–213. Only minor revisions have been made. Reprinted by permission of Routledge, Taylor & Francis Ltd, http://www.informaworld.com.
2   The Hindu Right in India is seen as subscribing to Hindu nationalism (Hindutva). While the main political party espousing this is the BJP, there are various other political and cultural organizations and movements including the RSS (Rashtriya Swayamsevak Sangh), VHP, Bajrang Dal, Durga Vahini and so on, that are together

seen as belonging to the Sangh Parivar (the Sangh family, where the Sangh, i.e. the RSS, is seen as the parent organization).
3   Dibyesh Anand, *Hindu Nationalism in India and Politics of Fear*, New York: Palgrave Macmillan, 2011.
4   India has a federal setup and Gujarat is a state in western India. In 2002, the ruling party in Gujarat was the BJP under the Chief Ministership of Narendra Modi. As anti-Muslim riots spread through Gujarat in the first half of 2002, the national media reported of clear complicity of Modi administration in the violence. Yet the federal government at that time, consisting of the BJP in a coalition, ignored and downplayed the severity of riots. After violence abated with more than two thousand Muslims killed and tens of thousands of people (mostly Muslim but quite a few Hindus too) displaced, BJP in Gujarat was confident of gaining electorally and called for an early election for the State Assembly. In this chapter, I am primarily interested in why such collective communal violence against minorities pays electorally. Why would Hindus who would not otherwise vote for BJP in the election, go out and vote for it even though the majority of the victims of violence are Muslims?
5   Rajeev Bhargava, ed., *Secularism and Its Critics*, New Delhi: Oxford University Press, 1998.
6   Christopher Jaffrelot, *The Hindu Nationalist Movement: 1925 to the 1990s*, New Delhi: Penguin, 1999; Amalendu Misra, *Identity and Religion: Foundations of Anti-Islamism in India*, New Delhi: Sage, 2004; John Zavos, *The Emergence of Hindu Nationalism in India*, New Delhi: Oxford University Press, 2000.
7   Thomas Blom Hansen, *The Saffron Wave: Democracy and Hindu Nationalism in Modern India*, Princeton: Princeton University Press, 1999, p. 4.
8   M. G. Chitkara, *Hindutva Parivar*, New Delhi: APH Publishing Corporation, 2003; G. S. Hingle, *Hindutva Reawakened*, New Delhi: Vikash Publishing, 1999; Rashtriya Swayamsevak Sangh, 'Mission & Vision' (2003), http://www.rss.org/New_RSS/Mission_Vision/Why_RSS.jsp [accessed 10 November 2004].
9   'Hindus! Where Will You Go Now?', n.d., *Sword of Truth*, http://www.swordoftruth.com/swordoftruth/archives/oldarchives/hindus.html [accessed 15 January 2004].
10 A. G. Noorani, *Savarkar and Hindutva*, New Delhi: Leftword, 2002.
11 'Muslims Don't Want to Live in Harmony, Says Vajpayee', *Rediff.Com*, 12 April 2002, http://www.rediff.com/news/2002/apr/12bhatt.htm [accessed 30 October 2004].
12 It would be simplistic to see this shift solely in terms of rise of Hindu nationalism. The changing global environment – the emergence of the United States as the sole superpower, dissipating of nonalignment movement, neoliberal globalization as the dominant regime – has led to liberalization, privatization and marketization. The establishment of neo-liberal orthodoxy in India has been an important part of this shift to the Right. See Aijaz Ahmad, *On Communalism and Globalization: Offensives of the Far Right*, New Delhi: Three Essays Collective, 2004.
13 For various intellectual positions see: Tapan Basu, Pradip Datta, Sumit Sarkar, Tanika Sarkar, and Sambuddha Sen, *Khaki Shorts, Saffron Flags*, New Delhi: Orient Longman, 1993. Paul Brass, *The Production of Hindu-Muslim Violence in Contemporary India*, New Delhi: Oxford University Press, 2003. Paul Brass and Achin Vanaik, eds., *Competing Nationalism in South Asia*, New Delhi: Orient Longman, 2002. Veena Das, 'Our Work to Cry: Your Work to Listen', in Veena Das, ed., *Mirrors of Violence*, New Delhi: Oxford University Press, 1990. Hansen, *The Saffron Wave*.

Samuel P. Huntington, 'The Clash of Civilization', *Foreign Affairs*, Vol. 72, No. 3 (1993), pp. 22–49, http://www.alamut.com/subj/economics/misc/clash.html [accessed 5 January 2005]. Jaffrelot, *The Hindu Nationalist Movement*. Sudhir Kakar, *The Colors of Violence: Cultural Identities, Religion, and Conflict*, Chicago: University of Chicago Press, 1996. Ashis Nandy, 'The Politics of Secularism and the Recovery of Religious Tolerance', *Alternatives*, Vol. 13, No. 2 (1988), pp. 177–194. Gyanendra Pandey, 'The Colonial Construction of "Communalism": British Writings on Banaras in the Nineteenth Century', in Veena Das, ed., *Mirrors of Violence*, New Delhi: Oxford University Press, 1990. Sumit Sarkar, *Beyond Nationalist Frames: Relocating Postmodernism, Hindutva, History*, New Delhi: Permanent Black, 2002. Ashutosh Varshney, *Ethnic Conflict and Civic Life: Hindus and Muslims in India*, New Haven: Yale University Press, 2002.
14 Pandey, 'The Colonial Construction'.
15 Anand Patwardhan, *Father, Son and Holy War*, Directed and Produced by Anand Patwardhan, India (1994), DVD.
16 David Campbell, *Writing Security: United States Foreign Policy and the Politics of Identity*, revised edn., Minneapolis: University of Minnesota Press, 1998; Keith Krause and Michael Williams, eds., *Critical Security Studies*, Boulder: Lynne Rienner, 1997; Ronnie D. Lipschutz, *On Security*, New York: Columbia University Press, 1995; Jutta Weldes, Mark Laffey, Hugh Gusterson, and Raymond Duvall, eds., *Cultures of Insecurity: States, Communities, and the Production of Danger*, Minneapolis: University of Minnesota Press, 1999.
17 Campbell, *Writing Security*; Michael Dillon, *Politics of Security: Towards a Political Philosophy of Continental Thought*, London: Routledge, 1996.
18 Tomlinson in Weldes, et al., *Cultures of Insecurity*.
19 Michel Foucault, *Discipline and Punish: The Birth of the Prison*, Alan Sheridan (trans.), London: Penguin, 1977; Michel Foucault, *Madness and Civilization: A History of Insanity in the Age of Reason*, London: Vintage, 1988.
20 Gyandendra Pandey, ed., *Hindus and Others: The Question of Identity in India Today*, New Delhi: Viking, 1993, p. 263.
21 The sample is distilled from anecdotal evidence, discussions with those with Hindu chauvinist leanings, academic literature on the Hindutva, and most importantly, from pro-Hindutva websites including http://www.hinduunity.org, http://www.hindutva.org, http://www.freeindia.org, http://www.organiser.org, http://www.swordoftruth.com.
22 Vinayak Damodar Savarkar, *Hindutva*, 7th ed., Mumbai: Pandit Bakhle, 1999, p. 26.
23 Kakar, *The Colors of Violence*, p. 107.
24 Brass, *The Production of Hindu-Muslim Violence*; Pradip Kumar Datta, '"Dying Hindus": Production of Hindu Communal Common Sense in Early 20th Century Bengal', *Economic and Political Weekly*, 19 June 1993, pp. 1305–1319; Kumari Jayawardena and Malathi De Alwis, eds., *Embodied Violence: Communalising Women's Sexuality in South Asia*, London: Zed, 1998; Kakar, 'The Colors of Violence', in David Ludden, ed., *Making India Hindu: Religion, Community, and the Politics of Democracy in India*, New Delhi: Oxford University Press, 1996; Pandey, *Hindus and Others*; Tanika Sarkar and Urvashi Butalia, eds., *Women and Right-Wing Movements: Indian Experiences*, London: Zed, 1995.
25 Reina Lewis, *Gendering Orientalism: Race, Feminity and Representation*, London: Routledge, 1996; Rana Kabbani, *Imperial Fictions: Europe's Myths of Orient*, London:

Pandora, 1986; Edward Said, *Orientalism: Western Conceptions of the Orient*, New York: Penguin, 1978.
26 See Note 12.
27 Chitkara, *Hindutva Parivar*, pp. 38, xi–xii.
28 Omar Khalidi, *Khaki and the Ethnic Violence in India*, New Delhi: Three Essays Collective, 2003.
29 Koenraad Elst, *The Demographic Seige*, Delhi: Voice of India, 1997, http://www.bharatvani.org/books/demogislam/part1.html [accessed 12 January 2011].
30 John Dayal, 'Indian Census: After Xenophobia, the Report Card of the Communities', *Countercurrents*, 12 December 2004, http://www.countercurrents.org/comm-dayal120904.htm [accessed 1 May 2010].
31 T. K. Rajalakshmi, 'The Population Bogey', *Frontline*, Vol. 21, No. 20 (2004), http://www.frontlineonnet.com/fl2120/stories/20041008006101600.htm [accessed 15 February 2005].
32 Rajmohan Gandhi, 'Blah, Blah, blood', *The Hindustan Times*, 4 July 2003, http://www.countercurrents.org/comm-gandhi040703.htm [accessed 10 February 2005].
33 Datta, 'Dying Hindus'.
34 Charu Gupta, *Sexuality, Obscenity, Community: Women, Muslims, and the Hindu Public in Colonial India*, Delhi: Permanent Black, 2001.
35 In this chapter I do not examine two issues that are related to the questions about Hindutva and masculinity. One is the Hindutva image of women in general and Muslim women in particular. The second is the role of Hindu women in Hindutva organizations and during communal riots. For various perspectives see: Paola Bacchetta, *Gender in the Hindu Nation: RSS Women as Ideologues*, New Delhi: Women Unlimited, 2004. Jayawardena and De Alwis, *Embodied Violence*.
   Urvashi Butalia, 'Muslims and Hindus, Men and Women: Communal Stereotypes and the Partition of India', in Tanika Sarkar and Urvashi Butalia, eds., *Women and Right-Wing Movements: Indian Experiences*, London: Zed, 1995.
36 Gupta, *Sexuality, Obscenity, Community*.
37 Bacchetta, *Gender in the Hindu Nation*, p. 101.
38 Butalia, 'Muslims and Hindus, Men and Women', p. 79.
39 David Ludden, ed., 'Introduction. Ayodhya: A Window on the World', in *Making India Hindu: Religion, Community, and the Politics of Democracy in India*, New Delhi: Oxford University Press, 1996, p. 16.
40 See the following sources for more details: 'Genocide Gujarat 2002', *Communalism Combat*, Vol. 8, No. 76 (2002), http://www.sabrang.com/cc/archive/2002/marapril/index.html [accessed 10 January 2005]; Javed Anand and Teesta Setalvad, eds., *Lessons from Gujarat*, Mumbai: Vikas Adhyayan Kendra, 2003; Harsh Mander, *Cry, the Beloved Country: Reflections on the Gujarat Massacre*, 2002, http://www.sabrang.com/gujarat/statement/nv2.htm [accessed 10 November 2004]; Threatened Existence: A Feminist Analysis of the Genocide in Gujarat, Report by the *International Initiative for Justice (IIJ)* (2003), http://www.onlinevolunteers.org/gujarat/reports/iijg/2003/ [accessed 15 January 2005]; Siddharth Varadarajan, *Gujarat: The Making of a Tragedy*, New Delhi: Penguin, 2002.
41 See Note 1.
42 The Hindutva forces have been agitating over building of a temple at the supposed birthplace of Lord Rama in Ayodhya, a town in North India. This town became infamous in 1992 when Babri Mosque (which allegedly was built by the Mughal ruler

Babur in sixteenth century over a Hindu temple) was demolished. The demolition was followed by serious anti-Muslim riots in various parts of India. The Ram Janmabhoomi campaign to build a temple at the site of the demolished mosque has been deployed by Hindutva forces, especially the VHP, in an attempt to mobilize Hindus. At the start of 2002 VHP had restarted the campaign despite the warnings that this would incite communal hatred. For analyses of the movement, see: Paul Brass, *Theft of an Idol: Text and Context in the Representation of Collective Violence*, Princeton: Princeton University Press, 1997. Ludden, *Making India Hindu*. Pandey, *Hindus and Others*.

43 Human Rights Watch, 'We Have No Orders to Save You', Vol. 14, No. 3 (April 2002), http://www.hrw.org/reports/2002/india/ [accessed 14 December 2004].
44 See Note 23.
45 Martin R. Cohn, 'India's "Lab" for Divisive Politics', *Toronto Star*, 26 October 2003, http://stopfundinghate.org/resources/news/102603TorontoStar.htm [accessed 12 February 2011].
46 For a detailed treatment, see Report by the *International Initiative for Justice (IIJ)* (2003).
47 Tanika Sarkar, 'Semiotics of Terror: Muslim Children and Women in Hindu Rashtra', *Economic and Political Weekly*, Vol. 37, No. 28 (2002), pp. 2872–2876.
48 An Independent Fact Finding Mission, 2002.
49 For detailed reports, see 'Genocide Gujarat 2002'.

7

Memories of Victimhood in Serbia and Croatia from the 1980s to the Disintegration of Yugoslavia

Slobodan G. Markovich

This chapter analyses the development of victimhood narratives in Serbia and Croatia in the 1980s and 1990s by examining historical experiences and narratives developed by influential intellectuals. It explores state-sponsored narratives and popular narratives among Serbs and Croats in royal Yugoslavia (1918–1941), the tragic experience of the Second World War and the subsequent development of communist myths. The development of victimhood narratives among Serbs and Croats is followed both in Yugoslavia and in émigré circles. The contributions and role of three disenchanted Yugoslav Communists is also analysed: Vladimir Dedijer and Dobrica Cosic in Serbia and Franjo Tudjman in Croatia. Victimhood narratives are seen as concomitant with the vacuum of values that followed the crisis of communism in Yugoslavia in the 1980s.

Although narratives of oppression appeared only a few years after the first Yugoslavia was created in 1918, they reached their climax in the territory of ex-Yugoslavia in the 1980s and 1990s. By the 1980s, these narratives were noticeable among all Yugoslav nations but were most widespread among Serbs and Croats. By the 1990s, they also strongly influenced Bosnian Muslims. Narratives of victimhood and genocide against Serbs were strengthened by the Serbian elite, who highlighted the traumatic experiences of the First and Second World Wars. In particular, they focused on the victims of Jasenovac concentration camp, run by the Ustasha Nazi regime of the Independent State of Croatia during the Second World War. Croatian narratives, in contrast, highlighted the oppression of Croats by the Serbian bourgeoisie in the first Yugoslavia (1918–1941) and similar oppression by Serbs in the second Yugoslavia. Parallel narratives developed among Croatian émigré circles focused on the Bleiburg massacre, an event that took place at the very end of the Second World War in which Yugoslav Partisans carried out retaliation against Croats.

These narratives have been the subject of several studies. The best documented is a monograph by David Bruce MacDonald entitled *Balkan Holocausts? Serbian and Croatian Victim-Centred Propaganda and the War in Yugoslavia*.[1] MacDonald demonstrated a thorough knowledge of opposing narratives, collected a substantial amount of data and provided far-reaching insights. Yet, his lack of factual knowledge of Yugoslav history and his inability to read texts in Serbo-Croat made it difficult for him to adequately frame events in their historical context or to distinguish between relevant and scarcely known participants in the debate. Another valuable insight came from Jasna Dragović-Soso, who provided a detailed and very-well researched intellectual history of Serbia and Yugoslavia in the 1980s. She dedicated a special chapter to 'the theme of genocide' which is of direct relevance to this chapter.[2]

In what follows, I will try to analyse two narratives of victimhood centred on Jasenovac and Bleiburg and put them into the context of the decaying Yugoslav communist state. I will also attempt to analyse the main protagonists who disseminated these narratives and their motives and will endeavour to trace how different and sometimes opposite narratives overlapped and fused. To properly set narratives within their historical background, I will also attempt to summarize the findings of historians to enable a full understanding of the narratives analysed.

Historical background: War trauma and post-traumatic narratives

To understand narratives that undermined Yugoslavia in the 1980s, one has to go back at least to the First World War, of which Yugoslavia was one result. The experience of the First World War ushered in a new era in European history (1914–1945) which the British historian Eric Hobsbawm called 'the age of catastrophe'. The British and the French remember it as 'The Great War', with experiences more traumatic for their populations than the Second World War. In The Great War, half a million British men under the age of thirty were killed; losses were notably high among the upper classes.[3] Although the German Empire and Russia had the highest casualties in absolute figures, Serbia had the highest proportional losses of all belligerents. No other country mobilized such a high percentage of its male population. Almost the entire male population between eighteen and fifty-five was drafted into forces totalling 822,000 men, of whom close to half were killed in the course of the war. Including civilian causalities, the dead approach one million, or a quarter of the total population.

Aldcroft and Morewood concluded that, 'in relative terms human losses in most other countries pale into insignificance'.[4] The bulk of victims were civilians who died as a consequence of the typhus epidemic of 1915. Some froze or starved to death during the Albanian campaign in the autumn and winter of 1915/1916. Many died of hunger and exhaustion during the Austro-German occupation, and some were killed in retaliations carried out by the occupying forces. As the American historian John Lampe put it: 'One way or another, half of Serbia's male population between the ages of eighteen and fifty-five had perished.'[5] The Albanian campaign later turned into an epic narrative and an important part of a foundation myth of the Kingdom of Yugoslavia. The number of Serbs killed in the First World War has never been the subject of discussion, and most estimates of the total number of Serbian dead are within the range of 1–1.25 million.⁶ The level of suffering was such that it was unnecessary to construct state-sponsored narratives of victimhood. Mere personal memories and reminiscences were enough to keep The Great War in popular memory as a period of utmost Serbian suffering.

In addition to the great losses, another difficult memory remained in Serbia. The bulk of the army, the majority of students and almost the whole political elite spent the last three years of war in a sort of exile in the Hellenic Kingdom, and in areas controlled by Britain and France. This traumatic experience strengthened aspirations among Serbian elites for the creation of a large and strong state of Yugoslavia to guarantee that a similar experience could not be repeated in the future.

After the First World War, a group of new states were brought into being by the Treaties of Versailles. They were the result of the spirit of that age expressed in the fourteen points advocating national self-determination drafted by American President Woodrow Wilson in January 1918. Among the new states were Czechoslovakia and the Kingdom of Serbs, Croats and Slovenes (later called Yugoslavia). These two countries were notable for their lack of ethnic majorities, since Czechs in Czechoslovakia amounted to 46 per cent of the total population and Serbs in the new kingdom represented just 39–40 per cent (44 per cent if we include Macedonians, whose distinct ethnic identity had not yet been clearly formed). Additionally, 24 per cent of the population of Yugoslavia in 1921 were Croats, 8.5 per cent Slovenes and 5.4 per cent Bosnian Muslims (claimed by both Serbs and Croats). Altogether 'Yugoslavs' (various South Slavs) constituted some 83 per cent of the total population. In both Yugoslavia and Czechoslovakia, common Slavic traditions were emphasized. In the Yugoslav version, this was a South-Slavic tradition from which Bulgarians were excluded (even though in the literal sense, 'Yugoslav' (South Slav) would include Bulgarians). The official position was that Yugoslavia was comprised of three tribes and one nation or 'three named people', a phrase used as early as 1916 by the Serbian Regent and, later, Yugoslav King Alexander.⁷ Yet, it meant that non-Slavs, (Germans, Hungarians, Albanians, Turks, and Italians) who comprised at least one eighth of the total population, were excluded from the official definition of the new state. The new ideology was most clearly manifested in the country's coat of arms, which was a combination of historical Serbian and Croatian coats of arms and a design that symbolized Slovenes. The anthem also consisted of four parts, of which the first and the last were taken from the Serbian anthem, *God of Justice*, the second from the Croatian anthem, *Our Beloved*, and the third from a Slovene song.

It proved more than difficult to connect 'Yugoslavs' into a unifying history. Two historical narratives, the Serbian and Croatian, clashed just months after the establishment of the new Kingdom in December 1918. There was a highly symbolic Croatian narrative insisting on the historical rights and national autonomy of the Croats, with long-held suspicion of political centres outside Croatia, and there was a narrative of victimhood among the Serbs, insisting that Serbians martyrs had served as the cornerstone for the future state.

The inability of Serbian political elites to accommodate the Croatian narrative provoked mutual national antagonism. The traumatic experience of the First World

War strengthened centralist tendencies in Serbia, and once the memory of Serbian victims had solidified, they entered the realm of the sacred. Any Croatian comment on Serbian victims was certain to provoke Serbian dissatisfaction and even revulsion. As a result, national fervour began which ended in the tragic murder of two deputies in the Parliament of Yugoslavia by a Serbian deputy from Montenegro in the building of the Kingdom's Assembly on the 20 June 1928. The most popular Croatian politician, Stjepan Radic, died as a result of his wounds several weeks later (in August), and the country was riled by nationalist turmoil. Conditions were such that even such an outstanding proponent of the unified state as King Alexander (nicknamed 'the Unifier' for a short time in 1928) considered letting Croatia secede.

Thus, two opposing narratives of Yugoslavia led to the first bitter incident in mutual relations. Needless to say, after his death, Radic was sanctified as a national martyr, while the general rise of right-wing extremism in Europe in the 1930s strengthened authoritarian tendencies throughout Yugoslavia. In the end, a new Serbian ruler, Prince Paul had to ascend the throne and grant substantial autonomy to Croatia in 1939. But this compromise came too late.

Although there was no consistent centrally planned cultural policy in the Kingdom of Yugoslavia, the state's very name was a sort of narrative. Originally it was called the Kingdom of Serbs, Croats and Slovenes, and the change of name in 1929 signalled increased efforts to fuse the three national identities into a single Yugoslav one. The problem was that the three separate national identities already existed, and the Croatian identity, as a central antagonist to the state-sponsored Yugoslav identity, was actually strengthened in Royalist Yugoslavia, particularly after the murder of Stjepan Radic. Officially it was claimed in Yugoslavia that there were three tribes that had united in 1918 into one nation. The main cultural protagonist of this new identity was Ivan Mestrovic, an internationally renowned Croatian sculptor. Like Alfonse Mucha

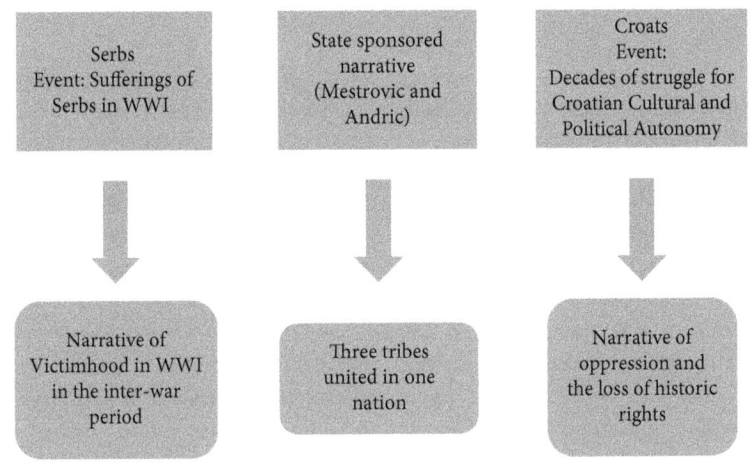

Serbs Event: Sufferings of Serbs in WWI	State sponsored narrative (Mestrovic and Andric)	Croats Event: Decades of struggle for Croatian Cultural and Political Autonomy
↓	↓	↓
Narrative of Victimhood in WWI in the inter-war period	Three tribes united in one nation	Narrative of oppression and the loss of historic rights

Figure 7.1 Kingdom of Serbs, Croats and Slovenes (1919–1929), Kingdom of Yugoslavia (1929–1941/1945)

of Czechoslovakia, Mestrovic drew his inspiration from a distant Slavic past that was seen as common to all three nations and from key events in national narratives of opposition to foreign domination, such as the Kosovo Battle. Additionally, a group of very influential Serbian and Croatian historians such as Vladimir Corovic, Stanoje Stanojevic, Viktor Novak and Ferdo Sisic and a well-known writer, Ivo Andric also disseminated Yugoslavism. Yet, their efforts proved insufficient.[8]

In inter-war Yugoslavia, Serbs clearly dominated administrative structures and the army. For example, in thirty-nine inter-war governments, Serbs occupied the office of prime minister thirty-eight times and Croats, not once. At the same time, 80 per cent of staff officers were Serbs by 1927, and the police force was 60 per cent Serbian. This domination was particularly disproportional in Vojvodina and Bosnia, both of which mainstream Serbian and Croatian societies viewed as their own. Slovenia was an exception, for the administration there was controlled by Slovenes. This explains both the dedication of Slovene elites to Yugoslavia and the increasing dissatisfaction of Croatian elites with the country. Despite the fact that Croatian symbols were fully included in the new state's symbolism; that Croats enjoyed a proportional representation in the Assembly; and that the Croatian language and Latin script were officially used, Croatian expectations were not met. Very soon, and particularly after 1928, mainstream Croatian narratives viewed Yugoslavia as a dungeon of the Croatian people.

For subsequent communist narratives on Royalist Yugoslavia, two features are of utmost importance. The first is that after an early success in elections of the Communist Party of Yugoslavia in 1920, the party was banned in December 1920. When the Yugoslav Minister of the Interior was killed the next year by a communist assassinator, the state began to persecute the Communist Party. Since the police force was mostly Serbian, Yugoslav Communists viewed Royalist Yugoslavia very negatively and saw the Serbian bourgeoisie as the primary culprit in their oppression. For the communist narrative, it was also significant that King Alexander allowed a large number of White Russian refugees to settle in Yugoslavia, sponsored their associations and harboured their army general staff in Yugoslavia.

The tragic burden of the Second World War

When troops of the Third Reich occupied the Kingdom of Yugoslavia in 1941, the country was already exhausted by inter-ethnic strife. Nazi Germany and Fascist Italy took advantage of this to further fuel national antagonisms by creating an 'Independent State of Croatia' (NDH) out of Croatia and Slavonia (including Srem), Dalmatia and Bosnia and Herzegovina. The Ustasha Party, the most extreme of the Croatian political scene, was placed at the head of the new state. What followed was an effort to create, through genocide, an ethnically pure state, cleansed of Serbs, Jews and Roma. Some recent estimates suggest that between 370,000 and 410,000 Serbs were killed in the NDH, along with around 75 per cent of the Jewish population.[9] However, mainstream publications in Serbia put the number of Serbs killed in the

NDH as high as one million. The truth, however, is that no one has ever been able to accurately estimate the number of Serbs or other Yugoslavs killed during the Second World War. Even organizations dealing with the Holocaust have come to contradictory estimates on how many Serbs were killed in NDH. This only fuelled a pamphlet war of competing narratives in émigré circles. The symbolic focal point of these debates became the number of victims killed in the Ustasha run concentration camp of Jasenovac.

In Serbia, additionally, there were two resistance movements, the communist movement under Soviet control, known as the Partisans and the Yugoslav Home Army, based mostly on traditional Serbian identity, and to a lesser extent on Yugoslav ideology. Popularly, but incorrectly known as Chetniks, this latter was led by the royalist Colonel Dragoljub Mihailovich. At the end of 1941, a civil war began between these two movements, ending with the victory of the Communists in the second half of 1944. A bloody revenge followed against ideological enemies, first affecting Montenegro and Serbia, and, in May 1945, Croatia and Slovenia. Many members of the political, cultural and economic elite were victims of this terror, and tens of thousands of Croatian and Serbian political refugees left the country. Additionally, many Serbian officers decided not to return to Communist Yugoslavia but remained in Western Europe. Thus, two great groups of émigrés were created: a Croatian group, notably in the countries that had sympathized with Nazi Germany such as Argentina and Chile, but also in Germany, and a Serbian group, consisting of both pro-Mihailovich and collaborationist forces in Anglo-Saxon countries, notably in Britain, the United States and Australia.

The two terrors: the nationalist one, conducted by Ustashe in Croatia, and the Communist one, conducted against ideological enemies throughout Yugoslavia, left deep scars and bitter memories. Additionally, acts of terror committed by local Chetnik commanders against Bosnian Muslims in Eastern Bosnia left bitter memories in Bosnia. The two émigré communities focused on different sets of events. Serbian émigrés focused on both Ustasha massacres of Serbs and communist retaliation, while Croatian émigrés mostly focused on massacres committed by Communists at the end of the Second World War. Two opposing narratives were created, and émigré propaganda based all their subsequent efforts on them. For Croats, the focal point became the Bleiburg massacre, while for Serbs the central point has remained Jasenovac, and to a much lesser extent the red terror of 1944/1945.

Communist myths

The Communist Party of Yugoslavia, which took over the country at the end of the war, developed its own narratives based on a series of myths. Although the Communist Party never went so far as to proclaim its own calendar, as did Fascist Italy, nonetheless, the year 1941 and the beginning of the Communist uprising became year zero. A new ideology was consecrated, and for this purpose five myths were employed and fully developed by the mid-1950s.

1. The myth of merciful revolution in which the majority of Yugoslavia's inhabitants participated and in which no mention of terror at the end of the war could be made, except in very few, carefully supervised publications.
2. The myth of the great personal role of the Yugoslav dictator, Josip Broz Tito in global history, particularly in the non-Aligned world, accompanied by his personality cult.
3. The myth of the outstanding geo-strategic position of Yugoslavia as a bridge between East and West.
4. The myth of the invincible Yugoslav Army.
5. The myth of 'brotherhood and unity', which included the postulation that war crimes were committed by bourgeois elements of all nations and that all national bourgeoisies were to be blamed equally.

All five myths were essentially Yugoslav and comprised the essence of Communist Yugoslavism, an attempt to create a new Yugoslav socialist nation. This attempt had clearly failed by the late 60s, when Croatian intellectuals refused to abandon their own name in a common language that was called Serbo-Croatian. Moreover, with the creation of a self-governing Kosovo and the Albanian political elite that began ruling it in the sixties, even the state's pan-Slavic anthem entitled 'Oh, Slavs' ceased to reflect reality, since one-eighth of the federation was neither populated nor ruled by Slavs. However, two central institutions of the communist dictatorship in Yugoslavia, the Communist Party and the Yugoslav People's Army, continued to exploit these myths. While the first three myths were specifically developed by Yugoslav Communists, the last two were only variations on previous myths of the invincible Serbian Army and one nation consisting of three tribes. The Communist Party insisted that atrocities during the war had been committed by the bourgeoisie of all nations. The Party saw inter-war Yugoslavia along Comintern lines as a dungeon of nationalities where the jail keeper was the Serbian bourgeoisie.

Tito's personality cult was one of the key Communist narratives, together with claims that the Yugoslav political system known as workers' self-management was unique and the most progressive in the world. Similar claims were made by all other communist countries that broke up with the Soviet Union, including Albania and China. Yet, Yugoslavia's openness towards the West led to the acceptance of this narrative by some leading leftists in the West. Moreover, Tito's cult was supported even by some Western countries such as Britain. It is important to note that both Tito and the Partisan movement in the Second World War had official biographies from which many episodes that could undermine the 'brotherhood and unity' narrative were excised. For instance, episodes such as Tito's participation in the Austro-Hungarian Army's drive against Serbian troops in 1914 or contacts with Germans during the Second World War were completely omitted.

These Yugoslav narratives were demolished between the late 1960s and mid-1980s, when two national movements re-emerged (in Croatia and in Kosovo). By the mid-eighties, Serbian nationalism re-emerged as well. This was exactly when narratives on genocide and victimhood started to gain momentum. The most difficult communist legacy in this field, one that has been felt ever since, is the tabooing of some of the most sensitive issues, including the question of genocide against Serbs, Jews and Roma in the NDH and the massacres of Croatian and other troops at the end of the Second World War. Banned in Communist Yugoslavia, narratives about these episodes were radicalized in émigré circles and through personal memories found ways to be expressed even in Communist Yugoslavia.

Debating the Jasenovac concentration camp

In Communist Yugoslavia, publishing works on the Second World War was permitted only to historians who were party members and demonstrated an inclination toward Marxist interpretations. Although groups of critically oriented historians did exist (particularly in Belgrade, Zagreb, Ljubljana and Sarajevo), they all had to stay out of any debate on the Second World War. Whatever the Communist Party of Yugoslavia (later called the League of Communists) proclaimed to be the official version of history had to be followed by communist historians, who were rewarded for their discipline by huge honoraria for their contributions. Since state commissions had, immediately after the war, established the official war losses of Yugoslavs, all historians dealing with the Second World War were obliged to use these figures.

The figures were, however, not based on serious research. According to testimony, published in 1999 by a retired professor of Notre Dame University, Vladeta Vuckovic, it was he who, in March 1947, while still a BA student in Mathematics, was put in charge fulfilling a request given to the Statistical Bureau of Yugoslavia. A request was made by top party ideologue Edvard Kardelj to prepare a report on Yugoslav war casualties during the Second World War. Vuckovic hastily (within two weeks) calculated total war losses of Yugoslavs at about 1,709,000. Yet, his calculations included not only casualties but also projected demographic losses (including unborn and missing persons). However, Kardelj, soon to become the leading Yugoslav ideologue, presented this estimation some weeks later at a conference in Paris as fact. There, he simply turned demographic losses into victims. Since no party report could be challenged, as soon as comrade Kardelj pronounced that 1.7 million Yugoslavs had been killed, that became the official estimate. Vuckovic claimed that his estimates were published in twelve copies of a confidential brochure for internal use only. Yet none of these copies has been found, and this prompted an ongoing debate on war losses in Yugoslavia in the late 1980s.[10] The debate, however, had by that time already been going on for decades in émigré circles.

The only serious effort in Communist Yugoslavia to establish the correct number of victims ended in failure. In June 1964, the Federal Yugoslav Commission for the Registration of War Victims was formed. The register of victims was carried out in November 1964 but in such a way that the methodology used excluded victims from military formations of defeated forces. The commission found 597,323 victims. No effort was made to collect data on who had done the killing, which in the opinion of leading Belgrade statistician Srdjan Bogosavljević 'reveals something of the motives of the then leadership of Yugoslavia: there was an unwillingness to stir up and bring into the forefront the barely pacified intolerance among nations that had reached its peak during the war'.[11] Actually, the result was worrying for Yugoslav Communists. If the official figure of 1.7 million victims was correct, then that would mean that more than one million people from anti-communist military formations had been killed. If it was not correct, then it would mean that official data on the Second World War could be challenged. In either case, the official interpretation of history would be seriously undermined.

The issue of crimes committed against Serbs in the NDH was raised by a prominent intellectual as early as 1948, when an eminent Croatian historian and professor at Belgrade University, Viktor Novak, published a bulky book in Zagreb entitled *Magnum crimen. Pola vijeka klerikalizma u Hrvatskoj* (Magnum Crimen. Half a Century of Clericalism in Croatia). It dealt in detail with crimes committed by Croatian Catholic priests during the Second World War. Most of the copies of it disappeared soon after. It was republished in Sarajevo in 1960 but could not be published in Belgrade until 1986. The debate was reopened in Serbia in 1985 when a Serbian political émigré, Bogoljub Kochovich, published his book in Serbo-Croat on war losses in Yugoslavia, in which he claimed, based on demographic calculations, that the number of Yugoslavs killed during the Second World War was 1,014,000. In his foreword to the third edition of his book, Kochovich noted:

> On many occasions I have made statements on myths among many so-called nationalists from all of the Yugoslav peoples 'that victims mostly belong to a single nation', or that 'victims were from one nation only'. Speaking on my figures on the actual losses among Serbs and Montenegrins, I have also written the following: 'For many so-called nationalists among the Serbs this will seem a 'scandalously' small figure.'[12]

Some critically oriented intellectuals accepted this figure as a way out of a long-running inflammatory polemic that had the potential to encourage new divisions and conflicts.[13]

Serbian victims in Croatia fall into a completely different category. They found themselves in the midst of the war of narratives in the 1980s and 1990s, and this has continued ever since. Therefore, it is not surprising that Kochovich's calculations have not been generally accepted and discussion continues. Discussion has been further complicated by the fact that many critically oriented historians have decided to stay out of this debate.[14]

In my opinion, there are two major reasons why demographic calculations may not be accepted for the estimation of the number of war victims. The first is that the period between two national censuses that has been used as a basis for the estimation was too long (1931 and 1948). This means that if the birth rate is estimated to be slightly smaller or higher, one will automatically get results differing on a scale of up to a hundred thousand victims (Kochovich himself recognized this fact). Additionally, one cannot positively estimate the number of refugees who left Yugoslavia in 1944–1945. Most importantly, the two censuses were made in two completely different polities. While the first census was organized in the semi-authoritarian Kingdom of Yugoslavia, the latter was organized in a totalitarian polity in which the communist secret police had the right to eliminate any internal enemy. One may realistically assume that with its resources, the Kingdom was not able to list the whole population, especially in rural areas and among inhabitants without permanent addresses. The second census was conducted at the moment when Yugoslav totalitarianism had reached its peak, and only a few could have escaped the census. In 1931, the census listed 13,934,038 inhabitants of the Kingdom of Yugoslavia. If we assume that the first census failed to list only 2 per cent of population, we get 280,000 more people. Had it missed 5 per cent, then the list of missing would include almost 700,000 people. It is for these reasons that demographic calculations can only be taken as opinion, no matter how professional their compiler.[15]

A more sensitive issue is posed by German sources. Some Nazi officials in Croatia complained that Ustasha persecution of Serbs was undermining the overall German policy in South-East Europe, and they compiled reports on Serbian victims in Croatia. For instance, in February 1942, a certain Von Horstenau assessed that, by that point, some 300,000 Serbs had been killed in the NDH, while another official called Neubacher claimed, in April 1944, that 750,000 had been killed. Thus, numbers used by Serbian historians are based on Nazi estimations. Here lies a real political problem. If any Serbian historian supported smaller figures, he would risk being accused of having even less sympathy for Serbian victims than some Nazi officials.

Yet, the problem of methodology has remained. Namely, the only serious way to establish the exact number of victims is to make lists of victims with their names, place and date of their death. Something like this has been done in Kragujevac, where severe German retaliation took place against the local population in October 1941. After two guerrilla movements in Serbia staged separate anti-German uprisings (the Royalists in May, and the Communists in July), an order to suppress the uprisings came from Berlin. On 16 September, Hitler demanded that, in occupied areas, 100 locals should be executed for every German officer or soldier killed, and fifty should be executed for every wounded German. In the period between 1 August and 5 December 1941, German troops killed 11,522 insurgents and executed 21,809 hostages in occupied Serbia.[16] The bloody autumn of 1941 has remained in the memory of the population of Serbia ever since. The most notorious retaliation took place in the central Serbian town of Kragujevac. Communist historians claimed that 7,000 persons were killed in the period 18–21 October 1941. This was based on the testimony of a person who survived execution, Mr. Zivojin Jovanovic. He testified at the Allied Military Court in Nuremberg in July 1947 that around 8,000 were murdered. Communist historians later accepted the figure of 7,000 and for decades it was an untouchable truth, and the Kragujevac massacre became a focal point in communist narratives of the anti-fascist struggle in Serbia. Thus, the Memorial Museum 'October 21' was established in 1953. After decades of carrying out its own research, the museum reached the conclusion that 2,795 hostages had been executed by German forces and that sixty-one persons survived the execution. Serbian and German historians fully agreed on the number of those who were executed in Kragujevac massacre.[17] This episode demonstrates that it is possible to reach mutually agreeable numbers even on a very sensitive issue.

The other good example is very recent. The number of casualties in the Wars for Yugoslav Succession (1991–1999) will soon be known, thanks to the work of three

NGOs from Sarajevo, Belgrade and Zagreb. The original estimation of 200,000–300,000 casualties during the Wars for Yugoslav Succession in Bosnia from 1992 till 1995 was resolved when the Sarajevo Research and Documentation Centre published its findings and established that total number of casualties, including missing persons, is around 97,207.[18] The centre has been able to identify the exact number of persons killed by nationality, region, gender, age and the military unit involved, and it is now very difficult even for nationalists to reject this list, although some have used it selectively.

Similar research could not be done by an independent commission in Communist Yugoslavia on the Second World War victims, since the Communist Party would not allow it. Yet, a commission existed and its findings from 1964 were classified as confidential, as was the case of the file on the Kragujevac massacre, which was only recently disclosed. In the 1990s, when this topic was very much debated, it was impossible to do serious investigation on the topic. Nowadays, too few survivors are left from the Second World War to carry out such research, and both documents and demographic estimates have proven to be relevant, but not sufficient, sources for making estimations. Therefore, one may regretfully say that the opportunity to compile an exact list of those who lost their lives in the Second World War has been missed. Estimations were and have remained estimations only. The absence of exact data in this sensitive field is likely to prolong radical narratives on genocide.

In Communist times, discussion of massacres was a favourite topic in émigré circles. The two principal adversaries of Yugoslav communism were the Serbian and Croatian émigré communities. In contrast to the Croatian post-WWII political emigration, which was more or less unified in defending the legacy of the NDH, the Serbian post-WWII political emigration was, and has remained, deeply divided between the majority of those who supported General Mihailovich (mostly in the United States), and a very vocal minority of those who supported the Serbian fascist movement of Dimitrije Ljotic during the Second World War but remained Yugoslavs and wanted to re-establish pre-war Yugoslavia. Moreover, the Serbian émigré community was hostilely divided between those who supported the Serbian Orthodox Church run from communist Belgrade and those who supported the rival Serbian Orthodox Church independently run from the United States. There were also small groups of pro-Yugoslav emigrants gathered around the journal *Naša reč*, who advocated a new democratic and federal Yugoslavia. Bogoljub Kochovich was an émigré belonging to the latter group.

Discussions of Bleiburg

At the end of the war in May 1945, there was a massive movement of NDH troops trying to escape towards Austria, accompanied by civilians. They continued to fight for six days after the capitulation of Nazi Germany and thus were the last axis army to surrender in Europe, on 15 May 1945. Other anti-Communist troops and Germans also endeavoured to escape Tito's Partisans. British troops handed them over to Yugoslav authorities. The number of Croats who were handed over was estimated by Croatian émigré sources to be in the hundreds of thousands, and various authors have suggested figures between 180,000 (Ivan Babic) and 410,000 people. Most German authors assessed the total number of those who were handed over (a broader group including Slovenes, the Yugoslav Home Army and Montenegrin Chetniks, in addition to Croats) at around 200,000. For their part, Yugoslav Communists acknowledged that between 74,000 (of which 24,000 were civilians) and more than 100,000 persons were encircled in the last days of the war, and the Yugoslav Veterans Association provided a figure implying that about 116,000 Croatian troops were captured along with 20,000 members of various Serbian and Slovene formations.[19] Jozo Tomasevich, who studied this affair for years, came to the following conclusion:

> The fact is that it is absolutely impossible to establish the exact number of Croatian soldiers and civilian refugees who tried to flee to Austria but were forced to surrender to the Partisans.[20]

Tomasevich, however, accepts Zerjavic's estimate that, in addition to 10,000 Serbs and Slovenes, around 60,000 Croats were killed at the end of the war, including 50,000 in Bleiburg and 10,000 at Viktring. In any case, 'the tragedy of Bleiburg', or 'the Bleiburg massacre' as it came to be known in émigré circles, was the key propaganda tool of pro-Ustasha émigré organizations during the Cold War and is an issue that still deeply divides Croatian society. A typical example of the passion the debate evoked may be found in Ante Beljo's phraseology. Beljo called Bleiburg the 'Croatian Holocaust'.[21] Beljo's book is mainly a selection of patriotic and jingoist paragraphs from various Croatian authors. A typical definition of the Beleiburg massacre is provided in a book by George J. Prpić (*Tragedies and Migrations in Croatian History*, Toronto, 1973):

> In 1945 the same West delivered them in Bleiburg mercilessly to 'Operation Slaughterhouse', the bloodiest orgy in Balkan history. Of all tragedies, Bleiburg was the greatest in Croatian history. It resulted in the death and exodus of over one million men, women, and children. As long as we exist as a nation, Croatians will remember this horrible genocide.[22]

Another Croatian émigré, Bruno Ante Busic, published a paper in 1980 on Croatian losses in the Second World War.[23] The importance the Yugoslav Communist Secret Service attributed to this debate can be seen from the fact that Busic was assassinated in Paris on 16 October 1978, very likely by the Secret Service. Since the archives of Federal SDB (Agency of State Security) are still not available, one cannot say how many Serbian and Croatian émigrés were killed by the Yugoslav secret service, but it seems quite likely that it was the Federal Yugoslav Secret Service and its branches in the Yugoslav republics that stood behind most of the murders in the émigré community. This only strengthened anti-Communist sentiments among Croats in exile and gave the impression of an almost everyday war with Yugoslav Communists who were mostly seen as Serbs.[24]

A very important role in this debate was played by the Croatian scholar and former Communist general, **Franjo Tudjman (1922–1999)**. By the late sixties, he claimed

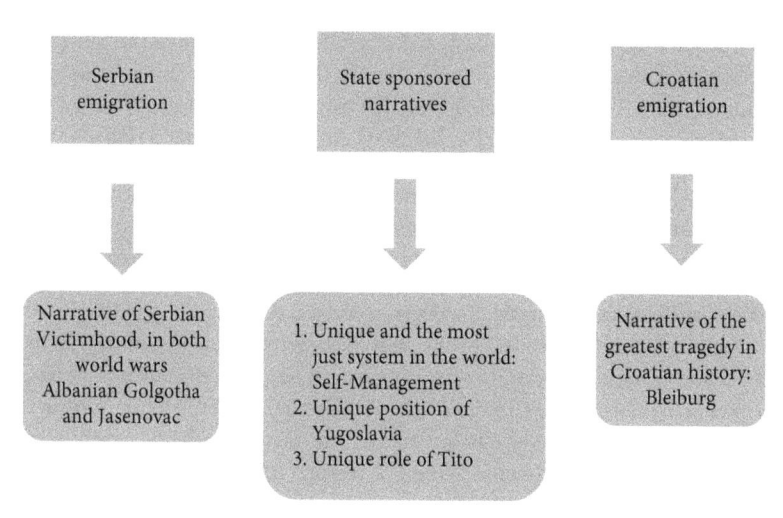

```
┌─────────────┐      ┌─────────────┐      ┌─────────────┐
│  Serbian    │      │State sponsored│    │  Croatian   │
│ emigration  │      │  narratives  │     │ emigration  │
└──────┬──────┘      └──────┬──────┘     └──────┬──────┘
       ↓                    ↓                    ↓
┌─────────────┐   ┌──────────────────┐  ┌─────────────┐
│Narrative of │   │1. Unique and the │  │Narrative of │
│  Serbian    │   │  most just system│  │the greatest │
│Victimhood,  │   │  in the world:   │  │tragedy in   │
│in both world│   │  Self-Management │  │Croatian     │
│wars Albanian│   │2. Unique position│  │history:     │
│Golgotha and │   │  of Yugoslavia   │  │Bleiburg     │
│Jasenovac    │   │3. Unique role of │  │             │
│             │   │  Tito            │  │             │
└─────────────┘   └──────────────────┘  └─────────────┘
```

Figure 7.2 Federative People's Republic of Yugoslavia (1946–1963), Socialist Federal Republic of Yugoslavia (1963–1991)

that the total real loss of population of Yugoslavia was between 700,000 and 800,000, which was the lowest figure of Yugoslav war losses ever. By the seventies, Tudjman had become a prominent figure in Croatia. In his youth, he had joined the Partisan movement, in 1941. His father died under unclear circumstances in 1945, but family tradition claimed that he was killed by the Yugoslav Communist Secret Service – OZNA. In the late fifties, Tudjman became a leading military historian and, in 1960, he was promoted to the rank of Major General. In 1961, he became the director of the Institute for the History of the Labour Movement of Croatia, and thus joined the ranks of privileged Yugoslav Communist historians, and became a lecturer at the University of Zagreb in 1963. Yet, he became active in the movement known as Croatian Spring from its onset in 1967 and for his nationalistic views was expelled from the League of Communists and arrested in 1971. But apparently Tito himself effected his early release. He was again arrested in 1982.

The obsession of Croatian émigrés with the Bleiburg massacre, and efforts to exonerate Ante Pavelic, the Ustasha Fuhrer, prompted a well-known German leftist political philosopher Ernst Bloch to remark in *Der Spiegel* (3 February 1985): 'Croats who live in West Germany are almost all fascists'. This provoked a very angry response from Franjo Tudjman, and Croatian émigrés.[25] His response firmly established Tudjman's reputation in Croatian émigré circles and facilitated his cooperation with them in spite of his Partisan background. In 1989, Tudjman published his book *Bespuća povijesne zbiljnosti* (*Wastelands of Historical Reality*), in which he dedicated many pages to what he termed 'Jasenovac's mythical figures'. He also expressed the opinion that estimations of six million Jewish victims in the Second World War were based on 'emotionally biased testimonies'. Among such testimonies, Tudjman included the claim by N. Levin that 770,000 people had been murdered in Jasenovac, of whom 20,000 were Jews 'although it is otherwise stated that Jews from Croatia were by

German request deported to the East, and partially found refuge in the Italian zone'.[26] He also assessed the data on Jewish victims in Auschwitz and Majdanek as 'unreliable'.[27] Yet, Tudjman, who obviously made a contribution to Holocaust denial, did not try to inflate the number of Croats killed in Bleiburg. As D. B. MacDonald notices:

> In reviewing Croatian interpretations of the NDH, we find two conflicting forms of propaganda. One is overtly pro-Ustaša, while the other is cautiously against it, but puts more effort into minimising its importance than into condemning it.[28]

As a former communist general, Tudjman belonged to the latter group. His contact with Croatian émigré circles led to the most bizarre combination of narratives that only a person with his background could produce. Being himself a former Partisan and a person who had been, like Croatian émigrés, persecuted by the Communists for his fight for the nationalist cause, he also has a father who (according to the family narrative) had been killed by Communists. Having a strange admiration for, and protection from, Tito, he struggled to unify all these conflicting personal experiences. In 1989, he was able to connect the three mutually antagonistic narratives into one in his most famous and controversial book, *Wastelands of Historical Reality*. He connected: (1) the inter-war Croatian narratives of suffering in the Kingdom of Yugoslavia that he had previously covered in his PhD thesis; (2) Croatian émigré narratives of massive crimes committed against Croatians, and a minimizing of Serbian and Jewish casualties, and; (3) the communist narrative of Josip Broz Tito. Thus, he completed a seemingly impossible task of bringing together, in the same symbolic field, the bourgeois leader of Croatian Peasant Party Vladko Macek, the NDH *Fuhrer*, Ante Pavelic, and the leader of Yugoslav Communists, Josip Broz Tito, all of whom were depicted as carrying out the same task: building Croatian statehood.

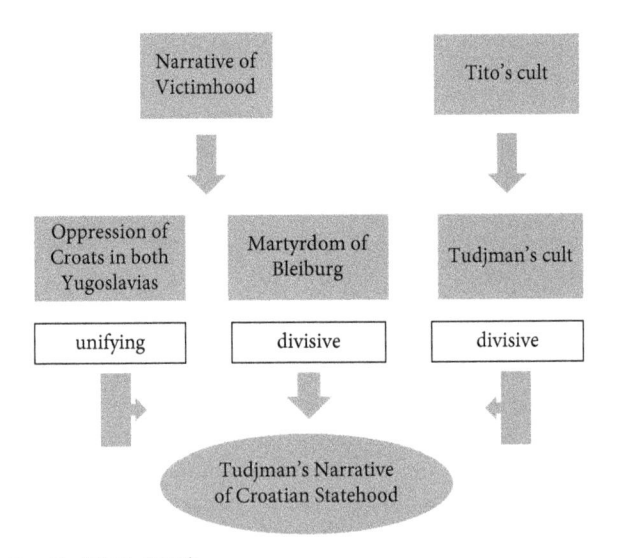

Figure 7.3 Croatia (1989–1999)

Speaking of Croatian émigré narratives on Bleiburg, one needs to acknowledge that the communist tabooing of this subject only made things worse, since, by the outbreak of war in 1991 the lack of a single serious piece of research on the Bleiburg massacre meant that anyone could claim virtually anything.

The coming of Milosevic to power in Serbia

As a recent study of the rise of Milosevic demonstrated, his coming to power in 1987 did not signal any particular change in already existing patterns of authoritarianism. It also had nothing to do with subsequent nationalist mobilization, which had, as N. Vladisavljevic put it, 'unfolded principally due to pressures from below'.[29] The pressure from below began to be felt immediately after 1981. In the 1970s, around 50,000 Serbs left the Serbian province of Kosovo subsequent to Albanian political elite taking control of the province after 1966. An equal number of Albanians moved to Kosovo in the period 1966–1986. In 1981, a combination of social and national rallies took place in Kosovo, in which Kosovo Albanians openly displayed their discontent and demanded that Kosovo be made a republic within Yugoslavia. This status, according to the Yugoslav constitution of 1974, theoretically included the right to self-determination. By this time, Kosovo was solidly set as the most underdeveloped region in Yugoslavia – an area that, in 1971, had only 32 per cent of Yugoslav average gross national product, with the gap tending to increase.[30] These Albanian rallies were soon suppressed but led to the re-emergence of grassroots dissatisfaction of Serbian elites in the 1980s. Discontent was encouraged by the deepest economic crisis in the history of Communist Yugoslavia, coinciding with the death of the Yugoslav dictator, Tito, in 1980. The austerity measures implemented to satisfy the World Bank and the International Monetary Fund meant a substantial reduction of a living standard that, in the 1970s, had reached a level comparable to some of the less developed West European countries.

By the early eighties, nationalism had already penetrated all historical narratives. This became most clearly visible in the preparation of a revised edition of the biggest Yugoslav cultural project – *Enciklopedija Jugoslavije*. Since 1980, debates on the project had emerged between Albanian, Serbian, Montenegrin and Bosnian Muslim authors. Although Serbian authors' objections were in the mid-eighties principled, by the late eighties they also became nation-centred. The main board of the *Encyclopaedia* finally disintegrated in 1990–1991. In the meantime, Slovenia published its own first volume of the *Encyclopaedia of Slovenia* in 1987, and even the Serbian autonomous province of Vojvodina decided to publish its own encyclopaedia.[31] In other words, before it disintegrated politically in the early nineties, Yugoslavia had disintegrated culturally in the eighties.

Another sign that Tito's cult was cracking in Serbia was demonstrated at the burial of Aleksandar Rankovic in 1983. Rankovic had been a notorious chief of secret police and Tito's deputy who was dismissed in 1966 when he became a real threat to Tito's own dictatorial position. In the popular imagination of many Serbs, the dismissal of

Rankovic took place only because he was a Serb, while Tito was a Croat. Rankovic's funeral was attended by tens of thousands of mourners in Belgrade, and even the state-run Radio Television Belgrade had a report on it despite the fact that the Communist Party in Serbia had wanted to ban reporting on the funeral.

The next indication of popular rejection of the official 'Brotherhood and Unity' policy came in 1985, when the Serbian writer Danko Popovic published a book on an imaginary Serbian soldier, Milutin, who tells a life story which reflects the Serbian discontents of the 1980s. Milutin only followed the Serbian victimhood narrative of the Great War that had never been encouraged in Communist Yugoslavia but had never been forbidden either. Thus, for instance, a great historical spectacle had been made in 1964, entitled *Marsh na Drinu* (A March to the Drina River), to commemorate the 50th anniversary of Serbian victory in the Battle of Tser (Cer) over the Austro-Hungarian Army.

The Book on Milutin followed the path paved by another significant Serbian figure, Dobrica Cosic, who will be discussed below. It was supposed to offer reflections of an ordinary Serb who was surprised that those who attacked Serbia in 1914 from the other side of the Drina 'spoke our language'. This was an obvious reference to Croats in general, and more particularly to Tito, whose participation in the Austro-Hungarian Army in 1914 had been kept a state secret for decades. *The Book of Milutin* was published as an unpretentious literary effort in 1985 with a print-run of only 2,000 copies. Yet, in 1986 it became a bestseller, with nineteen additional editions of which three reached 20,000 copies and two 30,000 copies.[32]

Though the opening up of the Second World War traumas was more threatening, it was unavoidable. The fact that the communists had tabooed certain the Second World War events just made them more fascinating and attractive to the general public in the 1980s. Thus, by the time Milosevic came to power, both narratives were already strongly rooted: one speaking of Serbian martyrdom in the First World War, and the other of Serbian victims in the Second World War, with a suggestion that Yugoslav Communists intentionally forbade any discussion of genocide against the Serbs. By 1988, the stream suggesting exoneration of General Mihailovich gained momentum.

Unlike Tudjman, Milosevic, a former banker, was not an intellectual but a technocrat who demonstrated a surprising mastery of political power. Apart from his speeches, he never published a thing. Also, with the exception of the period 1988–1989, when he participated in various rallies, he did not often make public appearances or give interviews. Therefore, one can hardly speak of any narrative of his own. Rather than creating narratives, as did Tudjman, he became a potent symbol of a newly emerging self-confident Serbia, and during his entire career as the most influential man in Serbia (1987–2000), he only touched occasionally on some segments of popular narratives that were constructed by his associates. To understand the narratives that developed, one has to analyse works not by Milosevic but by other prominent Serbs who enjoyed intellectual influence. Here I will analyse two disillusioned Serbian Communists who both advocated the democratization of Yugoslavia; both dealt with Serbian sufferings in the two World Wars, and both had a huge following in Serbia.

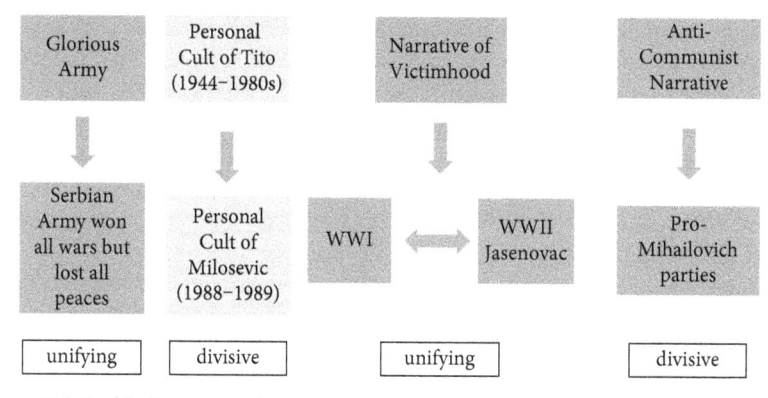

Memories of Victimhood in Serbia and Croatia 133

```
[Glorious Army] → [Serbian Army won all wars but lost all peaces] (unifying)

[Personal Cult of Tito (1944–1980s)] → [Personal Cult of Milosevic (1988–1989)] (divisive)

[Narrative of Victimhood] → [WWI] ⇔ [WWII Jasenovac] (unifying)

[Anti-Communist Narrative] → [Pro-Mihailovich parties] (divisive)
```

Figure 7.4 Serbia (1985–1991)

The first intellectual I will discuss about is **Vladimir Dedijer (1914–1990)**, a Serbian historian and a semi-dissident figure who published in 1981 his second volume of *New Contributions to the biography of Josip Broz Tito*. Before his clash with the Communist Party, Dedijer had published eulogies of Tito: one in Serbo-Croat, *Josip Broz Tito. Contributions to a Biography*, and the other in English, *Tito Speaks*, both published in 1953. The following year he sided with the prominent Communist Milovan Djilas, who had broken with the party. Dedijer was tried but got only a suspended sentence and left the Party. Initially, in 1955, he was prohibited from leaving the country, but two years later he was allowed to visit Manchester. Later, Tito found him useful in the English-speaking world as a promoter of his policies.

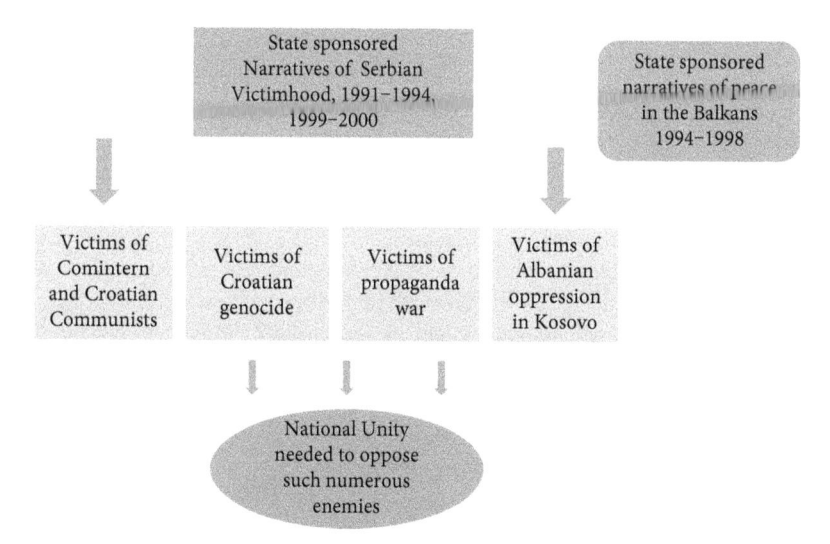

```
[State sponsored Narratives of Serbian Victimhood, 1991–1994, 1999–2000]
    ↓                ↓              ↓
[Victims of      [Victims of   [Victims of
 Comintern        Croatian      propaganda
 and Croatian     genocide]     war]
 Communists]

[State sponsored narratives of peace in the Balkans 1994–1998]
    ↓
[Victims of Albanian oppression in Kosovo]

    ↓       ↓       ↓
[National Unity needed to oppose such numerous enemies]
```

Figure 7.5 Serbia during the rule of Slobodan Milosevic (1991–2000)

Till the end of Tito's life, Dedijer remained loyal to official versions of Tito's biography that was very much based on his own account. Yet in 1981, soon after Tito died, Dedijer revealed that Tito had been a soldier in the Austro-Hungarian army in 1914 and also that Communists had held secret negotiations with German troops in Zagreb during the Second World War. Official historiography in Communist Yugoslavia had claimed that, with the exception of the Communists, all other Yugoslav military forces in the Second World War had collaborated with the Germans. This was a huge blow to the cult of Tito, just a year after his death.

Dedijer also claimed that around 700,000 Serbs were killed in Jasenovac. Yet one can hardly accuse Dedijer of a premeditated effort to inflate Serbian figures. He was not so much interested in numbers as in the very phenomenon of genocide. Thus, for instance, in his book on the Vatican and Jasenovac, published in 1987, Dedijer did not offer 'any specific estimate of wartime losses in Croatia or Yugoslavia'. On the other hand, the apparently exaggerated figure of 600,000–700,000 people (mainly Serbs) killed in Jasenovac was provided by Dedijer's associate Antun Miletic, who made the best documented monograph on the Jasenovac concentration camp.[33] Therefore, one might assume that both Dedijer and Miletic really believed these numbers and that both were just following earlier official communist figures.[34]

Dedijer was apparently obsessed with human suffering worldwide and he dealt not only with Ustasha genocide against Serbs but also with genocide in general. While he worked in the Russell Tribunal, he also wrote on the killing of the Vietnamese people:

> What I have read about the manner in which the war is being waged in Vietnam, the photographs I have seen, Russell's terrifying documentation on the chemical and bacteriological warfare going on there, led me to the conclusion that once again an Asian nation, a small nation, with an ancient culture is being exterminated by the most up-to-date weapons.[35]

He published, together with Antun Miletic, a lengthy volume on what he saw as Chetnik genocide against Muslims in the Second World War, in which Ustashas also took part.[36] Working in the Russell Tribunal, he became convinced that genocide began in pre-historic times, as soon as the first civilizations emerged along great rivers. He also began collecting, together with Antun Miletic, materials on crimes committed against Bosnian Muslims by the Kingdoms of Serbia and Montenegro after 1912, and he planned to publish a volume on genocide against Slavic Macedonians in the twentieth century. Yet his death in 1990 stopped these projects.

One may, however, still assign Dedijer the responsibility for the establishment of the Tito cult, albeit more for the cult abroad than in Communist Yugoslavia. On the other hand, it was again Dedijer who decisively contributed to the destruction of the cult of Tito, thus personally facilitating, although not at all intentionally, the fusion of Communist and nationalist narratives in Serbia.

The other author to be considered is **Dobrica Cosic (1921–2014)** who joined the Partisans in 1941 and, after the Second World War, became a deputy of the Serbian and Yugoslav parliaments and a member of the Central Committee of the League of Communists of Serbia (1965–1968). In this first period of Communism, he believed in internationalism and solidarity. For him, Yugoslavism was a local expression of Communist supra-nationalism capable of transforming and modernizing Yugoslav society. Until the mid-1960s, he viewed himself as a Yugoslav 'who was prepared to deny Serbianness in the interest of Yugoslavism'.[37]

He gradually and painfully realized in the mid-1960s that neither non-Serbian writers in Yugoslavia nor the League of Communists of Yugoslavia nor even its leader Josip Broz Tito were much interested in strengthening a supra-national Yugoslav identity. This led him to express increasing concerns about the future of Serbian culture and the Serbian nation. In May 1968, at a plenum of the League of Communists of Serbia, Cosic spoke like a sceptical Communist believer. He stated that the national question would 'remain a problem and preoccupation of future generations as well', and warned that 'unless democratic forces of socialism score a final victory over bureaucratic and petit bourgeois forces and deluges, there could flare up among the Serbian people an old historic aim and national ideal – the unification of the Serbian people in a single state'.[38] Two months after his speech, he left the Communist Party, and by that act he became a dissident. He was never arrested after he left the party. Indeed, he gradually became the most popular writer in Serbia.

His reputation as the most influential Serbian writer was firmly established in the 1970s. It was through him that the Serbian narrative of victimhood in the First World War was perfected. In 1972–1979 Cosic published a widely read saga in four volumes entitled *Vreme smrti* (A time of death), celebrating Serbian martyrdom in the Great War. In arguing that death had been built into the very foundations of the Kingdom of Serbs, Croats and Slovenes, he took a familiar Serbian narrative and poured it into a powerful literary form. This narrative became well established not only among Serbian intellectuals but also among the reading public.[39] Not surprisingly, it was precisely in the period when he was creating his the First World War saga that Cosic launched a formula that was, in a simplified form, attributed to him. It is that Serbs win wars but are not able to win the peace. In 1977, in his inaugural speech following his election to membership of the Serbian Academy, he said:

> The meaning of the liberation battles and victories on the battlefields of this century were denied in peace; peace has been understood as an opportunity to fulfil various selfish goals under various illusions and excuses.[40]

In the eighties, Cosic was one of key figures of Serbian political and intellectual opposition expressing itself through the Writer's Club. He led what he later called the Belgrade Opposition Circle. In the eighties, this circle tried to encourage democratization in Serbia and Yugoslavia. Cosic himself attempted to make alliances with similar groups in Zagreb and Ljubljana, but his efforts failed due to his own obsession with the preservation of Yugoslavia.

He reiterated his victimhood narrative on many occasions. In December 1988 he said:

There is no country in Europe for the creation of which (1914–1918) and for whose renewal and transformation (1941–1945 and 1948–1958) more victims have been laid and more hopes have been invested than for Yugoslavia.[41]

Also, on many occasions he mentioned that Serbian victims in the First World War totalled one third of the population of Serbia.[42] Originally a supra-national idealist, he gradually began to be preoccupied with his own nation. As N. J. Miller noticed:

Titoism betrayed his faith in the transformative value of communism, and his response was to shift the object of his idealism from the revolution to his nation.[43]

In 1992, after Yugoslavia disintegrated, Serbia's strongman Slobodan Milosevic agreed that Cosic would become the first president of what was left of Yugoslavia. Thus, Cosic became president of the Federal Republic of Yugoslavia, consisting of Serbia and Montenegro. He was impeached when he came into conflict with Milosevic in 1993. Yet, he continued to play a prominent role in intellectual circles in Belgrade throughout the nineties and even after the democratic changes in 2000.

In Cosic's case, it was he who unleashed what he had originally feared: the potent weapon of Serbian nationalism through a victimhood narrative. He did it unintentionally, in an internal debate with his own conception of communism.

Some reflections on genocide and victimhood narratives

The 1990s has been the focus of Western scholarship on the victimhood narratives of Serbs and Croats, or rather the period when the Wars for Yugoslav Succession took place. Yet victimhood narratives developed much earlier. They were fully developed as early as the 1970s by disenchanted Communists who were in search of their own identity, and who in most of cases had no intention of harming any other group. These narratives, for their part, repeated motifs from similar narratives that arose in the period between the two world wars.

Research on the comparative histories of various small Balkan nations has led me to believe that the history of a small nation is by definition a series of traumatic events. These traumatic events have a tendency to become focal points of historical memory. Toward the end of the Communist period, the focus on traumatic past events was facilitated by the crisis of Communist values and the disintegration of the Yugoslav secular religion, Titoism. As soon as the prevailing value system had been shaken, a reinterpretation of history was undertaken as an effort to fill the value vacuum. This task was performed by disenchanted Communists.

From the point of view of the results of the Wars for Yugoslav Succession that cost tens of thousands of lives in 1990s, victimhood narratives seem to have an ominous potential. Yet, they originally appeared in a different context of peace, mainly as a way to challenge Communist monism and as an effort to neutralize Communist Party-sponsored narratives and taboos.

The breakdown of the Communist value system led to efforts to introduce neo-traditionalism, attempts to re-establish vaguely understood values that existed before but with new interpretations. Once these vague efforts were coupled with victimhood narratives, they led an ethnification of politics: the tendency to see ethnicity as the primary political identity. Naturally, ethnification was particularly powerful in ethnically mixed areas and less influential in urban centres and ethnically homogenous areas. Ethnification in turn facilitated a competition in victimhood narratives between major ethnically defined antagonists – in our case, between Croats and Serbs in Croatia and Yugoslavia; between Serbs, Croats and Muslims in Bosnia and Herzegovina; and between Serbs and Albanians in the Serbian province of Kosovo.

Loaded with historical symbolism, victimhood narratives appeal to deep components of the human psyche. With their focus on victims, these narratives unavoidably raise the issue of the responsibility of perpetrators. Sacralization of victims is coupled with the Otherization of those who are held responsible. The usual simplified division of social reality into 'us' and 'them' may, under certain conditions, facilitate placing whole ethnic groups into those who are responsible for the deaths of 'our' sacred victims. A vacuum of values makes ideal conditions for this to happen. Those 'responsible' are classified as Others. In everyday human categorizations there is, indeed, a hierarchy of Otherness, ranging from incomplete self to the radical (fully dehumanized) Other. Victimhood narratives effectively help this categorization to reach a stage that is as radical as possible, or, in sociological terms, in which ethnic distance becomes as wide as possible.

Once we start to deal with 'our sacred identity' versus dehumanized Others, two new components emerge: insecurity and a sense of mission. The sense of mission is related to our identity which needs to be protected from possible future attacks by the same group that had previously been categorized as responsible for tragic events in the past. Thus, one starts to live in a symbolic field that makes the individual feel insecure as he is constantly under the pressure of historical symbolism focused on his/her own victims and the potential threat that a similar experience may be or is just about to be repeated. The dehumanization of Others strengthens the impression that the threat is imminent. This is exactly what happened in the major ethnic communities in Yugoslavia in the late 1980s, culminating in the Wars for Yugoslav Succession (1991–1995, 1998–1999). Victimhood narratives play an important role in this vicious cycle. Horrible atrocities committed against Serbs during the Second World War, particularly in the NDH, and harsh Communist retaliations against Croats at the end of the war contributed to the full traumatization of Serbian and Croatian communities. Both lived through victimhood narratives, nurtured them and made every possible effort to keep them alive. Franjo Tudjman proved to be an excellent mediator between Croatian émigré narratives and domestic narratives. This meant émigrés' narratives played a stronger role in Croatia than they did in Serbia where there was no need to import victimhood narratives, since influential intellectuals had developed them domestically. What was gradually imported to Serbia in the 1980s were narratives of the royalist forces, which only divided and antagonized the public and created opposing camps of victimhood narrators. The experience of Yugoslavia indicates that victimhood narratives precede ethnification of politics, but this does not mean that they cause it. They simply seem to be an unavoidable precondition but certainly not the sole cause.

The case of the ex-Yugoslavia in the 1980s and 1990s demonstrates that the strengthening of victimhood narratives is concomitant with a vacuum in values. It also shows that focusing on victimhood may contribute to serious conflicts and even wars. Still, the causes of wars seem to be more deeply rooted in concrete political, cultural and economic contexts, and victimhood narratives seem only to be a symptom of a more general crisis.

Notes

1. David Bruce MacDonald, *Balkan Holocaust? Serbian and Croatian Victim Centred Propaganda and the War in Yugoslavia*, Manchester: Manchester University Press, 2002.
2. Jasna Dragović-Soso, *'Saviours of the Nation': Serbia's Intellectual Opposition and the Revival of Nationalism*, London: Hurst and Company, 2002; see also Jasna Dragović-Soso, 'Intellectuals and the Collapse of Yugoslavia: The End of the Yugoslav Writers' Union', in Dejan Djokic, ed., *Yugoslavism: Histories of a Failed Idea 1918–1992*, London: Hurst and Company, 2003, pp. 268–285.
3. Eric Hobsbawm, *Age of Extremes*, London: Abacus, 1995, p. 26.
4. Derek H. Aldcroft and Steven Morewood, *Economic Change in Eastern Europe Since 1918*, Aldershot: Edward Elgar Publishing Ltd, 1995, p. 11. Most Serbian sources estimate the death toll at 28 per cent of the total population, or 1,200,000 in absolute figures.
5. John R. Lampe, *Yugoslavia as History: Twice There Was a Country*, Cambridge and New York: CUP, 2000, p. 109.
6. The recent estimation provided in *Enciklopedija srpskog naroda* (Encyclopaedia of the Serbian People) gives the figure of 1,248,136 Serbs from the territory of the Kingdom of Serbia and 286,753 from the territory of Austria-Hungary. *Enciklopedija srpskog naroda*, Belgrade: Zavod za Udžbenike, 2008, p. 1038.
7. Lampe, *Yugoslavia as History*, p. 132. See also Slobodan G. Markovich, 'The Legacy of King Alexander I of Yugoslavia', *Balcanica*, Vol. XL (2009), pp. 201–206.
8. The best known work in English on cultural policy in Yugoslavia in the inter-war period is: Andrew Baruch Wachtel, *Making a Nation, Breaking a Nation: Literature and Cultural Politics in Yugoslavia*, Stanford: Stanford University Press, 1998; see also Andrew Baruch Wachtel, 'Ivan Meštrović, Ivo Andrić and the Synthetic Yugoslav Culture of the Inter-War Period', in Dejan Djokic, ed., *Yugoslavism: Histories of a Failed Idea 1918–1992*, London: Hurst and Company, 2003, pp. 238–251.
9. Stevan Pavlowitch, *Hitler's New Disorder*, London: Hurst and Company, 2008, p. 34; Lampe, *Yugoslavia as History*, pp. 211–212.
10. Vladeta Vučković, 'An Introduction: In the Name of Love Among People', in Dr. Bogoljub Kočovićed, *Nauka, nacionalizam i propaganda* (*Science, Nationalism and Propaganda*), Second enlarged edition, Paris: Editions du Titre, 1999, pp. 8–14.

11 Srdjan Bogosavljević, 'The Unresolved Genocide', in Nebojša Popov, ed., *The Road to War in Serbia: Trauma and Catharsis*, Budapest: CEU Press, 1996, pp. 146–159.
12 Bogoljub Kočović, *Sahrana jednog mita. Žrtve Drugog svetskog rata u Jugoslaviji* [*A Burial of a Myth. Victims of the Second Wold War in Yugoslavia*], Belgrade: Otkrovenje, 2005, p. iii.
13 A leading Serbian émigré publicist of pro-Yugoslav orientation, Desimir Tosic, who returned to Yugoslavia in 1991 was the main advocate of Kochovich's book in Serbia. See also Srdjan Bogosavljević who, in 'The Unresolved Genocide' (pp. 150–151), found Kochovich's and Zervjavic's studies had the best argumentation. Most recently the British subject specialist Stevan Pavlowitch concluded that 'the number of deaths in Jasenovac remains a subject of controversy' but in a footnote on the same page he quotes only those estimations that put the number of deaths around 100,000 and implicitly accepts that number. Stevan Pavlowitch, *Hitler's New Disorder: The Second World War in Yugoslavia*, London: Hurst and Company, 1988.
14 The most popular recent history of the Serbs estimates that the most realistic figure for Jasenovac victims is 700,000. It also quoted the findings of the post-war Croatian Commission for the Investigation of Crimes committed by Occupation forces and Collaborationists that established that in Jasenovac between 500,000 and 600,000 people were killed. Dusan T. Batakovic, ed., *Histoire du Peuple Serbe*, Lausanne, Paris: L'Age d'Homme, 2005, p. 314. *Enciklopedija srpskog naroda* claims that at least 500,000 people of different nationalities were killed, but three lines later it says the recent most studies indicate that 982,680 Serbs were killed in Jasenovac. It also quotes German estimations of which one from March 1944 speaks of 750,000 Serbs who were killed in Croatia. *Enciklopedija srpskog naroda*, p. 442.
15 One should also note that Serbia launched a public campaign in 2010 encouraging Roma families to list themselves in official registers, such as registers of births. This indicates that even in 2010 some families in Serbia were not officially registered and therefore were not be listed in the census organised 2011. The situation is certainly not better in other parts of ex-Yugoslavia, and one can only imagine what conditions were like in 1931. However, one can also assume that in 1948, out of simple fear, under conditions of a totalitarian polity, far fewer people dared to avoid registration than in 1931, when there were no severe sanctions for failing to participate in the state census.
16 Pavlovitch, *Hitler's New Disorder*, 2008, p. 67.
17 Станиша Бркић and Ненад Ђорђевић, 'Крагујевачки октобар 1941', in *Геноцид у 20. Веку на просторима југословенских земаља* [Stanisha Brkich and Nenad Djordjevich, 'Kragujevac October of 1941', in *Genocide in 20th Century on the Territory of Yugoslav Lands*], Belgrade: Museum of Genocide Victims and Institute for Recent History of Serbia, 2005, pp. 143–144. The official site of the Memorial Park – Kragujevac October also states that 2,794 men, women and children from Kragujevac and nearby villages were killed on 19–21 October 1941, http://www.spomenpark.com/index.php [accessed 30 April 2010].
18 http://www.idc.org.ba/index.php?option=com_content&view=section&id=35&Itemid=126&lang=bs [accessed December 2010].
19 Jozo Tomasevich, *War and Revolution in Yugoslavia, 1941–1945: Occupation and Collaboration*, Stanford: Stanford University Press, 2001, pp. 757–761.
20 Tomasevich, *War and Revolution in Yugoslavia*, p. 763.
21 Ante Beljo, *Genocide: A Documented Analysis*, Sudbury: Northern Tribune Publishing, 1985, p. 14.

22 Beljo, *Genocide*, p. 299.
23 Bruno Busic, 'Demographic Losses: Croatian Casualties in Croatia and Yugoslavia', *Hrvatski list* (Lund), No. 11–12 (1980), pp. 46–53 and 'Population Losses During the War', *Hrvatski knjizevni list*, No. 15 (1969), quoted from Tomasevich, *War and Revolution*, p. 794.
24 In 1985 the Croatian émigré, Ante Beljo, dedicated his book to the memory of Bruno Bušić and re-published, a list of fifty-seven Croats, 12 Serbs and 4 Albanians who were, in his opinion, killed by the Yugoslav Communist Secret Service. The list was originally published in a book by Hans Peter Rullman called *Assassinations Commissioned by Belgrade* (Hamburg, 1981). Beljo, *Genocide*, pp. 347–348.
25 Franjo Tuđman, *Bespuća povijesne zbiljnosti. Rasprava o povijesti i filozofiji zlosilja*, Zagreb: Nakladni zavod Matice Hrvatske, 1989, pp. 119–121.
26 Tuđman, *Bespuća povijesne zbiljnosti*, p. 156.
27 Tuđman, *Bespuća povijesne zbiljnosti*, p.157.
28 MacDonald, *Balkan Holocaust?*, p. 138.
29 Nebojsa Vladisavljevic, *Serbia's Antibureaucratic Revolution: Milosevic, the Fall of Communism and Nationalist Mobilization*, London: Palgrave Macmillan, 2008, p. 74.
30 Lampe, *Yugoslavia as History*, p. 336.
31 Dragović-Soso, 'Saviours of the Nation', pp. 73–77.
32 According to the date of on-line catalogue of the National Library of Serbia the first twenty editions were published in a total of 179,000 copies, excluding the 19th edition for which there are no data on circulation.
33 Tomasevich, *War and Revolution*, p. 726.
34 Another expert who very much contributed to high figures was Milan Bulajic. In 1986 the trial of Minister of Interior of the Independent State of Croatia Andrija Artuković of Zagreb reopened the question of Ustasha crimes against Serbs. Dr. Milan Bulajic, a legal expert on genocide wrote in 1988/1989, a series of four volumes entitled *Ustaški zločini genocida i suđenje Andriji Artukoviću 1986. Godine* (*Ustasha Crimes of Genocide and the Trial of Andrija Artukovic in 1986*).
35 Jean-Paul Sartre and Vladimir Dedijer, *War Crimes in Vietnam*, Spokeman Pamphlet no. 12, The Bertrand Russell Peace Foundation.
36 Vladimir Dedijer and Antun Miletić, *Genocid nad Muslimanima*, Sarajevo: Svjetlost, 1990.
37 Nicholas J. Miller, 'The Nonconformists: Dobrica Ćosić and Mića Popović Envision Serbia', *Slavic Review*, Vol. 58, No. 3 (Fall 1999), pp. 515–536, esp. pp. 517–518.
38 Milan Nikolic, ed., *Sta je stvarno rekao Dobrica Cosic* [*What Dobrica Cosis really said*], Belgrade: Draganic, 1995, p. 7. The speech was delivered on 29 May 1968 at the 14th session of the League of Communists of Serbia.
39 The novel went through numerous editions in the 1970s and 1980s.
40 Miller, 'The Nonconformists', p. 524.
41 Nikolic, *Sta je stvarno rekao*, p. 8. A presentation at the round table organized by Knjizevne novine [Literary Gazette] in December 1988.
42 Nikolic, *Sta je stvarno rekao*, p. 18. Presentation made in the town of Krusavac in Central Serbia on 19 January 1991.
43 Miller, 'The Nonconformists', p. 533.

8

Insecurity, Victimhood, Self and Other: The Case of Israel and Palestine

Ilan Pappe

Insecurity is not a *terra incognita* in the Israeli-Palestinian conflict. It is a space often visited by many members of both societies. Jews and Palestinian alike are more than visitors to this space; they are permanent inhabitants of it. It is a kind of Lunatic Park where you can choose your favourite site. The most popular one seems to be the basest and ugliest site of them all, the one that opens a direct and unmitigated channel from the land of fear to the land of hate – the fear of the 'Other'. The Other in this context is constructed as the very antithesis of a strictly defined national self. In the particular case of the Israeli-Palestinian conflict, otherness not only raises questions of identity but also of history and legitimacy.

The following is a schematic overview of the process by which the construction of Israeli-Jewish national identity and the institutionalization of a particular hegemonic discourse in social and popular culture entailed the constitution of a Palestinian/Arab self as its demonized 'other'. Since the connections between the history of Zionism and the formation of Israeli national identity have been amply discussed elsewhere, I will focus on the implications of presenting Arab identity as the Other of the Israeli-Jewish national identity for potential reconciliation in contemporary Israeli society.[1] For this purpose I will explore the relationship between victimhood, justice and the ongoing conflict until today. In the process, I will also argue that from today's perspective, the rootedness of this discourse of otherness and its prevalence in Israeli-Jewish popular culture is forming a key obstacle to a just and equitable solution to the current conflict.

Fear, victimhood and otherness

The suppression of difference and the construction of an Other are critical to the imposition of a hegemonic national identity. In the particular case of Israel, this formulation took on an added significance that was painfully exposed in the early 1950s. Beginning in the nineteenth century, and elaborated upon much more significantly following the creation of the state of Israel in 1948, Arab identity came to be constructed as the 'hated other', of Israeli-Jewish national identity, symbolizing everything that Jewishness was not. This juxtaposition ran into trouble when Israel encouraged about one million Arab Jews to immigrate. There was a conscious effort to de-Arabize these Arabs immigrants: they were taught to scorn their mother tongue, reject Arab culture and make an effort to be Europeanized.[2]

This approach to identity, that is of constructing an Other as the negative pole of oneself, was further reinforced through Israeli historiography specifically in the ways it dealt with Jewish terrorism in the Mandatory period or with Jewish atrocities in the 1948 war. Given that terrorism is a mode of behaviour that Israeli Orientalists attribute solely to the Palestinian resistance movement, it could not be part of an analysis or description of chapters in Israel's past. One way out of this conundrum was to accredit a particular political group, preferably an extremist one, with the same attributes of the enemy, while exonerating mainstream national behaviour. As such, Israeli historians and Israeli society at large were able to admit to the massacre in Dir Yassin, committed by the right wing Irgun, but covered up or denied other massacres carried out by the Hagana – the main Jewish underground from which the future Israel Defence Forces was formed.[3]

In the same vein, this dilemma is further exemplified in the Israeli treatment of the issue of victimhood especially in the light of current events. Acknowledging the Other's victimhood, or much more than that, recognizing yourself as the victimizer of the Other is the most frightening ghost train one can embark upon. Until recently, most Israeli Jews have been unable, or simply refused, to entertain such ideas. As I have argued elsewhere, the Israeli TV series, *Tekkuma*, celebrating Israel's jubilee in 1998, was the first popular attempt to ponder the possibility that Jews were not only the ultimate victims of the twentieth century but also its victimizers. This was done by allocating space on TV to propose another possible narrative of the history of Palestine. Although this was a very cautious attempt, which did not deviate too much from the dominant Zionist narrative, it was enough to cause a massive outcry throughout Israeli society and from all the political parties against the series' editors and producers.[4]

My contention here *is that* acknowledging the atrocities committed against the native inhabitants of Mandate Palestine, and which led to the eventual formation of modern Israel, is a vital and necessary station in the socialization of the Jews in Israel, no less, than the horror destinations, to which high school children in Israel are forced – and one hopes that at least some of them seek – to visit in Holocaust Europe. This process that is the acknowledgement of the Other as a victim, and which requires two very different references on both sides, has been absent both in the Israeli and the Palestinian attitudes. In both instances, but for similar reasons, there has been a profound resistance to this move.

For the Israeli Jews, recognizing the Palestinians as victims of Israeli actions is deeply traumatic. This form of acknowledgement, which recognizes the injustice involved in the death and displacement of the land's native inhabitants, not only questions the very foundational myths of the state of Israel and its motto of 'a land without a people for a people without a land' but also raises a panoply of ethical questions with significant implications for the future of the state. In other words, this fear of recognition is deeply rooted in the Israeli-Jewish perception of what had happened in 1948, the year Israel was founded as independent nation state on part of mandate Palestine and where, according to mainstream and popular Israeli historiography, early Zionists settled an empty land making 'the desert bloom'. Here, this fear of recognition is also profoundly connected to one of the founding myths of Israeli society: that of David fighting the Goliath in a hostile environment. More importantly, the inability to acknowledge Palestinian trauma is also vitally connected to the manner in which the Palestinian narrative tells the story of that year, the year of the *Nakbah* (Catastrophe) in the Palestinian national narrative where the loss of lives and homes continue to be lived. Had this victimhood been related to the natural and normal consequences of a long lasting bloody conflict, Israeli-Jewish fears from allowing other side to become a victim of the conflict would not have been so fierce. From such a perspective, both sides would have been victims of 'the circumstances' or any other amorphous, non-committal concept which absolves human beings and particularly politicians from taking responsibility. But what the Palestinians are demanding and which in fact has become a *condition sine qua non* to many of them – but not of course to the present leadership of the Palestinian authority – is that the Palestinians be recognized as the victims of an Israeli evil. Losing the status of victimhood in this instance has both political implications on an international scale but more critically existential repercussions for Israeli-Jewish psyche. It implies recognizing that they had become a mirror image of their worst nightmare.

As for the Palestinians, recognizing the Israelis as victims implies not only acknowledgement of the Israeli Jews as a community of suffering whose victimization by European, namely German, evil does not justify victimizing the Palestinians but may explain a chain of victimization that would lead to a decrease in Holocaust denial on the Palestinian side. Palestinian reluctance to fully acknowledge the Holocaust and its importance in the constitution of an Israeli-Jewish psyche stems from a fear of sympathizing with the Other's suffering, after years of demonizing and degrading this Other while portraying the self as the Other's victim.

This fear of mutual recognition becomes more acute and is more critically articulated in public discourse in times of 'peace', for which such recognition is in fact a prerequisite. This became manifestly evident with the launching of the Oslo 'peace process' which even though was marketed as a reconciliation process, was in fact, as Naom Chomsky argues, nothing more than 'a military rearrangement of life than a genuine reconciliation' concluded by pragmatic political elites.[5] However, the very representation of that process as peace was enough to arouse the fears associated with the victimization of the Other and the vilification of the self. This will become more evident shortly.

History: Invisible and indivisible

In the imbalance between Palestinians and Israelis this last twin process of Other-victimization and self-vilification is dreaded more on the Jewish Israeli side. It requires recognition of the Palestinians as the victims of Israeli deeds, and not as most Israeli scholars, even of the Zionist Left, would put it down to circumstances.[6] Educators, historians, novelists and cultural producers in general, have willingly employed this discourse of ultimate and exclusive victimization, thus voluntarily contributing to this misrepresentation of historical processes. They all in one way or another helped to construct and preserve the national narrative, ethos and myths of Israeli society during times of war, or warlike times. This approach manifests itself in the tales told by child minders on Independence day and Passover; in the curriculum and text books in elementary and high schools; in the ceremonies of freshmen and the graduation of officers in the army; in the historical narrative carried in the printed and electronic media as well as in the speeches and discourse of the politicians; in the way artists, novelists and poets subject their works to the national narrative; and in the research produced by academics in the universities about Israeli reality in the past and the present.[7]

Liberal Zionists in Israel also adopt this particular posture. For them, peace and reconciliation translate into the need for mutual recognition between the Israeli and Palestinian national narratives, and the way to achieve this goal is to make divisible everything that is visible: land, resources, blame and history into a pre-1967 when we the Jews were Right and Just and a post-1967 when You the Palestinian are Right and Just. In other words, while the events which preceded and led to the foundation of modern Israel in 1948 not only remain unquestioned but in fact are justified, those following 1967 and the continued Israeli occupation of the territories conquered during this period (that is the West Bank and Gaza) are deemed unacceptable.

Viewed from this perspective, victimhood in the Israeli-Palestinian conflict can also be divided into those two historical periods. This same approach of the Israeli-Jewish liberal camp is then applied to the history of the conflict. Jews are the victims of the earlier and more distant chapter in the history of the conflict, namely the pre-1967 era while Palestinians are the victims of its more recent chapter, post 1967. The periodization is very important since the earlier period is considered to be the more important one; and thus being just then, in the formative period of the conflict, justifies the existence of Zionism and the whole Jewish project in Palestine. At the same time, it also doubts the wisdom and morality of Palestinian actions in that period, questioning their national narratives and implicitly their 'rights'. Even though Zionism may have 'misbehaved' in subsequent times, its actions do not cast doubt on its very essence and justification.

However, peace and mutual recognition entail bridging over the invisible, hence the indivisible, layers of history, guilt and injustice. Blame cannot be divided, not if peace and reconciliation mean respect for the Other's narrative. The Palestinian narrative is that of suffering, reconstructed on the basis of living memory, oral history, a continued exilic existence and the more tangible effects such as property deeds, faded photographs and keys to homes they can no longer return to. These historical narratives are read backwards through the prism of contemporary hardships, in the occupied territories where residents are subjected daily to house demolitions, sudden arrests, expulsions and more recently to daily atrocities committed by the Israeli army; and in exile, where they are subjected to the whims of their host countries and in some instances denied even their most basic civic and human rights. Through this prism, Zionism, or Israel, has come to represent absolute evil and the ultimate victimizer. How can this image be divided in the businesslike approach to peace, preached by American and Israeli peacemakers?

It cannot of course. When peace is discussed in such a context, one should appeal to ways in which communities of suffering, worldwide, reconcile with their victimizers. The narrative of suffering is an interpretative construct describing a collective evil in the past, often employed for the political needs of a given community in the present, in order to improve its conditions in the future. In order to avoid a reductionist view of the narrative of suffering, I will add that in the case of the Palestinians especially, as well as other communities which continue to live the aftereffects of the original action, this narrative also has a redemptive value – for the communities themselves. However, and as the case of the Holocaust has shown, the way this narrative is manipulated by cultural production and political actors for political ends is another issue which I will not discuss here.

In most contexts, this narrative is reproduced with the help of educational and media systems, a commemorative infrastructure of museums and ceremonies, and is preserved through a variety of discourses.[8] Even though it can serve a community in conflict, it is more difficult as means for reconciliation.[9] In the case of the Palestinians, living under occupation or in exile, commemoration takes on myriad, and sometimes unexpected, forms. Lacking the basic infrastructure, and in the absence of a *terra firma* on which to establish these rituals, commemoration takes form in the Occupied Territories most explicitly in crowding the calendar with significant days that have to be commemorated: days such the Balfour Declaration, the Declaration of Independence, the End of the Mandate, the Partition Resolution and the day of *Fatah*'s (the Palestinian Liberation Organization) foundation. In exile and often lacking the political, economic and civic rights necessary, retelling the narrative takes on its own local colour. In Lebanon for example, where the Palestinian presence is viewed as a serious threat to the country's sectarian balance, and hence long term political stability, the mass graveyard of the Sabra and Shatila massacres, where 2,000 residents of the camp were massacred following the 1982 Israeli invasion by right-wing members of a Lebanese militia under the watchful eye and protection of the Israeli army, has been used as a massive garbage dump for the past eighteen years. Every year it is cleared up in September, but it usually takes activists from outside the camp to generate some memorial event before it disintegrates into a dump again. More recently, children in these same camps have transformed the commemoration of the *Nakbah* through a re-telling of their own personal narratives and imaginative re-constitutions of the Palestine they wish to return to. In another exilic community in Tunis, a group of Palestinian activists transformed their private living rooms between 1983 and 1993 into live museums of the catastrophe, which had befallen their people. In each living room, a small corner was set up representing their own narrative and discourse of national identity. In yet another example, in Cambridge, Massachusetts, Palestinians and others have come together in recent years on 13 December, the anniversary of the first *intifada* to relay their own personal stories.

At times of conflict, suffering and victimhood become a most significant element in constituting collective identity as well as destroying the collective memory of the Other. The negation of the Other, his or her suffering and catastrophes, is a constitutive element in shaping national identities.[10] Violence and Fear are therefore important factors in constructing collective memories, in their reproductions, dissemination and inclusion or exclusion in or from a given historical reality and balance of power. Or, to be more precise the above assertion applies mainly in situations of conflict over the definition of identity in a given territorial entity as well as over definition of the territory itself – in other contexts, this is not necessarily the case.

In the case of Israel and Palestine, controlling the collective memory of both groups is part of the violent and existential struggle for national survival. The effort to shape collective memory is therefore a dialectical process motivated by the fear of the Other and the wish to negate it. Part of this process is a complete takeover of the victim's status, enjoyed by the other side, and the negation of its suffering. Recognizing the other side as a victim of your actions is part of the healing or reconciliation process.

Fear therefore plays a motivating role in the violence exercised daily in the struggle over narrative, memory and victimhood. Victimizing the Other and negating its right for the position of a victim are intertwined processes of the same violence. Those who expelled Palestinians in 1948 deny the ethnic cleansing that took place. An ethnic cleansing that included the destruction of more than 500 villages, city neighbourhoods, the expulsion of almost a million people and the massacring of thousands.[11] And so the self-declaration of being a victim is accompanied by the fear of losing the position of the Jew as the ultimate victim in modern history.

Fear, justice and retribution

What is the essence of that Israeli fear? The most difficult part of it is the need to recognize the cardinal role the Jewish State played in making the Palestinians into a community of suffering. The next step would be to consider the means to accept the implications of such a step. How can it be done?

I will suggest here three possible ways, out of probably many others through which the violent element in the relationship between the two communities can be extricated. I looked in a comparative way for guidance and advice in the realm of civic and international law, sociological theories of retribution and restitution and finally cultural studies so as to better articulate the dialectical relationship between collective memories and their manipulation.

The very idea of considering the 1948 case in the realm of law and justice is an anathema to most Jews in Israel. In fact, this mere suggestion would sow panic and horror amidst this particular community. However, I do believe that to achieve some form of actual reconciliation, this step has to be taken. What would most frighten Jewish society in Israel in the very association of its past conduct with such procedures and theories is the probable implication and inclusion of some of its members in the category of war criminals. When hearing for the first time about the 1948 massacre committed by Jewish soldiers in the Palestinian village of Tantura, the Israeli philosopher Asa

Kasher declared that the perpetrators should be regarded as war criminals.[12] Tantura, however, was not the only massacre and certainly not the worst of them all.

But Kasher was unique in his response. Veterans of the Israeli unit participating in the Tanatura massacre have sued for libel the researcher in whose MA thesis the massacre is described. Similarly, any reference in the Israeli press to expulsion, massacre or destruction is usually denied and attributed to self-hate and service to the enemy in time of war.[13] This reaction includes members of academia, the media and the educational system as well as most political circles. These reactions reveal the depth of the fear that pervades Israeli society that some of its members may be implicated in actions the likes of which have been condemned by the entire world, including prominent members of Israeli society.

So one can see how such associations and insinuations antagonize visually and acoustically many Jews in Israel and how little is the incentive to ride that ghost train in the land of fear back to the past. Given the present imbalance of power between the Palestinians and the Israelis, where the Israeli government effectively controls territorial access as well as all vital resources, any potential incentive to face up to this past diminishes considerably. To assess how frightening such an experience might be for Israeli-Jewish society, we can attempt to conjure up the possible media treatment of Israeli past conduct. Let us imagine the debate or treatment of such a case on Television or Radio. In the end of the previous century, the Public TV channel in America (PBS) recorded a new series of chapters in an excellent programme called 'Inside the Law', which takes place on the premises of the Law school at New York University (NYU). Those new chapters were devoted to 'Justice, Restitution and Reconciliation in a Violent World'. The first chapter in this series dealt with litigation arising from genocide and other crimes against humanity: the Holocaust and beyond. It recognized the *sui generis* status of the Holocaust compared to other atrocities. However, when it broke down such horrors into the distinct ingredients of which destruction in such contexts was comprised: social fabric, careers, culture, real estate and so on, it put these aspects on the same level of guilt.

One of the best means of approaching this quantification of suffering was offered by the Israelis and Germans in their preparation agreement. An agreement that included pensions calculated according to inflation across the years, estimation of real estates and other aspects of individual loss. A different set of agreements was concluded about translating into money, in the form of grants to the state of Israel, of the collective human loss. In his writings, the Palestinian activist, Salman Abu Sitta, has begun using this approach to estimate the real value of assets lost in the *Nakbah*.

The second chapter in this series dealt with the potential tribunals that could handle such litigation and lawsuits. It focused on Pinochet and Milosevic. It asked the question: should war crimes and other atrocities be the subject of international jurisdiction or domestic jurisdiction? The third chapter entitled 'Nation Building: Moving beyond Injustice' dealt with atrocities committed by regimes in transition periods between occupation and liberation. The fourth chapter pondered the right of international intervention in local conflicts in the wake of evidence on atrocities or crimes. It worried about US actions masquerading as international actions thus exploiting such situations.

Now, let us imagine legal experts of collective crimes introducing the Palestinian *Nakbah* among the case studies of ex-Yugoslavia, Rwanda and Chile as the subject for discussing the procedures necessary for the rectification of past evils. There are today Jews in Israel who are willing to watch such programmes, but they are undoubtedly a significant minority, even if they are larger in numbers than ever before.

The reason these people are a minority lies in the persistent power Zionist ideology still has on the Jewish public in Israel. This ideology, preached from kindergarten to school, produced a very pious self-image about Zionist morality and Palestinian immorality. Its level of sophistication varies according to education, socio-economic status and function. But its overall message does not. In the Israeli society, overt support by Jews for the Right of Return for Palestinians; for a Truth commission on the *Nakbah*; or for the trial of Israelis for war crimes committed in 1948 are instances that cannot be legitimized or accepted as part of everyday knowledge. Accordingly, and as Foucault argues in another context, advocates of such unpopular positions, which challenge a majority stronghold over what is admissible into the public realm, are assessed as ideologically deviant or mentally ill.

But maybe this is asking too much. And yet it is difficult to find non-retributive paradigms of justice. The Rwandan author, Babu Aynido, in his article 'Retribution or Restoration for Rwanda', published in January 1998 in the journal *Africanews*, dealt with the International Criminal Tribunal for Rwanda (ICTR) and elaborated upon one possible strategy for achieving justice:

> Suffice it to say that the retributive understanding of crime and justice, upon which the ICTR is founded, is discordant with the world view of many African communities. To emphasize retribution is the surest way to poison the seeds of reconciliation. If anything, retribution turns offenders into heroes, re-victimizes the victims and fertilizes the circle of violence.

Ayindo, here is inspired by Howard Zher's book, *Changing Lenses*,[14] in which he is strongly against the pro-punishment judicial system. One of the questions Zher raises and that is picked up by Ayindo in his discussion of the Rwandan case is relevant to our contemplation of the means by which Jews in Israel could overcome their fear of facing the past. He asks, should justice focus on establishing guilt or should it focus on identifying needs and obligations? In other words, can it serve as a re-regulator of life where life was once disrupted? Ayindo states clearly that Justice cannot be made to inflict suffering on victimizers, let alone their descendants, but to cease suffering from continuing. This claim that Zher considers revolutionary, explains Ayindo, is easily understood by many people in Africa, as the only reasonable way of dealing with victimhood. Even if one cannot compare between the genocide committed in Rwanda to the crime of 1948 Palestine, and its continued aftereffects, the mechanism of reconciliation itself is relevant.

Ayindo distinguishes between two models in this context: the tribunal in Rwanda which deals only with the past, and does not enable a reconstruction of relationships there, and the truth committee of Bishop Desmond Tutu in South Africa, which he prefers, because it pays attention to the future. The power underlying the Truth commission, according to Ayindo, lies both in its disinclination to inflict heavy penalties, and in its insistence on discussing future relationships between different communities in South Africa. In contrast, the first model, the Rwanda tribunal, is the fastest and surest way of turning the victims into victimizers themselves.

A second way of overcoming this fear to face the past is offered by the American psychologist Joan Fumia, whose work focuses on the transformation of attitudes in conflictual situations.[15] She bases her work on the relationships which develop between offenders and victims in the American legal system, based on a recently introduced new procedure, which offers victim-offender mediation. This method involves a face-to-face meeting between offender and victim (obviously unsuitable for murder cases and thus not appropriate for genocidal cases but rather more adaptable to the Palestine case). However, the most important part of the procedure is the readiness of the offender to accept responsibility for his acts. Thus, the deed itself is not the focus of the process but its consequences. The search in this method is for restorative justice, defined as a question of what can the offender do to ease the loss and suffering of the victim. It is not a substitute for the criminal proceedings nor, in the case of Palestine, an alternative to actual compensation or repatriation but a supplement to any final solution. Fumia claimed that in South Africa, this model was successfully implemented.

Israeli responsibility for the *Nakbah*, if it were to be discussed, which at the present stage is unlikely, as part of the attempt to reach a permanent settlement for the conflict, would obviously not reach the international court, as did the cases of Rwanda and ex-Yugoslavia. At least, this is what one can assess given the way the *Nakbah* is perceived by governments in the United States, Canada and Europe. These political actors have so far accepted the Israeli peace camp perspective on the conflict, as elaborated above. However, governments in Africa and Asia have different views on this, and the situation may change. But as long as this balance of power remains as it is now, one doubts the possibility of establishing a truth commission à la South Africa. But the demands of the 1948 Palestinian victims would remain in a very dominant position on the peace agenda, whether or not this procedure is followed. This outcry would continue to face the offenders. Moreover, the fear of the offender would have to be taken into account in order that the settlement of the conflict can move from the division of the visible to the restoration of the invisible.

The third route that could be possible has already been hinted at, in the beginning of this chapter. This would include the need for a dialectical recognition of both communities as communities of suffering; the demand that Israel recognize its role in the *Nakbah* can be accompanied by a parallel request that the Palestinians show their understanding of the importance of Holocaust memory for the Jewish community in Israel. This dialectical connection has already begun by Edward Said:

> What Israel does to the Palestinians it does against a background, not only of the long-standing Western tutelage over Palestine and Arabs... but also against a background of an equally long-standing and equally unfaltering anti-Semitism

that in this century produced the Holocaust of the European Jews... We cannot fail to connect the horrific history of anti-Semitic massacres to the establishment of Israel; nor can we fail to understand the depth, the extent and the overpowering legacy of its suffering and despair that informed the postwar Zionist movement. But it is no less appropriate for Europeans and Americans today, who support Israel because of the wrong committed against the Jews to realize that support for Israel has included, and still includes, support for the exile and dispossession of the Palestinian people.[16]

The universalization of the Holocaust memory; the deconstruction of this memory's manipulation by Zionism and the state of Israel; and the end of Holocaust denial and underrating on the Palestinian side can lead to the mutual sympathy Said talks about.[17]

However, it may need more than this to convince the Israelis to recognize their role as victimizers. From the start, the self-image of the victim has been, and continues to be, deeply rooted in the collective conduct of the political elite in Israel. It is seen as the source for moral international and world Jewish support for the state, even when this image of the righteous Israel on the one hand and the David and Goliath myth on the other became quite ridiculous after the 1967 war, the 1982 invasion of Lebanon and more recently the *intifada*. And yet the fear of losing the position of the victim, remains closely intertwined with the fear of facing the unpleasant past and its consequences. This is further compounded by the fear of being physically eliminated as a community, consistently nourished by the political system and substantiated by Arab hostility.

Israel's nuclear arsenal, its gigantic military complex, its security service octopuses, have all proved themselves useless in the face of the two *intifadas,* the guerrilla war in south Lebanon and the Gaza Strip. They are useless as means of facing an ever frustrated and radical million and a quarter Palestinian citizens of Israel or the local initiatives of refugees unable to contain their dismay in the face of an opportunist Palestinian Authority and a crumbling PLO. None of the weapons, nor the real or imaginary fears that have been produced, can face the victim and his or her wrath. More and more victims are added daily to the Palestinian community of suffering, in the occupied territories – in Israel itself and in south Lebanon. The end of victimization, with all its political implications, the admission of the Other into a national discourse and the recognition of the role of Israel as victimizer are the only useful means of reconciliation.

Notes

1   Ilan Pappe, 'Zionism in the Test of the Theories of Nationalism and Historiography', in Pinchas Ginosar and Avi Bareli, eds., *Zionism: Contemporary Controversy*, Beersheba: University of Ben Gurion Press, 1996, pp. 223–224 (Hebrew).
2   Ella Shohat, '*Mizrahim* in Israel: Zionism from the Standpoint of its Jewish Victims', *Theory, Culture & Ideology* Vol. 19, No. 20 (1988), pp. 1–35.

3   Ilan Pappe, 'Post-Zionist Critique: Part I: The Academic Debate', *Journal of Palestine Studies*, Vol. 262 (Winter 1997), pp. 29–41.
4   Ilan Pappe, 'Israeli Television Fiftieth Anniversary Series: Tekumma: A Post-Zionist Review?', *Journal of Palestine Studies*, Vol. 27, No. 4 (Summer 1998), pp. 99–105.
5   Noam Chomsky, *Powers and Prospects*, London: Pluto Press, 1996, pp. 159–201.
6   Benny Morris, *Righteous Victims*, New York: Knopf, 1999.
7   Ilan Pappe, 'Post-Zionist Critique: Part III: Popular Culture', *Journal of Palestine Studies*, Vol. 264 (Summer 1997), pp. 60–69.
8   See for example the ways on which Holocaust Memorials have been used to constitute collective memory as well as advance particular political ends in James E. Young, *The Texture of Memory: Holocaust Memorials and Meaning*, New Haven and London: Yale University Press, 1993.
9   This concept was first developed in Elizabeth Fau, *Community of Suffering and Struggle, Women, Men and the Labor Movement in Minneapolis, 1915–1945*, Chapel Hill: University of North Carolina Press, 1991).
10 See the articles in Bo Sarth, ed., *Memory and Myth in the Construction of Community*, Florence: European University Institute, 1999.
11 Ilan Pappe, 'Were They Expelled?: The History, Historiography and Relevance of the Refugee Problem', in Ghada Karmi and Eugene Cortran, eds., *The Palestinian Exodus, 1948–1988*, London: Ithaca, 1999, pp. 37–62.
12 Teddy Katz was interviewed in *Maariv*, together with Asa Kasher and others, on 21 January 2000; more details can be found in the news section of www.Arabia.com.
13 Ilan Pappe, 'Breaking the Mirror: Oslo and After', in Haim Gordon, ed., *Looking Back at the June 1967 War*, Westport: Prager, 1999, pp. 95–112.
14 Howard Zehr, *Changing Lenses; A New Focus for Crime and Justice*, Ontario: Herald Press, 1990.
15 Joan Fumia, 'Restitution versus Retribution: The Case for Victim-Offender Mediation, Conflict Resolution', *Suite101.com*, published for the first time in October 1988, reporting the Victim-Offender Program (VORP) at work in US legal system.
16 Edward Said, The *Politics of Dispossession*, London: Chatto and Windus, 1994, p. 167.
17 Peter Novick, *The Holocaust in American Life*, Boston Houghton Mifflin, 1999; Norman Finkelstein, *The Holocaust Industry, Reflections on the Exploitation of Jewish Suffering*, London: Verso Books, 2000.

9

Resistance Narratives: Palestinian Women, Islam and Insecurity

Maria Holt

In response to their traumatic experience of dispossession in 1948, stateless Palestinians adopted several modes of resistance. They developed a meta-narrative of suffering and resilience; they constructed an identity rooted in belonging to the territory of historic Palestine; and they embarked on a militant campaign to liberate the occupied homeland. Their efforts to resist the obliteration of their identity, by an enemy with its own strong counter-narrative of entitlement, have included tactics deemed illegitimate by outside observers and many Palestinians themselves. The involvement of Palestinian women in acts of violence has provoked unease, as it seemed to throw into question women's traditional role as preserver of national identity and protector of the family. This chapter explores Palestinian women's justifications for what others term 'atrocities'. Their arguments are supported by references to Islam as an indicator of identity and promoter of activism. However, random acts of violence by Palestinians, aimed at ending the Israeli occupation, can also be seen, in the context of this book, increasingly as expressions of deep insecurity. Far from espousing a 'moral' cause, the use of indiscriminate violence suggests the disintegration of Palestinian claims to justice; this is further reinforced by the involvement of women as defenders and perpetrators of terror as a weapon of resistance.

Narratives of loss and injustice

In October 2007, I met a Palestinian woman called Souad[1] in the West Bank city of Ramallah. At the time, Souad was thirty years old; she was married with three children and was working as a journalist. Two years earlier, her husband, a computer designer at al-Najah University in Nablus, had been imprisoned by the Israeli authorities; the Israeli army also demolished the family's home. This experience left Souad feeling profoundly helpless; it also caused her to think about her own role as a Palestinian woman living under military occupation with few means at her disposal to challenge that occupation. One important tool she possesses is her own voice; during our conversation, she referred to the dignity and steadfastness of Palestinian resistance and, in particular, the efforts of Islamic resistance groups, such as Hamas and Islamic Jihad. Under other circumstances, Souad may not have identified herself as an Islamist but her experiences had forced her to conclude that, in her words, 'Israel will never accept any peace agreement that threatens its security, so it is a waste of time to continue negotiating. Palestinians have the right to return to their homeland and they believe that, with God's help and the Islamic movement, they can realize their objective.'[2]

Telling stories 'about the past, our past, is a key moment in the making of ourselves',[3] and Souad's story is such a 'key moment', in the sense that it embodies a 'narrative of resistance' on three distinct levels: firstly, it is a factual account of events surrounding the arrest of her husband and demolition of her family home, and the feelings of trauma and helplessness these events caused; secondly it is an expression of opinion as a way both of making sense of her experience and also signalling defiance as an agenda for action; and, thirdly, it reiterates a larger narrative of Palestinian loss and rights. But her words also imply a deepening sense of insecurity as Palestinians struggle to maintain the morality of their cause while engaging in acts which have been termed 'illegitimate' or even 'terrorist'. Violence 'always has a context', which 'dictates both the range of public memory and political uses of the past',[4] and it is likely that Palestinian memory has been harmed by current vulnerability and perceived loss of 'morality'.

Souad's narrative of injustice is richly evoked in the words of another woman, who arrived in Lebanon in 1948, aged four; she remembers her mother saying to her that

> I must not pick oranges from the grove nearby. I was puzzled and insisted on knowing why. My poor mother, with tears streaming from her eyes, explained: 'Darling, the fruit is not ours; you are no longer in Haifa; you are in another country'... For the first time I began to question the injustice of our exile... I, as a dreamer living on the bare subsistence provided by a UN blue ration card... stand as a witness to Zionist inhumanity. I charge the world for its acquiescence in my destruction.[5]

The child grew up to be possibly the most famous Palestinian woman 'terrorist', Leila Khaled. Her narrative, like Souad's almost sixty years later, illustrates how Palestinian scars 'have accumulated like layers of sedimentary rock, each marking a different crisis – homelessness, occupation, war, dependency', and how resistance has been constructed and articulated.[6] What is striking is the presence of women's voices in the creation of a Palestinian national narrative utilized to justify acts of resistance ranging from speech and diplomacy to violent revolution.

In the face of mounting insecurity, in terms of living conditions and future prospects for a just resolution of the conflict, as well as the continuing Zionist project to delegitimize and obliterate their national identity, Palestinian women adopt various modes of resistance to protect themselves and their children. They confront efforts to negate their identity through memory, solidarity and steadfastness. Resistance is practised also by constructing a national narrative of 'Palestinian-ness' and it is here that women play a key role. Some scholars suggest that women's voices 'often differ significantly in form as well as content from dominant discourse',[7] but I would argue that they frequently embody similar themes, although women find it more difficult to be heard. In this chapter, I will discuss how ways of enacting and narrating 'resistance' have changed, in form and content, over time and, through their resistance narratives, the impact women have had on the performance of national identity; I will test the hypothesis by examining processes by which Palestinian women's voices 'are routinely suppressed or manage to emerge',[8] and by hearing what those voices say.

In order to address the increasingly vulnerable nature of Palestinian national identity and the narratives developed to ensure its survival, I will focus, firstly, on meanings of 'narrative' and of 'resistance' for Palestinian women and how these are contextualized; next, I will reflect on the link between identity and what Palestinian poet Mahmoud Darwish called the 'blessings of memory',[9] the remarkable stories told by women about their own lives and the life of Palestine itself and how these strengthen the ability to resist; thirdly, I will consider shared experiences of suffering, in exile and under occupation, and, in particular, the role of morality; and, finally, I will explore the specific modes of resistance adopted by women which enable them to challenge adversity, in the Palestinian territories and the Diaspora, in order to create a more tolerable future for themselves and their families. Beyond survival, resistance narratives are sometimes used to justify acts of violence, such as the 'terrorism' practised by Leila Khaled in the 1970s and the more recent and controversial use of suicide bombing against Israeli military and civilian targets. I will argue that, through their actions and their stories, women are pushing at the boundaries of 'acceptable' behaviour and thereby expanding understandings and methods of articulating 'resistance', but they do so within an environment of insecurity and crisis.

Rich tapestry of voices

In 2006–2007, I conducted two ethnographic research projects: the first explored Palestinian refugee women's lives in the camps of Lebanon in terms of memory, identity and change[10]; and the second examined the effects of Islamic resistance movements on Palestinian women in the West Bank.[11] During several fieldwork visits, I interviewed a total of 120 women, ranging in age from 18 to over 90, in towns, villages and refugee camps.[12]

I recognize that to discuss 'women' as an undifferentiated category appears to disregard the wide variety of women's experiences in Palestine and the Diaspora and, therefore, risks essentializing 'Palestinian women'. But I am seeking to engage in a particular sort of debate, one that takes *narrative* as a starting point. The prevailing narrative, in Scott's words, is 'the *self*-portrait of dominant elites as they would have themselves seen'.[13] However, as he argues, the 'recovery of the nonhegemonic voices and practices of subject peoples requires... a fundamentally different form of analysis than the analysis of elites, owing to the constraints under which they are produced'.[14] In the context of patriarchal Palestinian society, the majority of women are still expected to assume particular roles and therefore lack an authoritative 'voice'; even though the situations of violent and unresolved conflict that prevail in Lebanon and the Palestinian territories have permitted some women to engage in less traditional activities, this has not radically altered the notion of 'a woman's place'. Spivak argues that if, 'the subaltern has no history and cannot speak, the subaltern as female is even more deeply in shadow'.[15] While acknowledging that '[o]utside experts lack the deep nuanced knowledge that comes from...simply being in place'[16], this ethnographically based study intends to make a small contribution towards challenging narrative exclusions.[17] The focus of this chapter is on the practice of resistance and how it is articulated by women; diversity and creativity can be found in the rich tapestry of women's voices.

'A plurality of resistances': Articulating the narrative of 1948

Armed resistance is used 'to defend our people's rights and to force Israel and the international community to accept that our narrative of 1948, and our Palestinian rights, are of no less value than the rights or narrative of any other'.[18]

In this section, I will look more closely at how 'narratives of resistance' are enacted in the Palestinian context. The narrative form has been consciously adopted by Palestinians, who insist that 'our past history is an important source of our conception of ourselves; our self-knowledge, our conception of our own character and potentialities, is to a large extent determined by the way in which we view our own past actions'.[19] Narratives, stories and life histories are used, firstly, to make a case for the restoration of justice; secondly, to address the rising levels of insecurity felt by Palestinians as a result of their ongoing homelessness; and, thirdly, to set out a plan of action. However, it is likely that they are articulated differently by women and men. Whereas 'history', in the formal, 'account of real happenings' sense, tends 'to exclude marginal groups such as women', the majority of 'village storytellers were women'. Men, the ones with authority 'to speak and represent', usually assume the responsibility of recounting the national story of Palestine, while mothers and grandmothers relate the 'small' details of how life used to be.[20] Various authors have noted the absence of women's voices in the construction of the national narrative. Swedenburg, for example, speaks of men as 'the primary authorities...on local history and public affairs in general'.[21] Palestinian women's memories 'have rarely found a place'; their 'voice' tends to be conflated with maternal sacrifice and not taken seriously; they are likely to be excluded and their concerns often minimized or disregarded altogether.[22] One concludes, therefore, that communal identity is largely a male construct with little reference to the particular experiences of women.

But 'narrative' has other connotations. Palestinians are aware that their narrative of injustice is constantly subordinated to the more powerful Zionist 'narrative of 1948'. Power, as Bresheeth observes, 'is not only exercised over the land and its people, it also controls the story, its point of view, and the meta-narrative of *truth* and *memory*'.[23] The destruction of the Palestinian landscape has turned memory into an antagonistic process between competing versions of history. Yet power also engenders resistance. 'In this context, the power of the West, of an ascendant civilizational model, often forces others to look for means of resistance.'[24] In order to examine some of the ways in which Palestinians have sought 'means of resistance', to challenge the Western 'civilizational model' and the Israeli 'narrative of 1948', I have adopted Foucault's suggestion of 'taking the forms of resistance against different forms of power as a starting point'.[25] I am interested in looking at 'the resistances resulting from [...] various antagonistic interactions' in order to understand how power relations work.[26] Foucault argues that 'there is a plurality of resistances, each of them a special case [...] They are the odd term in relations of power; they are inscribed in the latter as an irreducible opposite'.[27] For Palestinian women in the West Bank and Lebanon, resistance operates at several levels, not only against Israeli power and violence but also in opposition to the 'universalizing characteristics' of Western feminism and, in some cases, against the anonymous, 'objective' violence of the Islamic system.[28]

Unlike the experiences of Leila Khaled and the secular Palestinian Front for the Liberation of Palestine (PFLP) in the early 1970s, Palestinian resistance in the late twentieth and early twenty-first centuries has been increasingly expressed and performed through the medium of Islam, whether in terms of authenticity or militant struggle. The national narrative of resistance is expressed through Islamic idioms which act as tools of legitimation and empowerment. My research reveals that, as members of a victimized population, many Palestinian women support the activities of Islamic resistance movements; they are aware that their position has been seriously undermined by Israeli policies. In the West Bank, for example, early marriage for girls is increasing as female students are forced by the prevailing economic and security situation to give up their education; women's mobility has been restricted by practices such as military checkpoints and the 'separation wall'. In Lebanon, the 2006 Israeli invasion resulted in massive loss of life and the destruction of homes and infrastructure. And although Palestinian communities were not directly targeted on this occasion, the memory of the war has led to widespread anxiety about the future. In response, many Palestinians are turning to Islam to make sense of an increasingly uncontrollable situation.

From as early as the 1920s, women have played an active role in the Palestinian national struggle and have contributed to the narrative of survival.[29] However, as Peteet argues, 'a gendered distinction appears in the practice of violence'.[30] Women certainly participated in activities aimed at ending the Israeli occupation of the West Bank and Gaza Strip, but their responsibilities have differed from those of men. In September 2000, Palestinians in the West Bank and Gaza Strip embarked upon a violent uprising, a second *intifada*, against the Israeli occupation. The following years witnessed the escalation of violence by the Israeli army and a corresponding increase in militant activities by the Islamist groups Hamas and Islamic Jihad. As a result of the increased use of violence by both sides, the position of women has been seriously undermined. Many women responded to their growing vulnerability by shifting their support to the Islamist political model. A high percentage of women actively contributed towards Hamas's resounding victory in the January 2006 Palestinian parliamentary elections, and many celebrated the group's 'victory' over Israel in the December 2008–January 2009 Gaza war. Islamic organizations in the West Bank and Gaza Strip have actively recruited and mobilized women. For example, they have established programmes to instruct women 'in Islamic culture, philosophy, law and religion', and 'to educate women in proper Islamic behaviour and the running of an Islamic home'.[31] It is likely that such activities permit women living in harsh and fearful conditions to feel they have some control over their lives.

Jamila is a twenty-year-old English literature student at Birzeit University in the West Bank. During the first *intifada*, her father, who was a member of the camp club at Jalazoun refugee camp near Ramallah, was arrested by the Israelis and imprisoned for six months, in her words, 'just for giving aid to refugees'. During the 2002 Israeli invasion of Ramallah, there were bulldozers outside her house, which has four stories and is near the camp, and they were afraid the house would be destroyed. On one occasion, the soldiers did not wait for her father to answer the door – they blew it up. Another time, her uncle's wife was driving her car late at night, as she was preparing for her son's wedding, but there was a curfew and she was killed. In 2006, Israelis soldiers invaded Jamila's house for two months; they took control of the roof of the house and sometimes sat in the living room with guns aimed at the family. The Israelis 'treat Palestinians as savages', she remarked, 'and this is why Islamic resistance movements began'.[32] Jamila's account illustrates very well the construction of a narrative of justification; the brutality of the Israeli occupation caused intense feelings of powerlessness and victimization for her family and this, as she says, 'is why Islamic resistance movements began'.

The 'blessings of memory'

How does a mother confirm her intimate recollections of childhood in Palestine to her children, now that the facts, the places, even the names, are no longer allowed to exist? (Edward Said)[33]

Hammer argues that memory and identity are connected; both, she suggests, 'are bound to historical contexts and have to be seen as constructions, intended and developed for particular purposes. They are subjective phenomena, changed over time, shared and contested'.[34] Although Palestinians' 'memories of a common origin […] give them a ground, and a symbolic repertoire, for identity, it is their experiences which … provide references for those symbols and a landscape for that ground'.[35] Identity is linked to feelings of belonging and community, an attachment to the land and, as Bowman says, something that took shape out of individual experience. It evolved into a shared national identity rooted in traumatic experience and also a personal identity based on memories. Palestinian women, both those who live in Palestine and abroad, possess a rich store of memories and these became central 'for the preservation of Palestinian identity in the diaspora',[36] as in the example of Leila Khaled's memory of the orange trees in Haifa.

It was women who told me about Palestine-as-homeland. In Lebanon, memories are characterized by nostalgia for a way of life and a place that no longer has any tangible link to reality while, in the West Bank, there is a sense that the homeland remains tantalizingly close. Those old enough to remember Palestine before 1948 described life in traditional village or rural settings, while younger women repeated the stories of their mothers and grandmothers, often in vivid and compelling detail. These narratives of belonging contribute to the sustaining of a scattered community. Historical memory 'is a collection of narratives transmitting what a people "knows" about its shared past. It is fluid and plural and, like a highway, constantly under construction and repair'. At the same time, '[n]arratives composing historical memory are partial and frequently contradictory'.[37] Oral historians alert us to the dangers of memory; as Thelen notes, '[i]n a study of memory the important question is not how accurately a recollection fitted some piece of a past reality, but why historical actors constructed their memories in a particular way at a particular time'.[38] This is particularly true in the case of Palestinian narrators, for whom the accuracy of recollection is less significant than the underlying message.

During my fieldwork, what came across to me most strongly were feelings of continuity, familiarity and nostalgia. A good example is Umm Nasif, who is seventy-five years old and lives in a former hospital building in the Sabra area of Beirut. She was born in Lydda in Palestine and remembers that there were figs, lemons, olives and gooseberries; there were also schools and hospitals, although most girls did not attend school and she herself did not learn to read and write. Umm Nasif left Palestine when she was fourteen, but she still feels that her country is Lydda which, she observed, is now an airport.[39] This raises the question of how memories such as Umm Nasif's affect identity today. As Rosemary Sayigh notes: 'The village – with its special arrangements of houses and orchards, its open meeting-places, its burial ground, its collective identity – was built into the personality of each individual villager to a degree that made separation like an obliteration of the self.'[40] Pre-1948 Palestine meant not only landscape and an abundance of fruits and vegetables but also a familiar way of life. Many women compared a settled, harmonious life in their own land with the uncertainties and humiliations of exile. They referred to customs associated with marriage and death, to styles of dress and cuisine, all of which impart a solid feeling of identity in the sense of knowing where one belongs. Their possession and dissemination of these precious memories, to family members and strangers, constitutes a powerful form of resistance and also a strong narrative of entitlement.

The familiar life was violently interrupted and effectively ended by the *nakbah* ('catastrophe') of 1948, when the majority of Palestinians were forced to flee from their homes and land. Many women regard this event as 'the end of history as "being", and the beginning of another kind of history they named "tragedy" or "destiny" or "God's will"'.[41] At that time, Palestine was a predominantly rural society and identity, therefore, was strongly associated with the land. Swedenburg argues that an 'individual's loss of land to Zionist colonization came to be regarded as an affront to the *national* honour ... these constituents of the (male) individual's identity – family, honour, land, women – resonated with the aura of the nation'.[42] But what implications does it have for *women's* notions of identity? The sense of dislocation following 1948 has had a pronounced effect on their identities. For example, Samira, a 37-year-old woman in Bourj el-Barajne camp in Beirut, said that 'being a refugee means being homeless, insecure, different from others; other people treat you with pity and fear'.[43] Similarly Nayla, a 42-year-old woman in Balata camp in Nablus, said she considers that all Palestinian refugees, wherever they live, are living under occupation; they do not have the freedom to express their Palestinian identity and are never treated well.[44]

This notion of identity as lack of freedom recurs repeatedly in the narratives of camp women. Huda is a 46-year-old midwife with one son. She has spent all her life in Lebanon and now lives in Bourj el-Barajne camp in Beirut. When I interviewed her in June 2006, she told me that her parents were young when they left Palestine in 1948. They took the keys of their house and told their children about the happy life they had in Palestine. Huda said that she regards Lebanon as 'only a country where I have to live while I wait to return to my own land'. A person without a homeland, she added, is exposed to suffering and poverty. If any hostilities break out, they have to hide their Palestinian identity. Following the 2000 Israeli withdrawal, she visited the Lebanese-Israeli border, she told me; her son tried to reach through the fence to touch Palestinian land.[45] This poignant image of continuing dispossession fuels a grand narrative of suffering.

Refugee women, whether they are located in the West Bank or Lebanon, tell stories of change, of how they and their families were abruptly uprooted from their places of belonging and plunged into terrifying uncertainty. These stories tend to emphasize the dislocation between an identity of attachment and the shattering or loss of identity, which has implications of violence. Mariam, a woman who was born in Palestine in 1936 and now lives in Beirut, told me about her childhood in Jaffa. She described hearing bombs and shooting at night, people shouting. In April 1948, she recalls, they headed north, through a landscape of explosions and overturned vehicles. Her family, like Huda's, took the keys of their homes and left most of their possessions behind, confident that the problem would soon be solved. She never saw her home again.[46] Even women who did not personally experience the *nakbah* are able to recount the stories of their parents' or grandparents' flight from Palestine and even to evoke the *smells* of their homeland. In Beirut, I met Wafa who, although she had spent all her life in Lebanon, had a strong image in her mind of her family's village in Palestine. A few years ago, she said, someone had a video of a wedding in her village, but she did not want to see it because she feared the reality might be disappointing. However, during the 2006 war between Israel and Hizbullah, the village was shown on the television; her son told her, 'look, it's our village'; even though people were being killed, she said, she felt happy because the village looked exactly like it did in her imagination; she could even smell it.[47]

Women's narratives chart the journeys undertaken by Palestinians into exile. They include many small details of how people coped. Asma in al-Am'ari camp in Ramallah, said that, when they first came to the camp, they lived in tents; people arrived from different villages, she said. UNRWA[48] issued cards to the refugees; they built a school and gave the pupils a glass of milk every day.[49] Similarly, Umm Mahdi, a 67-year-old widow in Bourj el-Barajne camp, recalled that, after reaching southern Lebanon on foot in 1948, her family moved to Tyre, where they were given tents; a truck brought bread, fish and other supplies from the UN and Red Crescent.[50] Several women described how the tents gradually became more solid structures, but still could not replace the homes they had left behind. Memories such as these are recounted as painful, humiliating and unjust. For example, some of the women living in Lebanon recalled the discrimination they had experienced from local Lebanese. The early generations, as Bowman notes, 'learned their identity through suffering intolerance and harassment at the hands of their unwilling hosts, the Lebanese authorities'.[51] Memories form the central core of Palestinian identity, but are experienced as both tragic and empowering; Palestinians use their memories of violent dispossession as a reminder of the unity of shared suffering and also as motivation for collective action. However, as Islah Jad says, there has been a fragmentation of Palestinians as a national community and an increase in enforced localism; people in one area often do not know what is going on elsewhere.[52]

As I listened to women in Lebanon and the West Bank, I noticed that their memories sometimes contain an element of dissent. For example, Umm Mahdi in Bourj el-Barajne camp, when recalling her family's flight from Kabri in northern Palestine, remarked on how Palestinians had been poorly served by their leaders. One of the respected men in her village, she said, told people to leave and they would be able to return after a week. 'He sold Palestine to the Israelis', she concluded bitterly.[53] Umm Saleh in the same camp, now aged seventy-seven, recalled how the Palestinian fighters were unable to protect the villages.[54] Occasionally one senses a thread of betrayal and disappointment running through women's narratives, highlighting what Julie Peteet calls the 'sacrificial nature of mothering'; in her discussion of 'mothering in the danger zone', she argues that women occupied a position as national activists that was regarded as being less central than 'formal masculinist militancy'.[55] This role reflects their perceived incapacity as formal history-tellers. But it is thrown into question by the image of the 'unnatural' Palestinian mother, who urges her sons to die for the cause. This is well illustrated in the account of the mother of a twenty-three-year-old suicide bomber. When invited to respond to news of her son's death, she said: 'I was very happy, when I heard. To be a martyr, that's something.'[56]

A narrative of heroism

The women of Palestine will resist this monstrous occupation imposed on us at gunpoint, siege and starvation. (Jameela Al-Shanti)[57]

In response to displacement, Palestinians began to construct a narrative of heroism, which was reinforced by local and international media. Scattered and demoralized Palestinians were determined to demonstrate that the Palestinian people as a unique national entity were not going to disappear. Edward Said has written that exiles 'are cut off from their roots, their land, their past... [They] feel, therefore, an urgent need to reconstitute their broken lives'.[58] They do this through the recounting of a national story. The 'narrative of heroism' was enriched by the actions of fighters such as Leila Khaled, but it has also been coloured by tragedy and failure, and this requires an explanation. Following the expulsion from Lebanon by the Israelis of the Palestine Liberation Organization (PLO) in 1982, a counter-narrative began to be articulated which, although it acknowledged Palestinian victimization, also incorporated qualities of survival and ways of fighting back other than armed struggle. Counter-narratives of the nation, as Bhabha observes, 'disturb those ideological manoeuvres through which "imaged communities" are given essentialist identities'.[59] It is through such 'disturbances', I think, that we can begin to appreciate the more subtle contributions made by women.

An inspiring example of women's contribution to the narrative of resistance may be observed during the 1982 Israeli invasion of Lebanon, when Palestinian women performed countless vital functions. After the Israeli military bombarded the Ain el-Hilweh refugee camp in Sidon, the camp was evacuated and some of the refugees took shelter in a local hospital. But the hospital was attacked too. Women in these places, said Siham, an activist in her late 50s,

> were cooking, washing clothes – it provided a basic level of survival. They brought flour to make bread. It was distributed to all the people. There were no male adults to take care of the family so the women had to do it [...] It was a big responsibility for women. Life was hard at that time; three or four families had to live together.[60]

The role of Palestinian women during this period, explained Khadija, a resident of the camp, was 'to take care of their families after the imprisonment of the men'.[61] Women also worked to rebuild the destroyed camps, sometimes with their bare hands. In Khadija's words:

> Journalists came. They saw how the women were cleaning the camp and trying to make it feel like home. When they saw women cleaning and using cement to rebuild the houses, they asked why we were doing it. The women replied that we were working like this because the young men were in prison. Slowly we were able to rebuild the houses so that our families could return.[62]

In 1982, women also 'organized small but vocal demonstrations and marches to protest the arrest or disappearance of their sons and husbands'.[63] These narratives illustrate the extraordinary resilience displayed by many women in a very dark period of Palestinian history. Similarly, during the first *intifada* in the West Bank and Gaza Strip (1987–1993), women participated in innovative ways in resisting the Israeli occupation. The narrative being expressed was one defiance and exasperation. For instance, women took part in protests and confrontations with the Israeli army; they were central in organizing and maintaining essential services, such as education for children and students, the provision of health care and the distribution of basic foodstuffs. Their work was social but also political, and their behaviour, as in Lebanon, challenged traditional forms of social control such as the family and the patriarchal nature of society. Raja Shehadeh has spoken of the strength of women such as these; 'they have the least to lose', he writes, 'and no ego to be pampered [...] They have been used to [...] oppression by men from the day they were born'.[64] It is striking that, despite patriarchal oppression, many Palestinian women have found a 'voice' which they are using to create a more nuanced narrative.

An example of a refining of the national narrative took place in June 2007, when violent clashes erupted between Fatah and Hamas for control of the Gaza Strip. Many Gazans, appalled by the violence, took to the streets to protest. According to former Palestinian Legislative Council member Dalal Salameh, women played a key role in these confrontations; they tried to prevent the factions from firing at each other. The women behaved as nationalists, she said, and were courageous.[65] Fatima, an activist in Ramallah, also referred to the demonstrations in Gaza; ordinary people, she recalled, including many women, took to the streets to protest.[66] This event illustrates a deterioration of communal solidarity, thus causing a fracturing of national identity and concomitant rise of insecurity. By raising their voices, women have sought to defuse the tension inherent in intra-Palestinian violence.

Finally, if we look at the refugee camps of Lebanon today, we can see the diverse supportive and constructive activities undertaken by women. Many women in the camps speak of being weary of politics. Political and military struggles, they argue, have failed to retrieve the homeland or solve the conflict. In the meantime, there are many practical pressures on them: to ensure the well-being of their children; to protect their own rights in an environment which remains intensely patriarchal; to care for the elderly and vulnerable members of their community; and, above all, to tell the story of Palestine to the world. At the same time, despite their resilience, they cannot escape the deepening sense of crisis currently afflicting the Palestinian national entity.

The majority of women, whether they are encountering the Israeli occupation on a daily basis or watching helplessly from the camps of Lebanon, see their primary identity in terms of motherhood. For example, according to academic Fadwa al-Labadi, during the first *intifada*, everyone practised resistance in ways that were mainly non-violent. There were good relations between families and within families. Now this has deteriorated. The second *intifada* witnessed a completely different sort of struggle; it was no longer the grassroots, but instead became an armed struggle, and this had a big impact on gender relations. Many women, she emphasized, do not believe in an armed struggle.[67] She is correct that women tend to incline more towards non-violent resistance, as we saw in the intra-Palestinian conflict in Gaza in 2007 and in Ain el-Hilwe in 1982. However, this is by no means always the case; Leila Khaled was not the only woman fighter; several of the women I met in Lebanon proudly recounted their own experiences as militant resisters. This raises the question of how the narrative of resistance has been shaped to accommodate women who choose to practice violence and how their choices might come into conflict with notions of morality and appropriate roles.

Narratives of morality

In the run-up to the Palestinian elections of January 2006, women played a decisive role in the victory of the Islamist party Hamas. Having failed to end the Israeli occupation through negotiation, compromise or non-violent protest, many Palestinians – including women, who expressed frustration at their inability to play a meaningful role in the second *intifada* – have come to regard resistance that has the support of religion as being one of the few options available to them. In the opinion of Maha, a student at Birzeit University, people voted for Hamas because they need to see changes in all aspects of life. Islamic movements, she added, look at a woman in a different way than others; they look beyond her body to her mind and this is attractive to women.[68] During the election campaign, Hamas effectively mobilized women, who went from house to house persuading other women to vote for Hamas.[69] However, the blockage in the political process and the absence of security for ordinary Palestinian families has later generated intense soul-searching about the failure of religious parties to conduct a 'moral struggle'.

This raises the question of what exactly is meant by a 'moral struggle'. While it has become routine, in Israel and the West, to condemn 'Palestinian terrorism', what effect is the culture of destructive violence having on Palestinian society and identity, especially since the start of the second *intifada* in September 2000? And how is the tension between precious memories and current chaos affecting women's sense of identity and involvement? In order to explore women's unease and increasing helplessness in the face of violence, I want to discuss briefly the role of morality. An important indicator of identity for Palestinians is religion and specifically Islam. In the period before the first *intifada* and the emergence of Hamas, the Muslim Brotherhood in the West Bank and Gaza worked to create 'the preconditions for an Islamic moral order'.[70] Lisa Taraki argues that the Brotherhood was successful 'in bringing a significant number of young refugee camp and urban women out of their homes and into mosques [...] Increasing numbers of young women and even girls adopted the "uniform" of the Islamist movement'.[71] The reason why many women seemed to welcome the re-Islamization of society was, firstly, that the secular nationalist movement, embodied in the PLO, had failed to end the occupation; and, secondly, that the Islamist movement appeared to offer a more inclusive environment.

However, while a broad cross-section of Palestinians, across age, class, gender and geographic divides, supported and participated in the first *intifada*, and felt it to be a moral struggle, the waging of the second *intifada* was more ambiguous. Some observers have remarked on feelings of moral decay which are beginning to afflict the community. For Dalia, an activist in Ramallah,

> political parties who cover themselves with Islam spoil religion. People are losing confidence. The people who work in politics in Palestine have a lot of work to do to give people confidence back in the national struggle. They need to renew their vision. Popular resistance should be peaceful, not a few people fighting.[72]

It is here that the Islamist movement has come to play an increasingly significant role. According to Islah Jad at Birzeit University, the Islamist parties have never used bribes but, instead, they have relied on motivation and internal conviction. In the 2006 elections, people reported that Hamas were not corrupt; they were seen as moral and as trying to build a model human being and this attracted many Palestinian voters.[73]

Islamists appeal to female members of the community on several levels. Firstly, they address the issue of Palestinian victimization. To become a victim is shameful and this is something with which women have great sympathy. The Palestinian people feel that they have been victimized by Israel for more than sixty years without effectively being able to fight back. Since its election in 2006, the Hamas government has been victimized, say Palestinians, by the international community. Some women complain that, although it is based on correct Islamic principles, this government has not been given a chance to introduce beneficial policies. Secondly, Islamist groups appeal to women on the level of good moral behaviour. They encourage the protection of women and the promotion of appropriate female roles. According to Hanan, a 41-year-old mother of seven in Balata camp, the role of women in Hamas is very wide. They are regarded as strong and important. Before Hamas won the election, she said, women helped; now they are in the legislative and municipal councils.[74] Thirdly, these groups also strengthen notions of community and the role of the active citizen. Islah Jad observed that Hamas has been successful in spreading religious teaching; social networks have been created in which women invite other women to their homes; pre-election meetings took place in friendly and comfortable settings.[75] Finally, by rejecting traditional practices of corruption and ignorance, they present a compelling vision of modernity. In the words of Jamila al-Shanti, an elected Hamas member of the Palestinian Legislative Council: 'There are traditions here that say that a woman should take a secondary role – that she should be at the back ... But that is not Islam.'[76]

In the camps of Lebanon, too, many women express contempt for failed political projects and some are turning towards Islam but, in this case, in terms of enhanced religious knowledge rather than party politics. For example, according to Soraya, a 31-year-old unmarried woman in Bourj el-Barajne camp, women now have more knowledge about religion; they understand more. She herself gives religious lessons to children and talks to other women about their rights.[77] For women such as Soraya, a greater awareness of Islam creates self-respect and resilience. It enables them to contribute in important ways towards the well-being of the community, for example through teaching other women about their rights and by working with youth, elderly people, widows and the disabled to create more tolerable living conditions. But the Islamist vision has been thrown into question by Hamas's 2008 war with Israel, and the terrible destruction unleashed on the people of Gaza. In these circumstances, Palestinian women are portrayed as helpless victims, unable to protect themselves or their children, or worse as encouraging their children to become 'martyrs'. One senses that they have little say in the waging of war and thus have been disempowered or disabled. Looking at events in Gaza from outside, the refugees in Lebanon feel helpless anger; as they are beyond Israel's direct sphere of control, this is experienced as a further fracturing of 'national identity'.

The insecure conditions of life for Palestinians in the West Bank and Gaza Strip has been highlighted by the emergence of a new model of female militancy: the *shahida*. According to Berko and Erez, three major 'types' of female suicide bombers have been identified: the first group acts 'out of religious conviction', the second out of a need to retaliate for the death of a loved one and the third as a result of 'exploitation' by a militant group.[78] This observation, based on interviews with a small number of 'failed' women bombers incarcerated in an Israeli prison, appears to disregard the larger narrative of the perceived threat to Palestinian national existence, locating women's motivations in more mundane concerns. Other scholars have suggested reasons for the 'aberration' of the female suicide bomber, such as choosing martyrdom 'as a way to escape the predestined life that is expected of them',[79] or as a misplaced quest for equal status in Palestinian society.[80] As Brunner observes, 'the female martyr, the female suicide bomber, the female terrorist irritates gender roles by imitating what we are used to see men do'. In her view, however, this phenomenon, rather than subverting conventional representations, has 'helped to reinforce the traditional gender order'.[81] While religious conviction, revenge, coercion or the destabilizing of 'existing social realities and discourses' may be part of the complex web of reasons motivating women militants,[82] one cannot help but feel that there is also an element of desperation. Far from espousing a 'moral' cause, the use of indiscriminate violence suggests the disintegration of Palestinian claims to justice; this is brought into stark relief by the involvement of women as defenders and perpetrators of terror as a weapon of resistance.

Conclusion

In this chapter, I have tried to show how a Palestinian national narrative of resistance, which is also a gendered narrative, has been painstakingly constructed from the memories of pre-1948 Palestine, the stories of survival in the Diaspora and the active striving of women and men against Israeli policies of dispossession and obliteration in Lebanon and the Palestinian Territories. However, the solidarity of this narrative is threatened by violence, whether in the form of the intra-factional conflict, the controversial targeting of civilians by several Palestinian factions or the emergence of the female suicide bomber. While the Palestinian struggle for justice and resolution often appears hopeless, a disturbing new trend is apparent whereby Israel and its supporters are laying siege to and seeking to delegitimize the very core of Palestinian national identity. Rather than a moral struggle, the Palestinian narrative is portrayed as embodying terrorism, irrationality and unnatural motherhood.

By detailing the lived experiences of Palestinian women in the Occupied Territory and the Diaspora, I have sought to assess their roles both as guardians of the Palestinian resistance narrative, and also as voices of morality. But, as I have suggested, their voices have also been used to justify and celebrate violence, thus undermining the

Palestinian narrative of self-vindication by providing ammunition to its detractors. Although women's narratives reveal a strong resilience, they also reflect a growing insecurity, both at the precariousness of their situation and the means adopted to change it.

Notes

1   The names of all women interviewed for this paper have been disguised.
2   Interview, Ramallah, 31 October 2007.
3   Annette Kuhn, 'Family Secrets: Acts of Memory and Imagination', in Michael Rossington and Anne Whitehead, eds., *Theories of Memory: A Reader*, Edinburgh: Edinburgh University Press, 2007, p. 231.
4   Bruce B. Lawrence and Aisha Karim, eds., 'Theorizing Violence in the Twenty-first century', in *On Violence*, Durham: Duke University Press, 2007, p. 3.
5   Leila Khaled, edited by George Hajjar, *My People Shall Live: The Autobiography of a Revolution*, London: Hodder and Stoughton, 1973, p. 28.
6   Michael Slackman and Ethan Bronner, 'Trapped by Gaza Blockade, Locked in Despair', *New York Times*, 13 July 2010.
7   Susan Gal, 'Between Speech and Silence', in Joan Vincent, ed., *The Anthropology of Politics: A Reader in Ethnography, Theory, and Critique*, Oxford: Blackwell, 2002, pp. 213–221.
8   Gal, 'Between Speech and Silence', p. 215.
9   Mahmoud Darwish, *Memory for Forgetfulness: August, Beirut, 1982* (translated from Arabic by Ibrahim Muhawi), Berkeley and Los Angeles: University of California Press, 1995, p. 15.
10 Funded by the Arts & Humanities Research Council (UK).
11 Funded by the United States Institute of Peace.
12 In the West Bank, a total of fifty-eight interviews were conducted in Abu Diss, Ramallah, Nablus, Hebron, villages near Nablus and Hebron, refugee camps in Ramallah, Hebron and Nablus and Birzeit University. The age range was as follows: under 20: 7 (12.1 per cent), 20–30: 18 (31 per cent); 30–45: 14 (24.1 per cent); 45–65: 16 (27.6 per cent); over 65: 3 (5.2 per cent). In Lebanon, sixty-two women were interviewed in Bourj el-Barajne, Shatila and Mar Elias camps in Beirut, Ain el-Hilwe and Mieh Mieh camps in Sidon, Rashidiyya and Kasmiyya camps near Tyre. The age range was as follows: under 20: 8 (12.9 per cent); 20–30: 5 (8.1 per cent); 30–40: 11(17.7 per cent); 40–50: 14 (22.6 per cent); 50–65: 17 (7.4 per cent); over 65: 7 (11.3 per cent).
13 James C. Scott, 'Domination and the Arts of Resistance', in Bruce B. Lawrence and Aisha Karim, eds., *On Violence: A Reader*, Durham and London: Duke University Press, 2007, p. 200.
14 Scott, 'Domination and the Arts of Resistance', p. 201.
15 Gayatri Chakravorty Spivak, 'Can the Subaltern Speak?', in Bill Ashcroft, Gareth Griffiths, and Helen Tiffin, eds., *The Post-Colonial Studies Reader*, London and New York: Routledge, 2006, p. 32.
16 Society for International Development, 'Women and the Politics of Place: An Introduction', paper written for the International Development Research Project

Power, Culture and Justice: Women and the Politics of Place, Rome, July, 2001, http://www.eurofem.org/info/Politics.html (last accessed: 19 June 2014).
17 Rosemary Sayigh, 'Women's Nakba Stories: Between Being and Knowing', in Ahmad H Sa'di and Lila Abu-Lughod, eds., *Nakba: Palestine, 1948, and the Claims of Memory*, New York: Columbia University Press, 2007, p. 138.
18 A senior Hamas leader (quoted in Alastair Crooke, *Resistance: The Essence of the Islamist Revolution*, London: Pluto Press, 2009, p. 195).
19 P. Connerton, *How Societies Remember*, Cambridge: Cambridge University Press, 1989, p. 22.
20 Sayigh, 'Women's Nakba Stories', p. 137.
21 R. Hammami, 'Gender, Nakbe and Nation: Palestinian Women's Presence and Absence in the Narration of 1948 Memories', *Review of Women's Studies*, No. 2, Birzeit University: Institute of Women's Studies, 2004; Ted Swedenburg, *Memories of Revolt: The 1936-9 Rebellion and the Struggle for a Palestinian National Past*, Minneapolis: University of Minnesota Press, 1995, p. 175.
22 Ahmad H. Sa'di and Lila Abu-Lughod, eds., *Nabka: Palestine, 1948, and the Claims of Memory*, New York: Columbia University Press, 2007, p. 8; Julie Peteet, 'Icons and Militants: Mothering in the Danger Zone', in Therese Saliba, Carolyn Allen, and Judith A. Howard, eds., *Gender, Politics and Islam*, Chicago and London: The University of Chicago Press, 2002, p. 151.
23 Haim Bresheeth, 'Te Continuity of Trauma and Struggle: Recent Cinematic Representations of the Nakba', in Ahmad H. Sa'di and Lila Abu-Lughod, eds., *Nabka: Palestine, 1948, and the Claims of Memory*, New York: Columbia University Press, p. 157.
24 Fouad Ajami, *The Arab Predicament: Arab Political Thought and Practice Since 1967*, Cambridge: Cambridge University Press, 1981, p. 16.
25 Hubert Dreyfus and Paul Rabinow, *Michel Foucault: Beyond Structuralism and Hermeneutics*, Chicago: University of Chicago Press, 1982, p. 211.
26 Azza M. Karam, *Women, Islamisms and the State: Contemporary Feminisms in Egypt*, Basingstoke: Macmillan Press, 1998, p. 4.
27 Michel Foucault, *The Will to Knowledge: The History of Sexuality Volume One*, London: Penguin Books, 1976, p. 96.
28 Slavoj Žižek, *Violence*, London: Profile Books, 2009.
29 Ellen J. Fleischmann, *The Nation and Its 'New' Women: The Palestinian Women's Movement 1920-1948*, Berkeley: University of California Press, 2003.
30 Julie Peteet, 'Male Gender and Rituals of Resistance in the Palestinian Intifada: A Cultural Politics of Violence', in Mai Ghoussoub and Emma Sinclair-Webb, eds., *Imagined Masculinities: Male Identity and Culture in the Modern Middle East*, London: Saqi Books, 2000, p. 116.
31 Sara Roy, *Failing Peace: Gaza and the Palestinian-Israeli Conflict*, London: Pluto Press, 2007, pp. 178-179.
32 Interview, Birzeit University, near Ramallah, 3 November 2007.
33 Edward Said, 'Reflections on Exile', in Russell Ferguson, Martha Gever, Trinh T. Minh-ha, and Cornel West, eds., *Out There: Marginalization and Contemporary Cultures*, New York: The New York Museum of Contemporary Art and Cambridge, MA: The MIT Press, 1990, p. 23.
34 Juliane Hammer, *Palestinians Born in Exile: Diaspora and the Search for a Homeland*, Austin: University of Texas Press, 2005, p. 40.

35 Glenn Bowman, 'Tales of the Lost Land: Palestinian Identity and the Formation of Nationalist Consciousness', in Erica Carter, James Donald and Judith Squires, eds., *Space and Place: Theories of Identity and Location*, London: Lawrence & Wishart, 1993, p. 95.
36 Muhammad Siddiq, 'On Ropes of Memory: Narrating the Palestinian Refugees', in E Valentin Daniel and John Chr Knudsen, eds., *Mistrusting Refugees*, Berkeley, Los Angeles and London: University of California Press, 1995, p. 95.
37 Mary Ann Tetreault, 'Divided Communities of Memory: Diasporas Come Home', in Haideh Moghissi, ed., *Muslim Diaspora: Gender, Culture and Identity*, London and New York: Routledge, 2006, p. 82.
38 David Thelen, 'Memory and American History', *Journal of American History*, Vol. 75, No. 4 (1989), pp. 1117–1129.
39 Interview, Gaza Building, Sabra, Beirut, 25 January 2007.
40 Rosemary Sayigh, 'The Palestinian Experience: Integration and Non-Integration in the Arab Ghourba', Arab Studies Quarterly, Vol. 1, No. 2 (Spring 1979), p. 107.
41 Sayigh, 'Women's Nakba Stories', p. 144.
42 Swedenburg, *Memories of Revolt*, p. 79.
43 Interview, Bourj el-Barajne camp, Beirut, 1 June 2006.
44 Interview, Balata camp, Nablus, 16 June 2007.
45 Interview, Bourj el-Barajne camp, Beirut, 2 June 2006.
46 Interview, Beirut, 6 June 2003.
47 Personal interview, Beirut, 1 February 2007.
48 United Nations Relief & Works Agency for Palestine Refugees in the Near East, founded in 1950 to meet the day-to-day needs of Palestinian refugees.
49 Interview, al-Am'ari camp, Ramallah, 18 June 2007.
50 Interview, Bourj el-Barajne camp, Beirut, 3 June 2006.
51 Bowman (1993: 84).
52 Interview with Dr Islah Jad, Birzeit University, Ramallah, 31 October 2007.
53 Interview, Bourj el-Barajne camp, Beirut, 3 June 2006.
54 Interview, Bourj el-Barajne camp, Beirut, 1 February 2007.
55 Peteet, 'Icons and Militants', p. 147.
56 Quoted in Bruce Hoffman, *Inside Terrorism*, New York: Columbia University Press, 2006, p. 162.
57 Jameela Al-Shanti, 'We Overcame Our Fear', *Guardian*, 9 November 2006.
58 Said, 'Reflections on Exile', p. 360.
59 Homi K. Bhabha, *Nations and Narration*, London: Routledge, 1990, p. 300.
60 Interview, Ain el-Hilweh camp, Sidon, 7 June 2003.
61 Interview, Ain el-Hilweh camp, Sidon, 7 June 2003.
62 Interview, Ain el-Hilweh camp, Sidon, 7 June 2003.
63 Peteet, 'Icons and Militants', p. 139.
64 Raja Shehadeh, *The Third Way: A Journal of Life in the West Bank*, London: Quartet Books, 1982, p. 115.
65 Interview, Dalal Salameh, General Union of Palestinian Women, Nablus, 16 June 2007.
66 Interview, Ramallah, 14 June 2007.
67 Interview with Dr Fadwa al-Labadi, Al-Quds University, Jerusalem, 18 June 2007.
68 Interview, Birzeit University, near Ramallah, 3 November 2007.
69 Interview, Ramallah, 3 November 2007.

70 Lisa Taraki, 'The Islamic Resistance Movement in the Palestinian Uprising', in Zachary Lockman and Joel Beinin, eds., *Intifada: The Palestinian Uprising Against Israeli Occupation*, Boston: South End Press, 1989, p. 172.
71 Taraki, 'The Islamic Resistance Movement', pp. 173–174.
72 Interview, Ramallah, 14 June 2007.
73 Interview with Dr Islah Jad, Birzeit University, Ramallah, 31 October 2007.
74 Interview, Balata camp, Nablus, 16 June 2007.
75 Interview with Dr Islah Jad, Birzeit University, Ramallah, 31 October 2007.
76 Ali Abunimah, 'Engaging Hamas and Hezbollah', *Al-Aqsa Journal*, Vol. 10, No. 2 (2008), pp. 25–28.
77 Interview, Bourj el-Barajne camp, Beirut, 3 June 2006.
78 A. Berko and E. Erez, '"Ordinary People" and "Death Work": Palestinian Suicide Bombers as Victimizers and Victims', *Violence and Victims*, Vol. 20, No. 6 (2005), pp. 603–623.
79 Clara Beyler, 'Messengers of Death – Female Suicide Bombers', *International Institute for Counter-Terrorism*, 12 February 2003, http://www.ict.org.il/Articles/tabid/66/Articlsid/94/Default.aspx [accessed 24 January 2010].
80 Raphael Israeli, 'Palestinian women: the quest for a voice in the public square through "Islamikaze martyrdom"', *Terrorism and Political Violence*, Vol. 16, No. 1 (2004), pp. 66–96.
81 Claudia Brunner, 'Female Suicide Bombers – Male Suicide Bombers? Looking for Gender in Reporting the Suicide Bombings of the Israeli-Palestinian Conflict', *Global Society*, Vol. 19, No. 1 (2005), pp. 29–48.
82 Frances S Hasso, 'Discursive and Political Deployments by/of the 2002 Palestinian Women Suicide Bombers/Martyrs', *Feminist Review*, Vol. 81, No. 1 (2005), pp. 23–51.

10

The State and Intergroup Violence: The Case of Modern Iraq

Ali A. Allawi

State violence in Iraq against specific communities (and since 2003, intergroup violence) has been a recurrent feature of its modern history. The scale and scope of this violence has varied but generally trended upwards as the state consolidated its power and extended its reach. State violence peaked towards the end of the Iran-Iraq War in 1988 with the genocidal campaign against the Kurds and then with the crushing of the widespread insurrection of March/April 1991. Intergroup violence on the other hand, hitherto a rare occurrence, rose to horrific levels in the 2005–2007 period, following the collapse of the Iraqi state after the invasion and occupation of the country in 2003. The typology of violence and ethnic cleansing that has marked Iraq's modern history can be better understood by utilizing a theoretical framework that contextualizes the scale of violence employed and relates it to its effects and its target groups. Underlying this process of large scale violence is the fear and insecurity experienced by the holders of state power. The tentative nature of their power and the fact that it was acquired through violent means, often by coups, only magnified the sense of insecurity of the ruling groups. As power became ever more concentrated in the Baathist era, so did the level of the violence employed against target groups, fortified by a narrative that validated the violence employed. Fear and insecurity have continued into the post-2003 invasion era. The democratic forms by which the holders of power have legitimated their rule have not diminished their fear that power could slip away from them. At the same time, narratives that demonize other groups and have contributed to the disastrous spread and deepening of sectarian sentiments are no longer contrived by the state but are now part and parcel of the baggage employed by sectarian parties as well as insurrectionists and terrorists.

Slide into communal violence

Extraordinary levels of intergroup violence broke out in Iraq after the US invasion and occupation of the country, reaching an apogee of sorts in 2005–2007, and continuing to sputter fitfully, in a much diminished state, into early 2013. But as of writing, it has erupted once again to alarming levels. The scale of intergroup violence has challenged Iraqis' perception of themselves and their nation, leading to vehemently voiced denials that such acts could be committed by Iraqis. The often heard refrain was that Iraqis were a generally tolerant and accommodating people, and that the violence could only have come about as a result of foreign interference and conspiracies. At another level, many Western commentators and analysts blithely attributed the violence to historic antagonisms between rival sects and ethnicities that persisted into modern times. The reality, as always, is more complex and nuanced than the narrative of a well-adjusted society pushed into terrible discord by scheming politicians and foreign powers; or the counter-narrative of age-old antagonisms that refuse to die – ones whose obscure origins go back to the mists of time but still maintain their potency as a determinant of identity and behaviour.

For centuries, Iraq had been a home for a variety of ethnicities and sects. But by the beginning of the twentieth century, Iraq's population, at about 1.6 million people according to the rough 1919 British census, was a fraction of what it had been at its heights when Iraq was the centre of the Abbasid Empire. In spite of the diversity of the population, the fact remains that during Iraq's pre-modern period ethnic and religious conflicts, though not altogether absent, never reached the scale which resulted in mass killings and expulsions. Sectarian massacres, of Shias by Sunnis, and vice versa, did result when control over the country changed hands between the (Sunni) Ottoman Empire and the (Shia) Safavid Empire, but these were instigated as a matter of official retribution. Similarly, throughout the long Ottoman period, the *millet* system allowed for the official representation of the recognized religious groups even though the state systematically discriminated in favour of its Muslim subjects, and within this category, in favour of its Sunni Muslim subjects. Starting with the major modernizing reforms of the mid-nineteenth century, Sunni Muslim subjects of the Empire in Iraq, whether Arab, Kurd or Turcoman, did have access to power and office; and at the onset of the First World War, there were a smattering of Jews, Christians and Shia Muslims from Iraq holding high office in the Ottoman administrative structures, whether as provincial officials or parliamentary representatives. The large scale killings and ethnic cleansings of Armenians, and to a lesser extent Balkan Christians, that marked the declining years of the Ottoman Empire, did not stretch to the three Ottoman provinces out of which modern Iraq was created. In this regard, the Ottoman Empire's ethnic, religious and sectarian policies in Iraq, though hardly exemplary, were a good deal better than what subsequently transpired after Iraq was constituted as a modern state.

An analytical model

Iraq was declared a formally independent state in 1932, when the British mandate ended and the country was accepted into the League of Nations. Between 1918 and 1932, the direct presence of the British in Iraq and their influence over political and administrative decisions necessarily limited the ability of the central authorities to plan and instigate acts of violence or repression against parts of their population. For it has been the state, at least until 2003, that had been responsible in the main for initiating, encouraging and implementing the string of violent ethnic and sectarian episodes that have punctuated Iraq's modern history. I will employ a conceptual framework to assess and analyse the nature of the scope of the violence that has affected Iraq since its independence. This framework is based, in part, on the work of Michael Mann on ethnic cleansing and in particular on the model that he evolved to classify the types of cleansing and violence in intergroup relations.[1] However, I have substantially modified and elaborated on Mann's model to fit the circumstances of Iraq.

In Mann's model, an ethnicity is a group that defines itself or is defined by others as sharing common descent and culture. A nation is an ethnic group that has political consciousness and claims collective political rights in a given territory.[2] Mann's model postulates a matrix with three columns of varieties of ethnic cleansing (from 'None' to 'Total') ranged against six types of violence (from 'None' to 'Premeditated Mass Killings' – see Table 10.1). In the case of Iraq, both of Mann's categories apply, but a

Table 10.1 Types of violence and cleansing in intergroup relations

Types of Violence	Types of Ethnic Cleansing		
	None	Partial	Total
1. None	1. Multi-culturalism/ toleration 2. Consociational/ Confederalism	Partial abandoning of Identity, e.g., through voluntary official language adoption	Voluntary assimilation
2. Institutional coercion	Discrimination	1. Official language restrictions 2. Segregation	Cultural suppression
3. Policed repression	Selective policed repression	1. Policed partial repression of out-group's language and culture 2. Policed out-group settlement/ displacement	1. Policed total suppression of out-group's language and culture 2. Population exchanges 3. Policed deportations and pressured migration
4. Violent repression	Generalized policed repression	1. 'Pogroms', communal riots, some forms of rape 2. Violent settlement/ displacement	1. 'Wild' deportation & emigration 2. Biological: sterilization, forced marriage, some forms of rape
5. Unpremeditated mass deaths	'Mistaken' war, civil war and revolutionary projects, fratricide	'Callous' war, civil war & class war & revolutionary projects	Ethnocide
6. Premeditated mass killing	Exemplary and civil war repression, systematic reprisals	1. Forced conversion 2. Politicide 3. Classicide	Genocide

Source: From Michael Mann, *The Dark Side of Democracy: Explaining Ethnic Cleansing*, Cambridge University Press, 2005, p. 12

third one must be added: the *sectarian* group. In this instance, a sectarian group is one that is defined by a specific religious consciousness. It can share many of its beliefs with the dominant religious group but is also different from it in important doctrinal and ritualistic ways. Discrimination, persecutions and violence against such a group are manifested whenever the sect makes political demands or is seen as a political threat. There are other examples of focussed state violence against specific groups in Iraq – such as against religious minorities – and these will form the fourth peg of the model in Iraq.

In the analytical model that I have postulated for Iraq, I have expanded on the four often interlocking powers that are the drivers of ethnic cleansing: Ideology; Economic Power; Political Power; and Military Power. Ideology includes the mobilization of public opinion by reference to historical and cultural narratives and appeal to common norms, values and rituals. These are all juxtaposed against the target group. Economic power includes the appeal to material interests in the isolation and targeting of the object group. Military power implies the use of lethal violence against the target group. Political power implies the use of centralized regulation of social life to isolate the target group. In the expanded model, there are eight variables that can be used to assess an event of ethnic/sectarian/religious violence. They include: the nature of the violence: the scope and scale of the violence; the political/historical context; the ideological narrative employed; the role and response of the state; agency; the outcome or outcomes; and finally extenuating or special circumstances such as the degree of the threat posed to the central authority or to the community itself.

The events that I have chosen to reflect the unbroken line of extreme violence used against particular groups are by no means the whole story of violence in modern Iraq. Nearly every coup, attempted coup or revolution was accompanied by some level of violence, especially the revolutions of 1958 and 1963. But these could be excluded from the argument as the violence was primarily driven by political, class and ideological factors and not particularly connected with ethnicities or sects. The events are:

1. The Assyrian Crisis of 1933
2. The Jewish Pogrom (*Farhud*) of 1941
3. The Expulsion of Fayli Kurds and Iraqi Shias of Iranian origin, 1969–1981
4. The *Anfal* campaign against the Kurds of 1988
5. The Shia Uprising (*Intifida*) of 1991
6. Mass killings, expulsions and disappearances of civilians, 2003–2008

Case 1: The Assyrian Crisis of 1933

The Assyrian Crisis of August 1933 affected a large community of ethnic Assyrians, followers of Nestorian Christianity, who inhabited the northern borderlands between Iraq and Turkey.[3] The community, numbering then perhaps 50,000 in total, were composed mainly of refugees transplanted by the British to Iraq as a result of a failed uprising against the Turks during the First World War. A large number of their able-bodied men served in the Iraq Levies, a British-officered force that was used to protect British installations and assets in Iraq. Following Iraq's formal independence, the Assyrian officers of the Levies resigned en masse, fearful that the end of the mandate would compromise their condition in Iraq. They were supported by the Assyrians' spiritual leadership in demanding recognition of their community rights and their claims for a special autonomous status in northern Iraq. Skirmishes between the armed Assyrians and the Iraqi army and police continued for a period, culminating in a major battle where a large group of Assyrians, returning from temporary exile in Syria, attacked the Iraqi army at the border outpost of Dairbaun. The Assyrian revolt was crushed with considerable loss of life. A particularly horrible massacre of Assyrians took place in the village of Summayl, where 300 Assyrian men were killed by a detachment of the Iraqi army (Table 10.2).

Table 10.2 The Assyrian Crisis of 1933

Nature of Violence	– Battles between regular army, police, irregular government forces and armed Assyrians – Attacks on unarmed civilians and villagers by regular army and irregular and tribal forces
Scale of Violence	– Probably about 600 people killed, including 300 massacred in one single incident (Assyrians claim 3,000 killed) – About 5,000 refugees
Agents	– Iraqi military and police – Arab and Kurdish tribes
Ideology/Narrative	– Assyrians are British agents and mercenaries – An arrogant and unassimilable community – Unpatriotic and refuses to take Iraqi nationality – Aggressive and violent people, misled by their spiritual leaders – Narrative did not extend to the other established Christian communities in Iraq
Political/Historical Context	– End of Mandate – Test for an independent Iraqi government – Test for an untried Iraqi military – League of Nations concern about the rights of minorities in Iraq – Sympathy for Assyrian Christians in ecclesiastical circles in Britain as well as the general public
Role of State Actors and Public Opinion	– Forceful army commander backed by ministers. King opposed at first and then supportive – Great popular support for military action – Foreign outrage especially in Britain and Europe
Outcomes	– Decisive defeat of Assyrian revolt – Limited retributive action – Most Assyrians subsequently granted citizenship – Assyrian separate consciousness persists into present times fuelled by profound trauma of the 1933 Revolt

Utilizing Mann's basic model, the Assyrian revolt falls into the category of 'Violent Repression', with 'Partial Cleansing'. It is a borderline zone in which ethnic cleansing had partly and occasionally taken place. However, the element of persistency and continuity is lacking in this regard. It is an event-driven form of cleansing, a singular episode that had not occurred in a similar fashion before, nor one that was repeated, even in a substantially diminished form, in later times.

Case 2: The Jewish Pogrom (*Farhud*) of 1941

The Jews of Iraq were a long established community whose roots went back to the Babylonian exile. On the eve of Iraq's independence, they numbered nearly 120,000 people mostly concentrated in Baghdad.[4] They were probably the largest single community in Baghdad at the outbreak of the world war. Although not uniformly well-off, the community was prominent in the business, cultural and professional life of the country. They provided ministers and senior officials in the governments of Iraq during the mandate period. Following the death of King Faisal I, who followed a policy of befriending all communities, and the general climate of insecurity that affected Iraq's Christians during and after the Assyrian crisis, a noticeable unease spread amongst the Jews of Iraq. This was compounded by the rise of Nazism in Europe, and the increasing influence of extreme Arab nationalist and fascist-influenced movements in Iraq of the 1930s. Iraqi opinion was also greatly impacted by the plight of the Arabs of Palestine and the (increasingly violent) resistance there to the rising tide of Jewish immigration. A conscious anti-Semitic strain began to creep into the discourse of Arab nationalists of Iraq in this period. At the outbreak of the Second World War, Iraq followed a pro-British course until the advent in 1941 of a pro-Axis government under Rashid 'Ali Gailani. The subsequent confrontation with the British led to hostilities which ended with the occupation of Iraq by British forces, the overthrow of Rashid 'Ali's government and the return of the Prince Regent to power.

In the period between 30 May 1941 and 3 June 1941 a power vacuum developed in Baghdad with the British forces outside of the city and government of Rashid 'Ali in disintegration. On 1 June 1941, anti-Jewish riots erupted across Baghdad with widespread looting and indiscriminate killing. Nearly 200 Jews were killed and property damage ran into the millions of dollars. After the end of the Second World War, Iraq's Jews were increasingly affected by events in Palestine.

Following the establishment of the State of Israel, Jews were subject to a variety of restrictive laws and administrative orders. A law allowing the departure of Iraq's Jews to Israel was promulgated, on the condition that departing Jews renounce their Iraqi nationality. Between 1948 and 1951, nearly 90 per cent of Iraq's Jewish community of nearly 140,000 had left the country, mainly for Israel. The remaining Jews stayed on until the 1970s when the last of the community disappeared from Iraq (Table 10.3).

Table 10.3 The Jewish Pogrom (*Farhud*) of 1941

Nature of Violence	– Mobs often whipped up by a collapsing government – Looting, murders, some rape – Mainly concentrated in capital – Disproportionately affected poorer Jews – A few days duration before order was restored
Scale of Violence	– About 200 killed – Property damage estimated at £100,000 (about $20 million in present terms)
Agents	– Mobs with no clear leadership, mainly driven by desire for loot – De-mobilized soldiers – Members of *Futuwwa* movement, a paramilitary, youth organization
Ideology/Narrative	– Beginning of extreme Arab nationalist discourse in education and media – Widespread Anti-British and Pro-Axis sentiments – Depiction of Jews as fifth columnists for the British – Influence of Axis anti-Semitic propaganda
Political/Historical Context	– Failure of Rashid 'Ali's government and the flight of its key members – Security vacuum in Baghdad for a few days – British invasion of Iraq and defeat of Iraqi army – Reaction to growing Zionist settlements in Palestine – No serious previous incident of mob or organized violence against Jewish community – Reasonable intercommunity relationships – Jews well-represented in business, academic and official posts
Role of State Actors and Public Opinion	– Government collapse and Municipal Authorities unable to restore order – Order only restored after entry of British forces – Some government officials implicated in whipping up sentiment – Mobs drawn nearly exclusively from poorer quarters of capital – Many cases of Muslims protecting Jewish lives and property
Outcomes	– Traumatic effect on Iraqi Jewish community – Greater willingness on part of Iraqi Jews to consider the Zionist message – Shame and denial on part of Iraqis – Consolidation of sentiment of Iraqi Jewish 'separateness'

The responsibility of masterminding and directing the Jewish *Farhud* of 1941 cannot be entirely placed on the Iraqi government of the time. It was no doubt supported by individuals in the government who were extreme nationalists and anti-Zionists. But the government had effectively ceased to function when the mobs came out into the streets. In fact, the security vacuum in Baghdad was partly caused by the inexplicable decision of British forces not to enter the city. These forces had defeated the Iraqi army units that resisted them and were camped just outside of the city when the rioting took place. Lawlessness, rioting, looting and property destruction are frequent episodes in Iraqi history when order breaks down.[5] But the clear targeting of the Jewish community was unprecedented.

However, Mann's model does not quite apply to the 1941 inter-communal violence in Iraq. The category of 'Pogroms, communal riots, some forms of rape' obviously applies to the *Farhud*. However, in as much as it had only spotty encouragement by the state, and no other clearly identified political group or party was involved (apart from some members of the youth movement, the *Futuwwa*). It thus cannot be said to have been officially sponsored. At the same time, and unlike the Assyrian crisis of 1933, the *Farhud* had wide-ranging effects, primarily in psychological terms. For the first time in the modern history of Iraqi Jews, the Zionist idea began to take root. Previously, there was little or no interest taken by Iraqi Jews in the Zionist project in Palestine. Iraq was their homeland, and Zionism affected them only indirectly. After the *Farhud*, some Iraqi Jews began to seriously question the viability of their community in Iraq in light of the profound changes taking place in the Middle East. After the war, the memory and lessons of the *Farhud* became a potent weapon in the determination of the loyalty of Iraqi Jews towards Iraq as their natural home and towards the new state of Israel.

Case 3: The expulsion of Fayli Kurds and Iraqi Shias of assumed Iranian origin, 1969–1981

The 1924 nationality law, which sought to define who was an Iraqi, created problematic categories of citizenship. Basically, an Iraqi was defined as any person who was living in Iraq at the onset of independence and who had hitherto been – or his parents had been – a subject of the Ottoman Empire. A sub-category of citizenship was also recognized, namely Iraqis who were subjects of Persia but were living in Iraq at independence. The majority of such Iraqis were Arab Shias who chose to become Persian subjects to avoid Ottoman conscription. This sub-category of citizenship, known colloquially as *taba'iya* (or dependency), continued to define the citizenship of the holders' descendants.

The nationality law also left large groups of people, primarily Fayli Kurds, mostly living along the central borderlands with Iran, with no clear national status. Fayli Kurds, numbering around 500,000 by the 1970s, were a Kurdish speaking community, known in Iran as Luris, who professed the Shia creed, unlike the majority of Iraq's Kurds, who were Sunni. A significant number of Fayli Kurds, probably numbering around 150,000 at the beginning of the 1970s, also lived in the capital, Baghdad, where they were involved in the mercantile life of the city as well as in crafts and trades. Successive Iraqi governments had failed to resolve the nationality issue for the large number of stateless Fayli Kurds, and though infrequent cases of small scale deportations (numbering in the dozens) did affect the community, they had been mostly left alone by the Iraqi state.

The return of the Baath party to power in 1968 was accompanied by a far more strident anti-Iranian and extreme Arab nationalist rhetoric. A succession of events starting in the early 1970s, targeting the resident Iranian community in Iraq, where up to 30,000 Iranians who were permanently resident in Iraq, were expelled. This was followed throughout the seventies by increasingly aggressive measures against the Faylis. In the mid-1970s Iraq expelled around 40,000 Fayli Kurds to Iran, alleging they were Iranian nationals. However, following the Iranian revolution of 1979, the assumption of supreme power by Saddam Hussein, and the beginnings of the Iran-Iraq War, the expulsions became more systematic, and included Iraqi nationals with assumed Persian ancestry.

In 1980, decree 666 of the Revolutionary Command Council, stripped Fayli Kurds of Iraqi citizenship. Their properties were seized by the government. Between 220,000 and 300,000 Iraqi Fayli Kurds were expelled from their homes and were forced to march across the Iranian border into decades of exile and statelessness. Others became non-citizens in their own country. Many of the families that were deported to Iran were highly educated, economically successful and held high ranking positions in the government. While in Iran, many of these families lived in camps and were denied access to work, education and travel documents. They were even unable to register births, deaths and marriages.[6]

Following the invasion of Iraq in 2003 and the overthrow of the Baathist regime, the issue of the nationality status of Fayli Kurds and Iraqis with presumed Iranian ancestry was partly resolved by a new nationality law. The 2006 Iraqi Nationality Law repealed decree 666 and stated that all persons denaturalized by the former government should have their Iraqi nationality reinstated. However, the documentation required to have one's nationality reinstated onerous for many people, as it required proof of residency in Iraq under the 1957 census. According to the Iraqi Ministry of Displacement and Migration, since 2003 about 20,000 families (or roughly 100,000 individuals) have had their citizenship reinstated. But many have been unable to provide this proof of registration. During the war and subsequent disturbances, records were destroyed or lost, and in some cases, people were simply not included in the census (Table 10.4).

The expulsion of the Fayli Kurds and Iraqi Shias of presumed Iranian origin was a qualitative leap in the scale and size of the organized repression of the state. It also followed the vastly increased capacities of the state to undertake such large scale operations of ethnic cleansing, influenced by the totalizing nature of the Baathist state. Using Mann's model, this episode can be placed in the context of 'Policed deportations and pressured emigration'. However, it fell short of the total cleansing of this community. A small fraction continued to reside in Iraq as a result of exceptions made, either because of bribes, deliberate oversight by officials, incomplete records or political protection. In terms of the type of violence employed, the fourth of Mann's categories of 'violent repression' would apply. All-in-all, the expulsion of Fayli Kurds and Iraqi Shia of presumed Iranian origin lies at the edge of Mann's grey zones but still falls short of ethnocide or genocide.

Table 10.4 The Expulsion of Fayli Kurds and Iraqi Shias of Presumed Iranian origin, 1969–1981

Nature of Violence	– Imprisonments, concentration camps, deportations, expulsions – Killings, rape, torture, beatings, forced to march across minefields – Stripping of nationality rights – Sequestration of assets – All affected were Shia Muslims
Scale of Violence	– Killings in the hundreds, possibly low thousands – Rape incidents in the hundreds – Asset sequestration in the hundreds of millions of dollars – Approximately 100,000 people affected in total
Agents	– Secret police units – Regular police – Baath Party operatives – Use of informers
Ideology/Narrative	– Stateless people who are not Iraqis (Applies to Fayli Kurds) – Iraqis of assumed Persian (2nd Class Nationality) antecedents and therefore suspect in their loyalties – Appeal to Iraqi Arab patriotism (as against Iran) – Appeal to Arab nationalism and the Arabism of Iraq as part of Baath ideology – Indirect appeal to sectarian (Sunni) sentiments – Elimination of Iranian fifth columnists
Political/ Historical Context	– Ascendancy of Arab nationalist/Baathist ideology in the 1970s – Increasing tensions with Iran after 1979 revolution – Tensions with Shia religious establishment – Massive repression against Iraqi Shia political Parties
Role of State Actors/ Public Opinion	– Entirely organized and executed by central Government and Baath Party – Information black-out on actual measures taken – Positively received by Arab nationalist and most Sunni Arab opinion – Anxiety and Fear on the part of religious Shia and urban Shia opinion – Groups close to power benefitted from sequestered assets
Outcomes	– Large population movement to Iran and from Iran to other countries – Beginning of Iraqi exile and refugee communities around the world – Embitterment and divisions within Iraqi society – Return of some refugees after 2003 – Massive claims for compensation and restitution affecting the post-2003 governments

Case 4: The *Anfal* campaign against the Kurds of 1988

The Kurds of Iraq, accounting for up to 20 per cent of the population, had been a reluctant addition to independent Iraq. There were frequent tribal uprisings during the monarchical period, but none were serious or widespread enough to threaten the stability of the state. However, after the 1958 revolution, Kurdish demands for autonomy became more persistent, in line with the rise of Kurdish national consciousness. Large scale revolts flared up across northern Iraq from the early and mid-1960s. In particular, the 1973–1975 uprising represented a serious threat to the Baathist regime and was put down with extreme brutality. The revolt collapsed when the Shah's Iran withdrew its support to the rebellion.

However, with the onset of the Iran-Iraq war, the Kurdish leadership, taking advantage of the prevailing war conditions, rose against the central government, draining resources and manpower from the major frontlines in the south-eastern part of the country. As the war reached its apogee, the Baathist regime began to plan for draconian measures against the Kurdish civilian population, aimed at 'settling' the Kurdish issue once and for all. The plans laid out included widespread destruction of villages, population resettlements and mass killings. These plans were put into effect in 1988, as the Iran-Iraq war was winding down and the Kurds could no longer count on Iranian military and logistical support. The campaign, code-named *al-Anfal*, was launched in several phases in 1988 and 1989, although systematic measures against the Kurdish population had already commenced in 1986. The campaign was wide-ranging and brutal, involving the use of ground and air forces, destruction of countless villages and forced resettlements. In a frightening development, government forces used various types of poison gas against civilians. At Halabja, nearly 5,000 civilians were gassed by Iraqi forces.

In total, tens of thousands of civilians were killed during the *Anfal* campaigns, and about 4,500 Kurdish villages in areas of northern Iraq were systematically destroyed. The number displaced could have reached about a million, nearly a third of the country's estimated Kurdish population.[7] Estimates of the total casualties have varied from a high of a million deaths (almost certainly an exaggeration) to a more realistic number of between 150,000 and 200,000 people. During the *Anfal* war crimes trial of 2006–2007, the Iraqi prosecutors offered a number of 182,000 killed. The primary targets were men of battle-age, between sixteen and forty years old. The *Anfal* campaigns against the Kurds were considered by most international legal experts, as well as the Iraqi Special Tribunal, as constituting genocide.

The bitter memory of the *Anfal* campaign was behind the mass movement of the Kurdish population of Iraq to Iran and Turkey in 1991, following the end of the first Gulf war and the collapse of the uprisings in the South and the Kurdish north against the regime of Saddam Hussein. The *Anfal* became a determining factor in the demand for the Kurds of Iraq for a high degree of autonomy outside the security control of the central government and has been the main impetus behind the establishment of the Kurdistan Regional Government as a special autonomous region inside the state of Iraq (Table 10.5).

The *Anfal* campaign has all the hallmarks of genocide. Using Mann's model, the type of cleansing employed falls clearly under the 'Total' category. Nearly all the entries that Mann employed to classify Total Cleansing apply in the case of the *Anfal* campaign and its aftermath. Kurds were encouraged to become Arabized (voluntary assimilation); cultural rights of Kurds were denied (Cultural suppression); policed deportations and

Table 10.5 The *Anfal* campaign against the Kurds of 1988

Nature of Violence	– Mass summary executions and mass disappearance – Widespread use of poison gas – Wholesale destruction of villages – Deliberate destruction of the town of Qala Diza – Wholesale destruction of schools, hospitals and places of worship – Population movements – Cultural war against Kurdish language and forced Arabization
Scale of Violence	– Killings in the tens of thousands, possibly hundreds of thousands – Mass rape in the thousands – Destruction of the village base of Kurdish economic, social and cultural life – Entire villages resettled – Approximately 1,500,000 people affected in total
Agents	– Regular Iraq Army Divisions – Republican Guards Divisions – Secret police – Baath Party militia – Auxiliary Kurdish tribal forces – Rival Kurdish tribes
Ideology/Narrative	– Kurdish aspirations as threats to national unity – Kurds as a constantly rebellious people – Fifth columnists for Western powers, Israel and Iran – Kurdish nationalism as threat to Arab identity of Iraq – Kurds as targets of racist/ethnic slurs – Tribally minded and beholden to archaic leadership
Political/Historical Context	– End of Iran-Iraq war – Kurdish uprising of 1973–1975 – Failure of government attempt to split Kurdish leadership – Opportunity to settle the Kurdish problem by brutal suppression in a benign international environment (Most Western and Arab powers supported Iraq in the Iran-Iraq War and refused to give credence to allegations of genocide)
Role of State Actors/ Public Opinion	– Entirely organized and executed by central Government and Baath Party – Information black-out on actual measures taken – Positively received by Arab nationalist and most Iraqi Arab opinion when presented as national unity measure and aimed at international conspiracies
Outcomes	– A defining episode in modern Kurdish history – Massive displacement of Kurdish population – Fear and anxiety amongst Kurds, leading to demands for autonomy and self-government and self-defence capabilities – Cemented Kurdish consciousness and demands for specific Kurdish territorial boundaries – General recognition that genocide had been committed against the Kurds – War crimes trials in 2006/2007 with many culprits sentenced to death and executed

expulsions were commonplace; mass rape and forced marriages, especially by and with the internal security forces, occurred regularly; and, in the end, premeditated and systematic mass killings occurred as well. It falls well within the areas of Mann's model of darker shading, which is the domain of ethnocide and genocide.

Case 5: The Shia uprising (*Intifida*) of 1991

Adherents of Shia Islam are the majority of the Arab Muslims of Iraq and account for nearly 60 per cent of the total population of Iraq. The Shia as a community saw themselves as disadvantaged in independent Iraq and poorly represented in the decision-making ranks in the upper echelons of the Iraqi state; nor did majority Shia provinces, especially in the South of the country, fairly participate in the growth of revenues accruing to the government as a result of rising oil exports. Although the state did not openly espouse sectarian policies, the sense of disadvantage was widespread in the community, becoming more acute as Iraq launched its war against Iran. The attack by the Baathist regime on the mainly Shiite Islamist parties, the expulsion of Fayli Kurds and the marginalization and persecution of the Shia religious hierarchy, heightened the sense of discrimination, even though the Shia provided the majority of the conscripts to the Iraqi army during the Iran-Iraq war.

Following the defeat of the Iraqi army in Kuwait in the first Gulf War of 1991, and with initial encouragement from the United States and its allies, a major uprising erupted in southern Iraq in March of 1991. At its height, the insurgency had seized control of most of the southern provinces of Iraq. However, Saddam regrouped his Revolutionary Guard units, and supported by attack helicopters, which the Allies cynically allowed Iraq to fly, succeeded in crushing the uprising. The regime then embarked on an extensive and systematic campaign against the Shia population of the south, targeting in particular young men who were thought to be the backbone of the uprising.

The scale of repression was massive, involving reprisal killings, mass incarcerations, disappearances, destruction of shrines and neighbourhoods, creation of free fire zones and a widespread cultural campaign against the symbols and doctrines of Shiite Islam. From evidence of eyewitnesses and experts in the war crimes trials of the Iraq Special Tribunal and exhumations of mass graves after the 2003 invasion of Iraq, the number of people systematically killed in the great repression of 1991 amounted to nearly 100,000 people.[8] Other estimates put the figure higher at about 200,000 people killed or disappeared. The repression was extended in the mid-1990s to environmental warfare, including a systematic campaign to destroy the marshlands of southern Iraq by draining them. The primary drive for this was to deny the marshlands as cover and sanctuary for rebels against the regime (Table 10.6).

The violence used by the state in putting down the uprising of 1991 is unprecedented in Iraqi history. There were many actions throughout modern Iraqi history, such as in 1935, where the state was confronted by tribal uprisings in the South, but the scope of violence used to reassert the state's authority was in no way comparable to that of

Table 10.6 The Shia uprising (*Intifida*) of 1991

Nature of Violence	– Targeted killings, reprisals, revenge killings – Mass incarcerations in prison camps – Exemplary and collective punishments – Destruction of shrines, libraries and symbols of Shia Islam – Destruction of neighbourhoods – Environmental warfare
Scale of Violence	– About 100,000 killed and disappeared – Large refugee movement of nearly 300,000 people – Razing of the central parts of Karbala, an important shrine city – Dozens of mass graves in the south, the one at Muhaihil with 100,000 bodies – Drainage of vast areas of the southern Marshes, desertification and refugees
Agents	– Special Republican Guards forces – Regular Republican Guards units – Baath Party militias – Secret Police – *Mujahidin Khalq* units (Exile Iranian opposition group based in Iraq) – Some tribal units
Ideology/Narrative	– Iranian-inspired and led uprising – Shias are potential fifth columnists – Marsh dwellers are not really Arabs, of Indian origin – Uprising is not politically motivated but mobs in search of loot and vengeance – Shia Islam is deviant and needs to be cleansed
Political/Historical Context	– Defeat in the Gulf War – Retreating armies in a state of chaos – Collapse in law and order in the south – Disintegration of control by the security apparatus – Fear of extension of Iranian influence by the west and Saudi Arabia – US toleration of repressive violence used by the Baathist regime
Role of State Actors/ Public Opinion	– Conducted entirely by the government and its direct instruments – Uprising portrayed as the work of mobs – Implied sectarian base of uprising
Outcome	– South cowed but not pacified by the government – Heightening of sectarian tensions – Played significant part in Shia narrative of discrimination and prejudice – Major perpetrators brought in front of Iraq Special Tribunal on war crimes charges

1991. It also had a profound effect on the mind-set of the Shia of Iraq, and alienated the majority from the Baathist state. However it falls short of ethnocide or genocide.

In Mann's paradigm the violence is certainly extreme, involving premeditated mass killings, systematic reprisals and generalized police repression. There was also an element of cultural and religious suppression of Shia customs and rites, but these faded into the decade. Nevertheless, the repression did not spill over into group displacements or deportations, or forced conversions and pressured emigration. The repression of 1991 would fall into a borderline zone where the victims were a recognized group (a sect rather than a race or ethnic group) but where its scope did not reach that of the *Anfal* campaign in the 1980s. It therefore would not be classified as genocide or ethnocide, but an extreme form of sustained and organized violence designed to terrorize and cow a population.

Case 6: Mass killings, expulsions and disappearances of civilians, 2003–2008

The near civil war conditions that prevailed in Iraq after the US invasion and occupation of the country in 2003 differ markedly from the patterns of earlier intergroup violence. They took place at a time when central authority was non-existent, degraded or severely weakened. The state in its myriad manifestations, though involved in parts of the violence, was in no position to plan, organize and implement the violence in a systematic and directed way. While it is true that certain elements of the nascent Iraqi security forces did assist in the violence and ethnic cleansing prevalent in the 2004–2008 periods, one cannot say that this was a feature of state policy in any meaningful form. The state was simply too feeble and disorganized and prone to factional divisions to do be able to direct such violence. This was also the first time in modern Iraqi history that near civil war conditions prevailed in the absence of a strong centralized state, a feature of modern Iraq at least from the 1930s (Table 10.7).

The civil war that erupted in Iraq was greatly aided by both the collapse of the Iraqi state and the inability of the occupying forces to assert their authority and control over the country. At the same time, great shifts had occurred in Iraq that effectively undermined and destroyed the key assumptions that underlay the establishment of the Iraqi state in the 1920s. Iraq was no longer a centralized, explicitly Arab state, dominated by a narrowly based political and military class. The forces that emerged to reverse this condition to the *status quo ante* – or to preserve the new dispensation – were the bases of the unconventional civil war that erupted in the aftermath of the occupation.

There was little mass participation in the violence – in the form of riots or mob attacks for example. Many people claimed to be horrified by the explicit sectarian bases of the violence but very little was done to stop the expulsion of people, or turning entire neighbourhoods or districts into an ethnic or sectarian monochrome. As is normally the case, expellees from certain areas became the beneficiary of residences and homes of those removed or had departed from other areas. The exchange of population, though not formally acknowledged as such, was nevertheless extensive and played a large part in the final dampening of the violence, especially after mixed areas were transformed to the control of one sect or another.

Table 10.7 Mass killings, expulsions and disappearances of civilians, 2003–2008

Nature of Violence	– Terror Bombings of civilian targets – Suicide bombings – Targeted assassinations, kidnappings – Random murders – Sectarian and ethnic cleansing – Displacements and expulsions – Occupation of neighbourhoods and villages
Scope of Violence	– About 150,000 people killed – About two million displaced, in internal exile or refugees – Affected the central, northern and Western parts of the country (South and Kurdistan relatively peaceful)
Agents	– Foreign and local terrorists and jihadis – Former regime elements from the Baath party and security apparatus – Sectarian militias and paramilitary units – Some 'rogue' government units from the military and police forces – Foreign intelligence agencies
Ideology/Narrative	– Return of the former regime – Unacceptability of the new order – Demonization narratives (Shias/Sunnis/Christians), drawn mainly from religious/clerical figures – Defending the community rights from external threats
Political/Historical Context	– Invasion and Occupation of Iraq – Empowerment of the Shia – Collapse of the Iraqi state – Intervention from regional powers – Iraq as central to the *jihadi* culture and al-Qaeda operations – Bombings of religious shrines and symbols, especially Samarra – Emergence of civil war conditions
Role of State Actors/ Public Opinion	– No official state involvement – Many political parties and politicians involved – Involvements of 'rogue' security forces – Selective logistical, financial and military support for violence from Iran, Syria, Saudi Arabia – Sharp polarization of public opinion on sectarian and ethnic grounds
Outcome	– Population movements – Creation of ethnically cleansed neighbourhoods and districts – Entrenchment of sectarian divisions

Conclusion

One has to trawl far and wide to find serious incidents of intergroup violence in premodern Iraq. There are reported cases of riots between Sunni and Shia neighbourhoods of Abbasid Baghdad, but they were more in the nature of rivalries between districts and turf wars, rather than sectarian warfare. It is true that large scale massacres of Sunnis by Shias and vice versa did take place in the wars between the Ottoman and Safavid

Empires for control over Iraq. However, these were instigated and managed by the victorious armies, and subsided as quickly as they emerged. The Wahhabi invasion of southern Iraq in the late eighteenth century led to the sacking of the city of Karbala and the murder of most of its (Shia) inhabitants, but the Wahhabis were from the wilds of Najd and had no urban presence to speak of inside Iraq. Organized attacks or pogroms in pre-modern times against Iraq's main minorities, such as the Jews and Christians were very rare; and the Kurds were reasonably well integrated into the structures of the Ottoman Empire. The era of large scale violence against specific groups, instigated by the central authority, could therefore be safely said to have originated in the modern era, specifically after Iraq was constituted as a new state in 1921.

The pattern of violence against specific communities from the 1930s until the 1990s can be directly attributable to the power and centralizing and totalizing nature of the state. In fact, all the incidents of violence that were described, up to the near civil war in the post-2003 period, could be attributed to either direct state action or instigation. One can therefore draw the inference that the greater the central power of the state – even during a power vacuum, such as in the 1941 *Farhud* – the greater is the scale and scope the violence employed. Closely aligned to the power of the centralized state in the planning and instigation of large scale violence against specific groups is the issue of ideology or narrative employed to justify the violence.

In all cases, there was an elaborate 'justification' for the extreme measures employed against the target groups by reference to their disloyalty, treacherous activity and fealty to foreign powers and/or alien ideologies. The corollary to the demonizing of the target group is the adoption of an overarching defining vision for the state and country: a 'strong' centralizing state; an overt identification with Arab nationalism; a glorification of the military; refusal to recognize or formally acknowledge the notion of plural identities. Ranged against these notions was the reticence or unwillingness by ordinary society to carry these differences into action against 'deviant' or outsider groups. Iraq's history of accommodation between the sects and ethnicities was too long in the making to be brought down by a state-sponsored narrative of what being an Iraqi or Arab meant. This held with varying but declining degrees, during the monarchical period (to 1958) and the republican period (to 1968).

With the advent of the Baath party to power in 1968, the ruthlessness and single-mindedness with which a monolithic vision of Iraq was pursued, coupled with the increasing availability of resources, gave the state, for the first time, the power to significantly transform the country. And the scale and range of violence used against target groups leapt enormously – from the early expulsions of the Fayli Kurds to the *Anfal* genocide to the horrors of the 1991 uprising. The post-2003 intergroup violence might appear to be prompted by non-state actors, but it took place in a landscape that was severely affected by the ravages of the thirty-five year Baath dictatorship, which greatly degraded Iraq's history of intergroup accommodation and toleration. Thus, when the state apparatus was greatly weakened after 2003, the checks and balances that allowed for a degree of intergroup accommodation – especially between the Shia and Sunni communities – had also deteriorated, allowing for the rise of unprecedented intergroup violence.

A theme that runs through the course of modern Iraqi history is that of insecurity of the holders of power. There are only a few periods when those holding the political reigns did not succumb to the anxiety that their hold on power could slip at any time. This gnawing fear that they could lose power at a moment's notice – by the machinations of the imperial power; by tribal uprisings; by the work of a cabal of officers; by street demonstrations and riots; by conspiracies and plots of ideologically-driven parties – necessarily informed the response of the governing power to real or perceived threats. The frequent changes in cabinets during the monarchical period, the coups and counter-coups of the 1960s, the killings that accompanied the rise of the Baath to power – all contributed to the climate of crisis that were the backdrops to the violent acts of the state. Perhaps, the most confident period in the state's history was in its early days – during the Faisalian period – where the process of state formation and the uneasy alliance/balance of power between the Palace and the British High Commissioner mitigated against the abrupt overthrow of the established order. But other relatively quiescent periods were few and far between. This pervasive insecurity was a contributing factor to the overreaction of the state, frequently in the form of extreme, often unprovoked, violence against its perceived enemies.

Iraq's new democratic dispensation is not leading to the revitalization of easy intergroup relations. In fact the opposite seems to be happening and would vindicate the thesis that the process of democratization, with few exceptions, can only function effectively in ethnically homogenous states or states in which one ethnicity clearly prevails. The Kurds of Iraq have carved for themselves an autonomous state with its own defence capabilities and an agreed share of the national budget, giving them a high degree of financial independence. In effect, Iraq is a confederal state operating in the form of a federal state. At the same time, the principle of *muhassasa* – in effect the division of major state appointments and departments according to ethno-sectarian considerations – retrenches the ethnic and sectarian divides, at least at the political level. In effect, *muhassasa* and the creation of the Kurdistan Region are attempts to ensure advantage – and protection – to ethnic and sectarian groups in an environment where the central state has been weakened and where memories of violence and catastrophes are too recent to allow for anything but platitudes about intergroup harmony and accommodation to rule the day.

Notes

1 Michael Mann, *The Dark Side of Democracy: Explaining Ethnic Cleansing*, Cambridge, Cambridge University Press, 2005, in particular, pp. 1–34, where Mann sets out the argument for his model. Mann makes a persuasive case linking ethnic cleansing to the modern nation state, where the idea of the *ethnos* (the ethnic group) is equated with the *demos* (democracy).
2 Mann, *The Dark Side of Democracy*, p. 11.
3 See Khaldun S. Husry, 'The Assyrian Affair of 1933, Parts I and II', *International Journal of Middle East Studies*, Vol. 5, No. 2 (April 1974), pp. 161–176; and Vol. 5, No. 3 (June 1974), pp. 344–360.

4 Elie Kedourie, 'The Jews of Baghdad in 1910', *Middle Eastern Studies*, Vol. 7, No. 3 (October, 1971), pp. 355–361 and Sylvia G. Haim, 'Aspects of Jewish Life in Baghdad under the Monarchy', *Middle Eastern Studies*, Vol. 12, No. 2 (May 1976), pp. 188–208.
5 The best example of this is the widespread looting and destruction in Baghdad just after the 2003 American invasion.
6 Elisabeth Campbell, quoted in *Refugees International*, 2 April 2010.
7 *Genocide in Iraq – The Anfal Campaign against the Kurds*, Middle East Watch, Human Rights Watch, New York, 1993.
8 *Endless Torment: The 1991 Uprising in Iraq and Its Aftermath*, Human Rights Watch, New York, June 1992.

11

Islamophobia as a Securitization Narrative: The Exclusionary Logic of Imperial Geopolitics

Nafeez Mosaddeq Ahmed

Conventional conceptualizations of Islamophobia have failed to offer meaningful explanations of this phenomenon due to a theoretical focus almost exclusively on the existence of Islamophobic discourses themselves, without however contextualizing their existence in relation to the structural dynamics of the global political economy, global systemic crises and their connection to the dynamics of securitization. This is symptomatic of problems within the field of critical security studies which, once again, tend to reify the idea of securitization in a way that suspends discourses in isolation from the structures that both enable them and are enabled by them.

This chapter thus attempts to first establish the empirical evidence for a rising trend of Islamophobic discourses and the threat they pose for social cohesion in the UK and the West in general. The chapter then critically explores the utility of the concept of Islamophobia for understanding this phenomenon, before moving on to a discussion of the relationship of Islamophobia to processes of securitization.

While securitization and critical security theories offer a useful way to situate and make sense of the construction of threat, a number of theoretical gaps render conventional securitization theory incapable of actually explaining the past trajectory of rising Islamophobia as well as future potential challenges. The chapter thus suggests an outline of an approach to understanding Islamophobia as a securitization process driven by overlapping social crises in an increasingly unsustainable global political economy. It suggests that the insertion of the 'Islamic threat' in securitizing narratives (which encompass economic crises, the crisis of US hegemony, climate change, balances of demographic growth and even a 'clash of civilizations') is in itself a symptom of crisis and uncertainty. But these codes threaten to escalate into a self-reinforcing process, since hostile acts directed towards Muslims threaten to descend into a spiral of hostilities that could easily become genocidal.

The rise of anti-Muslim hostility in the United Kingdom

On 1 February 2011, BBC *Newsnight*'s Jeremy Paxman conducted a twenty-minute interview with Stephen Laxley-Yennon, aka Tommy Robinson, a founder and head of the English Defence League (EDL) – an extreme offshoot of the right-wing British National Party (BNP). The EDL's entire political programme focuses on stirring fears of a takeover of Britain by the forces of 'militant Islam' and the 'barbaric 7th century form of Shariah Law'.[1] In spite of its marginality, it would be naive to ignore the EDL's meteoric rise and its mounting support among white working-class communities, especially in the wake of the 2008 global financial crash.[2] Although difficult to quantify scientifically, one indication of this is that the EDL's Facebook page is followed by over 150,000 people.[3]

The rise of the EDL is a symptom of a deeper, long-term trend of social polarization along ethnic and religious lines, particularly between Muslims and non-Muslims. Indeed, this is confirmed by the remarks made by Prime Minister David Cameron on 5 February 2010, at a security conference in Munich, on the same day that the EDL marched in Luton – suggesting that terrorism was a function of failure of multiculturalism to integrate Muslims into British society.[4] A 2006 YouGov survey found that the number of non-Muslim Britons who believe that 'a large proportion of British Muslims feel no sense of loyalty to this country and are prepared to condone or even carry out acts of terrorism' had nearly doubled (jumping from 10 per cent to 18 per cent) within one year following the 7/7 terror attack on London. The number of non-Muslims who believe that 'practically all British Muslims are peaceful, law-abiding citizens who deplore terrorist acts as much as anyone else' fell from 23 per cent to 16 per cent in the same period. Further, 53 per cent of non-Muslims said they felt threatened by Islam (as distinct from fundamentalist Islamism) – up from 32 per cent in 2001.[5] Similarly, the 2009 Gallup poll finds that only 36 per cent of the general population believed that Muslims were loyal to Britain.[6] Other polls corroborate this disturbing trend. A 2010 YouGov survey found that 58 per cent of Britons link Islam with extremism and 69 per cent believe it encourages repression of women.[7] A 2010 study by the Islamic Education and Research Academy also found that three-quarters of the general population believed that Islam was negative for Britain, and that Muslims did not engage positively in society. About 32 per cent believed that Muslims are a major cause of community tension.[8]

Intriguingly, though, negative attitudes do not work only in one direction. A 2006 study by the Pew Global Attitudes Project found British Muslims more prone than other Muslim diasporas in the West to hold negative perceptions of Westerners. Between 50 and 70 per cent of British Muslims perceived Western populations as 'selfish, arrogant, greedy and immoral'; just over half said Westerners were violent. Less than half thought that Westerners were respectful of women, and only 32 per cent viewed Jews in a favourable light.[9]

This rising trend of social polarization illustrates that the prevailing British public discourse on Islam is fundamentally concerned with the religion's compatibility with the liberal secular values of modern Western societies. Fringe groups like the BNP and the EDL have been able to feed off a growing sense of suspicion within wider society towards Muslim minorities. This unease is in turn linked to a persistent narrative depicting Islamic values as regressive, violent and oppressive. Ironically, this narrative and the related far-right rhetoric have been fuelled by Islamist extremist groups themselves, particularly networks linked to the proscribed al-Muhajiroun group, currently operating as 'Muslims Against the Crusades'. The EDL grew out of a response to a March 2009 protest against Royal Anglian Regiment troops returning from Afghanistan.[10] On the ten-year anniversary of the 9/11 attacks, both 'Muslims Against the Crusades' and the EDL held simultaneous and clashing demonstrations outside the US embassy, appallingly marring the remembrance service for sixty-seven British victims of 9/11.[11]

Finally, it is critical to recognize that the regressive narratives upheld by both far-right and Islamist extremist groups, fuelling negative images of Islam and Muslims, are also linked to concrete entrenched practices of social exclusion, through which Muslim communities have become increasingly marginalized from mainstream society[12] – and also to the rise in anti-Muslim hate crimes. Studies show that 69 per cent of British Muslims of Pakistani or Bangladeshi ethnic origin live in poverty, compared to 20 per cent of white people. According to the Office of National Statistics, unemployment rates for Muslims are higher than those for people from any other religion, for both men and women. Muslims have the highest male unemployment rate in Great Britain, at 13 per cent. The unemployment rate for Muslim women at 18 per cent is about four times the rate for Christian and Jewish women (4 per cent in each case). Muslims aged sixteen to twenty-four years have the highest unemployment rates and are over twice as likely as Christians of the same age to be unemployed.[13] A series of studies by the Joseph Rowntree Foundation similarly finds that two-thirds of ethnically South Asian Muslim children in Britain are impoverished. In families with at least one breadwinner, 60 per cent of ethnic Bangladeshis and 40 per cent of ethnic Pakistanis are in income poverty, compared to just over 10–15 per cent of white people.[14]

Social exclusion is linked to institutional discrimination. Another survey sponsored by the Joseph Rowntree Charitable Trust, undertaken by Ameli, found that 80 per cent of British Muslims had experienced discrimination, up from 45 per cent in the late 1990s.[15] These findings are corroborated by Ansari who documents deteriorating conditions in British Muslim 'access to education, employment and housing' along with a 'worrying rise in open hostility' from non Muslim communities.[16]

Parallel with the growing problem of social exclusion of Muslim communities is the phenomenon of rising anti-Muslim hate crimes. In 2010, Lambert and Githens-Mazer found that the majority of anti-Muslim hate crimes are not reported to police due to lack of confidence in the authorities and unawareness of police interest. Since 9/11, anti-Muslim hate crimes are now more prevalent than crimes against blacks and Asians broadly. Due to the problem of under-reporting, the report authors estimate that the number of actual anti-Muslim hate- crimes is likely to be far higher than that documented by official records. They conclude that 'assailants of Muslims are invariably motivated by a negative view of Muslims they have acquired from either mainstream or extremist nationalist reports or commentaries in the media' and that 'the major motivating factor for violence against Muslims is a negative and false belief that Muslims pose a security or terrorist threat'.[17] In other words, underlying the widening social polarization between Muslim and non-Muslim communities is a perception of Muslims as a security problem.

The underdevelopment of 'Islamophobia'

A range of studies indicate that the diverse phenomena affecting Muslim communities are in fact facets of a single overall social process, conveyed through the concept of 'Islamophobia'.[18] While sociological debates on the conceptual utility and coherence of Islamophobia continue, the increasing prevalence of prejudice and discrimination towards Muslim communities in the West over the last two decades is testament to the reality of the phenomenon it is supposed to capture – regardless of these squabbles.

The idea of Islamophobia conveys the sense of a distinctive form of racism and bigotry targeted specifically at members of Muslim communities, reinforced by negative stereotypes about Islam. In 1997, the Runnymede Trust offered its seminal definition of Islamophobia as a set of attitudes: Islam is perceived as a static, unchanging monolithic block; it is separate and 'other'; it lacks values in common with other cultures; is inferior to the West; and is irrational, primitive, sexist, violent, aggressive and supportive of terrorism. Hostility towards Islam is used to justify discriminatory practices against Muslims and the exclusion of Muslims from mainstream society, such that anti-Muslim hostility becomes normalized.[19] In 2004, the Council of Europe defined Islamophobia as 'the fear of or prejudiced viewpoint towards Islam, Muslims and matters pertaining to them. Whether it takes the shape of daily forms of racism and discrimination or more violent forms, Islamophobia is a violation of human rights and a threat to social cohesion'.[20]

However, as Maussen points out, there are important theoretical reservations for the use of the catch-all term Islamophobia to encompass so many diverse phenomena. Primarily, the term 'groups together all kinds of different forms of discourse, speech and acts, by suggesting that they all emanate from an identical ideological core, which is a "fear" or a "phobia" of Islam'. This amounts to a form of ideological reductionism which, however, fails to offer any further or deeper explanation of why this irrational fear of Islam has come about and how it refracts through myriad different social structures into such a wide array of different exclusionary behaviours and processes. Maussen notes that while 'these different kinds of discourse and speech' – such as negative media portrayals of Muslims, legislation impacting primarily or inordinately on Muslims and sporadic acts of public violence against Muslims – may well be 'related and feed into one another, but we cannot simply equate them all and treat them as comparable illustrations of a core ideology named "Islamophobia." ' There is therefore a need to 'distinguish speech and discourse on the one hand, from acts on the other hand'. While discourse and speech may be demeaning, it should not be conflated with 'policies which limit the religious freedoms of Muslims, or with acts of violence, such as burning mosques or attacking Muslim girls who wear the headscarf'.[21]

This sort of critical evaluation of the application of the term Islamophobia raises important issues highlighting the underdevelopment of the concept as a sociological category capable of providing a credible theoretical explanatory framework by which to understand the diverse phenomena of anti-Muslim hostility and discrimination. Clearly, while there may be compelling reasons to conclude that many of these phenomena are indeed motivated by a general irrational fear of Islam and Muslims – the causal origins of this irrational mind-set are largely ignored in the literature that endorses the concept of Islamophobia. Furthermore, the mechanisms through which this presumed mind-set manages to encompass such a diversity of processes, institutions and behaviours not only in a single society but indeed across multiple societies simultaneously, remains unexplained. In effect, Islamophobia becomes a self-reinforcing circular concept, in which anti-Muslim hostility is generated by nothing more than an irrational hostility towards Muslims – effectively, Islamophobia creates Islamophobia.

Although the conceptual definitions and theoretical efficacy of Islamophobia is therefore still hotly contested in academic literature, it is indisputable that there has been a meteoric rise in anti-Muslim hostility and discrimination on a global scale. According to the European Union Agency for Fundamental Rights, which has monitored this phenomenon since 2001, Islamophobia in the form of discrimination and violence specifically towards members of Muslim diaspora communities in the EU has increased dramatically. In particular, anti-Muslim prejudice in EU countries is manifest not simply in regressive ideological perspectives leading to acts of violence but also in tangible exclusionary patterns in housing, education, and employment.[22] A report co-sponsored by the University of California, Berkeley, Center for Race and Gender, similarly found evidence that Islamophobia in the United States is an increasingly powerful force in the political landscape, negatively affecting Muslims in terms of employment, education and housing as well as hate crimes and profiling by security agencies.[23]

The overall picture is of an increasing sense of unease, fear and hostility between Muslims and non-Muslims over the last decade. Overwhelmingly, this has coincided with a mainstream media narrative in which Islam and Muslims are increasingly projected as 'a threat to traditional British customs, values and ways of life', because 'there is no common ground between the West and Islam'.[24] Another study by Cardiff University's School of Journalism of UK press coverage of British Muslims from 2000 to 2008, found that 'the bulk of coverage of British Muslims – around two thirds – focuses on Muslims as a threat (in relation to terrorism), a problem (in terms of differences in values) or both (Muslim extremism in general)'. Further, it concluded that: 'Four of the five most common discourses used about Muslims in the British press associate Islam/Muslims with threats, problems or in opposition to dominant British values.'[25] A similar study of Islamophobia in the American media concluded that 'media stereotyping' after 9/11 'primed Americans to understand the 9/11 attacks as representative of Arab political culture and Islamic devotion', and was 'an important factor in the backlash that afflicted these communities post-9/11'. The study further documents an 'alarming deterioration in Islamophobic hate speech in the media' up to 2006.[26] A 2008 World Economic Forum study of the way 'Muslim-West' relations are covered across global media in a total of twenty-four Muslim-majority and non-Muslim-majority countries found that 'negative coverage was 10 times more frequent than positive coverage' with Muslims being 'associated with fundamentalist and extremist activities more than six times as often as other religious protagonists'.[27]

Corporate media's increasing demonization of Islam and Muslims is not occurring in a silo but is being driven very much by the agendas of government and security agencies. On the one hand, corporate media relies relatively uncritically on government and security agencies for its information on foreign policy and intelligence matters, including terrorism.[28] On the other hand, there have been direct efforts from security agencies to influence the media. Since 1990, for instance, the Pentagon has bribed, pressured and censored Hollywood film-makers to adapt story lines to support its propaganda.[29] As Jack Shaheen notes, 'Today's image makers regularly link the Islamic faith with male supremacy, holy war, and acts of terror, depicting Arab Muslims as hostile alien intruders, and as lecherous, oily sheikhs, intent on using nuclear weapons. When mosques are displayed onscreen, the camera inevitably cuts to Arabs praying, and then gunning down civilians.'[30]

Here, the mainstream media plays a critical function in ideologically linking the international to the domestic, in particular, the trajectory of Western foreign policy in Muslim-majority theatres across the Middle East and Central Asia as well as the processes of Islamophobia and radicalization experienced within Muslim diaspora communities in the West. On the one hand, Islamophobic media narratives buttress anti-Muslim public opinion at home, alienating Muslims and fuelling the extremist rhetoric of far right groups. Simultaneously, images of devastation and destruction from Muslim-majority theatres of war such as Iraq and Afghanistan also distress and anger Muslim diaspora communities, further exacerbating the alienation. In effect, the media acts as a symbiotic link between Islamophobia at home and abroad, as it mediates extremist rhetoric from neoconservative and right-wing factions and the official language of government and security agencies and politicians to pander to Islamophobic public opinion on political issues such as immigration and terrorism.

Thus, there is perhaps no clearer instantiation of the security-dynamics of Islamophobia than the actual activities of Western security agencies. After the US Department of Justice passed a regulation allowing indefinite detention on 20 September 2001, nearly 1,200 Arabs and Muslims were secretly arrested and detained without charge.[31] The US National Security Entry-Exit Registration System (NSEERS) 'call-in' programme required male visitors from twenty-four Arab and Muslim countries and North Korea to register with INS offices. No terrorists were found, yet over 13,000 of the 80,000 men who registered were threatened with deportation, and many were 'detained in harsh conditions'.[32] In the United Kingdom, more than a thousand Muslims have been detained without charge under antiterror laws, out of which only a handful have been convicted of terrorist offences. Worldwide, thousands of Muslim men – victims of the CIA's extraordinary rendition programme – are being detained without charges 'in secretive American-run jails and interrogation centres similar to the notorious Abu Ghraib Prison' under conditions which violate the Universal Declaration of Human Rights, the Geneva Conventions on the Treatment of Prisoners and the UN Standard Minimum Rules for the Treatment of Prisoners.[33]

Such practices accompany Anglo-American military engagements in predominantly Muslim theatres of war, regions often described as dangerous failed zones harbouring potential Islamist terrorists planning to inflict apocalyptic forms of mass destruction on Western civilization.³⁴ Such military engagements also tend to result in the indiscriminate killings of predominantly Muslim civilians and correlate invariably with their strategic location vis-à-vis contested energy reserves in the Middle East, Central Asia and Northwest Africa.

Iraq provides a case-in-point. From 1991 to 2007, the total civilian death toll in Iraq as a direct and indirect consequence of Anglo-American invasions, socio-economic deprivation, infrastructure destruction and occupation amounts to approximately three million over a period of sixteen years.³⁵ The scale of this violence is thus larger than some of the most well-known cases of twentieth century genocide, such as in Kampuchea, Yugoslavia and Rwanda. As Walt points out, estimating the number of Muslims killed directly or indirectly by US forces over the last thirty years suggests at least 100 Muslim fatalities for every US one. He thus observes: 'When you kill tens of thousands of people in other countries – and sometimes for no good reason – you shouldn't be surprised when people in those countries are enraged by this behavior and interested in revenge.'³⁶

This argument amply refutes the assumption that foreign policy has no relationship to terrorism and violent radicalization. In particular, taking a broader historical view of the continuity of US-UK interventionism in the Gulf region going back to 1991 demonstrates not only the immense scale of the violence inflicted upon Iraqi civilians but also illustrates that British interventionism in the region preceded the emergence and proliferation of Islamist-inspired terrorist attacks against Western targets.

Thus, Ralph argues that the massive military violence that has been inflicted predominantly on the civilian populations of Muslim-majority regions is only possible by their having been 'Islamophobically' constructed as having lives that are of less value compared to those of Western citizens.³⁷ But while the irrational fear of Islam and Muslims is clearly a significant factor in all these disparate phenomena, Islamophobia as a sociological concept offers little by way of a coherent causal explanation of how or why these phenomena are escalating simultaneously.

Islamophobia as securitization

It is therefore imperative to recognize that Islamophobia is distinctive precisely as a unique form of securitization targeted specifically at Muslim communities in the context of the particular objectives, interests and anxieties of powerful political actors. Indeed, Islamophobia cannot be understood as a sociological category without situating it in the context of the evolving socio-political relations of global imperialism, which in turn explain the political dynamic of the securitization of Muslim communities.

Wæver's seminal concept of *securitization* referred to a 'speech act' – an act of labelling – whereby political authorities identify an *existential threat* that, because of its extreme nature, justifies moving beyond conventional security measures within the public rule of law, thus permitting the execution of extra-legal emergence powers that are henceforth 'above politics'.³⁸ Thus, Buzan et al. argued that 'the priority and the urgency of an existential threat' permits the state to resort to consistent 'violations of rules that would otherwise have to be obeyed'. Securitization thus legitimizes the state of exception and the suspension of democracy.³⁹

In the early 1990s, Willy Claes, then NATO Secretary-General identified 'Islamic fundamentalism' as a new threat to Western Europe replacing the defunct USSR.⁴⁰ By the late 1990s, a number of hearings had been held in the Congress and Senate on the Islamist threat from the Middle East and Central Asia.⁴¹ The publication of Samuel Huntington's influential essay on the 'clash of civilizations' was a decisive turning point in the solidification of this strategic thinking.⁴² After 9/11, security agencies increasingly generalized the threat of Islamist terrorism as being, despite its marginality, nevertheless *widely dispersed throughout Muslim communities*, necessitating comprehensive regimes of surveillance, policing and, in some regions, counter-insurgency.

A sensitive briefing paper published by the Pentagon agency, Counterintelligence Field Activity (which operated from 2002 to 2008, after which its activities were subsumed by the Defense Intelligence Agency), argued that 'political Islam wages an ideological battle against the non-Islamic world at the tactical, operational and strategic level. The West's response is focused at the tactical and operation level, leaving the strategic level – Islam – unaddressed'. The paper concludes that 'Islam is an ideological engine of war (Jihad)', and 'no one is looking for its off switch' due to political 'indecision [over] whether Islam is radical or being radicalized'. Attempting to review the Qur'an and Prophetic traditions, the paper infers that 'Strategic themes suggest Islam is radical by nature... Muhammad's behaviors today would be defined as radical'. Western policymakers can no longer afford to overlook the 'cult characteristics of Islam'. Indeed even Islam's advocacy of charity – the principle known as Zakat considered an obligatory 'pillar' of Islam – is described as 'an asymmetrical war-fighting funding mechanism'. The only reason that the United States has failed to suffer scattered insurgent terrorist attacks – as opposed to the single, concentrated and catastrophic attack of 9/11 – is primarily due to its relatively small Muslim population. Accordingly, the threat of such insurgency will increase as the Muslim minority grows and gains more influence. The Pentagon cites successful and attempted terrorist attacks in Britain, along with the predominantly Muslim riots in France, as examples.⁴³

Thus, Tim Savage, division chief at the State Department's Office of European Analysis argues that Europe's Muslim population is expected to double while its non-Muslim population is projected to fall by at least 3.5 per cent. At worst, he speculates that by mid-century Muslims might outnumber non-Muslims not only in France but throughout Western Europe. European intelligence analysts already estimate that up to 2 per cent of the continent's Muslims – half a million people – are involved in extremist activity. This number, for which no corroborating evidence exists, is so huge according to Savage not because of the role of Islamic fundamentalism *per se*, but rather simply due to the inevitable 'chemistry resulting from Muslims' encounter with Europe [which] seems to make certain individuals more susceptible to recruitment into terrorist activities'. Therefore, he implies, terrorists are supposedly born simply from the identity crisis generated by Muslim immigration to Europe – 'A larger group of terrorists by far is recruited from the masses of young men, many of them middle-class, who experience a sort of culture shock in Europe and become radicalized "born again" Islamists'.⁴⁴

Security agencies are preoccupied with population politics not only in the context of the alleged dangers posed by the rising number of Muslims in the United States, Britain and Western Europe but also in terms of rising populations in the South in general and intensifying population movements towards the West as people attempt to escape the calamities created by climate change, food insecurity and resource scarcity. In this sense, security agencies project a direct connection between the question of civil unrest, global crises and rising populations of 'Others', particularly Muslims.

According to then-CIA Director Michael V. Hayden, rising world population and immigration 'could undermine the stability of some of the world's most fragile states, especially in Africa, while in the West, governments will be forced to grapple with ever larger immigrant communities and deepening divisions over ethnicity and race'. Noting the projected 33 percent growth in global population over the next forty years, he warned that regional friendly oil-exporting regimes 'like Nigeria and Libya will be forced to rapidly find food, shelter and jobs for millions, or deal with restive populations that "could be easily attracted to violence, civil unrest, or extremism."' Corroborating the fears described above, he added that rising world population would also have a debilitating impact within the West due to growing ethnicity differentials between shrinking and expanding population groups:

> European countries, many of which already have large immigrant communities, will see particular growth in their Muslim populations while the number of non-Muslims will shrink as birthrates fall. 'Social integration of immigrants will pose a significant challenge to many host nations – again boosting the potential for unrest and extremism,' Hayden said.⁴⁵

Furthermore, Muslim communities – both diasporas in the West and Muslim-majority countries in strategic regions of the Middle East, Central Asia and North Africa – are perceived to cut across the fault lines of increasingly complex non-traditional security challenges such as climate change, energy depletion, water shortages and food insecurity. A recent US Army War College study makes reference to Huntington's clash thesis, arguing that while it 'captured the possibilities' already emerging in the 1990s:

> the future and its implications are even darker than what Professor Huntington suggested.... The confluence between the world's greatest reserves of petroleum and the extraordinary difficulties that the Islamic world is having, and will continue to have, in confronting a civilization that has taken the West 900 years to develop will create challenges that strategists are only now beginning to grasp.⁴⁶

In other words, there is a direct link between Western energy interests, the 'War on Terror', and the West's military preoccupation with the Muslim world. For example, the US Joint Forces Command draws attention to the danger of global energy depletion through to 2030. Warning of 'the dangerous vulnerabilities the growing energy crisis presents', the report concludes that 'The implications for future conflict are ominous'.[47] Once again, the subject turns to demographics: 'In total, the world will add approximately 60 million people each year and reach a total of 8 billion by the 2030s', 95 per cent accruing to developing countries, while populations in developed countries slow or decline. 'Regions such as the Middle East and Sub-Saharan Africa, where the youth bulge will reach over 50% of the population, will possess fewer inhibitions about engaging in conflict'.[48] The assumption is that regions which happen to be both energy-rich and Muslim-majority will also be sites of violent conflict due to their rapidly growing populations.

A British Ministry of Defence report concurs with this assessment, highlighting an inevitable 'youth bulge' by 2035, with some 87 per cent of all people under the age of twenty-five inhabiting developing countries. In particular, the Middle East population will increase by 132 per cent, and sub-Saharan Africa by 81 per cent. Growing resentment due to 'endemic unemployment' will be channelled through 'political militancy, including radical political Islam whose concept of Umma, the global Islamic community, and resistance to capitalism may lie uneasily in an international system based on nation-states and global market forces'.[49]

The exclusionary logic of securitization

Thus, the securitization of global crisis leads not only to the problematization of particular religious and ethnic groups in foreign regions of geopolitical interest, but potentially extends this problematization to any social group which might challenge prevailing global political economic structures across racial, national and class lines. The previous examples illustrate how securitization paradoxically generates insecurity by reifying a process of militarization against social groups that are constructed as external to the prevailing geopolitical and economic order. Due to the geopolitical significance of Muslim-majority regions to imperial interests and their links to Muslim diasporas in the West, this securitization process overwhelmingly focuses on the externalization of Muslims. Hence, a simple discursive analysis of Islamophobia is insufficient to understand its causal dynamics.

For the mere identification of a security issue does not necessarily correspond to an objective threat, but represents the interests of power. This also means that the state of exception cannot simply be unilaterally decreed by the sovereign, but that the act of speech must conform to a normative grammar of security by a position of authority speaking to an audience that understands and is convinced by this act. Thus, the specific socio-political relations that lead to securitization are under-theorized. As McDonald points out: 'The potential for security to be constructed over time through a range of incremental processes and representations is not addressed, and the question of why particular representations resonate with relevant constituencies is under-theorized'.[50] He notes that questions like 'Why are some political communities more likely to view certain actors and dynamics as threatening? What role do narratives of history, culture and identity have in underpinning or legitimating particular forms of securitization?'

are obscured.⁵¹ Yet answers to such questions must go beyond a form of discourse-reductionism focusing exclusively on 'narratives of history, cultural and identity', to explore the *political economy* with which these narratives are co-extensive. As Doug Stokes points out:

> While the WoT ['War on Terror'] is undoubtedly a discursive complex whereby modes of representation about terrorism, non-Western populations and the construction of stark boundaries (you are either with us or with the terrorists) operate to exclude and include, it is also intimately bound up with political and economic processes... Specifically, the wars launched in the name of counter-terrorism are not purely driven by certain hegemonic discourses, but are also part of the West's economic interests in oil, strategic interests in military bases in the Middle East and the desire to maintain American hegemony into the twenty-first century by controlling one of the crucial resource-rich regions for global capitalism.⁵²

In other words, the hegemonic construction of exclusionary discourses is always inherently politically constituted, and therefore by the same token, politically embedded and politically transformative. Rather than securitization only justifying the suspension of law to pave the way for *exceptional* measures outside the political, contemporary security constructions of 'Islam' and 'Muslims' show that it can also lead to a form of governmentality that permanently transforms the way in which populations are politically managed and reproduced.⁵³ The Paris school of Security Studies thus points out that securitization is equally about risk management, actively conducted by security professionals working across multiple social bureaucracies in the army, intelligence services, police forces, border controls, defence companies, insurance firms and so on. Their activities construct 'regimes of truth' which draw on 'numerical data and statistics, technologies of biometrics and sociological profiles of potential dangerous behaviour' to 'determine what exactly constitutes security', and whose expertise empowers them to advise state-leaders.⁵⁴ Securitization therefore 'works through everyday technologies, through the effects of power that are continuous rather than exceptional, through political struggles, and especially through institutional competition within the professional security field in which the most trivial interests are at stake'.⁵⁵

The Paris school thus highlights that the state-level 'speech act' privileged by the Copenhagen school cannot simply appear *ex-nihilo* as a discursive rupture that innovates a completely new 'regime of truth', but must emerge from prior 'normal' political processes therefore amplifying pre-existing exclusionary 'regimes of truth' in new directions. Yet while identifying the role of 'interests', 'institutional competition' and the status of the 'professional security field', the Paris schools offers no exploration of the concrete political and economic structures by which these are constituted, and how they thus interact with and relate to the operation of state power. By what socio-political relations is the expertise of security professionals privileged and sanctioned by the state? What historically specific social conditions prompt the construction of exclusionary 'regimes of truth' through processes of everyday political institutional struggles, as well as through extraordinary acts of state-level decisionism enforcing exceptional measures?

Furthermore, the sharp theoretical distinction between the Copenhagen and Paris schools collapses in the face of historical and empirical reality. Anti-Western terrorist attacks such as 9/11 prompt state-level emergency responses which, justified by the perception of unprecedented threat, lead to adoption of extraordinary military and police responses. Yet these responses do not merely suspend constitutional law in the face of emergency – they establish permanence precisely through exploiting the declared state of emergency to legitimize the *institutionalization of exceptional measures within the body politic*, thus purporting to permanently transform the constitutional order. Securitization, in other words, can lead to wholesale *militarization* of society. Of course, this is not to suggest that the suspension of elements of the constitutional order leading to its permanent transformation amounts to a wholesale annulment of democracy. Rather, this process of militarization encompasses the progressive institutionalization of exceptional extra-constitutional measures, and thus undermining the democratic system on security grounds, and continually threatening to subvert it further. Yet what remains unanswered here is the very nature of the political processes that drive securitization, their institutional origin, and the socio-political relations by which they are constituted.

Ultimately, the most significant underlying causal factor is a deepening perception of a fundamental social crisis. New conceptual developments in genocide studies throw further light on this in terms of the concrete socio-political dynamics of securitization processes. It is now widely recognized, for instance, that the distinguishing criterion of genocide is not the pre-existence of primordial groups, one of whom destroys the other on the basis of a pre-eminence in bureaucratic military-political power. Rather, genocide is the intentional attempt to destroy a particular social group that has been *socially constructed as different*.[56] In Hinton's words:

> Genocides are distinguished by a process of 'othering' in which the boundaries of an imagined community are reshaped in such a manner that a previously 'included' group (albeit often included only tangentially) is ideologically recast (almost always in dehumanizing rhetoric) as being outside the community, as a threatening and dangerous 'other' – whether racial, political, ethnic, religious, economic, and so on – that must be annihilated.[57]

In other words, genocidal violence is inherently rooted in a prior and ongoing ideological process, whereby exclusionary group categories are reconceptualized, constructed and 'Otherized' in accordance with a specific socio-political programme. The very process of identifying and classifying particular groups as outside the boundaries of an imagined community of 'inclusion', justifying exculpatory violence towards them, is itself a political act without which genocide would be impossible.[58] This recalls Lemkin's recognition that the intention to destroy a group is integrally conjoined to a wider socio-political project – or colonial project – designed to perpetuate the political, economic, cultural and ideological relations of the perpetrators in the place of that of the victims, by interrupting or eradicating their means of social reproduction. Only by interrogating the dynamic and origins of this programme to uncover the social relations from which that programme derives, can the emergence of genocidal intent become explicable.[59]

Building on this insight, Semelin demonstrates that the process of exclusionary social group construction invariably derives from political processes emerging from deep-seated *socio-political crises* that undermine the prevailing framework of civil order and social norms; and which can, for one social group, be seemingly resolved by projecting anxieties onto a new 'outsider' group deemed to be somehow responsible for crisis conditions. It is in this context that various forms of mass violence, which may or may not eventually culminate in actual genocide, can become legitimized as contributing to the resolution of crises.[60]

This does not imply that the current logic of securitization is necessarily genocidal. Rather, the same essential dynamics of social polarization and exclusionary group identity formation evident in genocides are highly relevant in understanding the radicalization processes behind contemporary mass violence. This highlights the fundamental connection between social crisis, the break-down of prevailing norms, the formation of new exclusionary group identities, and the projection of blame for crisis onto a newly constructed 'outsider' group vindicating various forms of violence.

Conclusion

Widespread government and public anxieties about the overlapping dangers of global recession, environmental degradation, resource depletion, food price inflation, violent conflict, terrorism, and so on, can often translate into a mistrust of prevailing institutions and norms. Depending on one's political orientation, this can lead to the projection of those anxieties onto specific institutions, norms, or even social groups. It is in this context that historians of mass violence point out that the processes that lead to genocide invariably commence with the eruption of a social crisis generating radical uncertainty, which is subliminally resolved by projection of blame onto social groups who begin to be constructed as outsiders. Their extermination, partial or otherwise, is thus increasingly viewed as a 'final solution' by which the perpetrator group exculpates itself and psychologically alleviates its anxieties about entrenched crises.[61]

In the contemporary global context, the securitization of Islam and Muslims driving the entrenchment of Islamophobia is itself being driven by a deepening perception of social crises at multiple levels of society, vindicating the sense of a fundamental failure of prevailing institutions and values. At the level of defence planning, the pre-9/11 official recognition of an ongoing and inevitable decline in US hegemony has been compounded by the emergence and prevalence of non-traditional security challenges whose dynamics are being accelerated precisely by the normal functioning of the US-dominated global political economy. The strategic imperative throughout the 'War on Terror' to shore-up an increasingly beleaguered

US hegemony through domination of the world's critical energy resources and transhipment routes has in turn focused the imaginations of security agencies on the problematic role of Muslim-majority regions. Simultaneously, the institutionalization of this paranoia about the security threat potentially posed by Islam and Muslims in the form of wide-ranging new domestic police-powers – combined with the corporate media's normalization of mass military violence in Muslim-majority regions as 'par for the course' required to defend Western civilization against terrorism – has generated a parallel paranoia throughout Western societies. This irrational paranoia grows and becomes increasingly targeted and dangerous as global ecological, energy and economic crises – largely systemic in origin – continue to undermine the social fabric, to the impotence of the conventional paraphernalia of the Western political bureaucracy. This further fuels both government and public anxieties, and intensifies the securitization processes that drive the social polarization of insider and outsider groups, of which Muslims are the focal point.

In this context, does the conduct of actual Anglo-American military engagements in Muslim-majority regions, such as Iraq, Afghanistan, Somalia, Pakistan and so on, indicate an Islamophobic 'Muslim-centric' dynamic to such practices, evincing a tendentially genocidal logic, or is the systematic targeting of largely Muslim groups simply an accident of geopolitical interest? This discussion suggests that the answer is both. Processes of 'Otherization' due to securitization tend to become increasingly radicalized on the ground precisely in the context of increasingly violent socio-political contestations and social crisis. It is not a far cry to suggest that US wars in Muslim-majority theatres of war are therefore undergoing a process of radicalization, fuelled by both the difficulty and entrenchment of conflict in for instance Afghanistan and Pakistan, the terrorism that conflict inevitably generates, as well as the systemic non-traditional security challenges such as food, water and economic problems increasingly afflicting Muslim-majority regions.

This, of course, brings us to the thorny question, given our reference to the genocide literature, of how to conceptualize the *intentional* dynamic of much of this violence, particularly given that it often involves massive and indiscriminate killings of predominantly Muslim civilians. These killings are not only 'degenerate' in Shaw's sense of the foreseeable, tacitly-condoned collateral damage of technologized ways of war designed to minimize Western military casualties.[62] They also often include confirmed episodes of *deliberate* targeting of civilians as an integral strategy of war. Congressional testimony of US Army combat veterans in Iraq, for example, refers to 'free fire orders ... described by the soldiers who had been deployed during the invasion as coming from their commanders who told them "kill everything that moves" which included all civilians'.[63]

Even episodes of violence largely attributed to US incompetence may be more problematic, requiring more detailed empirical determination. Iraq expert Toby Dodge, for instance, emphasizes that a substantive portion of civilian deaths in Iraq was due to the escalation of violent sectarian conflict under the complete collapse of the administrative and coercive capacities of the Iraqi state, for which he primarily blames 'the United States' inability to reconstruct them'.[64] Yet, his analysis overlooks compelling evidence that at least to some degree, US forces intentionally brought about this collapse and exacerbated sectarian divisions as a strategy to weaken Iraq's capacity for self-determination, thereby consolidating its dependence on US security forces and legitimizing a permanent *de facto* occupation. Several credible journalistic and intelligence investigations argue that elements of the Bush administration envisaged a forcible division of Iraq along ethno-religious lines from the outset of its war-planning, and that for some years the United States actively backed an eclectic panoply of Shi'ite death squads and Sunni insurgents, both prime culprits in sectarian violence.[65] Cook, in this vein, suggests that at least in part the sectarian chaos in Iraq and the Middle East is the intended outcome of an imperial strategy of 'divide-and-rule'.[66]

On the other hand, clear differences in US and British approaches further complicate the picture and underscore again the need for a nuanced approach. While US forces in Afghanistan frequently call on air support, which has resulted in indiscriminate bombings of Afghan civilians. British forces have adopted precisely the opposite strategy, preferring to work on the ground, thus reducing reliance on air support precisely in order to minimize Afghan civilian casualties and hopefully increase popular support. In other words, even while at some level it seems plausible that Islamophobic processes of 'Otherization' due to securitization are at work, the dynamic of violence cannot be simplistically reduced to this, and each conflict on the ground generates its own specific trajectories that require careful explanation.

It would therefore be premature and unwarranted to causally reduce these disparate phenomena – the military violence of the 'War on Terror' in foreign theatres in Muslim-majority regions, its domestic corollary in counter-terror police powers focusing largely on Muslim diasporas, and the escalation of exclusionary paranoia and hostility towards Islam and Muslims from Western mainstream institutions – to an amorphous conception of 'Islamophobia'. While these processes should not simply be theorized as a single continuum of imperial Islamophobic violence tending potentially towards genocidal conduct, it is equally mistaken to ignore the fact that these phenomena are intimately interrelated.

This interrelation can only be understood in the context of the imperial socio-political relations of securitization – the deepening perception of social and global crisis, and the projection of anxieties towards these crises onto the geopolitical fault lines of an increasingly fragile US-dominated global political economy, which happen to cross Muslim-majority regions of the Middle East, Central Asia and North Africa. While contemporary Islamophobia, then, encompasses these different domestic and global processes, it is itself in some ways merely an ideological symptom of a global crisis of Western hegemony that is in many ways coming apart at the seams. Yet increasingly, the symptom is itself feeding back on and radicalizing the dynamic of the systemic processes by which it is generated. The overwhelming danger is that if present trends in the international system are permitted to continue – the normalization of imperial military violence abroad; the legitimization of draconian policing at home; and the unravelling of social relations due to the intensification of socio-political and economic crisis – these trends may well begin to culminate in increasingly genocidal outcomes.

Notes

1. See interview online at BBC Newsnight, 'Stephen Lennon on English Defence League's Mission', 2 February 2011, http://news.bbc.co.uk/1/hi/programmes/newsnight/9385015.stm.
2. Martin Smith, 'The BNP and EDL', *Socialist Review* (March 2010), http://www.socialistreview.org.uk/article.php?articlenumber=11183.
3. English Defence League Facebook page, http://www.facebook.com/English.Defence.League.EDL.
4. See for example my op-ed, 'Diversity Does Not Breed Terrorism – Politics Does', *Independent on Sunday*, 6 February 2010, http://www.independent.co.uk/opinion/commentators/nafeez-mosaddeq-ahmed-diversity-does-not-breed-terrorists-ndash-politics-does-2205649.html.
5. Philip Johnston, 'Islam Poses a Threat to the West, Say 53 pc in Poll', *The Daily Telegraph*, 25 August 2006.
6. Muslim West Fact Project, *The Gallup Coexist Index 2009: A Global Study of Interfaith Relations*, New York and London: Gallup and The Coexist Foundation, 2009, http://www.muslimwestfacts.com/mwf/File/118267/Gallup-Coexist-Index-2009.aspx.
7. 'YouGov Survey Findings', Inspired by Mohammed, July 2010, http://www.inspiredbymuhammad.com/yougov.php.
8. Hamza Andreas Tzortis et al., *Perceptions on Islam and Muslims: A Study of the UK Population*, London: Islamic Education and Research Academy, July 2010, http://www.iengage.org.uk/images/stories/ieraperceptionsonislam.pdf.
9. Pew Global Attitudes Project, *The Great Divide: How Westerners and Muslims View Each Other*, Washington, DC: Pew Research Center, June 2006, http://pewglobal.org/files/pdf/253.pdf. Also see Richard Wike and Brian J. Grim, 'Widespread Negativity: Muslims Distrust Westerners More Than Vice Versa', Pew Global Attitudes Project, 30 October 2007, http://pewresearch.org/pubs/625/widespread-negativity.
10. 'Luton "Parade Protestors" Were Members of Extremist Group', *The Daily Telegraph*, 12 March 2009, http://www.telegraph.co.uk/news/uknews/4976105/Luton-parade-protesters-were-members-of-extremist-group.html.
11. 'Muslims Against Crusades and English Defence League Clash at 9/11 Silence', *Metro*, 11 September 2011, http://www.metro.co.uk/news/875111-muslims-against-crusades-and-english-defence-league-clash-during-9-11-silence.
12. For a nuanced sociological definition of social exclusion and relevant disadvantage discourse, see Matt Barnes, *Social Exclusion in Britain: An Empirical Investigation and Comparison with the EU*, Hampshire: Ashgate, 2005.
13. Trades Union Congress, *Poverty, Exclusion and British People of Pakistani and Bangladeshi Origin*, London: Trades Union Congress Publications, 2005; Annual Population Survey, January 2004–December 2005, London: Office of National Statistics, 21 February 2006, http://www.statistics.gov.uk/cci/nugget.asp?id=979.
14. Guy Palmer and Peter Kenway, *Poverty Rates Among Ethnic Groups in Britain*, London: Joseph Rowntree Foundation, April 2007; Lucinder Platt, *Poverty and Ethnicity in the UK*, London: Joseph Rowntree Foundation, April 2007.
15. Saeid R. Ameli et al., *Social Discrimination: Across the Muslim Divide*, London: Islamic Human Rights Commission, 2004, http://www.ihrc.org.uk/file/1903718287_content.pdf.

16 Humayun Ansari, *Muslims in Britain*, London: Minority Rights Group International, August 2002, p. 3, http://www.minorityrights.org/download.php?id=129.
17 Robert Lambert and Jonathan Githens-Mazer, *Islamophobia and Anti-Muslim Hate Crime: A London Case Study*, Exeter: European Muslim Research Centre, 2010.
18 Lorraine P. Sheridan, 'Islamophobia Pre-and Post-September 11th, 2001', *Journal of Interpersonal Violence*, Vol. 21, No. 3 (March 2006), pp. 317–336; Scott Poynting and Victoria Mason, 'The Irresistible Rise of Islamophobia: Anti-Muslim Racism in the UK and Australia before 11 September 2001', *Journal of Sociology*, Vol. 43, No. 1 (March 2007), pp. 61–86; Liz Fekete, *Integration, Islamophobia and Civil Rights in Europe*, London: Institute of Race Relations, 2008.
19 Runnymede Trust, *Islamophobia: A Challenge for Us All*, London: Runnymede Trust, 1997.
20 Council of Europe, 'Islamophobia and Its Consequences on Young People', Seminar Report, Council of Europe, 2004, p. 6.
21 Marcel Maussen, 'Anti-Muslim Sentiments and Mobilization in the Netherlands. Discourse, Policies and Violence', in Jocelyne Cesari, ed., *Securitization and Religious Divides in Europe – Muslims in Western Europe after 9/11*, Submission to Changing Landscape of Citizenship and Security, Sixth Framework Programme of the European Commission, June 2006, pp. 100–142, http://www.libertysecurity.org/article1167.html.
22 EMCRX Report, 'Muslims in the European Union: Discrimination and Islamophobia', Vienna: European Monitoring Centre on Racism and Xenophobia, 2006, http://www.fra.europa.eu/fraWebsite/attachments/Manifestations_EN.pdf.
23 CRG and CAIR Report, *Same Hate, New Target: Islamophobia and Its Impact in the United States*, January 2009–December 2010, Berkeley, CA: University of California, 2011.
24 Greater London Authority, *The Search for Common Ground: Muslims, Non-Muslims and the UK Media*, London: Greater London Authority, November 2007.
25 Kerry Moore, Paul Mason, and Justin Lewis, *Images of Islam in the UK: The Representation of British Muslims in the National Print News Media 2000–2008*, Cardiff: Cardiff University, July 2008, p. 3, http://www.irr.org.uk/pdf/media_muslims.pdf.
26 Hussein Ibish, *Islamophobia: A Crisis of Hate Speech*, Washington, DC: Muslim Public Affairs Council, 2006, http://www.mpac.org/truthoverfear/special-report/index.php.
27 Sacha Evans et al., 'Media Coverage', in Nancy Tranchet and Dianna Rienstra, eds., *Islam and the West: Annual Report on the State of Dialogue*, Geneva: World Economic Forum, January 2008, pp. 102–106.
28 Edward Herman and Noam Chomsky, *Manufacturing Consent: The Political Economy of the Mass Media*, New York: Pantheon, 1988.
29 Diana Ralph, 'Islamophobia and the "War on Terror": The Continuing Pretext for U.S. Imperial Conquest', in Paul Zarembka (ed.) *The Hidden History of 9-11-2001* (Research in Political Economy, Volume 23), Emerald Group Publishing Limited, 2006, pp. 261–298.
30 Jack Shaheen, *Reel Bad Arabs: How Hollywood Vilifies a People*, New York: Olive Branch Press, 2001.
31 Ralph, 'Islamophobia', pp. 270–275.

32 Ralph, 'Islamophobia', p. 280.
33 Ralph, 'Islamophobia', pp. 280–290.
34 Lee Harris, *The Suicide of Reason: Radical Islam's Threat to the West*, New York: Basic Books, 2007.
35 Dan Lindley and Beth Osborne Daponte, *Iraqi Casualties from the Gulf War and Its Aftermath*, Cambridge, MA: Defense and Arms Control Studies Program, Center for International Studies, Massachusetts Institute of Technology, 1992; Andrew Cockburn and Patrick Cockburn, *Saddam Hussein: An American Obsession*, London: Verso, 2002; Eric Herring, 'Between Iraq and a Hard Place: A Critique of the British Government's Case for UN Economic Sanctions', *Review of International Studies*, Vol. 28, No. 1 (2002), pp. 39–56; Tina Susman, 'Poll: Civilian Toll in Iraq May Top 1M', *Los Angeles Times*, 14 September 2007, http://www.latimes.com/news/nationworld/world/la-fg-iraq14sep14,1,3979621.story?coll=la-headlines-world.
36 Stephen M. Walt, 'Why They Hate Us (II): How Many Muslims Has the U.S. Killed in the Past 30 Years?' *Foreign Policy*, 30 November 2009, http://walt.foreignpolicy.com/posts/2009/11/30/why_they_hate_us_ii_how_many_muslims_has_the_us_killed_in_the_past_30_years.
37 Ralph, 'Islamophobia'.
38 Ole Wæver, 'Securitisation and Desecuritisation', in Ronnie D. Lipschutz, ed., *On Security*, New York: Columbia University Press, 1995; Barry Buzan, Ola Wæver, and Jaape de Wilde, *Security: A New Framework for Analysis*, Boulder, CO: Lynne Reiner, 1998, p. 23.
39 Buzan et al., *Security*, p. 25.
40 Cited in Sami Zemni and Christopher Parker, 'European Union, Islam and the Challenges of Multiculturalism', in Shireen T. Hunter, ed., *Islam in Europe: The New Social, Cultural and Political Landscape*, Washington: Praeger, 2002, pp. 231–244.
41 Leon T. Hadar, 'The "Green Peril": Creating the Islamic Fundamentalist Threat', Cato Policy Analysis, No. 17, Washington, DC: Cato Institute, August 1992, http://www.cato.org/pubs/pas/pa-177.html.
42 Samuel P. Huntington, *The Clash of Civilizations and the Remaking of World Order*, New York: Simon & Schuster, 1998.
43 Paul Sperry, 'The Pentagon Breaks the Islam Taboo', *Front Page Magazine*, 14 December 2005, http://www.frontpagemag.com/Articles/ReadArticle.asp?ID=20539.
44 Timothy M. Savage, 'Europe and Islam: Crescent Waxing, Cultures Clashing', *Washington Quarterly*, Vol. 27, No. 3 (2004), pp. 28, 31–33.
45 Joby Warrick, 'CIA Chief Sees Unrest Rising with Population', *Washington Post*, 1 May 2008, http://www.washingtonpost.com/wp-dyn/content/article/2008/04/30/AR2008043003258.html.
46 Williamson Murrayed, 'Professional Military Education and the 21st Century', in *Strategic Challenges for Counterinsurgency and the Global War on Terrorism*, Strategic Studies Institute, Carlisle: US Army War College, September 2006.
47 US Joint Forces Command, *The Joint Operating Environment 2010*, Suffolk, VA: Joint Futures Group, 18 February 2010, pp. 24–29, http://www.jfcom.mil/newslink/storyarchive/2010/JOE_2010_o.pdf.
48 US Joint Forces Command, *The Joint Operating Environment*, pp. 12, 14–15.
49 MoD Report, *DCDC Global Strategic Trends Programme 2007–2036*, Swindon: Development, Concepts and Doctrine Centre, Ministry of Defence, December 2006,

updated and revised March 2007, http://www.mod.uk/NR/rdonlyres/94A1F45E-A830-49DB-B319-DF68C28D561D/0/strat_trends_17mar07.pdf.
50 Matt McDonald, 'Securitisation and the Construction of Security', *European Journal of International Relations*, Vol. 14, No. 4 (2008), p. 564.
51 McDonald, 'Securitisation', p. 573.
52 Doug Stokes, 'Ideas and Avocados: Ontologising Critical Terrorism Studies', *International Relations*, Vol. 23, No. 1 (2009), p. 88.
53 Jocelyne Cesari, 'The Securitization of Islam in Europe', *Challenge: Liberty & Security Research Paper*, Vol. 15 (April 2009), http://www.euro-islam.info/ei/wp-content/uploads/pdfs/the_securitisation_of_islam_in_europe.pdf; Luca Mavelli, 'Appropriation and Redemption in Contemporary Western Discourses on Islam in Europe', *St Antony's International Review*, Vol. 3, No. 2 (2008), pp. 74–93.
54 Didier Bigo, 'Globalized (in)Security: The Field and the Ban-Opticon', in Didier Bigo and Anastasia Tsoukala, eds., *Terror, Insecurity and Liberty*, New York: Routledge, 2008, p. 12.
55 Didier Bigo, 'Security and Immigration: Toward a Critique of the Governmentality of Unease', *Alternatives*, Vol. 27, No. 1 (2002), p. 73.
56 See Nafeez Mosaddeq Ahmed, 'Colonial Dynamics of Genocide: Imperialism, Identity and Mass Violence', *Journal of Conflict Transformation and Security*, Vol. 1, No. 1 (April 2011), pp. 9–36.
57 Alexander Laban Hintoned, 'The Dark Side of Modernity: Toward an Anthropology of Genocide', in *Annihilating Difference: The Anthropology of Genocide*, Berkeley: University of California Press, 2007, pp. 4–6.
58 Eric D. Weitz, *A Century of Genocide: Utopias of Race and Nation*, Princeton: Princeton University Press, 2003, pp. 2–3.
59 Raphael Lemkin, *Axis Rule in Occupied Europe: Laws of Occupation, Analysis of Government, Proposals for Redress*, Washington, DC: Carnegie Endowment for International Peace, Division of International Law, 1944, pp. 79–95.
60 Jacques Semelin, *Purify and Destroy: The Political Uses of Massacre and Genocide*, New York: Columbia University Press, 2007.
61 Semelin, Purify and Destroy, pp. 18–29.
62 Martin Shaw, *The New Western Way of War: Risk-Transfer War and its Crisis in Iraq*, Cambridge: Polity, 2005.
63 Kristofer S. Goldsmith, *Testimony of Former US Army Sergeant Kristofer Shawn Goldsmith*. Rayburn House Office Building, Room 2261, Washington, DC: U.S. House of Representatives, 15 May 2008, http://ivaw.org/publicdocuments/Transcript_WS_on_the_Hill.txt.
64 Toby Dodge, 'The Causes of US Failure in Iraq', *Survival*, Vol. 49, No. 1 (2007), p. 86.
65 Stratfor, 'United Jordan and Iraq Might Be Prime Post-War Strategy', *Stratfor Global Intelligence*, 26 September 2002; Robert Fisk, 'All This Talk of Civil War, and Now This Carnage. Coincidence?', *The Independent*, 3 March 2004; Michael Hirsh and John Barry, 'The Salvador Option', *Newsweek*, 10 January 2005; Seymour M. Hersh, 'The Redirection', *The New Yorker*, 25 February 2007.
66 Jonathan Cook, *Israel and the Clash of Civilisations: Iraq, Iran and the Plan to Remake the Middle East*, London: Pluto Press, 2008.

12

Killer Narratives in Western Popular Culture: Telling it as it is Not

Anas S. Al-Shaikh-Ali

The hostile stereotyping of Muslims is one of the oldest tropes in Western popular culture, almost as old as the negative stereotyping of the Jews. And it is getting to look ominously as dangerous. In recent years, Islamophobic narratives have been on the rise, and they pervade all genres of popular culture and the media: film, novels, television, newspapers, cartoons, etc. Furthermore, they have become more and more associated with violence and its reproduction and justification. The boundaries between Hollywood fantasies and atrocities committed on the ground in various theatres of war are becoming increasingly difficult to draw. But what is more remarkable is the apparent continuity in both form and motivation in the fabrication of stereotyping narratives across the centuries, as shown by fake travelogues of the nineteenth century and fabricated 'true life stories' dished out by contemporary religious fanatics. In this chapter, we chronicle and analyse this multi-genre phenomenon and explore the disturbing parallels between the frequency of these 'killer narratives' and the discourses that presaged the Holocaust and other modern genocides. Al-Shaikh-Ali concludes that unless something is done urgently to tone these narratives down (by stopping the fabrications, misinformation and incitement and by promoting appropriate counter-narratives), conflict and mass violence are sure to escalate.

Newspapers: Telling it as it is not

In 2011, as part of earlier ongoing investigations, some prominent British newspapers were accused of phone hacking, bribery and other unethical practices to obtain news stories for print. Public outrage led Prime Minister David Cameron to appoint Lord Justice Leveson in July 2011 to lead an official inquiry into the scandal. The Leveson report into *The Culture, Practices and Ethics of the Press*, published on 29 November 2012, stated that the Inquiry had 'heard sufficient evidence to conclude that some sections of the press have deliberately invented stories with no factual basis' and cited journalist complaints about 'top down pressure to fabricate stories...about celebrities and about Muslim issues that were published despite the knowledge that they were untrue'.[1]

This conclusion and the scandal engulfing Rupert Murdoch's News Corporation should come as no surprise, for inventing stories 'with no factual basis' with regard to Islam and Muslims, deliberate or otherwise, is nothing new. In fact flawed 'reporting' has been standard practice for centuries, but a particularly disturbing new trend was addressed in some detail by Edward Said in his insightful work *Covering Islam: How the Media and the Experts Determine How We See the Rest of the World* (1979). Said points to how a large proportion of the press coverage of the Iranian revolution and hostage crisis of the late 1970s was riddled with inaccuracies and factual distortion. In an updated edition of the work (1997), he added that the same distorted coverage characterized the reporting of the 1991–1992 Gulf War and the 1993 bombing of the World Trade Center. He notes:

> Not knowing the language is only part of the greater ignorance, for often enough the reporter is sent to a strange country with no preparation or experience, just because he or she is canny at picking up things quickly or happens already to be in the general vicinity of where front-page news is happening. So instead of trying to find out about the country, the reporter takes hold of what is nearest at hand, usually a cliché or some bit of journalistic wisdom that readers at home are unlikely to challenge.[2]

Media and 'experts' have tremendous weight, and what they say matters. Words and images have power as never before, and the experts and journalists who wield them often shape and dictate the opinion of the masses. And the challenge this poses is not restricted to trivial matters. Grave issues like mass killings are also impacted by this distorting lens of media expediency. 'Genocide' is an interesting example. When is mass killing 'genocidal' and when is it simply collateral damage in the name of bringing democracy to a region? That would depend on which side of the fence the journalist is and what viewpoint he/she or the editor determines readers should adopt.

In this regard, Glenn Grennwald points to the rise of the sham 'terrorism expert' industry, where such 'experts' are employed at think tanks, academic institutions and media outlets.

> They can and do have mildly different political ideologies but...ostensible differences in political views are totally inconsequential when placed next to their common group identity and career interest: namely, sustaining the myth of the Grave Threat of Islamic Terror in order to justify their fear-based careers, the relevance of their circle, and their alleged 'expertise'.[3]

From 'Barbary' to *Midnight Express*: Violently imagining the 'Turk'

Evidently the quality of 'expertise' has not improved much since one perceptive observer noted in the nineteenth century that 'the information provided by missionaries for the folks at home was biased and antipathetic'[4] and that many missionaries proceeded upon the assumption that the 'Terrible Turk' and other Muslim peoples in the Near East belonged to 'a retrograde race of Devil Worshippers'.[5] Cyrus Hamlin, an American missionary stationed in Turkey, 'lamented the influence of newspapers, pamphlets, and travel books upon opinions held by Americans about Turkey' and Turks which comprised 'half-truths', if not, at times, deliberate distortions.[6] He writes in his book *Among the Turks*: 'We all have a natural and noble tendency to believe what we read or hear, but when I take up Eastern news, I always pray inwardly, O Lord endow me with a suitable spirit of unbelief.'[7] As early as 1819, an anonymous 'Gentleman of Boston' had this to say:

> The unhappy prejudices of the Christian world against the professors of Mahomet's creed, which had been *instilled into my mind*, led me to fear a thousand dangers where none existed ... when the seaman approaches that part of Asia inhabited by the Turks, he may with safety bury all alarm, and rest satisfied that although he is not near a Christian country, still he will find among the inhabitants, all the virtues possessed by Christians with but few of their vices.[8]

Note that although 'the Turk' is specifically mentioned, often this was broadly understood to mean the wider Muslim populace and not just the Turkish people. It is generally widely known that many American 'travellers', 'reporters' and travel writers of the time were brazenly sending 'eyewitness accounts' and even producing travelogues of places they had in fact never set foot in. Most were in reality scribbling from the comfort of their armchairs, located in a European city, predominantly Venice, and relying on third- or fourth-hand accounts, which in many cases had been completely fabricated by those passing them on. Therefore, '...given most writers' source of information, it is not surprising that the Terrible Turk was portrayed as barbaric'.

Lady Mary Wortley Montagu, wife of the British Ambassador to the Ottoman Court (1717), did however set some of the record straight. Composing what have now come to be known as the *Turkish Embassy Letters*, she famously, or rather infamously, given the public reaction, wrote of Turkish women for instance:

> As to their Morality or good Conduct, I can say like Arlequin, that 'tis just as 'tis with you, and the Turkish Ladys don't commit one sin the less for not being Christians. Now I am a little acquainted with their ways I cannot forbear admiring either the exemplary discretion or extreme Stupidity of all the writers that have given accounts of 'em. 'Tis very easy to see they have more Liberty than we have ...[9]

Nevertheless, many travellers, reporters and travel writers repeatedly crossed the line between fact and fiction, ready to believe and spread 'almost anything that discredited the Turks'.[10] Sadly the accounts were regardless incredibly popular. Hamlin maintains that, 'the entire class of Levantines [who supplied information] were devoted enemies of Turkey and ... were congenitally incapable of telling the truth'.[11] Ironically many of these anti-Turk fabrications were taking place at a time when Turkey was fully supporting the American Union during the Civil War. Reacting to an attempt by a 'prominent missionary' to take action against the Sublime Porte because of '*alleged interference*' in missionary activities, an angry Secretary of State asked: 'Do you know, Sir, that Turkey is the only country upon the face of the earth which officially has supported the American government in these our trials?'[12]

Commenting on the negative impact of such bogus information in terms of causing bloody and tragic conflict affecting millions, Moore remarks:

> Reality frequently has no place in history. What causes a man to think, write, and speak as he does is often much more important. And, when these thoughts are translated into deeds, the truth may no longer matter for the deeds themselves become truth. Whether true or false information motivated these deeds is of little consequence. One daily encounters this perplexing problem of motivation. If issues are of sufficient importance, angry words, bloody noses, law suits, and even murder may follow... But, when these differences involve groups of individuals formed into nations, this becomes a matter of great import. It can mean peace or war for millions.[13]

Not surprisingly, the standard view of Turkey at the time is expressed in the following words which also capture the general tone:

> Reform of any kind is utterly impossible, it is contrary to the nature of the Turks. It is truly said that the only 'good Turk is a dead Turk,' for then he is incapable of injuring others in thought, word, or deed. It is a blot upon civilization and humanity of the Nineteenth Century, that a sensual and grossly immoral nation as the Turks, to whom rape and abduction are daily events, with a long and appalling record of bloodshed, cruelty and barbarity, should control several millions of Christians who are superior to them in character, intelligence and in every other respect.[14]

Moore also referred to another author, Ohan Gaidzakian, who presented Islam as a 'religion of the devil' and suggested that 'Turks talk of little but filth and smut, think only of flesh and lust. Mecca is nothing but a center of prostitution... to leave a man alive or a woman unravished is to be false to the precepts of Mohammed.'[15] Moore further referred to and quoted from several other authors and missionaries who have presented a very negative image of Islam and Muslims, deliberately fabricating and twisting information.

In addition to such material, poets and playwrights have also played an important part in developing negative and fantastic images of this nature. Although some were keen and careful not to stoop to such levels of falsification and dehumanization of Muslims, the majority did not hesitate to do so. The so-called 'Barbary conflict' helped produce at least ten plays between 1801 and 1841 on the subject. In the eighteenth and early nineteenth centuries, a large number of plays using Near Eastern material were produced both in Europe and the United States. Many were performed in New York and Boston, among other cities.[16] Some were even published for the Juvenile drama.[17] Interest in such plays was great on both sides of the Atlantic. For example, in the United

States, on 5 March 1805, 'Turks' (taken prisoners in North Africa), who arrived on the *John Adams* frigate, were 'dragged' to attend the 'appropriate' English play, *Blue Bears* (1798). Treated like animals, in fact dehumanized, they were seated 'in the stage-box cynosure of all beholders'. These prisoners of war were forced to attend several other 'appropriate' plays, which made use of Near Eastern material, as the 'public demand increased'. The 'atrocious taste of these proceedings', we are told, was 'only equaled by the vulgarity of the audience that flocked to the show' abusing the prisoners.[18]

Turkish film director Dervis Zaim's dissertation 'Representation of the Turkish People in the Film *Midnight Express*'[19] illustrates once again the one-sided depiction of the Turks as 'frightening' and 'ruthless' in Oliver Stone's 1978 film. The movie, which continues to be widely shown, depicts the highly disturbing and supposedly true-life account of Billy Hayes (an American citizen convicted of drug smuggling) and the horror of his experiences in a Turkish prison until his eventual escape to Greece. Years later, in an interview Billy Hayes admitted to Alinur Velidedeoglu that some of the scenes in the movie had been exaggerated or were not true.[20] Billy never claimed to have suffered any sexual violence at the hands of his Turkish wardens but did engage in consensual sex while in prison. Recalling similar distortions, Anwar Ibrahim (former Deputy Prime Minister of Malaysia) argues in *The Asian Renaissance* that 'No community has suffered more wrong from the information explosion' than Muslims, referring also to the portrayal of Arabs and Muslims as 'stern and menacing fundamentalists'.[21] For instance, Billy Hayes met many good Turks but this did not come across in the film. The clear-cut divide between what is good and what is bad uses violence committed by Muslims as its springboard. Granted, as Ibrahim states, 'Isolated incidents of violence and terrorism perpetrated by groups waving the fundamentalist or *jihad* banner will invariably stir up mass hysteria against Muslims'.[22] But the point is that incidents of violence are not peculiar to the Muslim world or Muslim people.

'Reel Bad Arabs'

A large number of films portray Arabs and Muslim non-Arabs with 'negative physical and moral characteristics – lustful, fanatical, irrational, cruel, scheming, unreliable, often cowardly, and always outwitted and defeated'.[23] In *Reel Bad Arabs: How Hollywood Vilifies a People*, Jack Shaheen analyses this 'unapologetic degradation and dehumanization of a people' in film, providing a powerful study of content dictating public perceptions and opinion. In this first comprehensive review of Arab screen images, Shaheen examines:

> virtually every feature that Hollywood has ever made – more than 900 films, the vast majority of which portray Arabs by distorting at every turn what most Arab men, women, and children are really like.[24]

In *The TV Arab*, he also examines over 100 different popular entertainment programmes, cartoons and major documentaries to showcase the level of stereotyping that viewers are inundated with across the networks.

Fake travel narratives and false reporting have developed many of the stereotypes that continue to be paraded by media and scholars today, intending to present the 'objective' views of novelists, play-writers, painters, and others, both in formal as well as informal education and popular culture. But if the source material is questionable, then of what credibility are their statements? Historical lies have allowed for historical stereotypes, but while lies can be corrected, *stereotypes in fact prevent the reconstruction of truth*. President John Kennedy was clearly aware of this. Frustrated at the hostile coverage he had received for being the first Catholic US President, he once declared:

> For the great enemy of truth is very often not the lie – deliberate, contrived and dishonest – but the myth – persistent, persuasive, and unrealistic. Too often we hold fast to the clichés of our forebears. We subject all facts to a prefabricated set of interpretations. We enjoy the comfort of opinion without the discomfort of thought.[25]

Continuous repetition of Muslim stereotypes down the centuries has not abated. I would even say it has escalated, the ramifications of the danger Kennedy pointed out notwithstanding. And neither has the practice of misrepresentation ceased. Much of the current reporting on Islam and Muslims is in fact a combination of the two, inherited stereotypes and blatant fabrications serving various political, religious and economic agendas.

Those who currently report and write on Islam and Muslims spreading disinformation and bias can roughly be divided into the following groups: those driven by religious or political agendas; those producing sensational material to maximize publicity or profit; and those ill-informed who base their views either on second or third hand information or shoddy research. The first and second categories contain many individuals, notoriously creative in inventing stories. The list includes scholars, faith leaders, journalists, politicians, parliamentarians, decision-makers, novelists, authors, etc.: that is, members of the cultural and political elite, to whom people turn to make sense of an enormously complex information age.[26] They have become the great filter through which the world is interpreted, because people are understandably unable to put the time and effort into studying what is being presented to them. This is the great shift, the reliance on news and casual 'experts' on a mass scale that Said was perhaps referring to.

Fiction writers add another contemporary 'thrillingly entertaining' dimension. Even when Turkey was an ally of the West, this negative portrayal never stopped but took different shapes and forms. For example, in Ian Fleming's bestselling novel *From Russia with Love* (1957), made into a block-buster James Bond movie, Bond's Turkish comrade in arms, Darko Kerim (supposedly a 'good Turk') is painted in dark colours. He works for British intelligence in Turkey and tries to help save Bond when the 'notorious Soviet SMERSH organization' decides to eliminate him. But he still appears as a shady character, who 'bribes and uses trickery' and then gets killed. There are many other examples of popular fiction titles published in the last three decades of the twentieth century (and into the twenty-first), with sinister Turkish characters.

But one rarely finds a good Turk or a positive image of any aspect of Turkish life and society. The rehashing and updating of old stereotypes and myths continues according to form. Some of these recently published titles include: Dale Brown's *Rogue Forces* (2009), Clive Cussler's *Crescent Dawn* (2010), George Mavro's *Operation Medina: The Jihad* (2011) and *Operation Medina: The Crusade* (2012), as well as a science fiction novel, Ian McDonald's *The Dervish House* (2010). Many are also published in other European languages; the most recent in French, for example, is Paul Fauray's *La Bombe Des Mollahs* (2012). A large number of these fiction titles use sinister images of Turkey (usually Istanbul) on the cover, mainly a silhouette of one of the famous mosques (Sultan Ahmet or Sulaymania) against a backdrop of fire overshadowed by menacing dark clouds.[27]

Islamophobia and the Holocaust: Disturbing echoes

Disinformation and bias can take many forms. For instance, in formal education it is not only what is being taught in schools and academia that can perpetuate stereotypes but also more importantly *what is not being taught*. In this way ignorance or misrepresentation of Islam and its values is maintained, which explains why it is still so widespread in the West despite advances in global communication. Utterly gross ignorance of this type allowed talk show host Robert Kilroy-Silk to attack Arabs by writing in a newspaper article headed 'We Owe Arabs Nothing', that they had in fact (living up to the title) contributed nothing useful or valuable to the world.[28] While this inaccurate and prejudiced claim did land him in some trouble, it was no doubt accepted by a sizeable segment of the readership who were unaware of the great contributions of a civilization whose legacy some of the finest scholars have paid tribute to.

Airing inflammatory anti-Muslim views to millions, hardly impartial though some semblance of debate is given, is now commonplace. In fact, in chapter six of *At War with Metaphor*, 'Hate Speak: Discourses of Dehumanization in Talk Radio', Steuter and Wills point to hate speech being institutionalized in recent years as part of mainstream media through radio and television talk shows.

> Violent inflammatory speech has become a staple of several talk radio shows that have risen to prominence over the last decade. The hosts of these programmes are profoundly influential in shaping opinion among the documented 100 million Americans who listen regularly.[29]

This is worrying because 'since 9/11, their prime target has been Muslims, particularly Arab Muslims', and because '[h]ate speech may fester within our social consciousness and prompt *violent action*'.[30]

President Kennedy's statement quoted earlier should be read a little more carefully for it also sheds light on a number of contemporary issues. These include racism, discrimination, bias, Islamophobia and anti-Semitism to list a few. They encompass both the fabrication of narratives that can lead to tragic consequences and the process of spreading them. Popular culture, both in the West and across the world, is spreading at breakneck speed, taking the form of novels, plays, cartoons, anecdotes, newspaper and magazine articles, movies, radio and television programmes, chat-shows, fiction and graphic fiction, social networking sites, etc., including material targeted at adults and the young. And in the wake of this 'friendly' roller coaster whose raison d'être is supposedly to entertain, is the generation of discrimination, leading ultimately to suffering, destruction, torture, death and massacre.

The Jewish holocaust is a vivid example. The tactics employed by the Nazis served them well and are sounding frighteningly familiar: the use of fabrication, lies, and stereotypes to dehumanize a particular 'other', in this case the Jews, to lay the groundwork for their eventual extermination. The Nazis believed in and practiced the 'teaching of intolerance' and 'anti-Semitism was taught before children were six or seven or eight'.[31] For example, we have the case of a children's story entitled 'Poisonous Mushroom', written by Nazi author Ernst Hiemer and illustrated by Nazi artist Fips. It was intended to 'indoctrinate young German children to despise and hate the Jews. The stories infiltrated the thoughts and beliefs of German children', portraying the Jews as 'evil and dangerous'.[32] Numerous other narratives of hate and stereotype were used by the Nazis in many forms of popular culture to generate the public consensus required for the 'final solution'. For there to be a 'solution' there has to be a 'problem' and some very talented writers are coaching discourse on Islam under this very framework. Nazi writings were 'killer narratives' in every sense of the term. Hideous and savage cartoons were also employed by the Nazis, with tragic consequences. Because, just as no one questions the power of political cartoons to persuade acceptance of a statement dressed up as caricature, so no one should underestimate the impact of cartoons to generate loathing and license dehumanization. Jewish cartoon rodents have simply been replaced with Muslim cartoon vermin. The use of disease imagery is often used to stir up the worst kind of paranoia, pointing to the source as a highly rotten entity threatening to poison what it comes into contact with.

The volume, *At War with Metaphor*, mentioned earlier, discusses these issues and the exact process of Nazi dehumanization of the Jews through cartoons.[33] In a chapter entitled 'Rallying Racism: Dehumanization and Genocide', the authors begin by citing a relevant quote from Sam Keen's *Faces of the Enemy*: 'In the scale of dehumanisation, we drop from the midpoint of the subhuman barbarian to the nonhuman, from the savage to the animal... The lower down in the animal phyla the images descend, the greater sanction is given to the soldier to become an exterminator of pests.'[34] The authors also refer to the work of Andreas Musolff, who argued that 'the Nazis' anti-Semitic metaphor system is a powerful demonstration of how stigmatisation and dehumanisation leads to genocide'.[35]

As an example of how cartoons are used in this dehumanizing process, the authors refer to a cartoon poster produced by the Danish Nazi Party during the Second World War urging extermination (see Figure 12.1).[36]

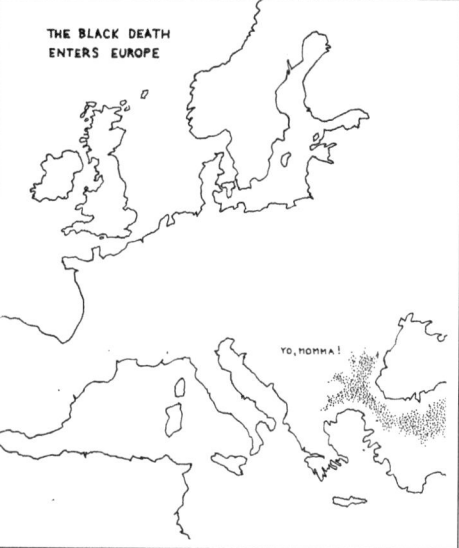

Figure 12.1 Danish Nazi Party Propaganda
Rotten Udryd Den. Translation: "Rats. Destroy Them"; a 1940s poster from occupied Denmark

Figure 12.2 Muslim Turks as also disease ridden rats threatening to engulf Europe (the black death having been brought over by rats)
The Black Death Enters Europe. © *www.CartoonStock.com*

They comment that

> the rat, drawn in painstaking detail down to the individual scales and bristles on its long tail, sits in the dark behind a wall peering out avariciously into the light through a jagged hole. The message of threat and invasion could not be clearer, they're in there, crouched in the dark behind our walls, ready to leap out and get us.[37]

Anti-Muslim Islamophobic imagery seems to be employing similar metaphors. See for instance Figure 12.2 which portrays Muslim Turks as rats too, threatening to engulf Europe, Black-Death style, ready to bring disease and death if admitted to the EU.[38] This is one example but its message is highly revealing. For it demonstrates that Nazi anti-Semitic style propaganda and use of genocidal narrative is being, at least partly, copied/imitated, and who knows to what end? (see Figures 12.3–12.6). Not only are Figures 12.3 and 12.4 particularly racist but more importantly note they are almost mirror images of one another despite the many decades separating them. Notice the hooked nose, dull yet devious expression, the heavy jaws, etc. This is surely not mere coincidence. Figures 12.5 and 12.6 are self-explanatory. The Jewish banker is no different to the Arab controlling the world's oil supply. Once again the similarities between the two images are striking.

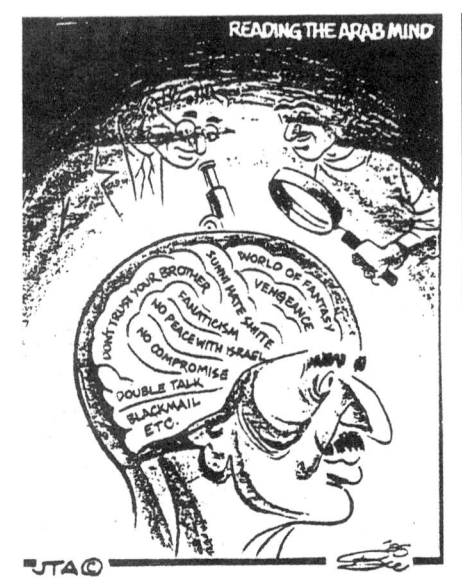

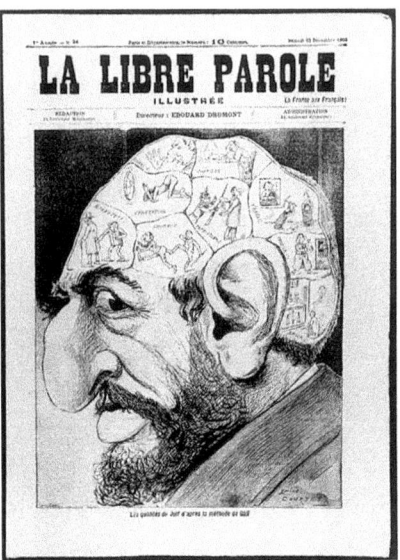

Figure 12.3 Reading the Arab Mind by Noah Bee. © JTA.
(The photo may not be reproduced without JTA's permission. More information about JTA is available on www.jta.org. If you would like to receive your FREE subscription to JTA's Daily Briefing sign up at http.//www.jta.org/briefing/index.htm)

Figure 12.4 Emile Courtet. Jewish Virtues According to Gall's Method (Les qualites du Juif d'apres la methode de Gall) 'La Libre Parole Illustre', Paris, December 23, 1893. The Jewish Museum, 1990 © 2014, © Photo SCALA, Florence.

Figures 12.3 and 12.4 are mirror images of one another, the devious minds of people with no values.

We can take an educated guess and we can certainly recognize the finger of accusation and blame. Muslims at the receiving end perfectly grasp the possibilities! Steuter and Wills comment correctly:

> There are many fertile examples of how enemies are made into the Other, dragged symbolically backwards down the evolutionary ladder until they, and the people who look like them, are no longer seen as human, but as insects or animal, germ or disease. This comes at a double cost. First, it fuels the kind of violence that has horrified us at Abu Ghraib, furthering the cycle of offense and retaliation. Second, it binds our imagination into an adversarial pattern that works against the humanity and creativity required to break free of the kinds of cyclical violence central to the war on terror.[39]

Ibrahim Kalin, a prominent Turkish intellectual,[40] recently warned: 'It would be a costly mistake to belittle and brush aside Islamophobic acts as marginal events to be tolerated

Figure 12.5 Jewish Banker / Jewish God is Money. Published in *Der Giftpilz* (The Poisonous Mushroom). *The image was also published in Fifty Questions on Antisemitism.* Publisher: Anne Frank House (2005). No copyright was cited.

Figure 12.6 Arab Oil. From *Best Editorial Cartoons of the Year*, 1975 Edition, edited by Charles Brooks ©1975 by Charles Brooks. Used by permission of the licenser, Pelican Publishing Company, Inc.

Figures 12.5 and 12.6 are once again mirror images of one another, the Jewish banker controlling the world's finances and the Arab controlling the world's oil supply.

under the guise of freedom of expression. Extremist discourse and hate-mongering against Islam and Muslims do lead to violence.'⁴¹

In 2000, I presented a paper entitled 'The Fiction of the Enemy Within' at an AMSS UK conference on *Muslims of Europe in the New Millennium: Multiculturalism, Identity and Citizenship* which discussed the development of an alarming new trend which is increasingly a feature of contemporary popular fiction plot lines. I refer here to the targeting of Muslim communities residing in the West, no matter what generation, as terrorists or potential terrorists, also referred to as the 'enemy within'. Using six novels, published between 1996 and 2000, as illustration, I attempted to demonstrate the irresponsible and potentially explosive nature of this theme. Sowing the seeds of suspicion, popular fiction writers are teaching readers to view the Muslim Other living and working among us as possibly treacherous and disloyal, without proper regard for evidence. This and other forms of media coverage and sensationalism increase already dangerously volatile levels of Islamophobia, negatively influencing the behaviour and attitudes towards these communities. *The Lion's Game*, published in 2000, presents us with a well-respected American Muslim academic, Professor Abdellah. He is suspected of being an 'enemy within' even though he does his best to help authorities by reading 'the mind of a terrorist' before the said terrorist is able to unleash further acts of terror. In one scene, a senior security agent acidly tells colleagues once Professor Abdellah has left the room: 'Someone like Ibin Abdellah was either a loyal American and valuable special agent, or he was a security risk. He was *almost undoubtedly* the former. But that *one per cent doubt*, like in marriage, gets bigger in your imagination.'⁴²

The impression given is that no matter how faithful one is to one's country, and no matter what one does, including endangering one's own life to protect fellow-citizens, there will always remain that *tiny possibility* –that one is a potential risk and could help and aid terrorism. The novel profiles several Muslims/Arabs as 'enemies within': 'An obvious security breach within the Trans-Continental operation at De Gaulle. In other words, an employee at Trans-Continental in Paris, *perhaps an Arab employee, of which there are many* in Paris, tipped off Yusef Haddad.'[43] The other five titles I referred to included, *The Enemy Within* (1996) by Larry Bond, *Day of Wrath* (1998) by Larry Bond, *Against All Enemies* (1998) by Richard Herman, *Tomorrow Belongs to Us* (2000) by Larry Collins, and *H.M.S. Unseen* (2000) by Patrick Robinson. The number has significantly increased since their publication.

The paper was presented over ten years ago but little has changed; in fact the trend has steadily grown. The popular American television series *Homeland*, winner of two Golden Globes in drama, is a prime example of how paranoia has mushroomed using popular culture to shift attention to Muslims being a hidden force, or an 'enemy within', in the process making something improbable now entirely plausible for the millions of fans it drew around the world. The show depicts a US Marine, Damien Lewis, a Muslim convert, not only suspected of being an Al-Qaeda affiliate but actually motivated to become so by a dislike and hatred for US foreign policy. Aileen Morgan, another Muslim convert, is also depicted as an 'enemy within' motivated by a love to commit acts of treason against the United States. This is not to be in denial of elements of this nature existing but to maintain that *Homeland* is flawed for blatant stereotyping and focusing on Muslim identity as the concomitant of terrorist inclination.

Promoting prejudice and hatred: Untrue 'True-Life Stories'

To return to the original point made in this paper, historical fabrications (some by missionaries and evangelists) have travelled with us down the centuries to emerge intact in new and even more malicious forms. One of these modern forms is that of the so-called 'True Life Stories' genre. Rather like nineteenth century false travelogues purporting to be true accounts, the majority, a little investigation reveals, turn out to be complete fabrications. And just as travel writers were supplied with information by those hostile to Islam, so with 'true life stories' we are given an anti-Muslim slant to produce a mixture of much of the same: seditious Muslims (the 'enemy within'), gross misrepresentation, stereotyping and distortion.

At the AMSS UK's First Annual Conference held in 1999, I presented a paper on the subject entitled: 'Fact, Fiction and Faction: The Fabrication of "True-Life Stories"'. *The Torn Veil: The Story of Sister Gulshan Ester*, the bestselling 'true story' of a Pakistani convert to Christianity as told to Thelma Sangster, was exposed as a work of bad fiction. A little bit of forensics was all it took to 'unveil' it, the author not bothering to get even basic facts right. The work contained gross geographical and other inaccuracies, errors even a person with limited knowledge of the Middle East would not have made, like the claim about Saudi oil resources being owned by individuals:

The plane touched down [at Jeddah] and there to meet us at the airport was my father's old friend, the Sheikh, with his big Chevrolet car. This Sheikh had eight wives and eighteen children living at his huge villa. Thirteen of his children were daughters and five were young sons. I believe he had others who were married or studying abroad. He had his *own oil well*, which supported them in luxury... we stopped to see the oil being pumped out of the ground in one place.[44]

Note, individuals in Saudi Arabia do not privately own oil wells, and to compound error, no oil wells exist in or near Jeddah, all being located in the eastern part of the country. This is one example of the many errors pointing to the account's fabrication. The blurb on an undated reprint (with a new cover) announces the story of 'a Muslim girl, imprisoned by her religion, her strict upbringing... the *classic true-life story* of Gulshan Esther who on becoming a Christian is miraculously healed', adding that since its publication in 1984 the book had 'sold over 200,000 copies worldwide'. Gulshan, we are told in the bio given of her on the back of both editions, 'lives in Oxford and travels widely speaking about her faith'.[45] In 1992, a sequel was published, *Beyond the Torn Veil*, this time written by Vita Toon.[46] This sequel, we are told in overly maudlin fashion, 'continues *the true-life story*' of a woman 'imprisoned on all sides by the Muslim religion, by its restriction on women' and 'traces her journey to England where she finds she can use her past experiences to share her Christianity among the country's growing Muslim community'. Upon reading the first edition I wrote to the publishers three times inviting Gulshan to speak at one of our conferences. Receiving no response, I wrote again in 1992 following publication of *Beyond the Torn Veil*. To date I have yet to receive a response or even acknowledgement to any of the letters. Meanwhile, the book marches on. There is a 2004 edition published by Zondervan Publishing House, which refers to her, for the first time, as originally a 'devout Muslim girl', giving her conversion further kudos.

A second title discussed was *Under the Guns in Beirut*[47] published in 1980 and presented on the back cover blurb as 'a *real-life drama story* of innocent people caught in the crossfire of war in the Middle East... a thrilling account of the mercy and protection of God in wartime stricken Lebanon... essential book for every believer who wants to more fully understand the explosive Middle East'. The author Terry Raburn, it is added, 'is now Pastor of a church in Florida'. Terry Raburn may or may not have been in Beirut between 1970 and 1974 when the events claimed took place, but I certainly was. And I can confirm (as can many of my colleagues also there at the time) that no Iraqi Muslim named Thomas existed at the AUB (where the events in the book are supposed to have taken place) at that time. In fact I completed my MA studies at the AUB during the years in question, and out of around fifteen Iraqi students (all known to me) there, none was named Thomas. Furthermore, the author should have known, or at least tried to culturally establish, that no Iraqi Muslim family (and even among the Iraqi Christian community this is rare) – and in fact no Muslim family anywhere – gives its sons Christian names such as Thomas, just as for instance, as a hypothetical example, no Christian family would name its sons Muhammad! Thomas, we are led to believe, was an AUB Iraqi Muslim who wanted to start an argument with a group of Christian missionaries holding a concert at West Hall:

> He was a Moslem and wanted an argument. When he found no one would argue he became angry and stomped out. The next morning he was sitting on the doorstep when Billy opened the chapel. Again, he presented a loud verbal challenge to Christianity and left infuriated when no one would debate him. But he was back Wednesday.

After several failed attempts to instigate an argument, he meekly confesses:

> He was from Iraq where there is little religious toleration. He had been taught to scorn and ridicule non-Moslems and to expect the same in return… he did not know what to do, but there was a hunger inside him for the spirit of toleration he had seen in us… the cold regimentation of Islam would not fall to the warm forgiveness of Christian love.[48]

The nonexistence of Thomas at the AUB is not the only mystery pointing to fabrication. Thomas' attitude of aggression and theological rivalry is hugely questionable primarily because Iraq has always historically been a model of religious toleration. Varying religious communities have lived peaceably in a melting pot of religious and cultural diversity, and never have Muslims, whether in formal or informal education, been taught to scorn and ridicule those of other faiths. So much so that leading members of the ruling party in Iraq at the time happened to be Christians with one of them becoming Foreign Minister, and Deputy Prime Minister. This situation only changed following the American invasion in 2003.

Unfortunately, this is not an isolated case. Many similar highly implausible and suspect titles of the same missionary genre claiming to be 'true life stories' are on closer investigation revealed to be outright fabrications, outrageous given the scope of the distortion.[49] But no matter how far-fetched, they will always have an avid readership.

Another even more blatantly false account is *A Soldier for Eden: From American Schoolboy to Arab Freedom Fighter*.[50] The author's short blurb on the cover flaps describes James Congdon as a 'writer and educator for many years' who 'has worked extensively in Europe and the middle East'. On the flap we also have a blurb which tells us that it is

> the incredible *true story* of an American schoolboy rescued from the Sahara, trained by Arab freedom fighters, primed to kill,… it was said that Qadaafi himself had honoured the boy with Palestinian nationality in recognition of his courageous determination to become a *young soldier*… fired with *Islamic zeal*, trained up as a crack commando, taught to disregard pain, privation and fear, in the bleak and inaccessible desert training camps of the Arab freedom fighters… a story of rare bravery and great adventure, of industrial intrigue and *methods of terrorism*.

In the story we find that he 'learned to speak Arabic and *hate Jews*'.[51] To lend authenticity the book contains many 'actual' photographs of the boy, Christopher Rustum, even a school photograph (when he was aged 'ten-and-a-half') taken six months before his arrival in Tripoli. Another shows him next to a tree which in reality never grows in the Middle East. After its publication, the book was 'given splash serial treatment in the bestselling *Sunday Mirror*'.[52] The BBC bought rights to turn the book into a film, only to discover that the whole account had been faked. But they made the film anyway, changing the title to 'Wind on Fire', claiming it to be 'inspired' by the albeit fake book. Eventually in July 1986, Macdonald Futura withdrew the book admitting: 'We've been misled... the book is a non-book... I have ordered all copies to be pulped'.[53] Further, the author's name 'has remained a mystery', although he had claimed his real name to be Peter Ebel and that he had written novels under the name Alan Scott.[54] More blatantly, the book's Introduction is attributed to a former Libyan Minister of education, who is non-existent! Although the book's publishers have 'exposed [it] as an elaborate hoax',[55] in which case it should have disappeared a long time ago, it is nevertheless still being sold on the internet. At the time of writing, copies are available on Amazon marketplace, eBay, AbeBooks, Alibris and other outlets.[56]

And fake factual accounts are not limited to political or missionary fiction. In fact, fantasies containing titillating tales of harem horrors are equally prolific. The erotic clichés of a sexualized East, under the guise of authenticity, take the guilt out of reading what is essentially soft porn.[57] And then there are spy novelists, doing their bit for deception, again using the guise of realism, and demonstrating the ability of novelists to make readers believe them and play an influential role in shaping public opinion. Debate over true-life accounts also continues with regard to the accuracy of Hollywood movies 'based on' true-life events, as in the case of *Midnight Express* mentioned earlier.

At the time of writing on current release worldwide is the movie *Captain Phillips*, the 'true-life account' of a US captain heroically offering himself as a hostage to armed Somali pirates who had overtaken his ship. 'The only problem, say some members of the real Capt. Phillips' crew, is none of it is true'.[58] Condemning the false version they point to an altogether different picture, arguing that 'the captain's wilful disregard for his crew's safety contributed to the attack'.[59] Yet Hollywood is little bothered with telling it like it is *not*, preferring to pay homage to supposed heroism at the expense of truth, reinforcing prevailing paradigms of Our noble values and the Other's barbarity. Hollywood is about heroes and villains, the complexities of human interaction, and the requirements of historical accuracy are often ignored in favour of one-dimensional characters and uncivilized Others. Furthermore, there is a 'longstanding relationship between the United States military and Hollywood – a symbiotic relationship in which each receives benefits from the others' work'[60] argues David L. Robb in *Operation Hollywood*, giving an 'unprecedented insight into the dark world of the military's shaping of public opinion and popular culture'.[61]

The Oscar winning film *Argo* by Ben Affleck is another case in point. Despite Hollywood acclaim for its 'realism', not everyone is entirely happy, to put it mildly, with its account of the Iranian Hostage Crisis of 1979 and the rescue of American diplomats being held there – aside from the Iranians (of course), the Canadians, the New Zealanders, and the British certainly are not:

> Upon its release in October 2012, the film was criticized for its claim that British and New Zealand Embassies had turned away the American refugees in Tehran. This claim was incorrect, as neither the British or New Zealand Embassies had turned the refugees away. In fact, the embassies of both of those countries helped them, along with the Canadians.... Sir John Graham, the then-British ambassador to Iran, said, 'My immediate reaction on hearing about this was one of outrage. I have since simmered down, but am still very distressed that the film-makers should have got it so wrong. My concern is that the inaccurate account should not enter the *mythology* of the events in Tehran in November 1979.'[62]

Conclusion

Recently, Pope Francis, having only been in office two months, canonized 800 'victims of an atrocity carried out by Ottoman soldiers in 1480', in which the 'Martyrs of Otranto' refused to convert to Islam and were subsequently beheaded.[63] Granted the list includes others also canonized but the focus of media attention has notably been on the 'Turks'. Fair coverage, taking account of growing undercurrents of hostility towards Muslims and their feelings of extreme vulnerability, could have softened the blow and eased tension. For instance, by discussing the fanaticism of the Spanish Inquisition and its toll on both the Jewish and Muslim populations of Spain, who incidentally were also given the same ultimatum of convert or else: the options being beheading, torture or burning at the stake. The historical record is abysmal. There is no monopoly on violence, just as there is no monopoly on mercy. Some great acts of compassion have been at the hands of Muslims, a jarring reminder for those who would prefer to live in a world of simple absolutes, enacting the Orwellian credo of 'All animals are equal, but some animals are more equal than others.'

A case in point is an Edict issued by Sultan Mehmet II El Fatih to protect the basic rights of the Bosnian people when he conquered Bosnia-Herzegovia in 1463:

> I, the Sultan Mehmet-Khan inform all the world that the ones who posses this Imperial Edict, the Bosnian Franciscans, have got into my good graces, so I command:
> Let nobody bother or disturb those who are mentioned, not their churches. Let them dwell in peace in my Empire. And let those who have become refugees be safe. Let them return and let them settle down their monasteries without fear in all the countries of my Empire. Neither my Royal Highness, nor my viziers or employees, nor my servants, nor any of the citizens of my Empire shall insult

or disturb them. Let nobody attack insult or endanger neither their life or their property or the property of their church. Even if they bring somebody from abroad into my country, they are allowed to do so. As, thus, I have graciously issued this Imperial Edict, hereby take my great oath. In the name of the Creator of the Earth and Heaven, the one who feeds all creatures, and in the name of the seven Mustafas and our great Messenger, and in the name of the sword I put, nobody shall do contrary to what has been written, as long as they are obedient and faithful to my Command.

Note the original Edict is still kept in a Franciscan monastery in the vicinity of Fojnica (Bosnia). It forms one of the oldest human rights declarations known in history – 326 years before the French revolution of 1789, and 485 years before the Universal Declaration of Human Rights of 1948.

To conclude, I have attempted to show that through contemporary popular culture (fiction, press coverage, television and media, cartoons, fabricated 'truelife stories' and a host of other genres) and some 'academic' discourse, the public are relentlessly being groomed to fear Muslims, to view them as a problem, social and international threat, seditious force and underground cell. Islamophobia is deeply troubling because to avoid a modern day re-enactment of the persecution and tragedy suffered by the Jews, the 'Islamic Question' must be seen for what it is: as largely a manifestation of racism and xenophobia, with a potential for creating and shaping conflict, suffering and mass violence.

On 24 May 2004, *Newsweek* magazine published a picture of a GI in Iraq, reading a hard copy of *Glorious Appearing* (the twelfth book in the best-selling 'Left Behind' series, an evangelical work that relates the story of Jesus' return to Earth to fulfil God's will by wiping out from the planet all those who did not believe in him, a form of en masse 'religious cleansing'). In a letter published by ISIM Newsletter, Elliot Colla wonders 'if some soldiers reading these books aren't thinking they're involved in the first stages of Armageddon'.[64] Once soldiers are indoctrinated, through popular culture, to view humanity through the lens of vermin imagery and imagine themselves as supermen and saviours above any code of morality, doing God's work even, is it any wonder that we witness chilling and horrific incidents like that of the gang rape of fourteen-year-old Iraqi girl Abeer Qassim Hamza al-Janabi by US soldiers on 12 March 2006? While she was being raped by his colleagues, Steven Green shot her parents and younger sister before he went to rape her and set her on fire. Later he admitted, '*I didn't think of the Iraqis as humans*'.[65] The level of brutality and depravity beggars belief. It serves as a warning that human beings are capable of great wickedness – all people irrespective of race, colour or creed. Justice was not served when journalist Daniel Pearl was decapitated leaving behind a pregnant wife. No matter what narrative his executioners chose to believe, nothing could legitimize this terrible application of punishment. For murder is not meritorious. And the question remains, who bears more responsibility for the killings: the direct perpetrators or the intellectual force(s) stoking the hatred, shaping opinion and producing the 'killer narratives', which in turn produce the killers incapable of real moral choice, who imagine themselves as 'superheroes' and 'saviours' dealing with 'vermin' according to the script they have been handed down? For the one without doubt compounds and underpins the other.

Notes

1. L. J. Leveson, *An Inquiry into the Culture, Practices and Ethics of the Press* (The Stationery Office (TSO), 2012), p. 674, http://www.official-documents.gov.uk/document/hc1213/hc07/0780/0780_ii.pdf [accessed 7 January 2013].
2. Edward W. Said, *Covering Islam: How the Media and the Experts Determine How We See the Rest of the World*, London: Vintage Books, 1997, pp. iii–iv.
3. Glenn Greenwald, 'The Sham "Terrorism Expert" Industry', http://www.salon.com/2012/08/15/the_sham_terrorism_expert_industry/ [accessed 7 January 2013].
4. Jean Haythorne Braden, 'The Eagle and the Crescent: American Interest in the Ottoman Empire 1861–1870', unpublished PhD dissertation, Ohio State University, 1973, p. iv.
5. Braden, 'The Eagle and the Crescent', p. iv.
6. Braden, 'The Eagle and the Crescent', p. 29.
7. Braden, 'The Eagle and the Crescent', p. 29.
8. David H. Finnie, *Pioneers East: The Early American Experience in the Middle East*, Cambridge, MA: Harvard University Press, 1967, p. 21. Italics are mine throughout the work unless indicated otherwise.
9. Secor, A., 'Orientalism, Gender and Class in Lady Mary Wortley Montagu's Turkish Embassy Letters: To Persons of Distinction, Men of Letters and C', *Cultural Geographies* (formerly Ecumene), Vol. 6, No. 4 (1999), pp. 375–398.
10. Finnie, *Pioneers East*, p. 16.
11. Finnie, *Pioneers East*, p. 16.
12. See John Hammond Moore, 'America Looks at Turkey', Ph.D. Dissertation, University of Virginia, 1961, p. 14.
13. Moore, 'America Looks at Turkey', pp. 1–2.
14. Alexander Hidden, *The Ottoman Dynasty*, New York: Nicholas W. Hidden, 1896. As quoted by Moore, p. 245.
15. Ohan Gaidzakian, *Illustrated Armenia and the Armenians*, Boston: n.p., 1898. As quoted in Moore, p. 246.
16. English theatre made use of Near Eastern people, subjects, costumes, music and décor as early as the 1750s. See Roger Fiske, *English Theatre Music in the Eighteenth Century*, London: Oxford University Press, 1973; and David Mayer, *Harlequin in His Element: The English Pantomime 1806–1836*, Cambridge, MA: Harvard University Press, 1969.
17. See George Speaight, *The History of the English Toy Theatre*, revised edn., London: Studio Vista, 1969.
18. See George C. D. Odell, *Annals of the New York Stage*, 15 Vols., New York: Columbia University Press, 1927, II, pp. 228–230.
19. *Örnek Literary Journal*, 1994, http://www.cypnet.co.uk/ncyprus/culture/mofa/cinema/dervishzaim/dz3.htm [accessed 7 January 2013].

20 'Billy Hayes Interviewed by Alinur Velidedeoğlu at the 1999 Cannes Film Festival', http://www.youtube.com/watch?v=pHjLMnGkedU [accessed 7 January 2013].
21 Anwar Ibrahim, *The Asian Renaissance*, Selangor, Malaysia: Times Books International, 1996) p. 42.
22 Ibrahim, *The Asian Renaissance*, p. 42.
23 Kamil Aydin, 'The Good, and the Bad and Ugly: Western Cinema Images', *The Fountain*, No. 4 (Winter 1993), http://www.fountainmagazine.com/Issue/detail/The-Good-and-the-bad-and-ugly-Western-Cinema--Images [accessed 7 January 2013].
24 Jack G. Shaheen, *Reel Bad Arabs: How Hollywood Vilifies a People*, USA: Olive Branch Press, 2009, p. 1. See also, Jack G Shaheen, *The TV Arab*, Bowling Green, OH: State University Popular Press, 1984.
25 Commencement Address, Yale University, 11 June 1962.
26 See Anas Al-Shaikh-Ali, 'Public Opinion and Political Influence: Issues in Contemporary Popular Fiction', *Citizenship, Security and Democracy: Muslim Engagement with the West*, London: AMSS and SETA, 2009, pp. 47–70; Anas Al-Shaikh-Ali, 'Islamophobic Discourse Masquerading as Art and Literature: Combating Myth through Progressive Education', *Islamophobia: The Challenge of Pluralism in the 21st Century*, Oxford and New York: Oxford University Press, 2011, pp. 143–172.
27 For the impact of popular fiction on public perception see Al-Shaikh-Ali, 'Islamophobic Discourse'.
28 Kilroy-Silk, 'We Owe Arabs Nothing', *Sunday Express*, 4 January 2004.
29 Erin Steuter and Deborah Wills, *At War with Metaphor: Media, Propaganda, and Racism in the War on Terror*, New York: Lexington Books, 2009, p. 132.
30 Steuter and Wills, *At War with Metaphor*, p. 132.
31 See Mary Mills, 'Propaganda and Children During the Hitler Years', www.nizkor.org/hweb/people/m/mills-mary/mills-00.html [accessed 7 January 2013].
32 Mills, 'Propaganda and Children'.
33 Steuter and Wills, *At War with Metaphor*.
34 Steuter and Wills, *At War with Metaphor*, p. 37.
35 Steuter and Wills, *At War with Metaphor*, p. 52. The work by Andreas Musolff referred to is: 'What Role Do Metaphors Play in Racial Prejudice? The Function of Anti Semitic Imagery In Hitler's Mein Kampf', *Patterns of Prejudice*, Vol. 41, No. 1 (February 2007), pp. 21–43.
36 Produced in Steuter and Wills, p. 53 as well as Jaap Tanja and Milly Schloss, *Fifty Questions on Antisemitism*, Amsterdam: Anne Frank House, 2005, p. 61.
37 Steuter and Wills, p. 52.
38 Of course the association with disease addresses profound European fears of the Black Death whose devastating death toll still lingers in the imagination.
39 Steuter and Wills, p. xvi.
40 Chief Advisor to the Prime Minister of Turkey and a fellow at the Prince Alwaleed Center for Muslim-Christian Understanding, Georgetown University.
41 'Islamophobia with a Thousand Faces', *Today's Zaman*, 21 September 2012.
42 Nelson Demille, *The Lion's Game*, London: Little, Brown and Company, 2000, p. 363.
43 Demille, *The Lion's Game*, p. 246.
44 Bob Hitching and Barbara Hitching, *The Torn Veil: The Story of Sister Gulshan Ester* as told to Thelma Sangster, Hants, England: Marshalls, Morgan and Scott, 1984, pp. 20–23.

45 See the back cover of the book.
46 *Beyond the Veil. Sequel to the Torn Veil.* Gulshan Esther with Vita Toon, London: Marshal Pickering, 1992.
47 Terry Raburn, *Under the Guns in Beirut*, London: Marshall, M. & S., 1985.
48 Raburn, *Under the Guns*, pp. 3–31.
49 See also Bilquis Sheikh (Richard Schneider), *I Dared to Call Him Father: An Incredible Journey of Discovery Begins when a High-Born Muslim Woman Opens the Bible*, Eastbourne, UK: Kingsway Publications, 1979; and Rob Hitching and Barbara Hitching, *Nejla: A True to Life Story of Love and Tragedy in the Middle East*, Kent, England: STL Books, 1984.
50 James Congdon, *A Soldier for Eden: From American Schoolboy to Arab Freedom Fighter*, London: Macdonald, 1987.
51 See Richard Brooks, 'The Terrorist Who Never Was', *The Observer*, Sunday, 16 July 1989.
52 Brooks, 'The Terrorist Who Never Was'.
53 Brooks, 'The Terrorist Who Never Was'.
54 Brooks, 'The Terrorist Who Never Was'.
55 Brooks, 'The Terrorist Who Never Was'.
56 See 'A Soldier For Eden: From American Schoolboy to Arab Freedom Fighter', http://www.amazon.co.uk/Soldier-For-Eden-American-Schoolboy/dp/B0015IPRK4 [accessed 7 January 2013]; 'A Soldier for Eden', http://www.abebooks.co.uk/9780356144016/Soldier-Eden-Congdon-James-0356144011/plp [accessed 7 January 2013]; 'Soldiers for Eden', http://www.alibris.co.uk/search/books/isbn/9780708836750 [accessed 7 January 2013].
57 Babs Rule, *Everyday Life in the Harem* first published in 1983 by Blond and Briggs Ltd, UK.
58 http://nypost.com/2013/10/13/crew-members-deny-captain-phillips-heroism [accessed 7 January 2013].
59 Ben Child, 'Captain Phillips "No Hero" in Real Life, Say Ship's Crew', http://www.theguardian.com/film/2013/oct/14/captain-phillips-tom-hanks-real-life-no-hero, [accessed 7 January 2013].
60 David L. Robb, *Operation Hollywood: How the Pentagon Shapes and Censors the Movies*, Canada: Prometheus Books, 2004, p. 13.
61 Robb, *Operation Hollywood*.
62 'Argo' (2012_film), http://en.wikipedia.org/wiki/Argo [accessed 7 January 2013].
63 'Pope Canonizes 800 Ottoman Victims of Otranto', http://www.bbc.co.uk/news/world-europe-22499327 [accessed 7 January 2013].
64 See Elliot Colla's response, in Letters to the Editor, *ISIM Newsletter*, 15, Spring 2005. For further details on this see Al-Shaikh-Ali, 'Islamophobic Discourse Masquerading as Art and Literature', p. 167.
65 See '"I Didn't Think of Iraqis as Humans," Says U.S., Soldier Who Raped 14-Year-Old Girl before Killing Her and Her Family', http://www.dailymail.co.uk/news/article-1340207/I-didnt-think-Iraqis-humans-says-U-S-soldier-raped-14-year-old-girl-killing-her-family [accessed 7 January 2013]. See also Fatima Bhutto, 'I Am Malala by Malala Yousafzai – Review', http://www.theguardian.com/books/2013/oct/30/malala-yousafzai-fatima-bhutto-review [accessed 7 January 2013].

Concluding Remarks

Abdelwahab El-Affendi

According to Helen Fein, the first question prospective genocide perpetrators ask themselves is: 'Can we get away with it?'[1] What our research here suggests is that they rather ask: 'Can we afford not to?' Actors possessed by nightmares about apocalyptic threats to their cherished world do not pose to think about the cost, nor do they contemplate limits on the levels of violence 'necessary' to counter the threat. The contributions to this volume have provided ample evidence of how being 'possessed' by visions of horror leaves little room for measured or considered action. Additional evidence comes from the ongoing carnage in Syria (and now Iraq and Egypt as well), where imagined nightmares drive the genocidal violence, but also explain the international community's tolerance of it. World leaders watch the carnage in Syria over drinks, just like a modestly interesting action movie. The horrors are dismissed because they are embedded in a broader narrative in which the victims are expendable, and alternative horrors lurking in the background ('extremism', chaos, etc.) are the more haunting nightmare.

Here, two threads of 'hyper-securitizing' narratives are evolving and merging in front of our very eyes, thus offering a 'laboratory case' for exploring how this type of narrative originates, evolves and works. The master narrative sustaining the Syrian regime (defiance to imperialism) overlaps with other 'unspoken' narratives about identities (sectarian, regional, religious, class). The (sectarian) inner circles of loyalists are fed clandestine (and now increasingly overt) narratives of insecurity, which warn that were the regime to fall, it would be their turn to become victims of genocide. This is a classic case in which genocidal violence is depicted as the 'lesser evil', the only protection against the *real* genocide. The regime has also persistently peddled stories about fighting Al-Qaeda and terrorism, mainly to secure international acquiescence in its atrocities, with increasing success, it has to be said. But the more salient and more effective narratives remain those of sectarian power rivalry, with Iran and Saudi Arabia vying for regional supremacy, and what Vali Nasr called the 'Shia Revival' reshaping the region.

As in other cases examined in this book, such nightmares have a tendency to turn into reality, since regime paranoia prompts ever-escalating genocidal atrocities, breeding in turn more resentment, resistance and more regime paranoia. As atrocity after atrocity failed to crush the current uprising, the Syrian regime continues to hysterically denounce the 'cosmic conspiracy' (*mu'amara kawniyya*) against it, and has abandoned any pretence of restraint in its response.

Do the Syrian propagandists who spin these tales of horror genuinely believe their stories? There is plenty of evidence to suggest that most were deliberate fabrications.

However, what is interesting is that many inside and outside Syria did espouse these narratives. (I use the term 'espouse' here, rather than 'believe', since it is questionable, for example, whether the sophisticated radical intellectuals in the West believe any of the myths concocted by the Asad regime about a joint Al-Qaeda/Mossad conspiracy to destabilize Syria.) This espousal provides interesting insights into how such narratives circulate and work, since they are then used to deny atrocities, or accuse the victims, or 'imperialist' designs. The line dividing 'believers' from 'sceptics' is also revealing, running as it does across sectarian lines in the region, and across old Western/anti-Western lines internationally. The lines that matter, however, are between those who see the atrocities and those who do not want to see them.

In intriguing ways, selectivity about narratives is usually identity driven, just as identities are mostly narratively constructed. You do not expect many Croats to buy into Serb narratives about Croat culpability in the Second World War genocides. But there are instances, as in the ongoing confrontations in Egypt, where we can observe identities coalesce around certain narratives (in this case, anti-Islamist versus pro-Islamist narratives), and then the new identities become more receptive of new narratives that have affinity to the original self-constituting narratives. We have witnessed here very dramatic shifts from narratives of mutual suspicion prior to the January 2011 uprising, to narratives of mutual acceptance and trust on the eve of the uprising and the period up to the end of 2012, when narratives of mutual demonization prevailed once more. A lot of it was deliberate machination by political actors with a clear purpose; but conditions of tension and mistrust made those narratives more acceptable. But there was nothing pre-determined about the prevalence of one set of narratives, since it is always possible to fashion and promote alternative narratives.

This in turn raises questions about the effectiveness of preventive measures versus legal sanctions, an issue taken up by Francis Deng in his substantive foreword. It is very much like Francis, in his generosity and conscientiousness, not to take our request to write a foreword lightly, and pen down the obligatory few lines of appreciation and commendation. Rather, he chose to engage deeply and energetically with the debate: questioning, probing and making important substantive contributions of his own. The foreword thus deserves to be a chapter in its own right, the more so since it has been written by the person manning the front line on behalf of the international community in its attempt to stem the tide of rising barbarism. He drew on his vast experience as Representative of the UN Secretary-General on Internally Displaced Persons (IDPs) for twelve years (1992–2004) and then as Special Adviser of the UN Secretary-General on the Prevention of Genocide (2007–2012), to highlight important points about the processes that presage mass violence, and also the best approaches to preventing or mitigating atrocities. It is well known that Francis played a pioneering role in developing the legal and theoretical framework which underpinned the doctrine of the Responsibility to Protect (R2P), formally adopted by the UN General Assembly in 2005. But if all this is not enough, Francis also draws on his personal experience and his vast work on the politics (and mythology) of his native Sudan, making his a truly remarkable contribution to this collective endeavour.

An important point Francis raises relates to the book's bias towards prevention. While accepting that prevention is paramount, he adds two caveats: first, it is at the level of identity construction that the seeds for atrocities are laid; and, second, legal sanctions and the prospects of punishment can act as a deterrent, as they are factored in elite calculations. With regard to the first point, his argument is that the very construction of exclusivist identities, even before it becomes surrounded by narratives of fear and insecurity, creates the conditions for conflict that could lead to mass violence. Work must thus start earlier, at the level of education, in order to put stops at the right points on this slippery slope.

The issues involved are indeed complex, but we believe the value of our contribution comes from pointing out that the construction of identity, the identification of threats and insecurities and the designation of potential victims, all take place in the context of interconnected framing narratives. The narratives are in turn embedded in a wider cultural and epistemological context. The Egyptian and Syrian cases indicate clearly how narratives of insecurity shape identity as well as being shaped by it. Vladimir Putin, Iran's Ayatollah and Chinese communists do not have a shared identity with Bashar Asad, but they have a shared story of solidarity against a common enemy: the 'West'.

Markovich's chapter on Yugoslavia highlights the uses of historical and religious myths and symbols to construct narratives of separateness. However, two specific elements contributed to the uniqueness of the Yugoslav case and the efficacy of the narratives. The first was the role of disillusioned Communist intellectuals, who enhanced the credibility of these narratives and immunized them against subversive counter-narratives by incorporating universalist and humanist components. (One can compare this to the role of ex-Trotskyites in the rise of American neoconservativism.) Second, one can discern the disproportionate role played by contests over statistics in the construction of rival narratives. This indicates how even 'scientific' arguments can be enlisted in the construction of narratives of insecurity and victimhood: whoever can provide more impressive statistics of higher number of victims on one side (and debunk the rival claims) can claim success. Here, we recall again how 'statistics' and historical revisionism are key tools of Holocaust denial.

Quibbles over statistics (and over 'naming') also figured prominently in recent debates over the mass in violence in the Sudanese region of Darfur.[2] De Waal did not focus on Darfur in his chapter, but brought out a more interesting and far more intriguing aspect of Sudanese narratives of self and victimhood, what he called the 'paradox of barbarism and civility' in Sudanese politics. In the process, he highlighted the less known but remarkable fact that 'communal violence' is very rare in Sudan. However, this is not as odd as it seems, since most societies have blind spots, leaving whole groups effectively outside the 'universe of moral obligation'. Just as the United States, Britain and France evolved narratives about the self which spoke of civility and democracy, while simultaneously endorsing slavery or genocide against colonial subjects, the Sudanese elite often seemed to believe that violence in the periphery did not count. As in the case of Darfur, often that violence was sub-contracted to various local militias, leaving elites belonging to warring communities to lead a relaxed life in major urban centres, mixing amicably at social occasions as war raged in the outlying areas: a sort of surreal 'Rick's Café Américain', a perennial haven of decadence and denial, as featured in Michael Curtiz's *Casablanca* (1942). As in the movie, there are limits to this double life, however. For with the widening and intensification of conflicts, the elites also began to enlist narratives about these conflicts in their own power contests, which threatens to 'bring the war home'.

In contrast to the Sudanese case, where narratives of grievance and victimhood co-existed with an actual practice of civility, in countries like Syria and Iraq narratives of harmony co-exist with realities of sectarian barbarism. Here, elites never tire of protesting their countries' 'tolerance' and primordial innocence of all sectarian grudges, blaming foreigners instead for fomenting the violence and promoting extremism. These narratives cannot be dismissed as mere illusions, since they form part of the coping strategies of the parties involved, and may even eventually contribute to restoring harmony and peace.

The interaction between narratives of insecurity and identity takes many forms. As Tsaaior indicates in his chapter on Nigeria, the telling and retelling of stories about formative traumatic events in Nigerian history (such as the series of coups and countercoups in 1966 and the Biafra war) can serve multiple purposes. The same story is told differently by different groups, while the same group can recount the same story differently for different purposes. Similarly, in Iraq, Kenya or India, historical/identity narratives relating to religion, sect, ethnic group, or connection to land can be told and retold in different ways, with different objectives and consequences.

The Indian case points to another important side of xenophobic narratives: their attempt to remould identities. The Hindutva militants not only attack the official narratives of secular democratic identity in the name of Hindu authenticity, but they also claim that the majority of Hindus need to be 'awakened' to their true identity. Violence is often seen as the tool to bring about this awakening. It is the same with Muslim extremist groups which do not see their communities as 'Muslim' enough. Islamophobia is the other side of this coin. Ironically, Breivik does not only rile against Norway's acquired multicultural identity, but even disavows its deeper Lutheran identity, calling on his country to revert to Catholicism. As Anand says about the Hindutva, the issue here is not to represent and defend a nation, but to fabricate one.

The same goes for the way 'Islam' and 'Muslim' identity figure in Islamophobic narratives, where the entity 'Muslim minority' is constructed of disparate (and internally heterogeneous) groups, such as Somali asylum seekers in Scandinavia, Bangladeshi immigrants in the UK or Turkish guest workers in Germany. The incongruousness of such constructs (as in 'Yugoslav Muslim') was brought home to me during an encounter in the mid-1980s with Bosnian Muslim activists, who spent hours briefing me about the victimization of Muslims in Communist Yugoslavia. At one point, I committed the impertinence of inquiring about the Muslims in Kosovo. My query was summarily brushed aside with a dismissive gesture: 'That is a totally different issue', I was told, before the discussion returned to Bosnia. It took me many years to understand what was meant then.

Again these revelations about how identities are constructed and also misconstrued have significant practical implications for the prevention of genocide and mass violence. For if, as this book shows, perpetrators of atrocities see themselves as 'superheroes' in a drama where grave existential threats loom, it is unlikely that the threat of future prosecution would figure highly in their calculations. But actual threats of force to stop them are sure to do. There is no room here to revisit the controversy about R2P, but I agree with Francis that a credible threat of external intervention to stop atrocities would certainly concentrate the minds of would-be genocidaires. If there was an actual, rather than imagined, 'cosmic conspiracy' to stop the Syrian genocide, then Asad would have stopped it just as he has handed over his chemical weapons in the face of credible threats.

But if it is narratives that frame action, then it is intuitive to argue that the first steps of preventive action should be to confront these narratives. This is not as easy as it seems. The construction of narratives is a highly creative process, with a great deal of indeterminacy and unpredictability as to how narratives evolve and gain acceptance. Narrative interventions must thus be carefully considered. Outsiders should be cautious when intervening in such 'sectarian' debates, lest they be accused of being part of the 'cosmic conspiracy' against this party or that. But understanding how these narratives are constructed, propagated and accepted, and how they work and achieve efficacy, is an important first step.

At the time of writing, another tragedy is unfolding that is of particular concern for both Francis and myself. I refer to the carnage in Southern Sudan, where elite political rivalry is fast turning into a vicious ethnic conflict, with mass atrocities already being perpetrated. As in the parallel crisis in Iraq, narratives of ethnic insecurity and victimization were quickly enlisted to shore up the respective shaky positions of rivals. It was possible, in both cases, for international observers to spot the various stages of escalation and intervene at the right time, especially given that the current cycles of violence mirrored earlier phases of escalation.

Of particular interest is that both Iraq and South Sudan were partial democracies with good relations with the West. Democracies are supposed to provide better forewarning of escalation due to their relative transparency, but in these cases, the warning signs were ignored. As we emphasized in this book, democracies are usually more resilient in the face of narratives of hyper-securitization, but they are also extremely vulnerable to them. This resilience/vulnerability was graphically illustrated by a bizarre incident in December 2006, when American radio talk show host Jerry Klein elicited, to his shock, an enthusiastic response from listeners to his hoax suggestion that American Muslims should be made to wear distinctive arm bands or have crescents tattooed on their foreheads. Klein said his listeners showed him why Germans looked the other way when Jews were being rounded up.[3] This was a clear indication that narratives can go – and take people with them – either way; and it depends on who is telling the story, and how 'good' it is, in all senses of the word.

The lessons of the Holocaust are always relevant, as Pappe reveals in his insightful chapter on Israel. For one thing, tragedies like the Holocaust transcend all narratives, as indicated by Theodor Adorno's famous remark that 'to write poetry after Auschwitz is barbaric'. In the face of such calamities, silence is more eloquent than any narrative. It is partially the terror of such an unspeakable event, and the fear of its repetition, which makes Israelis reluctant to embrace narratives that hint at an identity of perpetrators or, as Pappe put it, the fear of being their own worst nightmare. That is why, Pappe argues, even the most liberal Israelis find it difficult to espouse any narrative in which they admit having wronged the Palestinians. This adds another level of complexity to the way narratives of victimhood and insecurity function in relation to atrocities. For past atrocities could cast a shadow on the present, and fear of confronting responsibility can perpetuate conflict and hamper reconciliation.

Finally, we may have to look at our own 'narratives about narratives' in this book. A critical reading of the chapters would confirm the impossibility of finding an Archimedean external point from which to evaluate and judge the narratives being examined. The problem is compounded by the fact that most of the contributors are not entirely neutral with regard to the debates being evaluated, allowing for subtle biases in the analyses. A deeper analysis might even point to embryonic contests lurking behind the lines in these narratives, with the potential to flare up at a future time and possibly contribute to conflict. Looking at the chapters on Nigeria, India, Yugoslavia and Kenya, one can guess how probable narratives about unresolved issues (land ownership in Kenya) or past events (previous coups and civil wars in Nigeria, Sudan or Iraq, recurrent massacres in India) could be constructed and function to foster future conflicts.

At a more basic level, one cannot escape the narrative character of social science in general. Even before the so-called 'narrative turns', it was impossible to escape the narrative component of most scientific claims.[4] Even disciplines like physics and biology incorporate narratives as explanatory devices (Big Bang theory, evolution, etc.). Advocates of the 'narrative turn' see in this an advantage to be cultivated, rather than a problem. It has been argued, for example, that the employment of narratives in International Relations could contribute to a resolution of the agency–structure conundrum, since narrative can offer insights into the actors' reasoning, as well as accounting for contingency and unintended consequences. In addition to highlighting the way structures are reproduced and sustained through action, 'The story of action in narrative exemplifies and demonstrates the power and autonomy of agency and the actual effects of structures on action.'[5]

The focus on narratives can help avoid the problem of determinism that haunts most psychological or sociological explanations, since it preserves the element of choice even when psychological, sociological or contextual influences dispose individuals or groups to espouse particular narratives in preference to alternatives. In this context, one clue to how narratives are appropriated can be found in the way right-wing authors 'plagiarized' by Breivik distanced themselves from the man and his violence. Interestingly, the disclaimer was based largely on a report by court-appointed psychiatrists who found Breivik to be insane. This prompted one commentator to describe this as 'an odd strategy', since the right-wing bloggers involved 'are really saying that anyone who's willing to act on the warmongering ideas they promote – that is, anyone who listens to them seriously – must be crazy'.[6]

Many have rightly argued that branding Breivik and similar right-wing extremists 'insane' or 'lone wolves' appears to play down the contribution of incendiary right wing narratives (and even mainstream anti-immigrant or anti-Muslim rhetoric) to such murderous enterprises. This is the more so since the same circles making these arguments most vociferously reject similar attempts to de-link 'Muslim terrorism' from radical Islamist rhetoric. We have already referred to Richard Millet's provocative remarks about Norway's multiculturalism being responsible for Breivik's massacre, and his claim that the atrocity was 'without doubt what Norway deserved'.[7] Many rightly wondered what would be the reaction to comparable rhetoric which blamed the United States and its foreign policy for 9/11.

However, the point may be that when certain narratives of horror, no matter how far-fetched, are passively espoused by wide sections of opinion, the resulting gap invites extremists and vigilantes. When mainstream politicians speak about the dangers posed by immigration, for example, but do nothing about it, immigrants start to be attacked on the streets. Many recruits to violent radical Islamist groups ascribe their conversion to media and mainstream political rhetoric that deplored intolerable situations (in Palestine, in Iraq, in Bosnia, etc.) but did nothing about it. Given such narratives of apparent 'impotence' in the face of grave threats tend to incite 'heroic' action to fill the perceived gap, one can confidently predict that the ongoing televised genocide in Syria is going to generate extremist mass violence for years to come. It is a classic case of self-confessed impotence in the face of widely accepted narratives of unmitigated and intolerable horror. In this situation, will 'volunteers' proposing to do something about the massacres be deemed crazy, or just persons who took the narratives in question seriously?

To conclude, the revelations and insights in this book about the pivotal role narratives of insecurity play in inciting atrocities are only the beginning and not the end of the investigation in this matter. In spite of many important contributions to the debate on the construction of insecurity, there is much yet to be discovered about how these processes of construction operate. It is not enough to speak about the 'power of metaphors', or to engage in rarefied debates about 'speech acts', 'locution' and 'illocution'. The mere use of certain metaphors is not sufficient to explain the slide into barbarism (metaphors of 'long knives' and 'stabs in the back' are used quite often in democratic politics). We know that certain narratives turn men into killers, while others turn them into peace-makers. In this book, we have given many examples of both and how they unfold. As the above case of talk-show host Klein indicates, even one person can elicit proto-genocidal reactions from the public and then demonstrate the absurdity and disproportionality of that reaction, all within the space on one hour. There is yet a lot to be discovered about how this process works. And we hope that this book has offered enough pointers in the right direction in which research in this field should proceed. And in the meantime, we can all draw on the examples of the many authors of the good stories, satires, cartoons, etc., which are all very effective in deflating and neutralizing concocted horror narratives. And before and after, decent people always know what to do when confronted with problematic situations. Human decency may be very precarious and fragile, but it is also very resilient and creative.

Just as genocidal episodes tend to show how so many human beings can show courage and decency, the threat of atrocities also frequently elicit from decent people the right things to say at the right time to stem the slide towards barbarism. Let us hope that this book is a small contribution in that direction.

Notes

1 Helen Fein, 'The Three P's of Genocide Prevention: With Application to a Genocide Foretold-Rwanda', in Neal Riemer, ed., *Protection against Genocide: Mission Impossible?*, Westport, CT: Praeger, 2000, p. 46.
2 Mahmood Mamdani, *Saviors and Survivors: Darfur, Politics, and the War on Terror*, London: Verso, 2009.
3 Erin Steuter and Deborah Wills, *At War with Metaphor: Media, Propaganda, and Racism in the War on Terror*, Lanham, MD: Lexington Books, 2009.
4 Mark Bevir, 'Political Studies as Narrative and Science, 1880–2000', *Political Studies*, Vol. 54, No. 3 (2006), pp. 583–606.
5 Geoffrey Roberts, 'History, Theory and the Narrative Turn in IR', *Review of International Studies*, Vol. 32, No. 4 (2006), pp. 711–712.
6 Moustafa Bayoumi, 'Breivik's Monstrous Dream—and Why It Failed', *The Nation*, 2 May 2012, http://www.thenation.com/article/167682/breiviks-monstrous-dream-and-why-it-failed [accessed 19 June 2014].
7 Bruce Crumley, 'French Essayist Blames Multiculturalism for Breivik's Killing Spree', *Time*, 28 August 2012, http://world.time.com/2012/08/28/french-essayist-blames-multi-culturalism-for-breiviks-norwegian-massacre/#ixzz25VLCjLr0.

Authors' Biographies

Dr Francis M. Deng is the Permanent Representative of South Sudan to the United Nations. He served previously as United Nations Secretary General's Special Adviser on the Prevention of Genocide; Representative on Internally Displaced Persons; and as Human Rights Officer. He also served as Sudan's Ambassador to several countries and as Minister of State for Foreign Affairs. Dr Deng has authored and edited over thirty books and has received numerous awards, both at home and abroad.

James Tar Tsaaior is an Associate Professor and Chair of the Department of Mass Media and Writing in the School of Media and Communication, Pan-Atlantic (formerly Pan-African) University, Lagos, Nigeria, where he teaches creative writing, media/cultural studies and postcolonial literature. He is also the Director, Academic Planning of the University, and editor, *Journal of Cultural and Media Studies*. Between 2010 and 2011, he was a visiting Leverhulme and Isaac Newton Research Fellow, Centre of African Studies, University of Cambridge, United Kingdom, and a participant in the International Faculty Programme, University of Navarre IESE Business School, Barcelona, Spain.

Alex de Waal is executive director of the World Peace Foundation at the Fletcher School, Tufts University. Considered one of the foremost experts on Sudan and the Horn of Africa, his scholarly work and practice has also probed humanitarian crisis and response, human rights, HIV/AIDS and governance in Africa, and conflict and peacebuilding. During 2009–2012 he served as senior adviser to the African Union High-Level Implementation Panel for Sudan.

Kenneth Inyani Simala holds a Doctor of Philosophy degree in Kiswahili and is Associate Professor of Cultural Linguistics at Masinde Muliro University of Science and Technology in Kenya. He has done research and published in the area of language and how it affects and is impacted on by society. He writes on the interface between language, meaning, culture, communication and development.

Dr Dibyesh Anand is the Director of the Department of Politics and International Relations at the University of Westminster. His publications are in the areas of Global Politics, Identities, Tibet, China, Hindu Nationalism and Security. He is the author of *Geopolitical Exotica: Tibet in Western Imagination* (2007); and *Hindu Nationalism in India and the Politics of Fear* (2011).

Dr Slobodan G. Markovich is Associate Professor at the University of Belgrade. He co-edited collections with C. Popov and D. Zivojinovic, Bicentenary of Serbian

Diplomacy (2013) and with V. Pavlovic and E. Weaver, *Problems of Identities in the Balkans* (2006), and published *British Perceptions of Serbia and the Balkans 1903–1906* (2000). His research interests cover the construction of national and religious identities in SEE, British–Balkan Relations and the history of European pessimism.

Ilan Pappe is Professor of History, Director of the European Centre for Palestine Studies and Co-Director for the Exeter Centre for Ethno-Political Studies. Professor Pappé founded and directed the Academic Institute for Peace in Givat Haviva, Israel, between 1992 and 2000 and was the Chair of the Emil Tuma Institute for Palestine Studies in Haifa between 2000 and 2006. His research focuses on the modern Middle East and in particular the history of Israel and Palestine. He has also written on multiculturalism, critical discourse analysis and on power and knowledge in general.

Maria Holt is a Reader in Politics at the University of Westminster in London. Her research interests include the effects of violent conflict on women in the Middle East, women and Islamic resistance in the Arab world and Palestinian refugee women in Lebanon. Her most recent book, *Women and Conflict in the Middle East: Palestinian Refugees and the Response to Violence*, was published in January 2014.

Dr Ali A. Allawi is currently Visiting Research Professor at the Middle East Institute of the National University of Singapore. A graduate of MIT, the London School of Economics and Harvard (in civil engineering and planning), he was appointed minister of trade of Iraq in September 2003 before becoming in April 2004 Iraq's first post-war civilian minister of defence. He later held the post of minister of finance in the Iraqi Transitional Government from April 2005 to May 2006. His most recent book is *Faisal I of Iraq* (2014). He is also author of *The Crisis of Islamic Civilization* (2010). In May 2013, Allawi came fourth on *Prospect* magazine's list of the world's 'most original thinkers'.

Dr Nafeez Mosaddeq Ahmed is a bestselling author, investigative journalist and international security scholar. He is executive director of the Institute for Policy Research & Development, and author of *A User's Guide to the Crisis of Civilization*, among other books. He writes for the *Guardian* on the geopolitics of environmental, energy and economic crises on his Earth insight blog.

Anas S. Al-Shaikh-Ali is a founding member and current Chair of the Association of Muslim Social Scientists (AMSS UK), Academic Advisor and Europe Executive Director to the IIIT, and Vice-President of the Institute for Epistemological Studies in Brussels. He has an MA in English Literature (American University of Beirut) and a PhD in American Studies (Manchester University) and has taught Literature and Translation at universities in the Middle East. Dr Ali is a Fellow of the Royal Society of Arts, and is listed in *The 500 Hundred Most Influential Muslims* (2009–2013). In 2009, he was made Commander of the British Empire.

Dr Abdelwahab El-Affendi is a Reader in Politics at the Centre for the Study of Democracy, University of Westminster, London, and coordinator of the Centre's Democracy and Islam Programme. He was an ESRC/AHRC fellow in the Global Uncertainties Programme of Research Councils, UK, (2009–2012), and advisor to the African Union High Level Panel for Implementation in Sudan (2011–2012). Dr El-Affendi is a member of the ESRC Peer Review College as well as the editorial board of the Strategic Studies Series (UAE), and is on the editorial board of three academic journals. He is a co-author of the *Arab Human Development Report* (2004) and the author of *The Conquest of Muslim Hearts and Minds: Perspectives on U.S. Reform and Public Diplomacy Strategies* (2005). His most recent book is *Darfur: A Decade in Crisis* (2013).

Index

Note: The letter 'n' following locators refers to notes.

9/11 attacks 41, 45

Abdel Salam, A. H. 74, 89n. 4
abuse 5, 6, 21, 29
Addis Ababa peace agreement period 77
Adekeye, Adebajo 60, 71n. 21
Adibe, Jideofor 60, 71n. 20
Adorno, Theodor W. 38, 50n. 85, 235
Agamben, Giorgio 37, 50n. 76
Ahmed, Nafeez Mosaddeq 20, 191, 209n. 56
Ain el- Hilweh refugee camp, Sidon (Israeli military attack) 162
Ajami, Fouad 168n. 24
Aldcroft, Derek H. 118, 138n. 4
Alier, Abel 77, 89n. 13
Al-Shaikh-Ali, Anas S. 211, 229n. 26
Al-Shanti, Jameela 161, 165, 169n. 57
Ameli, Saeid R. 193, 206n. 15
Anand, Dibyesh 18, 47n. 5, 103, 113n. 3
Anderson, Benedict 34, 49n. 48, 49n. 50, 49n. 52-3, 55, 56, 70n. 7
Animal Farm 47
Ansari, Humayun 193, 207n. 16
anti-Muslim violence in Gujarat in 2002 103, 110–12
  see also India, Hindu Nationalism in
Apocalypse Now 41
Aradau, Claudia 35, 49n. 64
Arendt, Hannah 6, 11, 13, 14, 25n. 67, 26n. 82-3, 26n. 86, 32, 50n. 71
Assyrian Crisis of August 1933 174–6
Awolowo, Obafemi 61, 62, 63, 64, 71n. 24

Balata camp in Nablus 160
Bartov, Omer 10, 25n. 65, 32, 33, 41, 43, 47n. 4, 48n. 34, 49n. 36, 49n. 41
Beljo, Ante 128, 139n. 21, 140n. 22
Berko, A. 166, 170n. 78

Bhabha, Homi K. 49n. 49, 58, 71n. 15, 162, 169n. 59
bias 217
Bigo, Didier 9, 25n. 57, 49n. 61, 209n. 54-5
Bird, Michael Yellow 51n. 90
Bleiburg massacre 127–31
bloody autumn of 1941, Serbia 126
Blue Bears 215
Bogosavljević, Srđan 124, 139n. 11
Bourj el-Barajne camp in Beirut 159–60
Bowman, Glenn 158, 161, 169n. 35, 169n. 51
Breivik, Anders Behring 1–2, 4, 14, 15, 234, 236, 237
Brennan, Timothy 56, 57, 70n. 1, 71n. 9–10
Bresheeth, Haim 156, 168n. 23
Brunner, Claudia 166, 170n. 81
Buffy the Vampire Slayer 40
Buzan, Barry 25n. 55, 36, 38, 49n. 59, 50n. 66, 50n. 70, 50n. 84, 197, 208n. 39

Captain Phillips 225
Card, Claudia 5, 11, 12, 23n. 24, 24n. 28, 25n. 72, 26n. 74
Casablanca 234
Changing Lense 148
Chirot, Daniel 7, 24n. 38, 24n. 47, 24n. 51, 48n. 31
Chitkara, M. G. 108, 113n. 8, 115n. 27
Chomsky, Noam 44, 143, 151n. 5, 207n. 28
civil war in Sudan 77
Cohn, Martin R. 111, 116n. 45
Cole, Phillip 25n. 64, 26n. 79, 26n. 81, 34, 49n. 51
collateral damage 4, 31, 204, 212

collective trauma 7
communist myths 122–4
Comprehensive Peace Agreement (CPA) 77–81, 84, 87
Congdon, James 224, 230n. 50
conspiracy theories 29, 42–3
construction of self and victims 31–3
Cook, Jonathan 205, 209n. 66
Copenhagen School 9, 34, 35, 37
Covering Islam 212
Crescent Dawn 217
Croatia–Serbia victimhood 117
  Bleiburg massacre 127–31
  communist myths 122–4
  Jasenovac concentration camp 124–7
  Milosevic power in Serbia 131–6
  post-WWII political emigration 127
  reflections on genocide and 136–8
  tragic burden of Second World War 121–2
  war trauma and post-traumatic narratives 118–21
Crown Lands Ordinance of 1902 and 1915 98
Cry of the Owl 73

Darfur Peace Agreement (DPA) 79
Darfurian rebels in 2003 75, 78
  see also Sudan and South Sudan tragedies
Darwish, Mahmoud 155, 167n. 9
Davidson, Basil 60, 71n. 22
Day of Wrath 222
de Waal, Alex 17, 73, 89n. 14, 90n. 23, 90n. 30, 233
Debray, Regis 58, 71n. 14
Dedijer, Vladimir 117, 133, 134, 140n. 35, 140n. 36
DeLillo, Don 45, 52n. 120
democratization and internal conflict in African politics 93
Deng, Francis 89n. 1, 90n. 16, 232
disinformation 217
distrust 82–4
  see also Sudan and South Sudan tragedies
documentaries 28
Dodge, Toby 204, 209n. 64

Dr Zhivago 47
Dragovic-Soso, Jasna 118, 138n. 2, 140n. 31
Duchamp, L. Timmel 1, 23n. 3

El-Affendi, Abdelwahab 16, 27, 51n. 108, 89n. 3, 231
Entman, Robert M. 25n. 59, 94, 102n. 23
Erez, E. 166, 170n. 78
ethnic cleansing 4
Evans, Gareth 5, 23n. 23, 207n. 27
evil excesses 11–12
expulsion of Fayli Kurds and Iraqi Shias of assumed Iranian origin 178–80

Fadul, Abdul-Jabbar 86, 90n. 26
fatalism 84–7
  see also Sudan and South Sudan tragedies
fear 37–9
Fein, Helen 5, 24n. 26–7, 31, 48n. 20, 231, 238n. 1
Ferguson, Niall 54, 70n. 4
Foucault, Michel 37, 50n. 79, 114n. 19, 148, 157, 168n. 27
Freedman, Lawrence 6, 24n. 33
Fumia, Joan 149, 151n. 15

Gaidzakian, Ohan 214, 224n. 15
genocide
  defined 3
  and mass terrorism, conceptual clarifications 2–7
  of subjugation 4
Gerlach, Christian 3, 23n. 16
Giddens, Anthony 61, 71n. 23
Githens-Mazer, Jonathan 193, 207n. 17
grand narratives 5
grave crises 43
Greek tragedy 29
grievance 76–82
  see also Sudan and South Sudan tragedies
Gulag Archipelago, The 44

H.M.S. Unseen 222
Habermas, Jürgen 5, 6, 24n. 31, 44
Hammer, Juliane 158, 168n. 34

Herman, Edward S. 44, 52n. 115, 207n. 28
Hierbert, Maureen S. 30, 31, 32, 47n. 16, 48n. 33, 49n. 38
Hindu nationalism, see India, Hindu nationalism in
Hindutva movement 28
Hinton, Alexander Laban 38, 50n. 85, 202, 209n. 57
Hitler's Willing Executioners 10
Hobsbawm, Eric 56, 70n. 8, 118, 138n. 3
Hogan, Patrick Colm 42, 43, 51n. 102–3, 51n. 107
Horkheimer, Max 38, 50n. 85
Huntington, Samuel P. 20, 198, 199, 208n. 42
Huysmans, Jef 35, 37, 47n. 12, 47n. 13–15, 49n. 62–3, 50n. 77–8
hyper-securitization 34–7

'I Have A Dream' speech 47
Ibrahim, Anwar 215, 229n. 21–2
identity construction
  of self and victims 31–3
imagined communities 33
  nations as 33–4
Imperial British East African Company (IBEA) 97
Independence Day 40
India, Hindu nationalism in 103
  and communal violence 110–12
  Hindu rights 104–6
  'The Muslim' as danger, representing 107–10
  partition of 32–3
  productive discourse of security 106–7
insecurity, narratives of 6–10, 141
intergroup violence in Iraq after US invasion 171–2
Intifada 150, 157–8, 162–4
invasion of Ramallah 158
Iranian Hostage Crisis of 1979 225–6
Iraq (modern) state and intergroup violence
  analytical model 172–3
  communal violence 171–2
  types 173
Islam and insecurity, Palestinian women blessings of memory 158–61

narratives
  heroism 161–3
  loss and injustice 153–5
  morality 164–6
  plurality of resistances 156–8
  tapestry of voices 155–6
Islamo-fascism 42
Islamophobia as securitization narrative
  anti-Muslim hostility in United Kingdom 191–3
  Arabs and Muslim non-Arabs 215–17
  'Barbary' to *Midnight Express* 212–15
  and holocaust 217–22
  prejudice and hatred 222–6
  as securitization 197–200
  exclusionary logic 200–3
  underdevelopment 194–7
Israeli, Raphael 170n. 80
Israeli-Palestinian conflict
  fear and justice 146–50
  fear and victimhood 141–3
  invisible and indivisible 143–6
  otherness 141–3
  retribution 146–50

Jasenovac concentration camp 124–7
Jewish Pogrom *(Farhud)* of 1941 176–8
Justice and Equality Movement (JEM) attack 75
  see also Sudan and South Sudan tragedies

Kantian concept of diabolical evil 11–12
Kenya
  conceptualizing civic competence and 93–4
  and general elections 95–6
  land question 96–100
  narrative approach 91–2
  political discourse and ethnicity 94–5
Khaled, Leila 154, 155, 157, 158, 162, 163, 167n. 5
Kingdom of Serbs, Croats and Slovenes 119–20
Kingdom of Yugoslavia 119–20
Kopf, David 31, 48n. 26
Kragujevac massacre 126–7
Kressel, Neil 5, 24n. 25, 26n. 77, 26n. 92

La Bombe Des Mollahs (Paul Fauray) 217
Lambert, Robert 193, 207n. 17
Lampe, John R. 118, 138n. 5, 138n. 7, 140n. 30
Leila Khaled's memory of orange trees in Haifa 158
Lemkin, Raphael 202, 209n. 59
Leveson, L. J. 211, 228n. 1
liberalism 37–9

MacDonald, David Bruce 117, 130, 138n. 1, 140n. 28
MacIntyre, Alasdair 1, 6, 22n. 1
Magnum crimen. Pola vijeka klerikalizma u Hrvatskoj 125
Mahdist revolution 74
Mahmoud, Ushari 75, 90n. 24
Mann, Michael 25n. 63, 38, 48n. 21–2, 173, 181, 188n. 1–2
Mann's model 173
Markusen, Eric 31, 48n. 26
Martin, Andrew 24n. 37
mass atrocities 4–5
mass killings
  defined 3
  expulsions and disappearances of civilians 185–6
mass violence, defined 3–4
massacre, defined 3–4
Matrix, The 38
Maussen, Marcel 194, 207n. 21
Mazrui, Ali 59, 71n. 17
McCauley, Clark 7, 21n. 30, 24n. 47, 24n. 51, 48n. 31
McDonald, Matt 200, 209n. 50–1
media framing 44
Mein Kampf 42
Midlarsky, Manus I. 7, 24n. 40
Midnight Express 215
Miletić, Antun 134, 140n. 36
Miller, Nicholas J. 136, 140n. 37, 140n. 40, 140n. 43
Millet, Richard 1, 2, 3n. 5
Millet system 172
Milosevic power in Serbia 131–6
modern collective terrorism 5
Mombasa Republican Council (MRC), war of independence 97–8

Moore, Kerry 207n. 25
Morewood, Steven 118, 138n. 4
'Muslimness' 105–6

Nakbah (Catastrophe) in Palestinian national narrative 142–3
narrative communities 33–4
  graphic illustration 39
narrative-focused approach 10–11
narratives, defined 6
nation 55–7
nation-ness 56–7
National Salvation Revolution 83
Nigeria 53–4
  civil war narratives 65–6
  Igbo–Yoruba animosity 61–5
  imperial history 54–5
  military rule era (1984–1999) 66–9
  nation and nation-ness, theory of 55–8
  postcoloniality and nationhood 58–61
nightmares construction 28–9
Nosferatu, a Symphony of Horror 42

Ochieng, Philip 93, 101n. 20
Operation Medina: The Crusade 217
Operation Medina: The Jihad 217
Ordinary Men: Reserve Police Batallion 101 and the Final Solution in Poland 10
Orientalism 47
Oslo massacre 1–2
Oslo 'peace process' 143
Osofisan, Femi 59, 71n. 18–19
Ottoman administrative structures 172
Our Beloved 119

Palestinian elections of January 2006 164
Palestinian Front for Liberation of Palestine (PFLP) 157
Pappe, Ilan 19, 141, 150n. 1, 151n. 3–4, 151n. 7, 151n. 11, 151n. 13, 235, 236
Patwardhan, Anand 105, 114n. 15
permissive political culture 32
Peteet, Julie 157, 161, 168n. 22, 168n. 30, 169n. 55, 169n. 63
Petro, Patrice 6, 24n. 37, 51n. 93
political culture 32

popular culture narratives 39–42
Power of Nightmares, The 28

Raburn, Terry 223, 230n. 47–8
radical evil 11
Ralph, Diana 197, 207n. 29, 207n. 31–3, 208n. 37
Rashtriya Swayamsevak Sangh 112n. 2
red terror of 1944/1945 122
Reel Bad Arabs: How Hollywood Vilifies a People 215
refugee women 160
Renan, Ernest 34, 57, 71n. 13
Ricouer, Paul 57, 71n. 12
'Rivers of Blood' 1968 speech 44
Robb, David L. 225, 230n. 60–1
Rogue Forces 217
Rorty, Richard 1, 5, 23n. 4, 24n. 32, 37, 44, 46, 50n. 81, 51n. 111, 52n. 123

Sádi, Ahmad H. 168n. 22
Sageman, Marc 34, 49n. 54
Said, Edward W. 115n. 25, 149, 150, 151n. 16, 158, 161, 168n. 33, 169n. 58, 212, 216, 228n. 3
Savage, Timothy M. 198, 208n. 44
Savarkar, Vinayak Damodar 107, 114n. 22
Sayigh, Rosemary 159, 168n. 17, 168n. 20, 169n. 40–1
Schmid, Alex 3, 23n. 10–11
Schutz, Alfred 95, 102n. 24
Scott, James C. 167n. 13
securitization
  concept 197–200
  theory 9, 29, 34–7
    Schmittian interpretations 35–7
security 106
self 31–3
Semelin, Jacques 1, 3, 4, 7, 8, 22n. 2, 23n. 17, 24n. 39, 24n. 41–4, 24n. 49, 24n. 52, 25n. 53–4, 26n. 97, 43, 51n. 105–6, 203, 209n. 60–1
Sen, Amartya 32, 33, 49n. 40, 49n. 45–7
Serbia-Croatia victimhood 117
  Bleiburg massacre 127–31
  communist myths 122–4
  Jasenovac concentration camp 124–7
  Milosevic power in Serbia 131–6

reflections on genocide and 136–8
tragic burden of Second World War 121–2
war trauma and post-traumatic narratives 118–21
Settler Transfer Fund (STF) 99
Shaheen, Jack G 196, 207n. 30, 215, 229n. 24
Shehadeh, Raja 163, 169n. 64
Sheikh, Bilquis 223, 230n. 49
Shia uprising *(Intifida)* of 1991 183–5
Shklar, Judith N. 37, 50n. 80
Singh, Jyotsna 55, 70n. 5
skilful deployment of narratives 42–5
  receptiveness to narratives 43
  skilful re-telling of stories 42–3
  timing, context and delivery 44–5
Spivak, Gayatri Chakravorty 65, 156, 167n. 15
state and intergroup violence, case of modern Iraq
  analytical model 172–3
  communal violence 171–2
  types 173
Steuter, Erin 26n. 96, 217, 220, 229n. 29–30, 229n. 33–7, 229n. 39, 238n. 3
Stokes, Doug 201, 209n. 52
Straus, Scott 4, 23n. 13, 23n. 22
Sudan and South Sudan tragedies 73
  concept of 'Sudan' and 'Sudanese' 74
  distrust 82–4
  ethnic conflict 76
  fatalism 84–7
  grievance 76–82
  politics 75, 83
    civility and barbarity 75–6
    rules of civil elite politics 75
    provincial administration 75
    Sudan's democratic periods 74
Sudan Liberation Movement (SLM) 78
Sum of All Fears, The 40
Svendsen, Lars 8, 24n. 50, 25n. 73, 26n. 75
Swedenburg, Ted 156, 159, 168n. 21, 169n. 42
Synerton Land Plan of 1954 98
'systematic' murder 4

Tanatura massacre 147
Tanner, Victor 86, 90n. 26
Taraki, Lisa 164, 170n. 70–1
terrorism
  defined 2–3
Thelen, David 159, 169n. 38
threat 7
Tilly, Charles 74, 89n. 9
'Troubles' *(mashakil)* 86
Truman Show, The 39–40
Truth, Justice and Reconciliation Commission (TJRC) Report 99–100
Tsaaior, James 17, 53, 71n. 16, 234
Turko-Egyptian conquest of the Nile Valley 76–7
typhus epidemic of 1915 118–19

Umm Mahdi in Bourj el-Barajne camp 161
United Nations
  Convention on the Prevention and Punishment of the Crime of Genocide (UNCG; 1948) 3
  High-level Panel on Threats, Challenges and Change 2
US invasion of Iraq 171–2
US National Security Entry-Exit Registration System (NSEERS) 196
Ustasha massacres of Serbs 122

Valentino, Benjamin A. 3, 4, 23n. 14, 23n. 18, 48n. 25
Vladisavljevic, Nebojsa 131, 140n. 29
Vučković, Vladeta 124, 138n. 10
Vulliamy, Ed 34, 49n. 56
vulnerability 7

Wæver, Ola 25n. 55, 38, 49n. 58–9, 49n. 65, 50n. 84, 208n. 38
Walt, Stephen M. 197, 208n. 36
'war' *(harb)* 86
Wars for Yugoslav Succession 126–7, 137–8
Watson, Scott D. 9, 25n. 58, 51n. 112, 52n. 114, 52n. 116
Williams, Michael C. 25n. 56, 49n. 57, 50n. 82, 52n. 117
Williams, Raymond 57, 71n. 11
Wills, Deborah 26n. 96, 217, 220, 229n. 29–30, 229n. 33–7, 229n. 39, 238n. 3
Wimmer, Andreas 33, 49n. 42–4
World War Z 39, 40

YouGov survey 192
Young, Crawford 63, 66, 71n. 25–6
Yugoslavia, disintegration of 117–38
  see also Serbia–Croatia victimhood

Zionist ideology 148
Žižek, Slavoj 41, 51n. 100, 168n. 28

Lightning Source UK Ltd.
Milton Keynes UK
UKHW022021060320
359914UK00010B/1874